World Wide Web Design Guide

Stephen Wilson

Hayden
Books

World Wide Web Design Guide

Library of Congress Catalog Number: 94-73416
ISBN: 1-56830-171-5

97   96   95   4   3   2   1

Interpretation of the printing code: the rightmost double-digit number is the year of the book's printing; the rightmost single-digit number is the number of the book's printing. For example, a printing code of 95-1 shows that the first printing of the book occurred in 1995.

Dedication

This book is dedicated to Cathy, who constantly reminds me that the most important information is emotional and intuitive, and to Sophia, who thinks the Web is a place for spiders to play.

The Hayden Books Team

Publisher
David Rogelberg

Managing Editor
Pat Gibbons

Acquisitions Editors
Oliver von Quadt
Karen Whitehouse

Development Editors
Kezia E. Endsley
Eileen Mullin

Technical Editor
Sean P. Wingerter

Interior Designers
Fred Bower
Paula Carroll

Cover Designer
Jay Corpus

Production
Gary Adair, Kim Cofer, Dan Caparo,
Jennifer Eberhardt, Rob Falco, Joe Millay,
Erika Millen, Regina Rexrode, Christine
Tyner, Karen Walsh, Robert Wolf

Indexer
Bront Davis

Composed in *Triplex* and *MCP Digital*

About the Author

Stephen Wilson is a San Francisco artist and teacher who explores the cultural implications of new technologies. His interactive installations have been shown internationally in galleries and SIGGRAPH, SIGCHI, NCGA, Ars Electronica, and V2 art shows. His computer-mediated artworks probe issues such as interactivity, telecommunications; artificial intelligence and robotics; hypermedia and the structure of information; synthetic voice; and environmental and biological sensing.

He won the Prize of Distinction in Ars Electronica's international competition for interactive art. One example of his artwork is the "Is Anyone There?" event in which a computer called five San Francisco pay telephones every hour on the hour for a week and tried to engage people in conversations with digital characters.

He is an international co-editor of *Leonardo,* the international journal of Art & Science, and Professor of Conceptual Design and Information Arts at San Francisco State University. He teaches courses in art and technology, design of interactive events, telecommunications art, and Web design. He has been a developer for various high tech firms and a consultant to businesses, museums, and school districts on the integration of new technologies and Web design. In 1994, he was an artist-in-residence at the Xerox PARC research center working on projects related to the World Wide Web.

He has published extensively, including articles such as "The Aesthetics and Practice of Designing Interactive Events," "The Relationship of Cultural Theory to Art That Uses Emerging Technologies," "Interactive Art and Cultural Change," "Noise on the Line: Emerging Issues in Telecommunications Art", and "Research and Development as a Source of Ideas and Inspiration for Artists," and two books, *Using Computers to Create Art* (Prentice Hall, 1986) and *Multimedia Design with HyperCard* (Prentice Hall, 1991). Details about his writing and artworks can be found at http://userwww.sfsu.edu/swilson/.

Acknowledgments

The author would like to thank many people for making this book possible. Oliver von Quadt at Hayden for seeing the value of the proposal and Kezia Endsley for shepherding the book.

Eileen Mullin, my editor, for the hard work of helping consolidate all I wanted to say into a practical form that could fit between these covers and for using her love of the Web to guide the process. Sean Wingerter for technical review of the book and for contributing the Perl scripts in Chapter 7. Kevin John Black for rounding up the permissions from the Web authors whose work appears in the book. Kasey Asberry for searching for dead links. David Miller for reviewing early drafts of my chapters with a focus on what would be understandable to non-experts. Catherine Witzling for editing early versions. Students in my Art & Telecommunications courses for trying out early versions of the book and for their enthusiasm in exploring the Web. Web designers for allowing us to reprint Web pages illustrating their extraordinary work.

I also want to thank the Xerox PARC research center and their PAIR program for the artist-in-residency they awarded me that provided the incubation space for the ideas behind this book. Thanks to Rich Gold, director of the program, for creating this extraordinary opportunity for artists and researchers to investigate emerging technologies together.

Special thanks to Jock Mackinlay and Polle Zelleweger, the researchers who worked with me during the residency, for their willingness to share the intensity and insights of their own research and to engage with me in open-ended investigations of the cultural implications of the Web.

Thanks also to the researchers, hackers, freeware authors, Web fanatics, and dreamers who created the Internet and the Web not out of greed, but rather out of the love of intellectual challenge and wild ideas. I hope this book can encourage the next generation to continue this tradition of generosity.

Table of Contents

Chapter 3   Creating Hyperlinks   81

Chapter 5   Working with Sound on the Web   **153**

Chapter 8   Experimenting on the Web   247

Chapter 9   The Challenge of Web Design   273

Appendix B   Preparing Servers to Respond to Imagemaps   333

Appendix C   Examples of Scripts Responding to Web Forms   347

Index   359

Introduction

Designing for the World Wide Web

The World Wide Web is as close as we've come to cyberspace. But cyberspace requires designers who understand the way it works and who can invent its new landscapes.

Step by step, this book shows you how to design engaging Web pages efficiently and effectively. It gives you the tools and techniques you need to put eye-catching information online right away. You also develop a thorough understanding of how to present sound, video, and interactive events on the Web.

Throughout this book, you are asked to look at many different Web sites with a critical eye from a design perspective: How were these sites created? What makes them succeed visually and conceptually? How might they have been done differently? This book also introduces you to emerging technologies that enable you to create Web pages that go beyond anything you've already seen. Ultimately, this book helps you design Web sites that visitors find useful, inviting, and provocative.

Design in a Digital Networked Age

Many people without any formal graphic arts training are now designing and developing Web sites. In addition to attending to visual arrangement and readability, these designers need to keep in mind various technological issues such as access times and cross-platform file formats. If you are going to create effective Web sites, you too must understand these new challenges.

Design is a funny word. In its narrowest sense, the term is used to mean visual composition of 2-D images and 3-D objects. However, during the last 50 years an expanded view of design has emerged, represented by theorists such as Buckminster Fuller. Design can be seen as a process of integrating information from diverse fields. The goal is to create cohesive systems; visual appearance is only one factor. Web designers who restrict their efforts only to how their Web pages look tap only a small part of the Web's potential.

Therefore, this book helps you to consider a wider set of expanded design issues beyond visual and media composition. It provides the background material and tools necessary to be an innovator in a rapidly changing environment. Let's look at some of these issues.

Technology as a Source of Ideas

Computers, the Internet, and the World Wide Web are all examples of technological systems that provide great challenges and opportunities. Some readers may want to "black box" these tools—in other words, they're willing to deal with the technology as a mysterious black box whose inner workings are unimportant , as if to say, "Just tell me what I need to put in and what I get out."

My experience of teaching digital artists over the last 16 years has convinced me that this approach is not the most productive. Artists and designers who are going to be creative innovators with technological systems must know as much as they can about the underlying assumptions, history, and functional structures of the systems with which they work. Web designers need to immerse themselves in these emerging technologies, play with their capabilities, and let the possibilities stimulate their imaginations.

This book includes sections that explain the inner workings of these technological systems, such as how the Web accomplishes what it does. Many readers probably are quite adept at using hardware and software, but may not understand at a fundamental level how it works. I provide that technical background in a demystified, down-to-earth way. Even though it may not seem critical to creating a Web page, I guarantee it is useful as you get deeper into Web design.

Preparing to Participate in a Revolution

Navigating the Web can be so absorbing that many users lose track of time and space, lost in its surprises and delights, its frustrations and dead ends. As a Web designer, this is your audience. You can help shape this innovative publishing and performance medium. But you also need to broaden your horizon beyond the Web to understand the trends shaping its future and the ways it fits in the larger society.

Some consider the Web a revolutionary cultural development as well as a medium for spreading ideas on a large-scale basis. People who never thought of themselves as authors or designers can now make their work internationally available. This book aims to empower you to participate fully in that revolution by providing both the hands-on and analytical tools you need to be an information provider on the World Wide Web.

What Is Information?

What is information? Who needs it? Who can provide it? If you are going to be an information provider on the Web, you must confront these questions. You need to make your own decisions about what constitutes information worth publishing. And as a Web designer, you need to consider what constitutes useful or desirable information for your audience. You need to make sure your Web work makes sense in the larger context outside the Web.

In an information age, some say information is what people pay for. Specialized insider business newsletters can cost thousands of dollars an issue. Even before the Web, online information businesses were trying to make money selling access. Focused services such as Dialog and Lexis/Nexis were quite successful. However, general purpose online services such as CompuServe, America Online, and PRODIGY struggled at first to find a definition of information that expanded their appeal. Over time, these services began to enroll much larger user bases and entrepreneurs began to realize that online services could have mass appeal. The next generation of big player services such as eWorld and Microsoft Network joined in. The spread of the Internet and the Web to non-technical users raises the question again: "What information is sufficiently important to everyday life that people value it?" Some market analysts warn the present media craze about the appeal of online information is overstated, and only the

future can tell what online services will appeal to audiences in the long run.

The Web can provide some insight on what many define as information. Information providers seem to be responding to almost every facet of life—ranging from home, family, and community life to entertainment and business to research, art, and religion. Your challenge as a Web designer is to help shape the vision of what the Web is good for and to create new information resources that capture the imaginations of your audience.

The Structure of Information

Many Web sites offer a rather complex array of materials. There is rarely an intrinsic "right" way to organize such a body of information. Structural arrangements such as category headings, by their very nature, tend to impose hierarchies about the relative importance of the elements.

As an information designer, you need to consider structural questions as you plan a new Web site, including what information should be provided and excluded. What are appropriate categories for describing the available information to users? How should the visual and textual presentation of the Web site represent these structures?

The Web is not just a static structure; it is highly interactive. As a Web designer, you must help make decisions about this interactive process. The Web uses hypertext as the underlying model of how users pursue their interests. A brief definition of hypertext is that it is a non-linear system in which users can each pursue their own paths through material. Operationally, users do this by choosing among the hotlinks an author has indicated. Almost like a playwright, you must create the array of scenarios that users can experience.

You need to think about the following questions as part of the expanded design process: How should choices link together into various paths? What choices should lead to what other information? What text or images should serve as hotlinks? What navigational aids should be offered to users so they don't get lost?

These questions cannot be answered solely from the perspective of visual design. There are many disciplines that offer intriguing and useful viewpoints on these questions, including information science, psychology, human-machine interface design, cognitive ergonomics, information visualization, hypermedia, and interactive media arts. This research can give you new ideas to enhance the ways you think about Web design.

Communicating Online and On-Screen

You need to pay special attention to the ways that communicating via the Web is different from communicating via print. You must be sensitive to the nature of computer presentation of text and image—for example, limits on the readability of on-screen text and the limits of screen size. You must also optimize your presentation for the interactive realities of the Web. For example, you need to make sure your Web pages display well on a variety of computers, attend to the differences in speed of access users have, keep your site's information up-to-date, and offer information that works in an interactive hypermedia environment.

You may be reading this perhaps because you're considering becoming an "information provider." It's a pretty weighty-sounding term, but actually we all function as information providers in many aspects of our lives. We answer questions, make suggestions, express opinions, and share musings. Usually we don't formalize these activities and don't extend them far beyond our circles of acquaintances.

The World Wide Web allows any individual, group, or organization anywhere in the world who has something they think is of interest to make this information widely available to an international audience. The information provided can in some ways achieve as much exposure as that from large institutions. This new expansion of publishing is an unprecedented development. Just as the spread of reading and writing extended communication possibilities to everyday people, the increasing ability to publish on the Web can be considered another major event in the history of literacy.

What Is the Internet?

The Internet is the name given to the international network of interlinked computers that use a particular set of conventions for their communications called TCP/IP (Transmission Control Protocol/Internet Protocol). These conventions govern such things as how digital information is formatted at a basic level, how addresses are arranged so information can find its destination, how computers negotiate communication with each other, and how software programs must connect with the information being sent on the network.

There is no room here to present a full introduction to the Internet. For more information, consult one of the many excellent books explaining the Internet such as *The Internet Starter Kit* by Adam Engst (Hayden, 1994) or *The Whole Internet Catalog* by Ed Kroll (O'Reilly, 1994). Here I present only a brief overview, emphasizing those features that are most important to understanding the World Wide Web.

There are four features of the Internet that are crucial for Web designers to understand: Device independence, addressing conventions, decentralization, and Internet services.

Device Independence

Many people falsely envision the Internet as an extensive jumble of cables and computers. But actually the Internet was designed to be hardware-independent. That is, as long as the information being sent is formatted in accordance with the standards, it does not matter what kind of computer is sending or receiving the information or what kind of cable is used. Internet information can variously travel via fiber optics, microwaves, or satellite signals.

The Web's wide appeal builds on the Internet's device independence. To achieve this independence, each communicating computer must have the capability to understand the TCP/IP format—for example, by having an extension file that works with the operating system. The Web's present popularity and future promise are built on this device independence.

Addressing Conventions

The Internet relies on a naming system that can uniquely identify any computer in the world. Each host computer's address (known as an IP address) is a combination of a domain, subdomain, and individual computer address. The domain is the name given to the host that arranges and administers the Internet connection—for example, a university or online service provider. The administrators at each domain maintain a database for assigning the numbers within their domain. Each host's IP address is assigned a unique number (for example, 130.212.13.61), but most users use the host name, which is easier to remember (for example, www.infoarts.sfsu.edu).

This addressing convention is critical to the Web's ability to implement links. The Internet address of the computer that stores the resources is a crucial part of the URL (Uniform Resource Locator) address that the Web uses to find resources.

Decentralization

The Internet uses a decentralized model, which means there is no central computer through which all messages are sent. Using the TCP/IP protocols, computers on many dissimilar networks can exchange messages such as e-mail or data files quickly and seamlessly.

Each message is divided into many smaller packets, composed of data and a header that contains the sender and receiver address. Internet host computers monitor the passing electronic traffic by inspecting the address of each packet. If the packet is addressed to a computer in its own domain, the host takes it in and directs it to where it needs to go. If the packet is intended for another computer somewhere else, the host passes it along to another host closer to the ultimate destination. The process of jumps is repeated until the packet arrives at its intended address. The packets are reassembled into the original message and delivered to the user.

Internet Services

The Internet community has developed many programs and protocols to help users access resources and remote hosts. These include Telnet, FTP, Gopher, Usenet newsgroups, and the World Wide Web, among others. The Web is an integrated resource for accessing all these other tools and provides a user-friendly interface to access them. For example, many Web links are to Gopher servers.

What Is the World Wide Web?

The World Wide Web allows users to access information via hypertext documents that contain links to more documents. Running Web browser (also called client) software such as Mosaic or MacWeb, users activate an information link by clicking text or images with a mouse or by pressing an arrow key. After the user activates the link, the browser sends a request to the Internet-connected host computer (sometimes called the *server*) indicated in the link for the specific information. The server quickly sends the document and disconnects. The local computer must temporarily store and display the document. Contrary to what many users think, they are not continually connected to the server once the document has been received. Because the Web is built on the Internet's distributed client/server system architecture, these host computers can be located anywhere in the world.

Hypermedia

The Web's hypermedia system lets users send and receive data requests for text, image, sound, or digital video. Perhaps most importantly, the Web's range of coverage is extensible, so new data types or new kinds of services can be easily added.

The Web achieves some of its flexibility via browser configuration files that map the various data types that one might find on the Web to helper applications.

Origins of the term "hypertext"

Theodore (Ted) Nelson is a visionary who is credited with coining the term hypertext. His book Computer Lib/Dream Machines *(Mindful Press, 1974) described the importance of hypertext systems. He expanded this concept by mapping out a distributed interlinked hypertext system he called* Xanadu, *in which readers could follow their interests over a network to wherever relevant resources resided. Furthermore, anyone could publish their work in this interlinked system. The World Wide Web bears an uncanny resemblance to some essential features of Xanadu, which is no coincidence; some of the Web's developers acknowledge that Nelson's ideas influenced them strongly.*

There is a Web location called Xanadu devoted to Nelson's ideas. (http://peg.pegasus.oz.au/xanadu/). Nelson notes that networked hypermedia goes beyond a new technical system; it has more radical implications because it promotes populism (availability to all authors at low cost), pluralism (support of many points of view), unorthodoxy (encouragement of controversial subjects), and universalism (ideas spread in spite of geographical or other boundaries).

These helper programs work with browser and server software to add the functionality to handle various kinds of data, such as graphic images saved in a certain file format. Helper applications use an underlying Internet protocol called MIME (Multipurpose Internet Mail Extensions); a standardized method for organizing divergent file formats.

Web Protocols and Addressing

Web browsers shield users from all the details of addressing the requests and responses, formatting them for the Internet, negotiating between computers, and presenting the information on-screen. Like other Internet systems, the Web can operate because there is a set of conventions and protocols governing how requests and responses should be formatted and how the process of communication should proceed. The protocol that governs the communications between computers on the World Wide Web is called HTTP (HyperText Transfer Protocol).

HTTP includes a systematic and comprehensive way of identifying the location and appropriate access protocol for retrieving documents through addresses called *URLs* (Uniform Resource Locators). Each URL details an access path composed of three parts: the necessary protocol, the Internet address of the server computer that contains the resource, and the location of the resource in the host computer's local file directory system.

For example, the link pointer to the W3 organization's descriptions of the origins of the Web is http://www.w3.org/hypertext/WWW/TheProject.html. The http:// part identifies the resource as a native Web document. The next part gives the computer's host name (www.w3.org). The last part provides the file path location on that computer's directory structure (/hypertext/WWW/TheProject.html).

The language that defines the format in which individual documents must be prepared is called *HTML* (HyperText Markup Language). HTML is constantly under revision; currently, the standards for HTML 3.0 are being finalized and are nearing implementation.

Getting Prepared to be a Web Designer

This book helps you learn the practical and analytic skills you need to become a Web designer. Each chapter answers a set of questions that confront Web designers.

Design Implications of the Web

Chapter 1: How is Web publishing different from regular publishing? What should and should not be published on the Web? What can you learn from looking at other Web sites?

HTML and Linking Fundamentals

Chapter 2: How does HTML work? How can it be used to format text in a way that displays well on many kinds of computers? What new possibilities does HTML 3.0 offer?

Chapter 3: How can you use HTML to create hypermedia links that can access resources all over the world?

Working with Image, Sound, and Video on the Web

Chapters 4, 5, and 6: How do you offer images, sound, and video on the Web? How do you prepare these media to optimize them for the Web?

Advanced Interactive Events

Chapter 7: How can you make the most of advanced features such as CGI scripts, imagemaps, and fill-in forms?

Experimentation and Future Trends

Chapter 8: What can you learn from the artists and technologists who are experimenting with the Web's capabilities in areas such as telepresence, interactive media, collaboration, and alternative information structures?

Chapter 9: What makes a compelling Web site? What tips and guidelines are there for making engaging and effective Web pages?

Chapter 10: What's in store for the future of the Web? What technological trends must designers be aware of? How can you keep up with the Web?

Additional Resources

Appendix A offers an overview of how to conduct research on the Web to locate resources relevant to the development of your site, such as indexes and automatic search programs. Appendixes B and C contain some detailed information on creating advanced scripts and fill-in forms.

The Web as Cultural Experimentation

My most recent art projects directly relate to this book. I was invited to be artist-in-residence at the Xerox PARC research center. This think tank was responsible for many of the computer innovations we now take for granted—for example, graphical user interfaces (providing the origins of the Mac and Windows systems), networking, Ethernet, and PostScript. PARC researchers are still working on inventing the future.

During the residency my co-researchers, Jock Mackinlay, Polle Zelleweger, and I focused on the Web. We tried to understand how it functioned now and what it might become. This research led me to write this book to help others start designing for the Web. I hope it serves you well!

Chapter 1

Design Implications of the Web

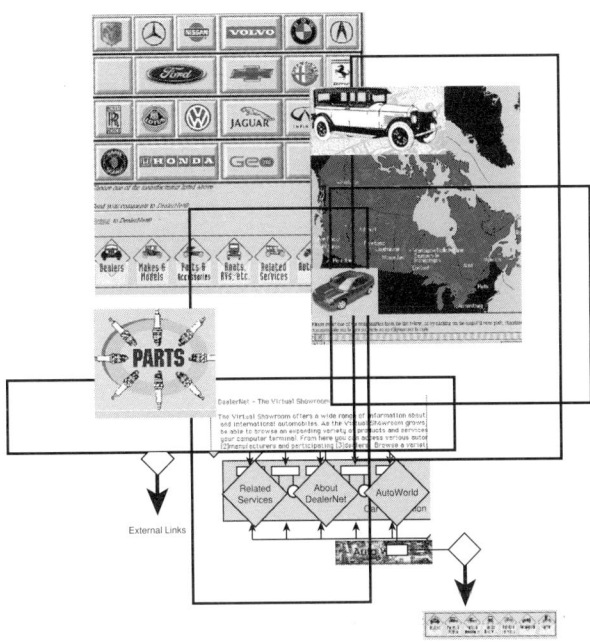

If you've already started surfing the Web, you've been intrigued, excited, and captivated. You've also been lost, bored, or maybe even disgusted. Some sites amaze you and make you want to return many times; others make you wonder, "Why in the world did they bother to put this on the Web?"

You've already started preparing to be a Web designer in one of the most important ways possible. You need to know the Web inside and out. You need to look at as many Web sites as you can—studying them from many perspectives. How do they change your ideas about what information is significant and how the Web might be used?

Reasons for Designing on the Web

As a Web designer, you can connect directly with an audience anywhere in the world. Groups or individuals with radical, unusual, or specialized interests can find interested audiences. Businesses with new products can advertise them immediately. Even traditional information providers can reach new audiences in new ways. In these exciting times of the birth of the Web, you can be part of this revolution.

At this early stage of the Web's development, just being a pioneer on the Web might suggest hipness or technological sophistication. Consider the businesses that bought ads on the first TV stations. They reached very few real customers, but they did create an innovator image for themselves.

As the Web matures, this appeal will fade. There will probably be many similar Web offerings. In a fast-evolving environment like the Web, it makes little sense to think of Web design as a one-shot deal. Web sites will need to change with the shifting cultural context and with constant technological innovation. This is something you need to communicate to those you work with as a Web designer.

Questions to Ask Yourself as a Web Designer

To respond adequately to the challenge of the Web, you can use concepts of *expanded* design. As you design your site, ask yourself about larger context of your site, its information structure, effectiveness of interactivity, and visual communication.

Here are some starting questions:

- **Surrounding Context:** What is the site's definition of significant information? Why is the site being created? Who do you think will be interested? What other sites cover related material? Does the international context of the Web have any special influence on this site? Without the Web, where would anyone go to find similar information?

- **Information Structure:** What categories of choices are offered? What conceptual frameworks seem to underlay those categories? How will you structure the information? How will you make that structure clear to Web visitors?

- **Interactivity:** How is interaction orchestrated? What hotlinks are there? How are navigational options made clear? What would be typical navigational scenarios?

- **Visual Impact:** On first view, what will be most noticeable about the site? What will engage visitors? How does the site's presentation work visually? How does its composition influence its effectiveness and appeal? What will visitors find new or surprising about your site?

Analysis of a Site

To explore expanded design, let's take a look at a Web site in detail. We look at DealerNet, a site devoted to automobile-related information. But we could have picked any site; the analysis process would be similar.

We'll analyze what the DealerNet designers did from several perspectives—conceptualizing who the target audience is and how their site fits into the larger context of the world outside the Web, interactive structure and the organization of information, visual impact and effectiveness, and designing to take advantage of the unique capabilities of new technologies.

Your best strategy for perfecting your Web design style is to become a compulsive Web navigator. Visit as many sites as you can. Look at sites that are close to your world and look at sites that have nothing to do with your interests. But don't just skim the surface. Study the sites to understand how the designers put them together, what assumptions they seem to have made, what innovative features they introduced, and what you might have done differently. This process of study and question asking is the first step in good Web design.

Web pages?

Often people will ask me to help them create a Web page. What they may not realize is that most Web sites do not consist of a single "page." The Web's interactive hypermedia structure promotes a less static design, which will probably consist of many "pages." Users will pick and choose links on their path through these pages to get to the information they want. It's a rare situation in which all the information can or should be presented on one page.

Even calling these information spaces "pages" is misleading. Many Web pages are viewed in a scrollable window and can contain much more information than you would find on a print page. Also, these pages are full of active links that have no equivalent on a print page. Most Web designers probably want to do more than create a single Web "page."

Who Is Your Site's Audience and What Is Its Surrounding Context?

The first questions to ask are

- What are the Web developers trying to do in creating this site?

- What audience do they hope to reach?
- What do they hope their audience will think or do? How are they positioning the site in the Web and in the real world?

Figure 1.1 shows the home page of DealerNet.

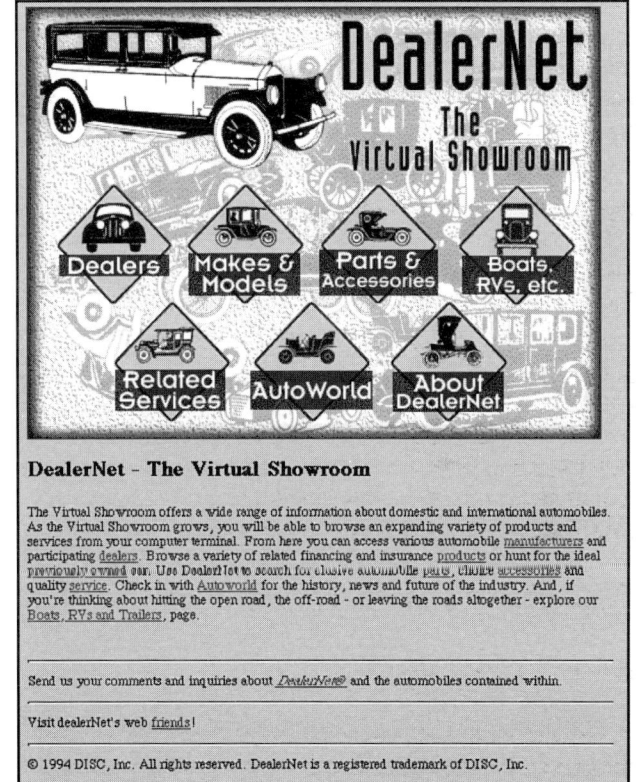

Martin S. Road, CEO.

Figure 1.1:

DealerNet's main access page.

`http://www.dealernet.com/`

The designers named their site DealerNet. The name focuses on the dealers rather than auto information in general because they may have two related audiences—dealers and buyers. They are selling the service to dealers, who have to be convinced that being listed in DealerNet is a good idea. Naming it DealerNet, instead of, say, AutoNet, makes the intended purpose clear.

Like so many designers on the Web, DealerNet's creators are constantly updating their site. When you visit, DealerNet will most likely look a bit different than shown here. Using the design analysis in this chapter, ask yourself if the changes have made the site stronger.

One goal of the site is to convince potential buyers that the dealers listed are good sources of information and ultimately good places to buy a car. But the Web is international; it is unlikely that Web visitors from faraway cities will buy their cars from these dealers. For local Web surfers, the sites can function as advertisements, buyer education, and buyer contact; for distant surfers, however, the site must function as something else. These distant buyers may use the data offered (for example, details about different model cars) to make a buying decision, but the DealerNet sponsors will not directly benefit. Maybe the designers hope to franchise the idea with many local nodes?

Let's look at how they position their appeal—what advertising sometimes calls the "pitch" or the "spin." Figure 1.1 shows their main sign-on image, built from monochrome illustrations of antique cars. This evokes nostalgia, possibly as a way of suggesting that old-fashioned virtues and value still apply. Nostalgia is of course only one of many potential pitches—for example, work utility, family usefulness, snob appeal, technological innovation, and fantasies of adventure, power, or sex.

It is hard to know if this latent meaning works as intended. To really find out, the DealerNet planners would have to conduct in-depth interviews with viewers. But often this is impractical and advertisers have no choice but to go with intuition. Nonetheless, pitch is important and you as a Web designer need to be aware of how you position your work. There are techniques that can provide you with "hit statistics" about your site indicating useful information about numbers of user visits to the various parts of your site, but they cannot tell you about the way your pitch is being received.

Where does DealerNet sit in the larger culture outside of the Web? How do potential buyers usually find out about cars? They talk to friends, look at cars on the street, read car and consumer magazines, and perhaps go to dealers to collect brochures. To figure out how much to trust a dealer, they may look around, watch interactions between salespersons and customers, or even talk to a representative.

How does this Web version compare? It lacks the personal approach of talking to friends, the sensual immediacy of seeing real cars, or scoping out a dealer. It does, however, satisfy the need for gathering official auto manufacturer information conveniently. Even more, this information is available on demand, 24 hours a day, every day of the week. As a stimulus for further development, the Web designers might ask how the site might serve some of those personal or unmet sensory functions.

Some futurists think that interactive technologies will change the face of advertising. Sellers will no longer need to spend money on mass untargeted ads and consumers will no longer be bothered by unwanted ads. Buyers and sellers will be able to collaborate. Once a potential buyer indicates an interest, the automatic "infomercial" systems will be able to send them information. Furthermore, consumers will be able to fine-tune the interchange by interactively requesting custom information—for example, viewing a representation of a potential purchase in the color they want or getting a comparison with other models. Also, the nature of information advertisers can offer will expand beyond narrow product information to include other useful related topics. See the section on responsibility in this chapter for samples of the other kinds of information DealerNet might have offered. These speculations about the future of advertising suggest experimental approaches that could be tried out in Web design today.

Your success as a Web designer will be limited if you restrict your job description to laying out the text and image of Web pages. Designers have always been known for breaking new visual ground. In the quickly changing, wide-reaching context of the Web, expanded design means asking questions such as: What is going on here? What is not going on that might be relevant? and What are the trends and the possibilities for the future?

Interactive Structure and the Organization of Information

As you begin to convert your text and pictures to hypermedia, you should think about how you'll address the following questions:

- How will your site organize the information it offers?
- What are the main categories of choice?
- What are the subcategories? What is linked to what?
- How can you navigate the information? How easy is it get around, to know where you are and where you might go?

A bias toward "structured" information

Realize that this search for immediate resolution of structure does represent a bias toward certain kinds of information. It assumes that efficiency and clarity are important. Such an approach seems to make sense in a site such as DealerNet that wants to facilitate potential buyer access to information.

There are other models for information structures. For example, in the arts a slow unveiling of information is often important. In a novel or film, the main focuses are not necessarily clear at the beginning. The resolution gradually develops and that is part of the joy. Similarly, in contemporary interactive CD-ROM works, the choices of the user determine what is revealed and what options are available at any subsequent time.

DealerNet does better than many sites in clearly presenting its information structure. The diamonds in its main index page (illustrated in Figure 1.1) prominently indicate there are seven main categories. The index pages of many other Web sites are very confusing; often there are hidden resources that can be found only with difficulty. DealerNet's main structure announces itself strongly.

Furthermore, the site uses this sevenfold division as its main interactive aid. Most pages at this site include a miniaturized version of the seven diamonds for quick movement. Once you understand the structure, you are never more than one click away from the main index page or from any of the other main categories. Figure 1.2 illustrates the miniaturized quick navigation panel. In many sites, there is no way to retrace your steps other than to use the *go back* option on the software (called a Web browser or client) you are using to browse the Web.

Figure 1.2:
DealerNet's quick navigational panel.

The site seems to support "index" scenarios as its primary navigational pattern. The user goes to the main index, picks one of the seven categories, goes to the local index for that category, goes to next level down, and then returns to either the local or the main index to select the next link. Figure 1.3 shows the local index under the category "Makes & Models." Figure 1.4 shows one of the dealer's listings that can be reached via either the "Dealers" or "Makes & Models" categories. Figure 1.5 shows a schematic of the relationships among the seven main sections of the site and their connections to outside information.

The information organization does present some problems. The seven diamonds imply a parallel structure with each item equally important. But that's not the case here. *About DealerNet*, *Related Services*, and *Parts & Accessories* do not seem as important as the all-encompassing *Dealers* category that contains the list of dealers and the information each offers. Some kind of visual differentiation (for example, size, color, or positioning) could have been introduced to clarify the relative importance, although the visual impact of the seven parallel diamonds would have been disrupted.

Makes & Models is another window for accessing the dealers. Instead of picking by dealer, users can pick by make and model, but they end up linking to the same place as before, the information pages offered by each dealer. The information

design might have been stronger if designers could have found some way to indicate that the choices led to the same body of information. But this challenge is difficult; hypertext structures with multiple points of access to the same information are complicated to represent.

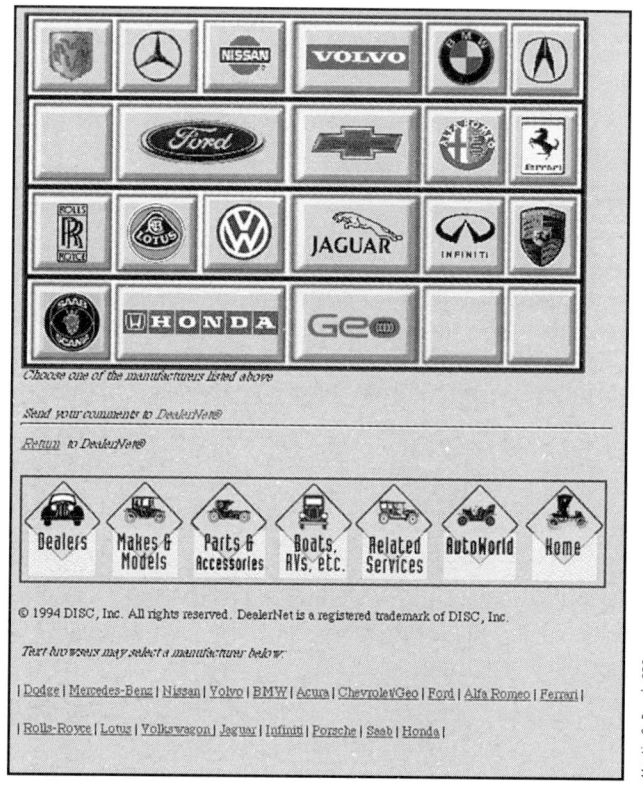

Figure 1.3:
Makes & Models category index.

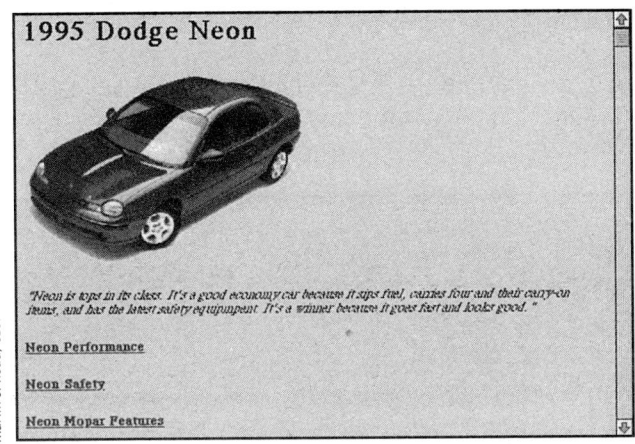

Martin S. Road, CEO.

Figure 1.4:
Sample listing from one of the dealers.

Boats & RVs appears like another major distinction that is not quite parallel with the other choices. RVs and boats seem to call for their own sites on a par with DealerNet. They seem included here as a not yet fully fleshed out example of future possibilities. (There were few offerings in each of these categories at press time.)

AutoWorld is the page that provides access to related Web information. This is a different kind of resource from information provided by the dealers. It might have been helpful to indicate that difference in the index image. Figure 1.6 shows the index to *AutoWorld* and a page with the resources it offers.

DealerNet focuses on offering unique *locally* generated resources. That is, much of the material at the site consists of the text and images created by DealerNet's designers and dealers rather than focusing on links to material available in other sites. Other Web sites primarily offer links to external resources. But offering external links poses another problem. Once the users click on an external link, they are gone from that site—out into Cyberspace. The next display they see on their screens will be from the external site. There most likely will be nothing on that page to indicate the original site. As they follow the links offered at this new place, they can end up even further away conceptually from the original starting place. This typifies the power and the chaos of hypermedia. Users can always use the *go back* or local history options on their Web client to return, but this requires an action that is outside of the links offered on their screens. Decisions about the relative emphasis on internal and external links is one of the challenges of information design on the Web.

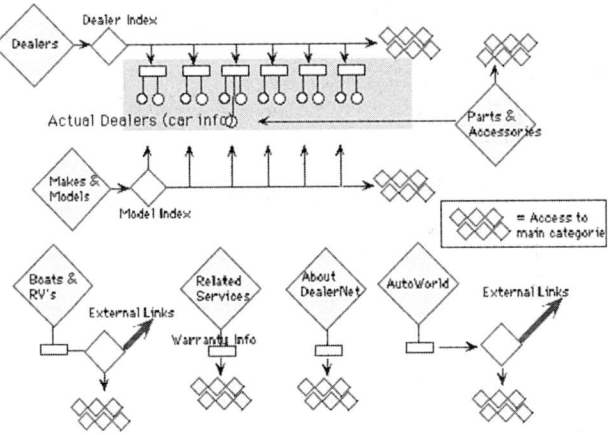

Figure 1.5:
Relationships between sections of the site and outside information.

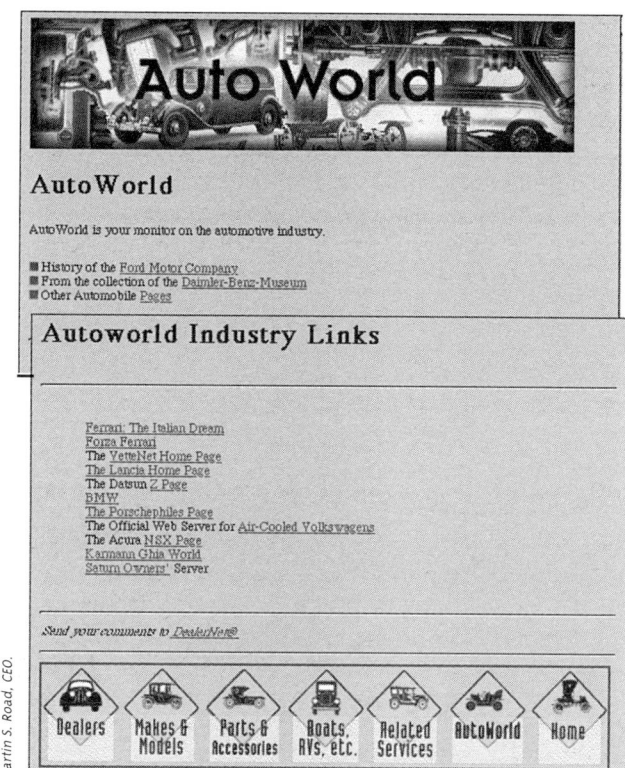

Martin S. Road, CEO.

Figure 1.6:
AutoWorld pages with access to outside Web resources.

DealerNet's designers attempted to deal with this dilemma by making access to external resources a two-step process. Accessing AutoWorld first takes you to a description of the resources before you can actually click on the link that goes outside. On this page there is a prominent choice to link back into DealerNet. This arrangement prevents the premature loss of DealerNet surfers to Cyberspace.

Compared to many other sites, DealerNet is easy to get around in. Its major categories are clear. Every page offers the user a chance to navigate back or move to other major categories.

Visual Impact and Effectiveness

As a Web designer, you'll want to take the following issues into consideration in order to create the right impression and elicit favorable responses:

- What is the visual appeal of the site?
- What do visitors notice first?
- How do text and images work together?
- How effectively do the displays communicate?

DealerNet's main signature graphic is much more carefully developed than many you find on the Web. The yellow diamonds set up a clear sevenfold division of categories, the antique cars communicate the auto focus of the site, and the background pattern of cars is interesting without being distracting. It is fun to look at and is not so simple that it is entirely grasped in one cursory glance.

The antique car imagery may have solved another problem for those who created DealerNet. Antique cars communicate the concept of automobile while avoiding specificity of brand, and can represent many different kinds of cars. Use of contemporary images might be a problem because the cars would be identifiable as specific models.

The main index and the makes and models index use an advanced Web capability called *imagemaps*. Imagemaps are images with coordinates mapped to perform different jumps depending on where you click on the image. For example, a map of the United States could contain different links for each state. When a user clicks on an image, the Web client application sends the coordinates of the click to the server application at the Web site. Special software reads these coordinates and sends back customized information that the designer has mapped to particular places in the image. For example, DealerNet's designers have mapped the seven diamonds on the index to link to the sections represented in the image. Chapter 7 explains the complexities of setting up this capability and describes the way it enhances interactivity.

The *Dealers* and *Makes & Models* categories take advantage of auto makers' logos and the decades of consumer recognition that go with them. Each dealer is represented with the logo of the cars offered. The main index for *Makes & Models* presents a fascinating grid of logos to click on (Figure 1.3). The car information sheet offered under each dealer uses a clear, informational graphics approach of thumbnail images and tables of data. Figure 1.4 shows an example of one of these offerings.

The site's presentation of text could be stronger. For example, the main index page presents a paragraph under the imagemap index that lists the categories and links. (Figure 1.1). The paragraph seems forced and not clearly organized. The DealerNet designers could have explored some of the list options available in HTML, the Web's authoring language, to present this text in a more visually interesting and clearer way.

Designing to Take Advantage of Diverse Technologies

DealerNet faces a dilemma. Much of the Web's appeal comes from its graphics. But many users access the Web with text-only browsers, such as Lynx, that do not display graphics at all. Even users with graphically oriented browsers might have relatively slow modem links and could reject the waiting time for these graphics to load. They might even deactivate image loading in order to speed access. Figure 1.7 shows DealerNet's Home Page as it would be rendered in a text-only browser such as Lynx. Compare this page with Figure 1.1, which shows the same page rendered by a graphical Web browser such as Netscape or MacWeb.

```
[1][IMAGE]
_____

DealerNet - The Virtual Showroom

The Virtual Showroom offers a wide range of information about
and international automobiles. As the Virtual Showroom grows,
be able to browse an expanding variety of products and services
your computer terminal. From here you can access various autor
[2]manufacturers and participating [3]dealers.  Browse a variet
financing and insurance [4]products or hunt for the ideal
[5]previously owned car. Use DealerNet to search for elusive
automobile [6]parts, choice [7]accessories and quality [8]servic
Check in with [9]Autoworld for the history, news and future of
industry. And, if you're thinking about hitting the open road, the
off-road - or leaving the roads altogether - explore our [10]Boa
RVs and Trailers, page.
_____

Send us your comments and inquiries about [11]DealerNet(R) and
automobiles contained within.
_____

Visit dealerNet's web [12]friends!
_____

(c) 1994 DISC, Inc. All rights reserved. DealerNet is a
registered trademark of DISC, Inc.
```

Martin S. Road, CEO.

Figure 1.7:
DealerNet home page as rendered by Lynx, a text-only Web browser.

None of these users will be able to use the main home page diamond graphic as an index. They won't see it. The text-only viewers will see the word "Image" and the deactivated graphics viewers will see a generic icon. DealerNet addresses these technological wrinkles by offering alternative text for each index. For example, a text list explaining the main categories and providing links to them appears below the visual index. It will be available to all users.

The *Accessories and Parts* section of the site employs the fill-in forms capability of the Web. Users can type in the year, make, model, and part description, their e-mail address, and other relevant information. The parts department of the dealer can then check availability, price, and other information and relay it back to the user. Figure 1.8 shows the parts index and information fill-in form from DealerNet.

At this point, the process by which the dealer responds to Web-submitted forms includes real people to check for the requested information. However, database technology already exists to implement an automatic information retrieval system. Although it is somewhat complex to link it to the Web, it could be done. Eventually human labor could be mostly excluded. Users would have automatic, 24 hour a day, 7 day a week access to parts information. Chapter 7 explains the complexities of setting up fill-in forms response systems.

Once Web technology enables secure credit card transactions, the entire process could be automated including the ordering, billing, and sending and inventory control on the dealer's side. You go on the Web; search for your part; if its available, you order it; and poof, it's on its way to you and your credit card is billed. If you work on cars, you know the frustration of searching for a part and the special annoyance of not being able to search outside of business hours. The Web can potentially change those problems.

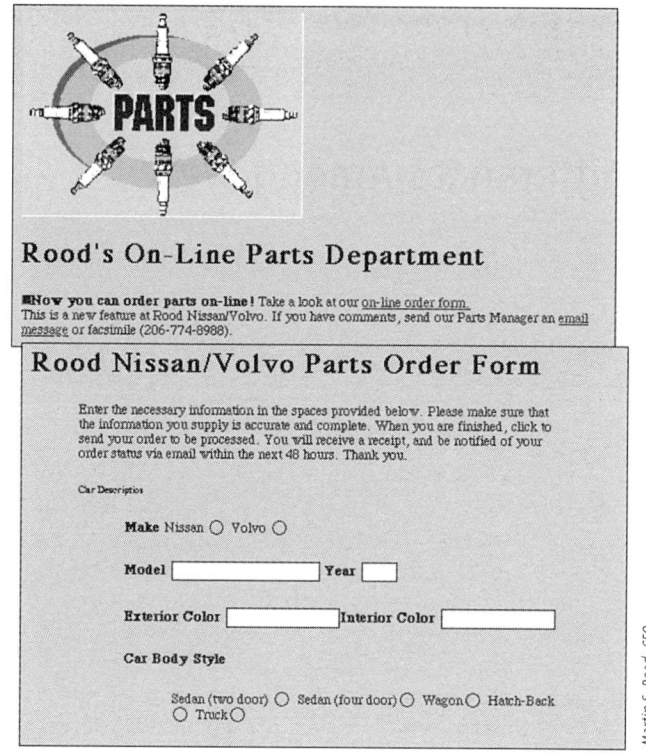

Martin S. Road, CEO.

Figure 1.8:
Parts index and fill-in information request form.

In its general car information section, DealerNet does not yet allow much customization of requests. The user cannot do much more than indicate make preference. The technology exists to do much more. For example, fill-in forms would allow the site to provide price quotes for the specific model with indicated options. The linkage of fill-in forms capability with scripted graphics would allow a personalized visual representation of the car a user was interested in—for example, customized by color or by placement in a particular background.

Differences Among Web Browsers

Designers working with interactive environments typically use an approach called *user-centered design*. This method stresses understanding of an experience from the user's point of view. It suggests designers adopt the user's perspective to the greatest extent possible and test extensively with potential users. These *client* or *browser* applications are the prime contact most people have with the Web and thus must be understood thoroughly. But users go Web surfing with a great variety of capabilities. Some are using text-only terminals with slow modem connections. Others are using state of the art workstations with fast, broad bandwidth network connections and full color, 21-inch display monitors. This section addresses the following questions to help you prepare for this variety:

- What are the basic and experimental capabilities of different Web browsers?
- What do you need to know about the ways users can customize their browsers?
- How are browsers likely to develop in the future?

Basic Functions of Web Browsers

Consider what browser application programs that run on the local computer must accomplish. They must know how to access Web servers connected to the Internet and to interact with the server software in order to request desired information. There are many different kinds of browser software that have been developed for different kinds of computers and operating systems. For example, Mosaic, Netscape, Cello, MacWeb, WinWeb, Lynx, and Windows all offer built-in browsers. Almost all major online service providers such as CompuServe, America Online, and PRODIGY now offer Web browsers customized to their service. All Web browsers, however, share a set of basic functions they must be able to perform, including the following:

- Send requests for information to Web servers in the proper Internet and World Wide Web formats.
- Receive information sent back from Web servers or display error messages to the user.
- Display that information in a way that preserves the design indications that the original author embedded in the documents.
- Provide a way for users to save documents that arrive via Web requests.
- Provide a way for users to store "bookmarks" or hotlist entries of locations they might want to visit again.
- Keep a history record of links that have been chosen and allow the user to reactivate past entries.
- Display possible links in a clear way, read user actions to choose those links, and send requests for the information based on those choices.
- Manage memory in ways to minimize downloading time (for example, by temporarily storing previously requested documents in local storage caches so they can quickly be retrieved when requested again).

There are Web browsers, such as Lynx, that will run on simple text-based terminals. Even these must provide the functions listed previously. The most popular browsers, however, take full advantage of the graphic user interface of the Macintosh, Windows, and UNIX X Windows environments. These allow user choices to be indicated via mouse clicking and they display images and other kinds of information types not supported by text-only terminals. They also add other experimental capabilities that were not part of the original specifications. Many advanced browsers can perform the following:

- Display inline images appropriately.

- Call upon "helper" programs to display information types that are not an intrinsic part of the Web (for example, sound, certain formats of images, or digital video).

- Allow users to extend the helper capability by indicating new programs to handle additional information types.

- Allow users to customize their computing environments (for example, by postponing inline image loading in order to speed downloading and by choosing font style and size conventions).

- Interpret user clicks on interactive "imagemaps" in order to send the specific click location to the server in a format that will allow the server to make custom responses based on where the image was clicked.

- Correctly display fill-in forms on the screen that allow the user to click selection buttons, pick from pull-down selection boxes, and type in responses. Send the user provided information back to the server in a format that will allow custom response.

- Provide quick access to frequently used Web services such as indexes, home pages, and the like.

- Provide for secure Web communications by encrypting transmissions and decrypting receptions.

These functions set the context for a user's experience with the Web. As a Web designer, you need to know what is available to users and what they really use. Most Web clients are designed so users can customize them. Each user can adjust the way the browser interprets information—for example, the bookmark list of frequently accessed sites; the helper applications used to play sounds or movies; the fonts, styles, and sizes of text that are mapped to standard Web styles; and how links are indicated. Understanding the kinds of modifications users can make to their browsers is important information about how the pages you design might end up. Study the browsers carefully. Do you know what all menu items and toolbar icons represent? Do you know what can be changed in the preferences and options? Figure 1.9 shows one of the preference dialog boxes from the Mosaic browser to illustrate the kinds of modification users can make.

Think about users carefully. Which functions do Web navigators use? How many deactivate image loading? How do users employ hotlists or bookmarks? How many adjust their screens or change the color or font mapping preferences? Many sections of this book will explore the possibility that users might customize their displays and offer strategies to address this possibility. Once you start to create Web documents, ask naive users to test your materials and talk you through their internal mental processes. Watch how they use browser functions in conjunction with your work. These observations will be valuable tools in refining your work.

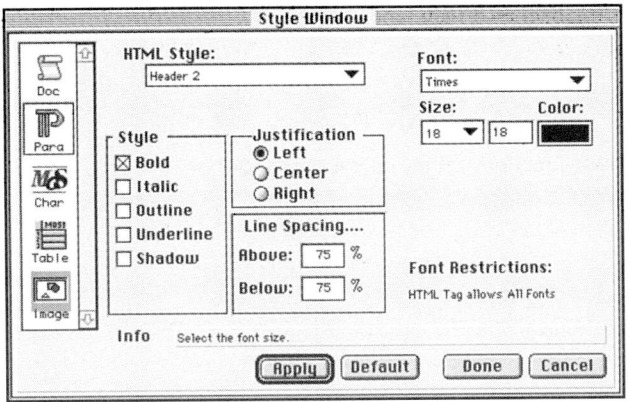

Figure 1.9:
Customizing the font display in Mosaic.

Future Developments in Web Clients

Developers are working hard to invent new versions of Web browsers, and users can expect great variety in the next few years. For example, browsers such as Netscape are offering instant tool palette access to Net directories and search engines. The Netscape browser also offers some features missing in Mosaic such as the ability to handle special HTML text and graphics "extensions" that are not part of the international standard. (These are discussed in more detail in Chapters 2 and 4.) The browsers offered by online services such as CompuServe have tried to create unified interfaces that integrate access to their unique internal information resources with access to Web sites.

Browsers also differ in the ways they address new Web developments. The Web community is constantly in flux—proposing new capabilities and working through the processes of formal international acceptance. At any given time, various browsers might differ in which proposed features they support prior to formal acceptance. For example, even though HTML 3.0 is still not formally accepted as an international standard, some browsers have already implemented some of the proposed features.

Remember that at the fundamental level all Web clients must perform the basic functions. Web browsers may differ in the interface, performance, and convenience features they offer, but they cannot offer radically new capabilities because the Web standard that guides authors and servers must also relate to many other client applications. As a Web designer, you must learn as much as possible about the variety of Web browsers available so you can design your pages to play well in as many contexts as possible.

What Should or Shouldn't You Publish?

You probably have some tentative ideas about information you want to put on the Web. As you surf the Web, you can see that there are almost as many reasons for Web publishing as there are different life activities—for example, education, community and government life, religion, entertainment, creative expression, or hobbies. As you discover how easy and satisfying Web publishing can be, you will most likely develop new ideas for the Web beyond your initial reasons. Any information that would be of interest or value to people beyond your immediate circle could be a candidate for the Web.

The Web revolutionizes publishing. *Anyone* can be an author. This sounds like a great idea... or does it? On one hand, you get access to a much greater variety of materials than you would see through traditional publishing alone, but you also have to wade through a lot of junk. How will you find the things you need? How will you decide what is worth your limited time? Turning these questions around from the perspective of you as publisher raises these questions: How will Web readers find my work? What will they think of my work if it is part of this mass of other authors? What is worth putting on the Web?

Everyone can be a reader. But we're used to thinking in more restrictive terms about who should be an author or information provider. Some analysts suggest that the Web challenges this assumption. The Web infrastructure simplifies the economics and practical details of distributing materials so that you can make materials available if you have basic computer access and knowledge of Web authoring processes. Others answer that the Web will quickly need to reestablish techniques for filtering, editing, and distinguishing worth or it will drown in its own undifferentiated flow. Being a Web designer at this early stage of its development puts you right in the middle of this debate.

The Web transfers the main responsibility for deciding what should be on the Web from large institutions to individuals. You will face these questions as you develop your own Web ideas. One major criterion is that Web offerings should be as clear and engaging as possible; this book aims to help you with that goal.

Taken to the extreme, anything anyone has to say could be published on the Web. Where do you stand on this? Since the Web represents such an experiment in culture, the answers are not always so clear-cut. Let's look at some of the issues you should consider in making judgements about what to put on the Web.

Public and Private Interest

Who will want to see what you publish? How big is the circle of interest? You might have information that is of vital interest to a specified group but of questionable value to others. Is it appropriate to put on the Web? What about very personal expressions?

Sometimes the answer seems easy: If you know that your materials are likely to have wide public interest or at least interest to an identifiable group, publish them. If not, common sense says don't put them on the Web. The evolving culture of the Web, however, challenges old assumptions about relevance; the circle of interest might be much larger than you expect. For example, there are educational projects underway in which school children are following the Web postings of remote research groups as a way of learning about the processes of science. Those research groups did not define students as their audience but the Web allows this new audience to define itself.

Figure 1.10 shows the home page of the Human Genome Project. This project is part of a worldwide effort by scientists to map the human gene structure. The scientists are making extensive use of the Web for professional communication of results and research issues, but it may also be of interest to many others.

What if you define your circle of interest very narrowly? Who do you want to see what you publish? Should it be private? The Internet and the Web are still by and large insecure communication networks. That is, anyone with appropriate software can monitor communications not aimed at them. Work is proceeding apace to create secure servers and clients that will use passwords and encryption schemes to guarantee secure communications. Until those systems are in place, sensitive information should not be published on the Web.

Human Genome Project, U.S. Department of Energy (public domain).

Figure 1.10:
Human Genome Project.
`http://www.er.doe.gov/production/oher/hug_top.html`

Technical Concerns: Target Audience Access and Media Capabilities

Does your target audience have Internet access? A lot of people don't even have computers or modems, let alone Internet access. It makes no sense to place materials on the Web aimed at audiences without appropriate access. Businesses especially are wondering if enough of their potential customers have Web access to warrant their entry into the Web.

The flux of the Web makes decision-making based on target audience access problematic. The population of Web users is rapidly changing, and placement of resources on the Web can itself stimulate new relevant audiences to get access. Thus, just because the target audience is not there today does not necessarily mean it never will be and that you should not publish on the Web.

Inequities in access

Many in the Internet and Web community are worried about inequities in Internet access. Within developed countries the economically disadvantaged are less likely to have Internet access than more privileged classes. Internationally, undeveloped countries have poor Internet access. When the Internet was a specialized geek world, this inequity was not so important. If the Web becomes as central to commercial, political, artistic, and intellectual life as many predict, this inequity becomes a critical problem.

Do your Web publishing plans include high quality multimedia such as high resolution images, sound, or digital video? High quality media files tend to be very large. Because the Internet is a relatively narrow pipeline that uses a store and forward technology to send data, these files can take a relatively long time to travel from the Web server to the browser's computer. Conditioned to a relatively fast time of Web browsing, users can become frustrated with the network realities of slow transmission times. As a result, Web designers often must make compromises in media quality (for example, reducing the length, frame size, or frame rate of their video). Some decide the Web is not ready for their work. Chapters 4 through 6 on Web media work clarify these limitations, show you how to work with them, and help you decide about your own media plans and Chapter 10 explains research underway to improve the media performance of the Web.

Intellectual Property

One of the most compelling attractions of Web publishing is exposure. Your work can be seen and appreciated all over the world. But what if your audience members appreciate it so much that they want a copy of it? Is there any way to protect, track, and get compensated for use of one's Web media creations? What is fair use? Conversely, what if you see work on the Web or elsewhere that would be useful for your work? Are you allowed to copy and use those resources?

Some see the World Wide Web as an intellectual property nightmare that is only going to get worse. The ease with which viewers can access media resources is one of its main appeals. Images, sounds, and digital movies are just a click away. On the user's end, the media arrive as independent files ready to be copied to the viewer's system and used. Once copied, these files can be manipulated and incorporated into other works as easily as original media files. Piracy is very easy if the user is so inclined.

As a Web designer you must address intellectual property issues. You must know when you have rights to use the creative work of others and you must give consideration to protecting your own work. Chapter 9 considers intellectual property rights in more detail.

Responsibility

The decentralized structure of the Web places an unprecedented responsibility for assessing the value of potential Web offerings on each individual designer or information provider. What a paradox! If everyone really published everything they thought was potentially interesting, all the voices might flood out each other. The deluge is already beginning. Many Web navigators complain that there is so much on the Web that they can't find what they want. Ironically, the Web's ability to give everyone a voice can end up with no one being heard.

Just because you can put anything you want on the Web doesn't mean you should. Are those potential Web pages really worth the information space they will occupy? Do they duplicate resources already available? Information space means that they become options for readers and indexes and thus must be considered when a Web navigator is looking for something.

Personal, organizational, and educational reasons for Web publishing

Most discussions about the value of Web publishing focus on the audience. Will the information you're going to provide be well received? Will it be useful or interesting to someone?

There are other reasons, however, to publish that have nothing to do with the larger audience. You might want to create a Web resource for personal reasons or for the positive value of the process on the group or organization that is involved regardless of how useful or interesting the Web pages are to any audience. For example, an organization's work on Web pages can help increase morale and clarity of mission. Similarly, many schools are undertaking Web projects for their educational value for the students who work on them rather than for their real worth to any larger audience. These are not necessarily reasons to refrain from publishing. You just need to be clear as a Web author what your real reasons are. Also, you should probably treat them as quasi-private and not announce these sites to the public in order to keep them out of the indexes.

Figure 1.11 shows the map selection page from the Web-based *Our Home* project, which has engaged children throughout Canada in documenting their local communities with image and text. Although the information will be of interest to anyone trying to learn more about Canada, it has even greater value for the children and communities involved.

So don't be a Web litterer. Do your research on what your site proposes to do and on what already exists. Make sure your site offers something unique to the Web community in its substance and its design. On the other hand, don't be unnecessarily conservative. At this young age, the Web needs designers willing to experiment and take risks to help shape its future directions. Responsibility reaches beyond negative injunctions. Designers have the responsibility to probe the new information and technological possibilities of the Web and to expand the vision of what Web sites can be.

Let's return for a minute to the DealerNet site. It could do more than it does. We could ask questions about the place of automobiles in the larger culture. There is nothing in this site about pollution, ecology, auto accidents, drunken drivers, urban congestion, or alternatives such as mass transit. There is little of the information you would find in *Consumer Reports*. The site does offer links to external Web sites in its "AutoWorld" category, but only in a restricted range. To the Web maintainers' credit, naming their site DealerNet was an upfront expression of their restricted point of view.

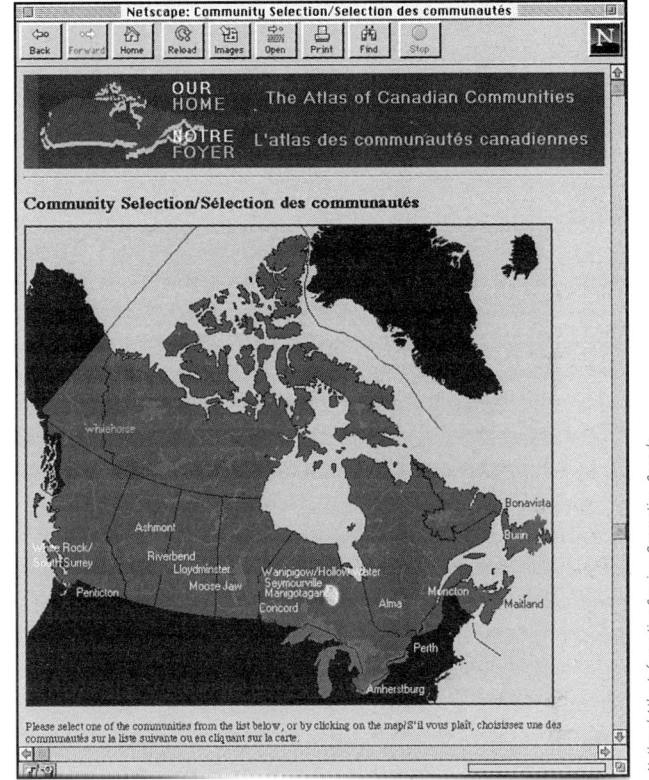

National Atlas Information Service. Geomatics, Canada.

Figure 1.11:
Our Home project documenting a variety of Canadian communities.
`http://ellesmere.ccm.emr.ca:80/ourhome/ourhome/`
`selectio.html`

Is it unrealistic to ask an auto dealer's Web site to include more general information? Perhaps, but some analysts think that in the coming information culture, consumers will expect broad conceptual reach. Some Web visitors might in fact be impressed that such a site defines its responsibility so broadly. Web designers can help those they work with to stretch their vision.

Figure 1.12 shows the U.S. Census Bureau's art posters commissioned as part of their "Stand Up and Be Counted" effort. Some might wonder what an art gallery is doing in the Census Bureau Web site; yet this is precisely the kind of expansion of vision encouraged by the Web of what kinds of information can be provided.

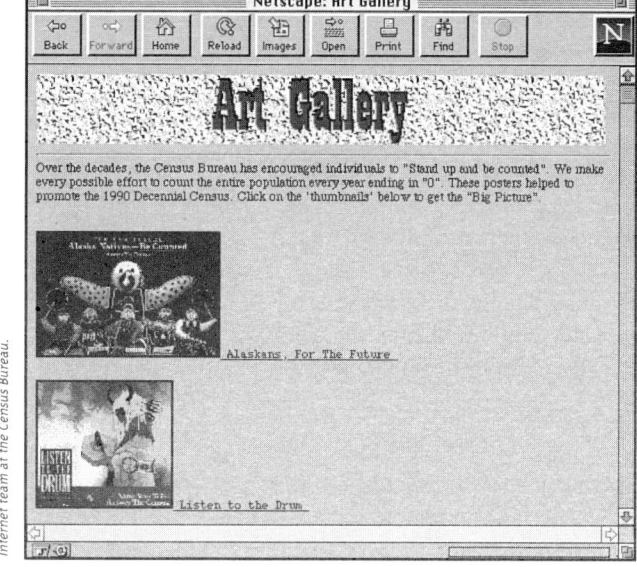

Internet team at the Census Bureau.

Figure 1.12:

Census Bureau Art Gallery Web site.
http://www.census.gov/gallery.html

Learning from the death of the railroads

The importance of a wide horizon line for designers is illustrated by the history of the railroads. Railroads were among the economic powerhouses of the American economy up to the 1950s. Most downplayed and ignored the spread of the automobile, airplane, and electronic communications. They arrogantly thought they did not need to look beyond the narrow boundaries of their business as it was conventionally practiced. A few railroads did take a larger view of how they might fit in a changing culture and early redefined their business as transportation, not railroading. The bulk of the dinosaurs who did not expand their perspectives are now bankrupt and extinct; the others are thriving.

Summary

Designing well for an online audience on the Web is difficult and challenging. You must broaden your technical and conceptual attention far beyond the layout of text and image. Your work must be visually engaging and clear but it must also respond the technological and contextual realities that surround the work. There is no other option if you are going to communicate effectively on the Web.

This chapter's process of preparing for Web design has asked you to:

- Consider the revolutionary opportunities and challenges faced by Web designers.

- Learn the expanded design approach, which includes asking questions about the context of site in the world outside the Web, its information structure, effectiveness of interactivity, and visual communication.

- Study a sample site (DealerNet) in detail to understand the process of designing for the Web.

- Examine differences and similarities among Web browsers in order to understand the user's experiences as they browse the Web.

- Analyze reasons for publishing and not publishing on the Web.

It's time to start creating Web pages. Chapter 2 introduces HTML, the major authoring language that will allow you to create pages that anyone in the world with a Web browser can view.

Chapter 2

HTML and Formatting Fundamentals

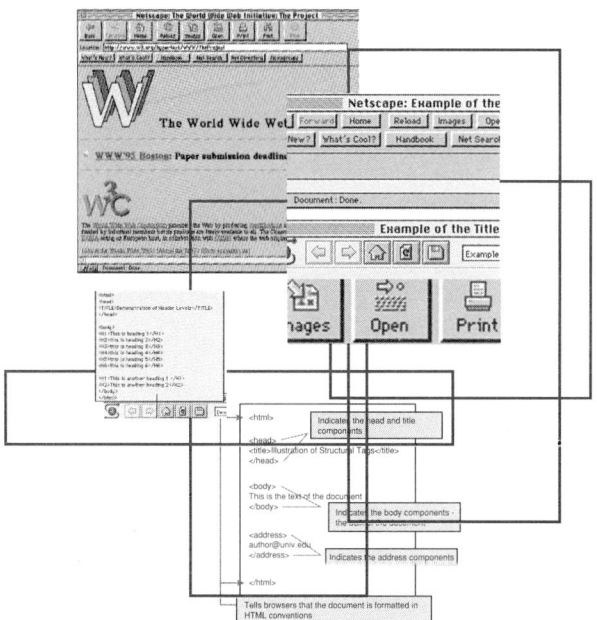

Imagine this dilemma. You've created a beautiful page of text with an image or produced an interactive hypertext document, and you want everyone to appreciate it. You've composed it in some particular application. Now, you want to convert it into a beautiful Web page. Where do you start? What tools do you need to do this? If you are asking yourself these questions, you have come to the right chapter.

Hypertext Markup Language (HTML) is the Web's authoring language that lets you click keywords or images to jump to other references in a page, access different Web pages altogether, play video, or listen to audio. You're going to be both amazed and frustrated by it. Because HTML is so central to creating Web events, several chapters focus on its inner workings:

- This chapter concentrates on formatting text for HTML.
- Chapter 3 shows you how to create hypertext links.
- Chapters 4, 5, and 6 teach the skills of using image, sound, and video on the Web.
- Chapter 7 explains HTML's advanced interactive features, including imagemaps and fill-in forms.

When you create resources for the World Wide Web, you need to remember that your viewers can be using any kind of computer anywhere in the world—ranging from super-computers to personal data assistants. The challenge of developing device-independent documents—that is, documents that maintain their visual appearance, format, and style regardless of the machine that reads them—is a big one. HTML helps the Web manage this automatic conversion from machine to machine.

HTML 3.0 and the Web's rapid changes

HTML is the international authoring standard for the Web and it is rapidly evolving. Internet committees such as the W3 committee and the IETF (Internet Engineering Task Force) are continually debating proposals for revisions yet to come. As a Web designer, you must decide what version of HTML you will use. You must pay attention not only to what you like or what looks good on your computer, but also to what your audience of Web readers is likely to have access to. The core of this book is built on standard HTML 2.0, which you can safely assume is universally available to the widest possible audience.

The section on HTML 3.0 later in this chapter explains the methods used by the Web community to enhance HTML and how to stay current with these new features. This book discusses the features in HTML 3.0 that are likely to become standard.

Getting Started

HTML uses *markup tags* contained in brackets to designate certain formats or styles for all the information on your Web pages. These tags are ASCII text indicators that you surround the text and images with. Most markup tags have an opening tag to mark the beginning of a formatting feature (e.g., <B> for boldface) and a closing tag that consists of the same indicator preceded by a slash (as in </B>). For example, surrounding the word *Important* with the HTML tags for bold like so:

<B>Important</B>

causes the word to appear bold when viewed by any user on any computer system in the world, no matter what Web browser is being used.

Note that you can create these HTML documents with any word processor; you just need to save your file in plain text (ASCII) format. Figure 2.1 presents a sample Web page and the page of text with HTML tags (known as the *source code*) that created it. Understanding HTML means learning what these tags are, the syntax for applying them, what their effects are, and creative ways for using them.

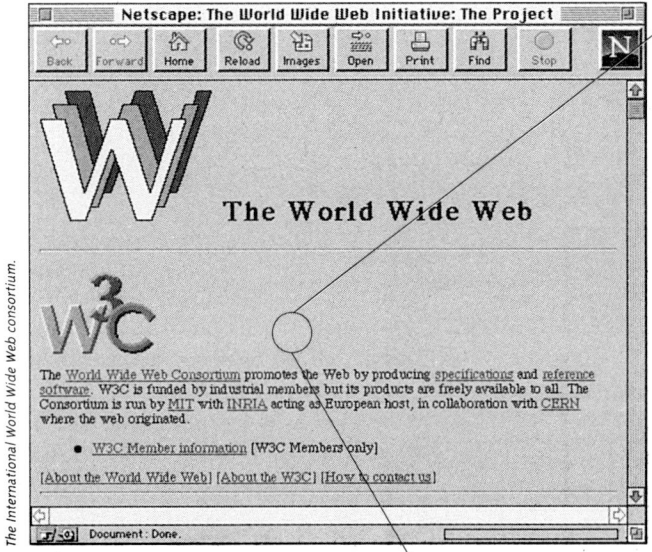

The International World Wide Web consortium.

Figure 2.1:

World Wide Web Initiative page displayed with the source code that created it.

http://www.w3.org/hypertext/WWW/TheProject

```
<HTML>
<HEAD>
<TITLE>The World Wide Web Initiative: The Project
</TITLE>
<! — Changed by: Karen MacArthur, 26-Jun-1995 —>
</HEAD>
<BODY>

<H1> <IMG alt="WWW" SRC="/hypertext/WWW/Icons/WWW/
WWWlogo.gif"> The World Wide Web</H1>


<hr>
<H2><img src="/hypertext/WWW/Icons/WWW/w3c_96x67"
alt="The World Wide Web Consortium"></H2>

The <a href="/hypertext/WWW/Consortium/">World Wide
Web Consortium</a> promotes the Web by producing
<a href="#zSpecifications">specifications</a> and
<a href="#zReference">reference software</a>.  W3C
is funded by industrial members but its products
are freely available to all.

The Consortium is run by <a href="http://
web.mit.edu/">MIT</a>
with <A HREF="http://www.inria.fr/">INRIA</A>
acting as European host,
in collaboration with <A HREF="http://www.cern.ch/
">CERN</A> where the Web originated.

<UL>
<LI> <a href="/member/WWW/Consortium/Member/">W3C
Member information</a>
 [W3C Members only]
</UL>

<P>
<a href="/hypertext/WWW/WWW/">[About the World Wide
 Web]</a>
<a href="hypertext/WWW/Consortium/">[About the
 W3C]</a>
<a href="hypertext/WWW/Consortium/Contact.html">[How
 to contact us]</a>

<hr>
```

Unfortunately, you have to give up WYSIWYG (what you see is what you get) control with HTML formatting. You'll need to toggle between your text editor and your Web browser to preview and proofread your Web pages.

This non-WYSIWYG frame of reference may take some getting used to, especially if you're used to seeing your formatting changes on the fly with page layout programs. But if you're a regular user of word processing or desktop publishing applications, you probably have at least a passing familiarity with the concept of style tags. If you have a typesetting background, you've probably had plenty of experience with code-based formatting. Many Web designers find it convenient to run their Web browser and their text editor side by side on their computer desktop, taking a break from coding to check out the formatting as necessary.

Some designers consider HTML a giant step backward. Others consider it a brilliant system for making work so widely available. Once you become comfortable with HTML and get over the shock of losing full control of your document's final appearance, you will find creative ways to exploit HTML's features, its possibilities, and work around its limitations, as illustrated later in this chapter.

Other markup languages

HTML has several precedents. Professional typesetters used proprietary markup tags for decades to instruct their specialized machines, such as the Compugraphic and Varitypers systems, how to render text. Many grew quite adept at being able to visualize what a page of text would ultimately look like by just looking at the tags. The UNIX programs TeX and Nrof still use a system of tags to instruct printers to produce text in the desired format.

SGML (Standard Generalized Markup Language) is another UNIX system for formatting text with special tags. These tags require authors to make obvious the structure of the text—for example, the logical levels of headers and their relationships to headers above and below them. HTML is technically a derivative or subset of SGML and future developments in the Web may be influenced by this relationship. For more information, see http://www.w3.org/hypertext/WWW/MarkUp/SGML.html.

Controlling Format and Appearance with HTML

In this section, you learn the following:

- What kinds of HTML tags exist
- How to apply tags to format text properly
- How to control lists, indentation, and spacing
- How to create visually appealing and effective documents with HTML

In the next chapter, you learn about the special tags that control the hypertext linking in Web documents. Building on these basics, you begin to see how to create your own style using HTML.

HTML tags also allow control of images, sound, video, and complex interactive events such as fill-in forms. Separate chapters address each of these.

In addition, there are many excellent online guides to writing HTML. Some of these resources are listed later in this chapter.

HTML Tags: General Considerations

Before actually trying out some HTML authoring, it is important to keep in mind the global style guidelines so that your text comes out as you have planned.

HTML uses the following conventions for almost all of its tags. Table 2.1 illustrates these general guidelines.

Table 2.1

Guidelines That Apply to Most HTML Tags

Guideline	Example
Angle brackets (less than "<" and more than ">" symbols on most keyboards) enclose the special formatting tags.	</H3><OL>
Most tags require *balancing*; that is, if a tag is used in front of some text, a closing member of the pair must be used at the end. With a few exceptions, the forward slash / is used as part of ending tags.	<B>This is an example of balancing a beginning tag with an ending tag </B>
HTML is case-insensitive, so the tags can be in upper- or lowercase.	</B> = </b>
Nesting logic must be carefully observed and some tags cannot overlap.	<H4><B>Inner tags end before outer tags do.</B></ H4>

Hands-On Process for Learning HTML

It is best to learn HTML with a hands-on approach. Turn on your computer and fire up your word processor and you'll be ready to start generating HTML pages. In this book, I illustrate examples showing you how to enter HTML straight from your word processor without any special software because that lets you understand HTML's fundamentals best. As you become more experienced, you can use one of the special HTML editors discussed in the section "Using HTML Editors and Converters," later in this chapter, which help automate some of the details.

Also launch your favorite Web browser such as Mosaic or Netscape. You do not need to be hooked up to your network or modem, but it's OK if you are. If your service provider charges you by the hour for how much time you spend online, though, you should definitely use your browser's offline (or local) mode for previewing your work.

Mosaic and Netscape have a special local mode ideal for testing Web pages in development. As you start the browser, it tries to make a network connection to its designated home page. Just choose the *stop loading* option. It returns an error message saying it can't connect. That's OK because you don't need any external access for this testing process.

Here are the typical steps in developing a simple HTML document:

1. Start up your Web browser and word processor (or HTML editing application).

2. Type the text to be formatted, or open a text file you want to use. For this introductory example, let's use a short two-paragraph excerpt with a title and a **heading as illustrated next.**

Type this text in your **word processor**:

```
Sample Text Page
An Example of Some Text to be Marked Up
When you create HTML, you must remember to apply
tags to the text or Web browsers will not render
what you have written the way you intended it.
You also must remember to indicate explicitly the
places you want paragraphs to break.
```

3. Now you're ready to start applying HTML tags. Don't worry if the tags themselves don't mean anything to you yet; they will all be explained fully later in this chapter. In our short example, you first add HTML structural tags that should be part of every HTML document—the <HTML>, <HEAD>, <TITLE>, and <BODY> tags and their corresponding closing tags. These tags describe your file as an HTML document and identify its title.

```
<HTML>
<HEAD><TITLE>Sample Text Page</TITLE></HEAD>
<BODY>
An Example of Some Text to be Marked Up
When you create HTML, you must remember to apply
tags to the text or Web browsers will not render
what you have written the way you intended it.
You also must remember to indicate explicitly the
places you want paragraphs to break.
</BODY>
</HTML>
```

4. Although you've defined the document and identified its title, you haven't done any formatting of the body of the text yet. To make "An Example of Some Text to Be Marked Up" a headline, type **<H2>** at the beginning of that line and a finishing tag **</H2>** at the end of that line. This line should now read as follows:

```
<H2>An Example of Some Text to be Marked Up</H2>
```

5. Now emphasize the words "must remember" by putting those words in boldface. Type **<B>** in front of "must" and put the closing tag **</B>** after the word "remember." This line should now read as follows:

```
You also <B>must remember</B> to indicate explicitly
the places you want paragraphs to break.
```

6. Now you need to indicate where each paragraph ends. The paragraph tag (<P>) usually indicates the *end* of a paragraph, and should be placed at the end, not the beginning, of each separate paragraph. In this example, type **<P>** after the words "...you intended it." Unlike most other tags, the **<P>** tag does not need a closing tag. Here is what the fully coded version of your document should look like now:

```
<HTML>
<HEAD><TITLE>Sample Text Page</TITLE></HEAD>
<BODY>
<H2>An Example of Some Text to be Marked Up</H2>
When you create HTML, you must remember to apply
tags to the text or Web browsers will not render
what you have written the way you intended it.
<P>
You also <B>must remember</B> to indicate explicitly
the places you want paragraphs to break.
</BODY>
</HTML>
```

7. You've just marked up this excerpt in HTML. Congratulations! Save the document as a plain text file. Your word processor should have an option in the Save or Save As dialog box for file type. Search there for an "ASCII Text" or "Text Only" option. Use .html (if you're using a Macintosh or .htm for a DOS/Windows platform) for the filename's suffix.

Note: You must remember to save the page in plain text format rather than the formats of your particular word processor (you can find this option in the Save dialog box under "File Type" or a similar wording). Otherwise, your Web browser will not be able to read your document. *No HTML formatting appears unless it is indicated with an HTML tag.*

8. Switch to your Web browser's window.

9. Open your HTML document within your Web browser. If you're using Mosaic, use the *Open Local* option under the File menu to access your file. (Note the menu choice might be named something else—for example, *Open File* in Netscape.)

Congratulations—you've just coded some HTML for the first time! Figure 2.2 shows the plain text version of this example and the text with HTML tags applied. Becoming an HTML guru will mean learning more tags and the rules for applying them, but the process will be fundamentally the same as what you did here. You'll always want to check your work in your Web browser to make sure you haven't inadvertently left out any brackets or forgotten to input a closing tag.

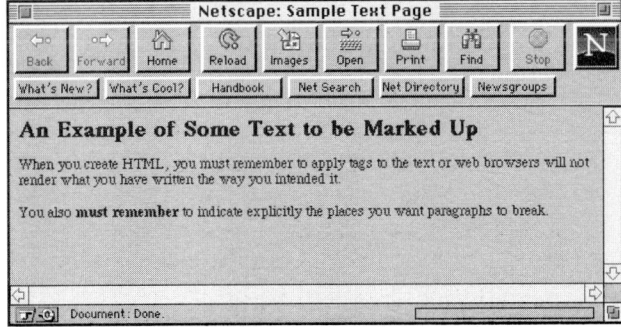

Figure 2.2:
An introductory exercise in applying HTML tags.

Document Organization Tags

The main purpose of the *Title, Head, Body, Address* , and *HTML* tags is to structure the various segments of a Web document. Title identification is important because many search programs search the Web looking only at the information contained in the title and/or head section.

In addition, Web developers working on new programs to help surfers process Web information indicate that these tags may have greater importance in the future. For example, the address tag (which usually contains information about the page's author) may enable automatic updating programs to contact the authors of pages without human intervention. Figure 2.3 shows a skeleton HTML document with these tags applied and Table 2.2 shows a summary of the structural tags. Note that the <HTML>, <HEAD>, and <BODY> tags have no impact on the way the other tags function.

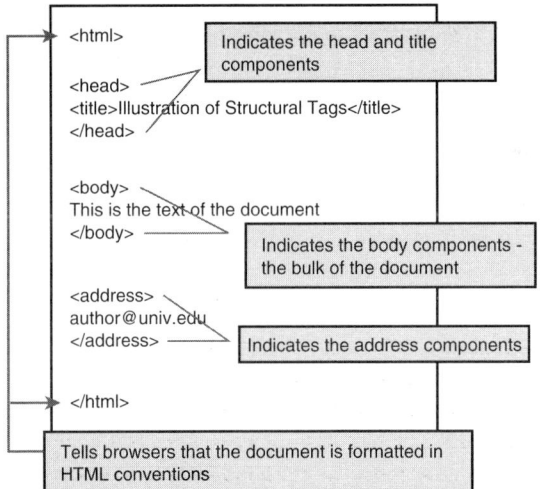

Figure 2.3:
Major structural components of HTML documents—title, head, body, address, and HTML tags.

Table 2.2

HTML Structural Formatting Tags

Beginning Tag	Ending Tag	Comments/ Exceptions
<HTML>	</HTML>	Indicates that text is marked up in HTML standard.
<HEAD>	</HEAD>	Encloses the head material such as title.
<TITLE>	</TITLE>	Title will appear in window header on browsers and in hotlists when saved.
<BODY>	</BODY>	Encloses the main part of page text.
<ADDRESS>	</ADDRESS>	Encloses the name and address of page author or maintainer.

<HTML>

The <HTML> and </HTML> tags serve to identify the markup language of the document. Typically, it is the first and last tag in a document and it has no visual effect. Currently, this tag does not serve much function because almost all Web documents are in HTML. Proposals in the Web community call for extending the protocols, however, to be able to deal with a variety of markup conventions.

<HEAD> and <TITLE>

Use the <HEAD> and </HEAD> tags to enclose the title and other material that you want to enclose in the title section.

The <TITLE> is the most important structural tag. As with other literary or artistic works, select a title carefully because it helps set the tone and readers' expectations for the document.

Moreover, titles have special uses in the Web context. Client applications store titles in hotlists and history lists. Several index services that find sites of interest use the title as the main indicator. In these situations, your Web site is picked (or skipped over) primarily because of its title.

You indicate a title by placing the tag <TITLE> in front of the title text and the suffix </TITLE> at the end. The title should be relatively short (no longer than 64 characters). Here is a sample of a title with its proper tags:

```
<TITLE> Example of the Title HTML Tag </TITLE>
```

Figure 2.4 shows the appearance of the title text in two browsers. They treat the title slightly differently, but both give it prominence. Note that while the title appears in the title bar of your window, it does not automatically appear in the body of the document. If you want it to appear on the page, you have to retype the text with an <H1> heading or some tag other than <TITLE>.

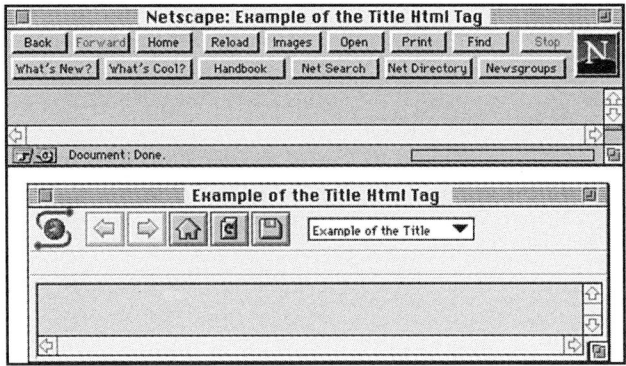

Figure 2.4:
Comparison of how two different browsers display title information.

<BODY>

Use the <BODY> and </BODY> tags to enclose the rest of the material except for the address. These have no visual effect, but do help to define the structure of your document.

<ADDRESS>

Use the <ADDRESS> and </ADDRESS> tags to indicate an address. Web etiquette urges you to include the e-mail address contact for readers. Addresses are usually placed at the top or end of Web documents. Line breaks inside addresses must be indicated with the paragraph tag <P> or break tag <BR>, discussed in the next section. The address tag is useful for some automatic systems that attempt to link Web documents with the e-mail address.

Browsers differ in the details of how they visually format addresses; one typical implementation uses italics, another may use bold. Indeed, all HTML styles will be subject to these kinds of minor differences among browsers. Browsers will try to logically represent your style choices, but the details of their actual visual representation may differ.

Headers

Authors traditionally use headings and subheadings to alert readers to logical relationships among sections of texts. Six levels of headers are available in HTML, numbering from the largest <H1> tag to the smallest <H6> tag. You indicate the header level of a fragment of text by using the tags <H1>, <H2>, <H3>, <H4>, <H5>, and <H6> and their corresponding closing tag (with /) to enclose the text. The following example shows some text marked for a level two heading:

```
<H2> This is heading 2 level text </H2>
```

You can use the header tags to enclose as much text as you want; you are not limited to one line. All text will be rendered at the same header level until you use the closing tag. If you want to break the headline into two lines at a particular point, you'll need to use the break tag <BR> to do so.

While HTML lets you designate formatting styles (like boldface and italics) and relative headlines (such as a first-level head, then several levels of subheads), the HTML 2.0 standards do not let you specify particular typefaces or font sizes. HTML 3.0 extensions, described later in this chapter, may help overcome this problem by giving Web designers some direct control over font size. Figure 2.5 shows the way one browser renders header tags.

Entering HTML text

Most of the figures in this chapter show samples of HTML coding and what the results look like in a Web browser. You will learn best, however, if you actually experiment with entering the text. As you move through the chapter, take these steps with each figure:

1. Launch your word processor and your Web browser.

2. Enter the source code illustrated in the figure, paying attention to applying the tags as indicated.

3. Save the text in text-only or ASCII text format.

4. Activate your Web browser and choose the "Open Local" or "Open File" option to access the file you have created.

5. Check to see that the results resemble those in the figure.

```
<HTML>
<HEAD>
<TITLE>Demonstration of Header Levels</TITLE>
</HEAD>

<BODY>
<H1>This is heading 1</H1>
<H2>this is heading 2</H2>
<H3>this is heading 3</H3>
<H4>this is heading 4</H4>
<H5>this is heading 5</H5>
<H6>this is heading 6</H6>

<H1>This is another heading 1 </H1>
<H2>This is another heading 2</H2>
</BODY>
</HTML>
```

You can use headers to indicate relative logical levels or primarily for their visual effects. Using them to indicate logical levels can be a great aid to readers; this helps the reader to navigate through your information, identify logical relationships, and focus attention. Some information presentations adopt themselves easily to this kind of hierarchical approach. For example, scientific and business essays are often based on logical underpinnings which fit well with this model of information. Other forms such as expressive arts and literature are not so easily adapted.

You can also use header tags simply to control visual appearance. For example, you will discover that sometimes

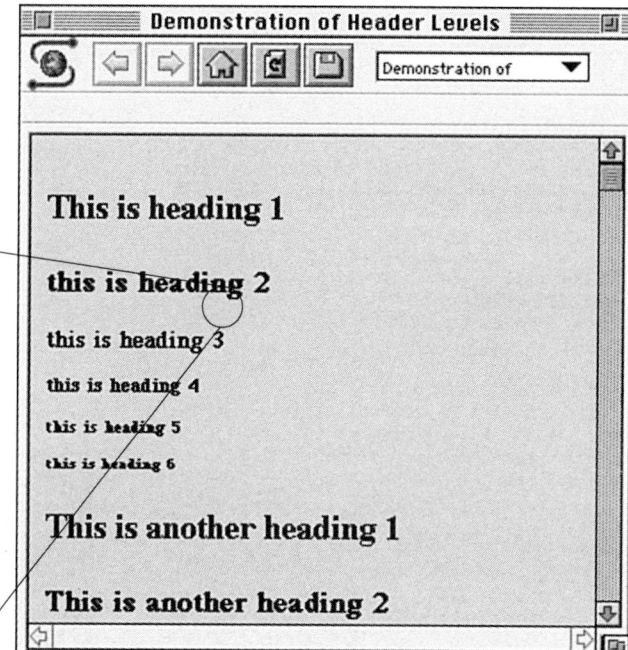

Figure 2.5:
HTML header tags and their interpretation in a browser.

the only way to render text at a particular size is to tag it at a specific header level. Unfortunately, when you use headers in this way, you work against their function as indicators of logical level. For example, some of the automatic "robot" information-gathering programs on the Web (described in Appendix A) make assumptions that header levels indicate logically equivalent divisions of a document that can be used to build an automatic summary. Use of header tags merely for their size effects will confuse the functioning of some of these programs. You must make your own decision about whether these programs' functions in creating summaries for you is more important than the visual effect you want.

Paragraphs and Line Breaks

When you're typing a letter on your word processor you might press the Return key when you get to the end of a paragraph, but you'll need to do more than that to indicate separate paragraphs in a Web document. You'll need to add a <P> paragraph tag, or force a line break with the <BR> tag, when you're ready to end a section of text and start on a new line. Figure 2.6 shows the way a Web browser will ignore all line breaks except those explicitly indicated with tags.

In most Web browsers, paragraph indications introduce more space between lines than a break. Unlike most other tags, the paragraph and break indicators do not need a closing tag. They are very useful for controlling the visual appearance of Web pages, as illustrated in Figure 2.7.

Line breaks can appear in other ways. As with most window-based applications, graphic WWW browsers automatically introduce visual line breaks when text reaches the side of the window—for example, in the way that word wrap works in a word processor. Realize, however, that these are not permanent breaks and their position will change as soon as anyone changes the window size. Permanent breaks must be indicated with explicit tags.

```
<TITLE>Disregard of document format & style</TITLE>

HTML Disregard of Document Formatting
that is not Indicated with Special Tags.

Paragraph 1:
This is an explanation of how standard formatting
is disregarded by html browsers. This document is
carefully formatted into paragraphs.

Paragraph 2:
Html browsers disregard all style and format
characteristics that are not explicitly indicated
with tags. For example they disregard the
returns that make these paragraphs.

Paragraph 3
The browsers will also disregard font, size, style,
and spaces between words. The table that follows is
lost.

Apples          Bananas  Carrots
Rhinos          Snakes   Tigers
```

HTML Disregard of Document Formatting that is not Indicated with Special Tags. Paragraph 1: This is an explanation of how standard formatting is disregarded by html browsers.. This document is carefully formatted into paragraphs.. Paragraph 2: Html browsers disregard all style and format characteristics that are not explicity indicated with tags. For example they disregard the carraige returns that make these paragraphs Paragraph 3 The browsers will also disregard font, size, style and spaces between words. The table below is lost. Apples Bananas Carrots Rhinos Snakes Tigers

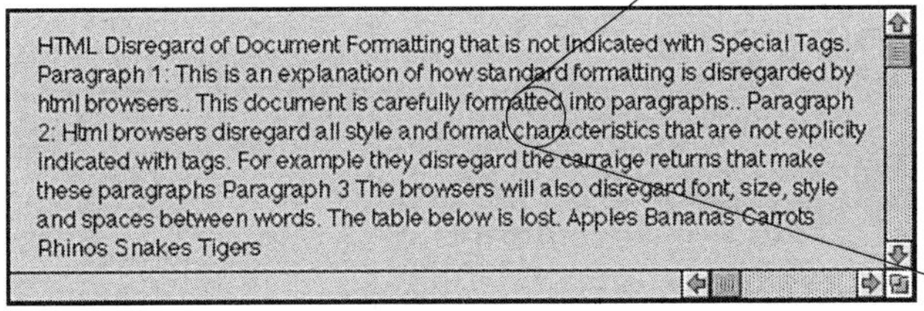

Figure 2.6:
HTML disregards paragraph indications in text.

```
<TITLE>Use of Paragraph Tags</TITLE>

<h1> Use of Paragraph Tags To Control Line Breaks
</h1>

<H2>This paragraph has no paragraph tags</H2>
Any desired line break must have
a paragraph marker placed after it.
Otherwise all line breaks in the text
are disregarded.

<H2>This paragraph does have paragraph tags</H2>
Any desired line break must have a tag<P>
Notice no closing tags are required<P>
Notice also that header tags imply line break
without indications.
```

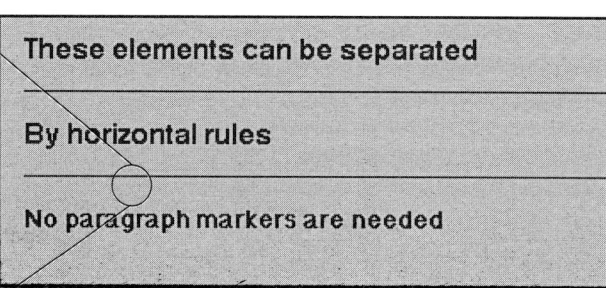

Figure 2.7:
Using the paragraph tag <P> to control appearance of new lines.

Horizontal Lines

Web designers use horizontal lines extensively to divide the screen into visual or logical regions. There aren't many such graphic capabilities in HTML, so the horizontal rule tag, <HR>, is a useful tool.

The tag name refers to the term *horizontal rule,* which is a typesetting term for a horizontal line. Netscape has proposed interesting extensions to the <HR> tag, including variations in style, thickness, and length of the line. (See the section on Netscape later in this chapter.) This tag requires no ending marker. Figure 2.8 shows the way you would mark up a page with the <HR> tag in order to produce horizontal lines.

```
<HTML>
<HEAD>
<TITLE>Demo of Horizontal Rules</TITLE>
</HEAD>

<BODY>
<H2>These elements can be separated</H2>
<HR>
<H2>By horizontal rules</H2>
<HR>
<H3>No paragraph markers are needed</H3>
</BODY>
</HTML>
```

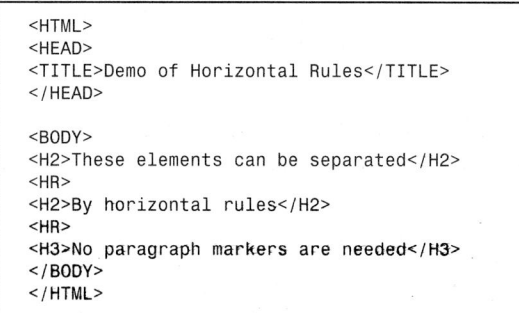

Figure 2.8:
Using the horizontal rule <HR> tag.

List Categories

Here's a list of reasons why lists are useful:

- They are visually interesting.
- They can be used to group similar items or ideas.
- The eye can easily scan lists and note equivalent items.

HTML offers a rich assortment of list styles including ordered, unordered, menu, directory, and definition lists. Each list has its own special formatting. For example, an ordered list automatically numbers each item on the list, while an unordered list adds a marker such as a bullet before each list item. A definition list is a good format for a glossary or a similar list where you want to first distinguish a word or line of text and then add an indented paragraph beneath. The items on a list can be as short as a single word or as long as you want. The menu and directory tags are likely to be phased out in HTML 3.0. Table 2.3 summarizes the list tags and Figures 2.9 to 2.11 show you concrete examples of the tags to apply and their results in a Web browser.

Table 2.3

HTML List Formatting Tags

HTML Tag Name and Start and End Tags	Comments/Use
Ordered List: <OL> </OL>	Each item is given sequential number (implies order is important).
Unordered List: <UL> </UL>	Each item is given a marker such as bullet (implies order is not important).
Definition List: <DL> </DL>	Each item consists of two elements: an indented first level header indicated with <DT> and then a second level text body indicated by <DD>, which is indented further (see Figure 2.11).
Menu List: <MENU> </MENU>	Each item is given an indicator such as a bullet (structural function to indicate menu items—looks much like unordered list).
Directory List: <DIR </DIR>	Each item is given an indicator such as a bullet (structural function to indicate directory items—looks much like unordered list).
List Item Indicator: <LI></LI>	Placed in front of each item in a list, except for definition lists.

Ordered Lists: The numbers in ordered lists are automatically generated by browsers as they interpret HTML. You indicate an ordered list by prefixing the tag <OL> before the first item and suffixing the tag </OL> at the end. Each item in the list is indicated by the tag <LI> as a prefix. You do not need an ending tag for <LI> in any of the lists where the tag is used.

Browsers will treat the text after the <LI> tag as an item in the list until it sees the next <LI> or the ending tag for the list. Your entries in the list can be simple phrases or sentences or can be composed of multiple lines separated by <BR> tags. Figure 2.9 shows HTML tags to apply for an ordered list along with its result in a Web browser.

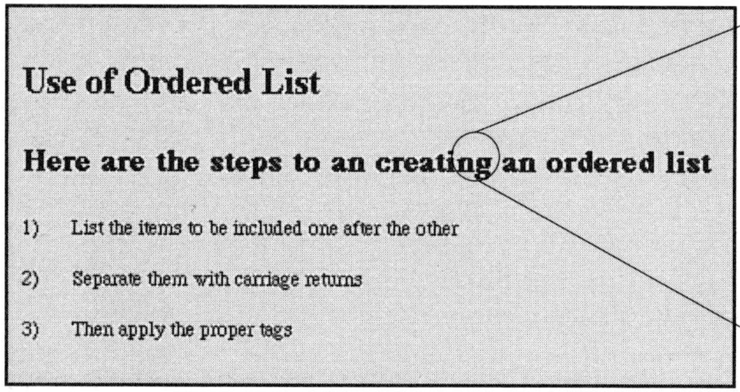

Use of Ordered List

Here are the steps to an creating an ordered list

1) List the items to be included one after the other

2) Separate them with carriage returns

3) Then apply the proper tags

```
<TITLE>Use of Ordered Lists</TITLE>

<H1> Use of Ordered List</H1>

<H2>Here are the steps to creating an ordered
  list</H2>
<OL>
<LI>List the items to be included one after the
  other
<LI>Separate them with carriage returns
<LI>Then apply the proper tags</OL>
```

Figure 2.9:
Ordered lists.

Unordered Lists: These function the same as ordered lists except that each item starts with an indicator such as a bullet, open square, or dash instead of a number. Just substitute the tags <UL> and </UL> for the <OL> tags. Figure 2.10 shows you how to create unordered lists.

Use of Unordered List
Features of unordered lists

- Looks just like ordered lists
- Except each line starts with marker, not number
- Appropriate when ordering in time or importance is wrong

```
<TITLE>Use of Unordered Lists</TITLE>

<H1> Use of Unordered List</H1>

<H2>Features of unordered lists</H2>
<UL>
<LI>Looks just like ordered lists
<LI>Except each line starts with marker, not number
<LI>Appropriate when ordering in time or importance
  is wrong</UL>
```

Figure 2.10:
Unordered lists.

Menu Lists: These visually appear much like unordered lists. Each item similarly starts with some kind of indicator and is indented from the left margin. <Menu> is the prefix tag, </menu> is the suffix, and you apply the <li> tag at the start of each item. HTML 3.0 is introducing some options to unordered lists that will allow menu and directory lists (discussed in the next section) to be eventually phased out.

Directory Lists: Directories appear much like unordered lists and menus except that no marker appears to start each item. That is, there is no number or bullet. Typically each item is 20 characters or shorter. They are marked in a similar way with the tags <dir>, </dir>, and <li>.

Definition Lists: These lists have a two-level format that lets you follow each entry's line of text with an indented paragraph. You might use this tag to format a list of terms, followed by their definitions.

Web browsers use two-tier indentation for these lists—the term or title line is indented and the elaboration sections have an even more pronounced left indent.

The <DL> tag starts one of these definition lists and a </DL> ends it. Each entry starts with a <DT> tag for descriptive line and a <DD> for the elaboration text that follows. <DT> tags must have at least one <DD> tag follow them. Some browsers recognize a <COMPACT> tag placed after the initial <DL> tag. This causes extra white space to be compressed.

Although this format was probably designed to render glossaries and lists of definitions, you can adapt it for its visual qualities. Figure 2.11 shows how to create a definition list.

```
<TITLE>Use of Definition Lists</TITLE>

<H1> Use of Definition Lists</H1>

<DL>
<DT>Defintion List Format
<DD>The definition list creates a 2 level indenta-
    tion so the first line appears as a mini-title and
    the material that appears on the following lines
    appears to be an elaboration.
<P>
<DT>Visual Advantage of Defintion List Format
<DD>This style creates a visually interesting
    format.</DL>
```

Figure 2.11:
Definition lists.

Nesting Lists

With HTML, you can include one list within another, as long as you close the internal, or "nested," one first. Let's say you wanted to organize a list of future research developments shaping the Web and include additional sets of lists under those category headings. Type the text shown in Exercise 2.1 in creating this nested list. Figure 2.12 shows what the results look like in a Web browser.

Exercise 2.1:

Creating a nested list

Step 1:

This list will identify some future trends for the Web, with nested lists naming examples for each one. Fire up your word processor, and enter the text for the title and the outline for your list:

```
Research Affecting the Future of the Web
Commerical exchange
Hardware innovations
Information access innovations
```

Step 2:

Add HTML structuring tags as described previously to identify this document as an HTML document and identify the title. You will also add <OL> and <LI> tags to identify your ordered list and the list items it contains:

```
<HTML>
<HEAD><TITLE>Future Web Trends</TITLE></HEAD>
<BODY>
<H1>Research Affecting the Future of the Web</H1>
<OL>
<LI>Commerical exchange
<LI>Hardware innovations
```

```
<LI>Information access innovations
</OL>
</BODY>
</HTML>
```

Step 3:

Next, add nested list items for each of the three items on your list. Your final HTML document should look like the following:

```
<HTML>
<HEAD><TITLE>Future Web Trends</TITLE></HEAD>
<BODY>
<H1>Research Affecting the Future of the Web</H1>
<OL>
<LI>Commerical exchange
<UL>
<LI>Encryption and digital signatures
<LI>Digital cash
</UL>
<LI>Hardware innovations
<UL>
<LI>Increased bandwidth
<LI>New sound and video techniques
</UL>
<LI>Information access innovations
<UL>
<LI>Information visualization
<LI>Intelligent software agents
</UL>
</OL>
</BODY>
</HTML>
```

Step 4:

Activate your Web browser and use the *Open Local* or *Open File* option to load and view the document you just created. Your document should be similar to the one pictured in Figure 2.12.

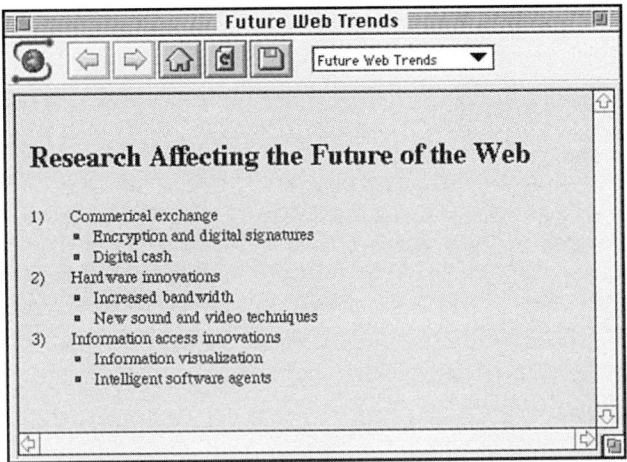

Figure 2.12:
Nested lists.

returns in your text. It also aligns everything at the left side of the window. Here's HTML to the rescue—sort of. The preformatted text and blockquote tags offer rudimentary capabilities of preserving some of the formatting from original word processed text and to align text in other places in the window.

The preformat style allows you to create text in which the carriage returns and spaces are preserved as you originally entered them. This style is different from most other HTML formats; within the preformatted text you are not required to use explicit tags for each formatting desired. For example, paragraphs do not require the <P> tag.

To preserve the spacing, Web browsers use a constant width font rather than one with variable widths. A fixed-width font resembles typewriter output. It can be very useful in situations where spacing is essential, as in representing some kinds of computer program code, and in simulating tables or columns until HTML 3.0 allows use of real tables.

You indicate this format with the beginning tag <PRE> and the end tag </PRE>. Paragraph <p> and break <br> tags should not be used within preformatted text.

Figure 2.13 shows you how to use the <PRE> format to preserve spaces between words and lines.

Preformatted Text

The tags discussed so far give you some control, but there are many times these tags won't do the job—for example, when you want particular kinds of spacing between words or lines. Standard HTML 2.0 disregards extra spaces and carriage

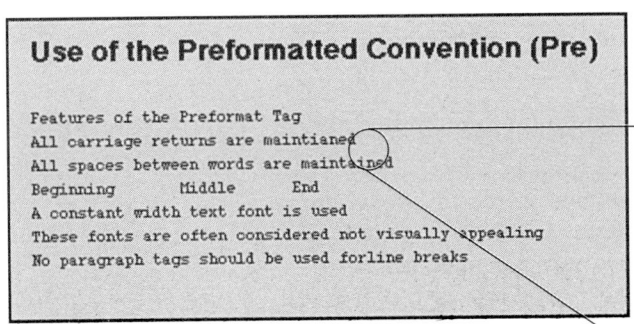

```
<TITLE>Preformatted Text</TITLE>

<H1>Use of the Preformatted Convention (Pre)</H1>

<PRE>
Features of the Preformat Tag
All carriage returns are maintained
All spaces between words are maintained
Beginning         Middle         End
A constant width text font is used
These fonts are often considered not visually appealing
No paragraph tags should be used for line breaks
</PRE>
```

Figure 2.13:
Preformatted text.

Blockquotes

The blockquote format is conventionally used for extended quotes—again preserving original formatting such as line breaks. In the Mosaic browser, the blockquote format left-justifies all text with a fixed left indentation for all lines.

You format these text blocks with the <BLOCKQUOTE> tag and end the text with </BLOCKQUOTE>. Figure 2.14 shows the method of applying the blockquote tag.

```
<TITLE>Blockquote Convention</TITLE>
<H1>Use of the Blockquote Convention</H1>

<H3><BLOCKQUOTE>
This format allows for extended quotes. Line breaks
must be indicated by the paragraph tag. Text is
indented a constant amount and left justified. Other
tags such as headers can be used to format the text
within the quote. In this example, all the text
appears at header 3 level.
<P>
The format is similar to the use of extended quotes
within normal written communication. The goal is
visually to separate the quoted material from the
regular text.</BLOCKQUOTE></H3>
```

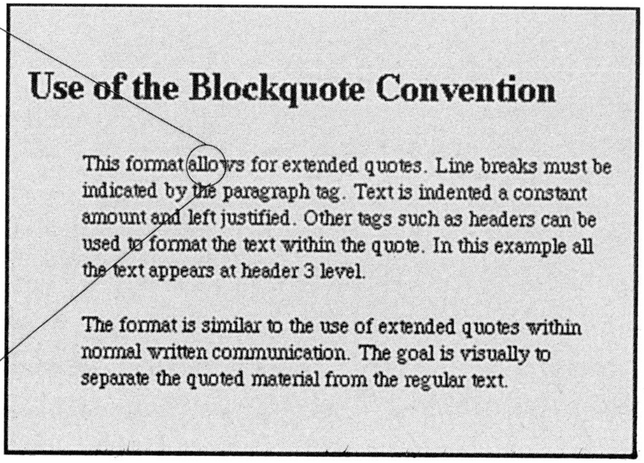

Use of the Blockquote Convention

This format allows for extended quotes. Line breaks must be indicated by the paragraph tag. Text is indented a constant amount and left justified. Other tags such as headers can be used to format the text within the quote. In this example all the text appears at header 3 level.

The format is similar to the use of extended quotes within normal written communication. The goal is visually to separate the quoted material from the regular text.

Figure 2.14:
Using the blockquote format.

Character Style Tags

Character style tags allow you to control the appearance of the text itself—for example formatting a word in **bold** or *italics*. This formatting can be applied to parts of text as small as a single letter.

Character style tags are generally divided into two categories: *physical* and *logical*. Physical styles are explicit references to typographic characteristics. The styles potentially supported include bold, italics, underline, and fixed-width typewriter font.

Logical styles can accomplish similar formatting, but they refer to the function of the text rather than the explicit typographic characteristics. The styles supported include: emphasized, citation, strong emphasis, code, sample, variable, and keyboard. As you've seen with many other HTML formatting tags, how logical styles are displayed may differ in various browsers. The style guide at the Mosaic home site urges HTML authors to use logical rather than physical styles because doing so allows easy unified style changes to a document—for example, a decision to make all <CITE> tags into bold instead of italics can be accomplished with one change.

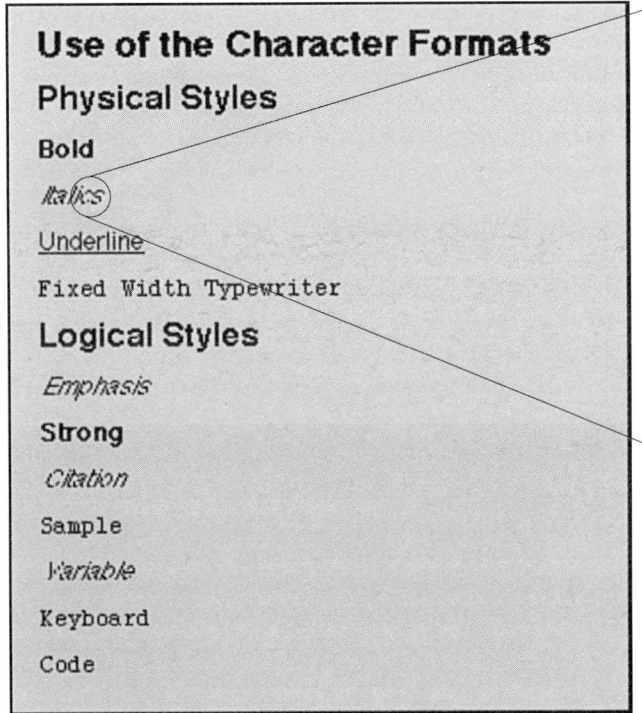

```
<TITLE>Character Formatting</TITLE>

<H1>Use of the Character Formats</H1>

<H2>Physical Styles</H2>
<B>Bold</B><P>
<I>Italics</I><P>
<U>Underline</U><P>
<TT>Fixed Width Typewriter</TT><P>
<P>
<H2>Logical Styles</H2>
<EM>Emphasis</EM><P>
<STRONG>Strong</STRONG><P>
<CITE>Citation</CITE><P>
<SAMP>Sample</SAMP><P>
<VAR>Variable</VAR><P>
<KBD>Keyboard</KBD><P>
<CODE>Code</CODE><P>
```

Figure 2.15:
Character formatting tags.

Table 2.4 presents the styles, their tags, and some information from the HTML specifications about the meaning of the style. Note that several of these formats originated in the computer science documentation world and may not be useful to the general public. Figure 2.15 demonstrates how to apply the tags and shows their results.

Table 2.4

HTML Physical and Logical Character Tags

Style	Tag	Function
Physical Styles		
Bold	`<b>`	Render text bold
Underline	`<u>`	Underline the text

continues

Table 2.4

Continued

Italic	<i> or <it>	Render text italics
Teletype	<tt>	Fixed width font
Logical Styles		
emphasis	<em>	Important
strong	<strong>	Really important
citation	<cite>	Citation
code	<code>	Example of fixed width program instructions
sample	<samp>	Literal characters (document what appears on-screen)
keyboard	<kbd>	Characters typed by a user as in an instruction manual
variable	<var>	The symbolic name of an entity that can assume various values
definition	<dfn>	An explanation of what a term means

Combined and Embedded Tags

You have to be careful about how you combine HTML tags. For example, you should always put anchor tags inside elements, instead of surrounding them on the outside.

Character style tags and linking anchors (discussed in Chapter 3) are examples of tags that are allowed inside of other structures. For example, you are advised not to embed header tags inside of lists. You can, however, use character styles inside of list items or within preformatted text. Here are some caveats in using character styles, however:

- You cannot use them inside of text marked with header tags; the header's own style will predominate and the character tags will be disregarded.

- The same logical style might be rendered quite differently in various browsers. For example, the <EM> tag will be shown as italics inside of Netscape and bold inside of Mosaic.

- Browsers differ on which physical tags they will allow to be used inside of other formatted sections. For example, both Netscape and Mosaic will reliably render the bold <B> tag inside of a list. Neither renders the italics <I> tag inside of a list and only Mosaic renders the underline <U> tag correctly.

- Multiple character tags used in combination with each other will often have unpredictable results—for example <b><u> bold underline </u></b> will not necessarily produce bold underlined text. Generally, the innermost tags take precedence.

HTML 3.0 standards will enforce consistency on the way browsers render character tags so that combinations of font styles are rendered as you expect. Figure 2.16 shows an example of using character formatting tags inside of a list structure.

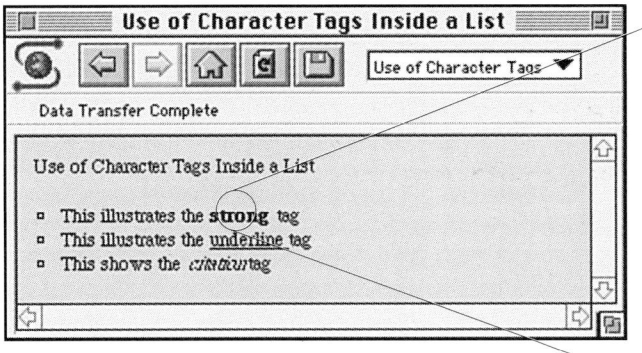

```
<HTML>
<HEAD>
<TITLE>Use of Character Tags Inside a List</TITLE>
</HEAD>

<BODY>
Use of Character Tags Inside a List<P>
<UL>
<LI> This illustrates the <STRONG> strong </STRONG>
   tag
<LI> This illustrates the <U> underline </U> tag
<LI> This shows the <CITE> citation </CITE> tag
   </UL>
</BODY>
</HTML>
```

Figure 2.16:
Use of character tags inside a list.

Special Characters and Escape Characters

There are several characters that HTML uses for special purposes, including, of course, the < (less than) and > (greater than) characters. Because these symbols are used to indicate tags, you cannot use them "as is" in HTML. Instead, you must use an *escape sequence* (so called probably because the user is trying to escape from its special meaning) to represent these characters. Other special characters such as graves, acutes, and umlauts must be represented by escape sequences as well.

Table 2.5 lists some common escape characters and their special escape sequence. The reference points to the official specifications for representing these characters.

Table 2.5

Escape and Special Characters

Character	Sequence
<	&<;
>	&>;
&	&amp;
"	&quot;
À Capital A, grave accent	&Agrave
Ã Capital A, tilde	&Atilde
Å Capital A, ring	&Aring
Ä Capital A, umlaut mark	&Auml
Æ Capital AE dipthong (ligature)	&AElig
Ç Capital C, cedilla	&Ccedil
á Small a, acute accent	&aacute

continues

Table 2.5

Continued

Character	Sequence
à Small a, grave accent	&agrave
â Small a, circumflex accent	&acirc
ã Small a, tilde	&atilde
ä Small a, umlaut mark	&auml
æ Small ae dipthong	&aelig
ç Small c, cedilla	&ccedil
¢, Cent sign	&#162;
£, Pound sterling	&#163
¥, Yen sign	&#165
©, Copyright	&#169
®, Registered trademark	&#174

Note: Table 2.5 lists the escape sequences for the accents, graves, umlauts, and other special characters that are linked to the letter a. The sequences for the other vowels follow the same pattern with the other letters substituted for a. For example, &Eacute will place an acute accent on capital E and &eacute will place an acute on small e. Also, the escape sequences with numbers refer to the standard ASCII mapping of characters to numbers. All the ASCII numbers can be used in escape sequences; the table illustrates some of the more frequently used symbols. Finally, HTML 3.0 will introduce the &copy (copyright), and &register (registered trademark) as alternatives for the escape sequences that use numbers for those symbols.

Official HTML Specifications with List of Special Characters
`http://www.w3.org/hypertext/WWW/MarkUp/html-spec/html-spec_9.html#SEC101`

Why special characters need special treatment

Internet communications are based on the standard ASCII conventions for communicating text. This convention does not include the special characters indicated on extended keyboards such as accent marks (graves, acutes, umlauts, etc.). Because these are not standardized, different computer systems might use different ASCII codes and keys to indicate them. Including the explicit tags described in this section to identify them means that each Web browser can adjust to the conventions of the system it is running on.

Comment Tag

Like most computer languages, HTML offers a comment option. This option is great for your notes and documentation. Text enclosed in this tag is ignored by browsers; users do not see it. However, it is always there for anyone looking at the source code for your HTML page. Commented text is designed to inform the person reading the source code; it does not serve as any sort of instruction to the computer.

Comments are indicated with the prefix tag <!-- and the suffix tag -->. Note that there is no closing > symbol on the prefix and no beginning symbol < on the suffix. Figure 2.17 shows use of the comment tag.

Use of Comment Format

Use of Character Formats Inside Lists

- This is an **emphasis** character.

- This is a *citation* character.

- This is a **strong emphasis** character.

```
<TITLE>Comments</TITLE>

<H1>Use of Comment Format</H1>

<!-- The lines that follow illustrate character
formats inside other formats.  This explanation does
not appear in the rendered html document because it
has the comment format attached. The computer
ignores it when it is time to render the document.-->


Use of Character Formats Inside Lists
<UL>
<LI>This is an <EM>emphasis</EM> character.
<LI>This is a <CITE>citation</CITE> character.
<LI>This is a <STRONG>strong emphasis
</STRONG>character.</UL>
```

Figure 2.17:
Using the comment tag.

More to Come: Other Tags

HTML tags that control hypertext linking, such as the anchor tags <A HREF=...> and <A NAME= ... > are discussed in Chapter 3. Tags that control images, such as the <IMG> tag are introduced in Chapter 4, and interactive events are explained in Chapter 7.

There are several other HTML tags that have fallen into disuse that are not covered here. If you are curious about them, you can learn more from the official HTML documentation on-line sources listed in the reference list that follows.

Online Information about HTML

- *Primers and tutorials for HTML*
http://www.ncsa.uiuc.edu/demoweb/html-primer.html
tutorial

http://fire.clarkson.edu/doc/html/htut.html

http://www.utirc.utoronto.ca/HTMLdocs/NewHTML/
intro.html

http://www.ziff.com/~eamonn/crash_course.html

http://union.ncsa.uiuc.edu/HyperNews/get/www/html/
guides.html

http://www.chem.emory.edu/html/html.html

- *Guides to advanced usage and developer tools*
http://www.hal.com/~barry/Links/html.html

http://oneworld.wa.com/htmldev/devpage/dev-
page.html

- *Official HTML specifications*
http://www.w3.org/hypertext/WWW/MarkUp/MarkUp.html

- *Style guides for HTML*

```
http://www.w3.org/hypertext/WWW/Provider/Style/
Overview.html
```

```
http://www.willamette.edu/html-composition/strict-
html.html
```

```
http://bookweb.cwis.uci.edu:8042/Staff/
StyleGuide.html
```

What's New in HTML 3.0

HTML is amazingly flexible for a light, device-independent standard, but even its earliest advocates were pushing for improved features from the start. Even before HTML 1.0 was adopted as a standard, developers were proposing "HTMLplus" extensions to HTML such as those now included in HTML 3.0 proposals.

Plans for HTML 3.0 include protocols for increased formatting control, new kinds of formats such as tables, mathematical expressions, and new characters such as strikethrough and the copyright symbol, and new capabilities for integrating images with text. The growing popularity and commercial possibilities of the Web have accelerated the pace of change.

Understanding and keeping up with Web changes

Understanding this change process is essential to your success as a Web designer. You need to know the current official HTML standard, the proposals for the next version that are in the process of being ratified, and unofficial experimental HTML features that have been introduced by innovating companies such as Netscape. You cannot decide in a vacuum which HTML capabilities to use in your documents. Because one of the most important goals of Web design is the creation of documents that will be viewable by the widest international audience, you must balance your desire to use advanced features against judgments of what capabilities Web users have at the current moment and are likely to have in the near future.

Let's look at how new HTML standards get officially ratified. Because the Web (as part of the Internet) is not a centralized, hierarchical system, it uses a distributed, participatory structure to institute changes to standards. Volunteer "working groups" convene online and in occasional face-to-face meetings to discuss changed standards. They create proposals. RFC (requests for comments) are circulated to gather the Web community's reactions. Eventually the new standard is ratified. This process takes time, so proposed changes can be pending for a long time. Developers of Web software often implement preliminary versions of proposed capabilities before official acceptance. The W3 organization has assumed responsibility for coordinating the development and ratification of standards. The reference list later in this section points to online sources where you can keep up with their work and all proposed changes to HTML. The shaping of Web standards is an open process that solicits active *participation by the Web community. If you have strong ideas about changes you would like to see in Web protocols, you can join the online standards groups. Chapter 10, "Web Research and Emerging Trends," also presents more detail about the W3 organization.*

Many commercial companies entering the Web arena are eager to introduce innovations and consider this pace too slow. They are not willing to wait. For example, Netscape Communications Company developed the Netscape Web browser that can process several useful, but non-standard, HTML formatting conventions. Some of these are unofficial implementations of proposed HTML 3.0 standards. Others are enhancements they have proposed for ultimate inclusion in HTML 3.0 or later standards. Although Netscape says they will work actively to win their inclusion in the official protocols, their ultimate acceptance is unpredictable.

Although these extensions are seductive and greatly enhance your ability to control Web pages, documents that contain them are rendered correctly only by the Netscape browser. By distributing its browser free to most users, Netscape has become the most widely used Web browser on the market. Still, you cannot always count on all Web users to use this browser—Mosaic, for example, still commands a sizable audience. Netscape says they will support the official standards once they are ratified, although they may still offer their special enhancements.

As one version of HTML approaches official ratification, newer versions will be in development. What advanced capabilities should you start using? You could start right now using those that are well-defined and already implemented in browsers such as Netscape. These are highly likely to be incorporated in the HTML 3.0 standard. You could use those that are implemented in Netscape (but not part of the official HTML 3.0 proposals) if you can accept that your readers who don't have Netscape will not see them as you intended.

The HTML 3.0 sections that follow give you a firm understanding of how the capabilities are likely to work and hands-on information about applying the tags—based on the official proposals at press time. Although many of these are likely to be accepted as presented here, some will be subject to change as the comment and ratification process proceeds. The text makes clear which capabilities are highly defined and likely to be ratified as presented here, which are still in a very tentative proposal stage and still subject to much change, and which are implemented as Netscape's enhancements, which may or may not become part of the official specifications. An essential part of your work as a Web designer requires staying up to date—checking online sources for current information about the development of HTML and about the details of tags and syntax. Also, before you try out the techniques described in these sections, be sure to check the documentation of the browser you are using to be sure it supports these HTML 3.0 capabilities.

Information about HTML Development and HTML 3.0

- *W3 organization information page on HTML*
`http://www.w3.org/hypertext/WWW/MarkUp/MarkUp.HTML`

- *HTML 3.0 official draft proposal*
`http://www.w3.org/hypertext/WWW/MarkUp/html3/CoverPage.html`

- *Presentation on HTML+ (concepts incorporated into HTML 3.0)*
`http://www.w3.org/hypertext/WWW/MarkUp/`
`htmlplus_paper/htmlplus.html`

- *Information on Netscape extensions to HTML*
`http://www.netscape.com/assist/net_sites/`
`html_extensions.html`

- *Netscape approach to standards*
`http://www.netscape.com/newsref/std/`
`standards_qa.html`

- *Information about mathematical expressions in HTML 3.0*
`http://www.w3.org/hypertext/WWW/MarkUp/html3/`
`maths.html`

- *Information about LINK and META features in HTML 3.0*
`http://www.w3.org/hypertext/WWW/MarkUp/html3/`
`dochead.html`

- *Information about style sheets in HTML 3.0*
`http://www.w3.org/hypertext/WWW/Style/`

- *Service that analyzes HTML documents to tell what level of HTML they comply with*
`http://www.halsoft.com/html-val-svc/`

- *W3 Organization description*
`http://www.w3.org/hypertext/WWW/Consortium/`

- *Charter of the official Internet working group on HTML*
`http://www.ietf.cnri.reston.va.us/html.charters/`
`html-charter.html`

- *IETF working group on HTML development e-mail archives*
`http://www.acl.lanl.gov/HTML_WG/archives.html`

HTML 3.0 Capabilities and Netscape Suggested Enhancements

HTML 3.0 features offer exciting new capabilities. This section stresses only those related to text formatting. New features related to linking, in-line images, and imagemaps are described in Chapters 3, 4, and 7 respectively.

Tables

HTML 3.0 implements an easy-to-use tables feature. This feature lends itself to much more than data summaries; you can also use tables as a way to flexibly format the placement of text in a window. HTML 3.0 allows you to define table captions, headers, cell format, and border presence. The cells can contain text, paragraphs, figures, lists, or other tables. The browsers use layout algorithms that dynamically size the table to take into account the details of what is in the various cells and the size of the window. The HTML 3.0 table structure is well defined and already implemented in Netscape and Mosaic. You can count on many Web navigators supporting this capability.

Exercise 2.2 shows you how easy it is to create a table in HTML 3.0. The best way to design a table is to sketch it first on paper. The table protocol's basic model asks you to move systematically through the table, row by row, specifying exactly what must appear on each row. Each row will start with the table row <TR> tag followed by designations of table headers and table data that make up that row. Figure 2.18 shows you what the table will look like when it is displayed by a browser. Table 2.6 summarizes all table-related tags, except for those related to alignment, which are described in the following section. The table to be generated in the exercise generates a small table about how many calories are in a serving of various snack foods.

Exercise 2.2:

Creating a table

Step 1:

Here you'll build a very simple table, with four rows and two columns, describing the caloric content of several popular snack foods. Type the text for your table as follows:

```
Are Your Favorite Snacks High in Calories?

Food            # of Calories
10 potato chips  105
2/3 cup pretzels 100
1/4 cup peanuts  210
```

Step 2:

Add HTML structuring tags to identify this document as an HTML document and identify the title. You should also add the <TABLE> beginning and ending tags to identify all the information as part of one table.

```
<HTML>
<HEAD><TITLE>Creating a Table</TITLE></HEAD>
<BODY>
<TABLE>
Are Your Favorite Snacks High in Calories?
Food            # of Calories
10 potato chips  105
2/3 cup pretzels 100
1/4 cup peanuts  210
</TABLE>
</BODY>
</HTML>
```

Step 3:

Now you're ready to add the <CAPTION> tag to identify the caption for your table, as follows:

```
<CAPTION>Are Your Favorite Snacks High in Calories?</CAPTION>
```

Step 4:

Type **<TR>** to create your first table row. The text in the first line of your table should be rendered as table headers, so type **<TH>** before the words Food and # of Calories. Here, you also made use of the <ALIGN=RIGHT> attribute to make the second header flush right. Use a closing **</TR>** tag to end the row. Headers are typically displayed in bold while data is displayed in plain text:

```
<TR><TH>Food<TH ALIGN=RIGHT># of<BR>Calories</TR>
```

Step 5:

On the next line, type **<TR>** to start the next row of the table. The text in this line should be rendered as table data, so type **<TD>** before the data that goes in each table cell. You also made use of the <ALIGN=RIGHT> attribute to make the data in the cells in the second column flush right. Repeat for all rows in the table. Use a closing **</TR>** tag to end the row. (Some versions of the HTML 3.0 proposals don't require a closing tag for <TR>, <TD>, or <TH>. Check the official specs as the standard moves to ratification.)

```
<TR><TD>10 potato chips<TD ALIGN=RIGHT>105</TR>
<TR><TD>2/3 cup pretzels<TD ALIGN=RIGHT>100</TR>
<TR><TD>1/4 cup peanuts<TD ALIGN=RIGHT>210</TR>
```

Step 6:

Save the document as an ASCII text file. Use .html (if you're using a Macintosh or .htm for a DOS/ Windows platform) for the filename's suffix. The HTML for your sample table document should look like the following:

```
<HTML>
<HEAD><TITLE>Creating a Table</TITLE></HEAD>
<BODY>
<TABLE BORDER>
<CAPTION><H3>Are Your Favorite Snacks High in
 Calories?</H3></CAPTION>
<TR><TH>Food<TH ALIGN=RIGHT># of<BR>Calories</TR>
<TR><TD>10 potato chips<TD ALIGN=RIGHT>105</TR>
<TR><TD>2/3 cup pretzels<TD ALIGN=RIGHT>100</TR>
<TR><TD>1/4 cup peanuts<TD ALIGN=RIGHT>210</TR>
</TABLE>
</BODY>
</HTML>
```

Step 7:

Activate your Web browser and use the *Open Local* or *Open File* option to load and view the document you just created. Your document should be similar to the one pictured in Figure 2.18.

Typically, normal tables have headers along the first row at the top and in the first column on the left. If you are using the table feature strictly for visual effect, you could place table headers anywhere.

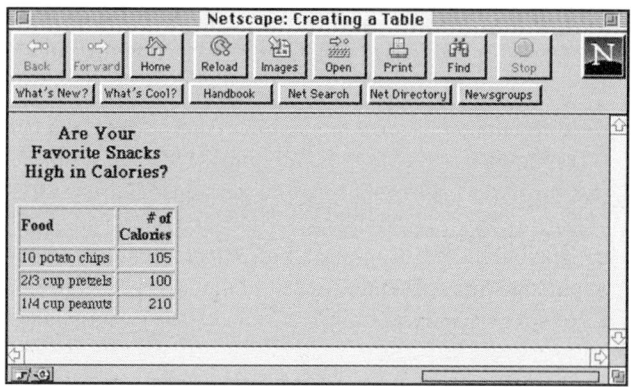

Figure 2.18:
Creation of a table.

You have many options for finer control. The next subsections show some options available for table design.

Lining up Table Headers

The previous exercise placed headers only along the top. Many tables also have headers on the side in the first column. Although you construct the table just as you did in the exercise, you must keep track of the total number of cells occupied, including the headers on the left side. You also must keep track of empty cells that you indicate to keep cells and headers lined up. Figure 2.19 shows a table with headers on the side and the top and illustrates the need to watch out for alignment.

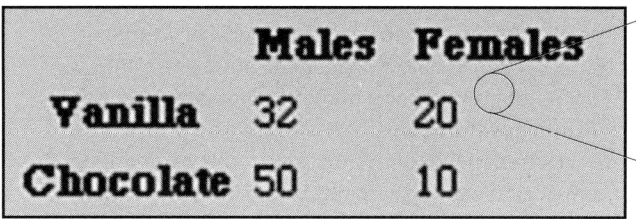

```
<TABLE >
 <TR><TH><TH> Males <TH >Females</TR>
 <TR> <TH> Vanilla<TD>32<TD>20</TR>
 <TR> <TH> Chocolate<TD>50<TD>10</TR>
</TABLE>
```

Figure 2.19:
A table with headers on the top and side. A blank <TH> tag is needed in the first row to bump the headers to the second and third columns.

Table Borders

You can control whether a table should have a border by including the word BORDER within the table tag. <TABLE BORDER> would be the starting tag for a table that included a border. The Netscape browser offers a border control not in the HTML 3.0 official proposals. You can manipulate the number of pixels for the border of a table by adding an indication after the BORDER option. For example <TABLE BORDER=9> would create a table with a nine-pixel border. Figure 2.20 shows the table illustrated in Figure 2.19 with a 9-pixel border.

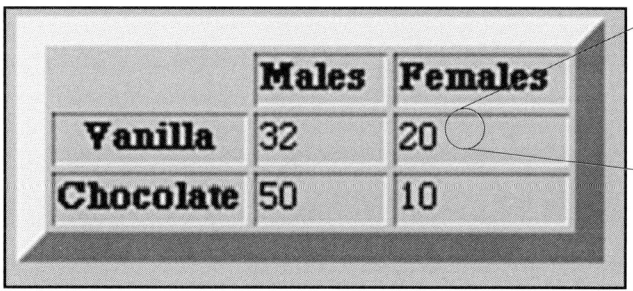

```
<TABLE  BORDER=9>
 <TR><TH><TH> Males <TH >Females</TR>
 <TR> <TH> Vanilla<TD>32<TD>20</TR>
 <TR> <TH> Chocolate<TD>50<TD>10</TR>
</TABLE>
```

Figure 2.20:
Controlling the border of a table.

Table Width

Normally Web browsers will use a sophisticated algorithm to assess how wide the user's window is and how much material is in the table to set up an appropriate width. You can override the algorithm by directly specifying the percentage of the window width the table should occupy by adding a WIDTH option within the opening <TABLE> tag such as <TABLE WIDTH=*n*%>. Figure 2.21 shows what you would type to set the width of a table to cover 80% of the window.

```
<TABLE  BORDER WIDTH=80%>
 <TR><TH><TH> Males <TH >Females</TR>
 <TR> <TH> Vanilla<TD>32<TD>20</TR>
<TR> <TH> Chocolate<TD>50<TD>10</TR>
</TABLE>
```

	Males	Females
Vanilla	32	20
Chocolate	50	10

Figure 2.21:
Controlling the width of a table.

Multiple Row or Column Table Cells

Tables can be much more complex than those illustrated so far. For example, you can specify any cell's size in rows or columns with an optional <ROWSPAN> or <COLSPAN> feature. You add this property to the <TH> or <TD> tags. Figure 2.22 shows what you would type to create a table in which the top

headers each span two columns. In this example the *Male* and *Female* headers are each divided into two sub categories by age. Line 1 and 2 of the table must start with empty header cells in order to position the column heads and subheads over the appropriate data cells. With these multirow and multicolumn options, you can create quite complex multilayered tables.

```
<TABLE Border>
<TR><TH ><TH COLSPAN = 2> Males <TH COLSPAN = 2
>Females</TR>
<TR><TH ><TH >Under 18 <TH >Over 18 <TH> Under 18
<TH> Over 18</TR>
<TR> <TH> Vanilla<TD>32<TD>20 <TD> 55<TD>22</TR>
<TR> <TH> Chocolate<TD>50<TD>10<TD>67<TD>33</TR>
</TABLE>
```

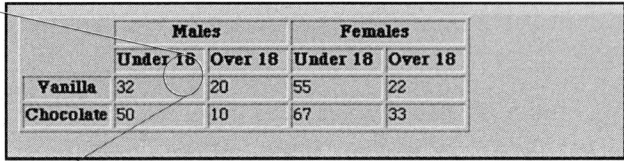

	Males		Females	
	Under 18	Over 18	Under 18	Over 18
Vanilla	32	20	55	22
Chocolate	50	10	67	33

Figure 2.22:
Use of multicolumn table cells.

Nested Tables

Note that the HTML 3.0 table specifications allow the inclusion of tables inside of other tables. The example that follows shows how you could create a table of 2 rows and 2 columns with an embedded table occupying the top left cell.

```
<HTML>
<HEAD><TITLE> Table within a table</HEAD></TITLE>
```

```
<BODY>
<TABLE BORDER>
<TR>
<TD>

<TABLE BORDER>  <!-- this is the embedded table for
 the top left cell --></TR>
<TR>
<TD>1<TD>2<TD>3</TR>
```

```
<TR>
<TD>4<TD>5<TD>6</TR>
</TABLE>
<TD> row1/column 2 data

<TR>
<TD>row2/column 1 data
<TD> row2/column 2 data</TR>
</TABLE>
```

Cell Spacing and Cell Padding

The Netscape browser offers some controls of data in cells and borders between cells. These are not in the HTML 3.0 official proposals. CELLSPACING allows you to control the number of pixels inserted between cells—for example <TABLE CELLSPACING=4>. CELLPADDING indicates the number of pixels inserted between the data inside the cells and their borders—for example <TABLE CELLPADDING=2>.

Using the Table Feature to Simulate Text Columns

The table can be quite useful for positioning text and graphic elements in the window. It need not be used only for data summaries. For example, you could very easily create a display that simulated three columns of text as they would appear in a newspaper. You would create a table of one row of three columns with no borders. The example that follows illustrates the code to create a table that accomplished this. The tags for each data section are put on separate lines for the sake of clarity.

```
<TABLE>
<TR>
<TD> This would be the text that would appear in
  column 1. It could go on and on...till its end.
<TD> This would be column 2 text. It could also be
  long...till its end.
```

```
<TD> Column 3 text could go here. You would have to
  work to make sure to adjust the lengths of each
  column. In this </TR>
</TABLE>
```

Remember, HTML looks only for tags to determine its formatting. HTML table tags and Netscape-enhanced table features are summarized in Tables 2.6 and 2.7, respectively.

Table 2.6

Table-Related Tags and Options

Tag	Function	Comments
<TABLE> </TABLE>	Marks the beginning and end of a table. A table can consist of rows and columns.	Attributes include WIDTH=% BORDER COLSPEC*.
<CAPTION> </CAPTION>	A label for the table.	Usually placed on top of table. Option is not required.
<TR> </TR>	Indicates a table row. Marks the beginning of a new row in your table.	Consider each <TR> in your table as a separate row.*
<TD> </TD>	Indicates table data. Indicates a new cell in your grid.	Consider each <TD> in your table between <TR> tags as a separate column.*

Table 2.6

Continued

Tag or Option	Function	Examples
</TH>	Indicates a table header. Usually used to label the columns and rows with text.	<TH> is interchangeable with <TD>*.

*This feature is still a tentative proposal.

**Some HTML 3.0 proposals don't require closing tags for <TR>, <TD>, and <TH>.

Table 2.7

Netscape Extensions for Tables

Tag or Option	Function	Examples
WIDTH=n (pixels) WIDTH=n%	Defines, in pixels, the width of a cell; also can be specified by percentage of window	<TABLE WIDTH=20>
CELLPADDING	Indicates, in pixels, a text inset between data and the cell borders	<TABLE CELLPADDING=2>
CELLSPACING	Controls the number of pixels inserted as a gutter between cells	<TABLE CELLSPACING=4>
BORDER = n (pixels)	Indicates in pixels the thickness of the table's border	<TABLE BORDER=4>

Alignment Control

HTML 3.0 lets you control, for the first time, the horizontal alignment of most kinds of HTML elements. This applies to headers, paragraph text, lists, preformatted text, blockquote, horizontal rules, tables, and images. Figures 2.23–2.27 show examples of using the alignment property, and Table 2.8 summaries the options.

> **Note:** At press time alignment options had been implemented for headers and images in both Netscape and Mosaic. The other alignment options—for example, lists, preformatted text, and table alignment are likely to be implemented in the near future. They might not yet work, however, with the browser you or your Web readers are using, so check before you build pages based on them.

Alignment of HTML Elements

The following exercise demonstrates the ease with which you will be able to horizontally align headers. You activate alignment by including an <ALIGN=> property inside the normal tags. Alignment options include left, right, center, and justify. Note that Netscape uses a slightly different syntax for centering, as shown in Table 2.8. Take a look at the source code that follows for the figure in Figure 2.23 to see how the different alignment effects are produced.

```
<HTML>
<HEAD>
<TITLE>Aligning Headers</TITLE>
</HEAD>
<BODY>
<H2 ALIGN=RIGHT>This header appears at the right of
  the window.</H2>
<H2 ALIGN=LEFT>This header appears at the left of
  the window.<H2>
<H2 ALIGN=CENTER>This header appears centered in the
  window.<H2>
</BODY>
</HTML>
```

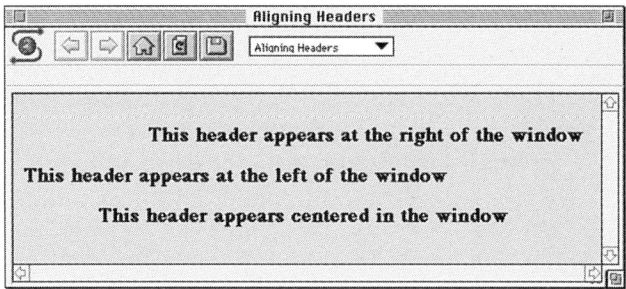

Figure 2.23:
Aligning headers.

Side by Side HTML Elements and the <CLEAR> Tag

Once the alignment option is fully implemented, other HTML text, tables, or images will be able to fill in the available space alongside rather than automatically starting below the text, as was true with older versions of HTML. For example, Figure 2.24 shows how a text header would appear alongside a table aligned on the right margin rather than below it.

Because text can fill in on the side of other elements, you must explicitly indicate when you want the new element to start below other elements. In HTML 3.0, you indicate this with the <CLEAR=> property. Options include <CLEAR=ALL> (for forcing a new element below all elements as was true in older versions of HTML), left (for moving below any elements sitting on the left margin), and right (for moving below any elements sitting on the right margin). Figure 2.24 shows what you would type to force a header to fill in on the side of a table aligned on the right margin and also how you would use the <CLEAR> tag to force the next line to be positioned below any other elements.

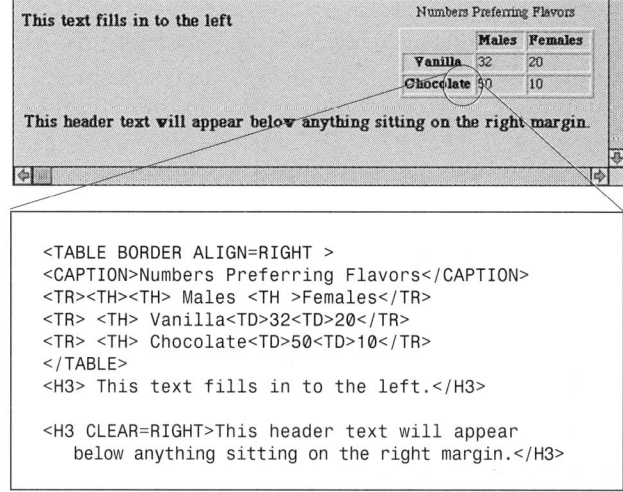

```
<TABLE BORDER ALIGN=RIGHT >
<CAPTION>Numbers Preferring Flavors</CAPTION>
<TR><TH><TH> Males <TH >Females</TR>
<TR> <TH> Vanilla<TD>32<TD>20</TR>
<TR> <TH> Chocolate<TD>50<TD>10</TR>
</TABLE>
<H3> This text fills in to the left.</H3>

<H3 CLEAR=RIGHT>This header text will appear
    below anything sitting on the right margin.</H3>
```

Figure 2.24:
Side by side HTML elements and the <CLEAR> tag.

You can also mark up your text so that the browser will find the next available space with a certain open space between it and other elements. You indicate this feature by using the <CLEAR= 100 pixels> or <CLEAR= 40 en> options. *En* is a printer's term that basically refers to the width of the letter "n" in the particular font you are using. The line that follows would place the header at the next place it could where there would be at least a 65 pixel space between it and any element on the right:

```
<H2 CLEAR=65 pixels>This header text will appear
  when there is a 65 pixel space to the next
  element on the margin.</H2
```

Web browsers, like word processors, usually automatically wrap lines of text when they come up against the right window boundary. With HTML 3.0 you can use the <NOWRAP> option to prevent a browser from wrapping the text. Usually the browser will just extend the text beyond the right window margin and offer the user a scroll bar to control viewing. This sample line would prevent a browser from word wrapping this line. You might use this feature if the connections between words in your sentence were something you would not want to broken up by word wrapping. The text would extend beyond the window border and users would need to scroll to see the rest of the line. Figure 2.25 illustrates what you would type to activate this feature.

```
<H3 NOWRAP>  No browser would wrap this text; it
  would keep going until you put in a BR or P tag.
</H3>
```

Figure 2.25:
Using the <NOWRAP> tag.

Tabs

HTML3.0 implements a new tab feature that allows you to specify tab positions and position text relative to them. To overcome the problem of varying font widths, the proposals call for a dynamic setting of tabs relative to other text. An author can name a tab stop by inserting a tab identification tag <TAB ID= *name*> in document text. Later tab calls will go to the position defined in the text with a <TAB TO=> tag. The lines that follow show a quick example. Figure 2.26 illustrates the use of this feature.

```
<p>Now is the time for all persons<tab id=ta1>to
  answer the call<br>
<tab to=ta1> What persons?<br>
```

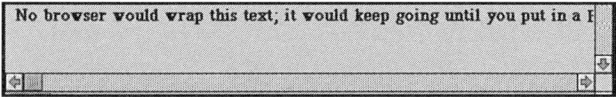

Figure 2.26:
TAB ID feature proposed in HTML 3.0.

The <INDENT> option allows control of tabs by distance in ens—for example <TAB INDENT=8> would start the text 8 en spaces from the margin. Tabs can also be used to align columns on decimal points. The tag <TAB TO t1 ALIGN= decimal> 143.44 will make sure the decimal point lines up at the tab stop t1.

Alignment Options Specially Related to Tables

You have already seen in Figure 2.24 how HTML's general alignment function can position tables in the browser's window just as it can position other HTML elements. In addition, there are several alignment options specifically relevant to tables. You can specify whether the caption should appear on the bottom of the table with the <CAPTION ALIGN=BOTTOM> option; the default places the caption on the top.

You can also specify the alignment of data within cells. Figure 2.27 illustrates what you would type to align a caption at the bottom of a table and to position the data within a table's cells. By default, header cells are centered and data cells are flush left. You can change this by including the <ALIGN> attribute inside the <TR>, <TH>, or <TD>. For example a <TD ALIGN=RIGHT> tag would cause the text in that cell to be aligned against the right cell border and putting a <TD ALIGN=CENTER> would cause the text to be centered. Putting the ALIGN=RIGHT property within the TR tag (<TR ALIGN=RIGHT>) would cause all cells in that row to be aligned against the right cell border. You can also determine vertical alignment with the <VALIGN> property.

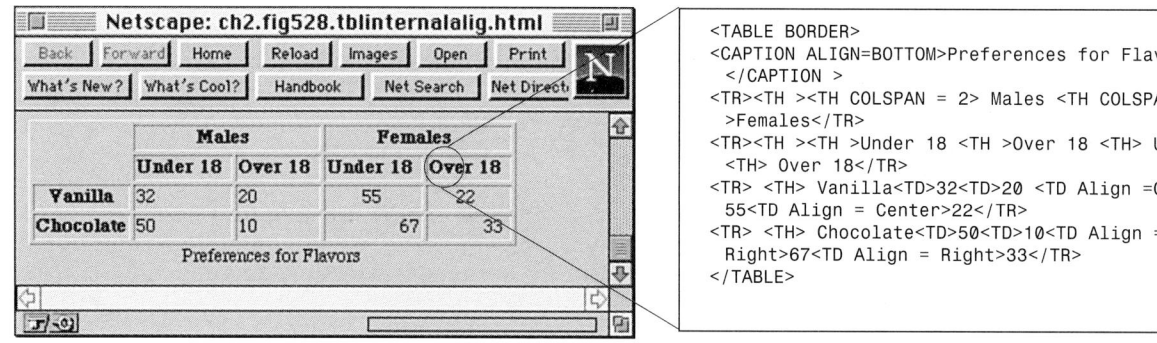

Figure 2.27:
HTML 3.0 alignment options used in tables.

Table 2.8

HTML 3.0 Alignment Control Options

Tag or Option	Function	Comments	Examples
ALIGN = (right, left, center)	Indicates horizontal alignment.	Can be used as an option in block elements, header, lists, preformatted text, tables, equations, and images. Default is left.	\<H2 ALIGN=RIGHT\> \<PRE ALIGN=CENTER\> \<BLOCKQUOTE ALIGN=JUSTIFY\>
CLEAR = (right, left, all) also,			
CLEAR=n, where n is the number of pixels between elements.	Use to indicate how far to move down before placing element.	If no ALIGN options are used, the default is CLEAR=ALL.	\<H2 CLEAR=RIGHT\> \<H2 CLEAR=ALL\> \<H2 CLEAR=10\>
TAB (ID=, TO, INDENT=)	Indicates a position in text where TAB should be set.	TAB ID= is the setting of the tab. TAB TO refers to TAB set with ID. TAB INDENT= refers to number of pixels to indent.	\<TAB ID=T1\> \<TAB TO T1\> \<TAB INDENT=10\>

continues

Table 2.8

Continued

Tag or Option	Function	Comments	Examples
NOWRAP	Indicates that browser should not attempt to wrap text when it meets the window right margin.	Can be used with all block elements, headers, lists, preformatted and block-quote text, and tables. Default is to allow wrapping.	<H2 NOWRAP>
<CENTER> </CENTER>	Use to enclose any elements to be centered.	Netscape's implementation is slightly different from the HTML 3.0 proposals in which ALIGN=CENTER is an attribute within a tag.	<CENTER> <H2>My Project</H2> </CENTER>

Table 2.9

Alignment Options Specific to Tables

Tag or Option	Function	Comments	Examples
TABLE ALIGN = (RIGHT, CENTER LEFT, BLEEDLEFT, BLEEDRIGHT, JUSTIFY)	Indicates alignment for the table as a whole.	Other HTML code will fill in avail-available space.	<TABLE ALIGN=RIGHT>
ROWSPAN = n COLSPAN = n	Use inside TR, TH, or TD to indicate number of rows or columns a cell should span.	Default is 1.	<TH COLSPAN=5>
TH, TD ALIGN = (RIGHT, CENTER, JUSTIFY, DECIMAL)	Use inside TR, TH, or TD to horizontally align the text or data within table cells.	Default for <TH> is centered; default for <TD> is <TH ALIGN=LEFT> left.	<TD ALIGN=CENTER>

Tag or Option	Function	Comments	Examples
TD VALIGN = (TOP, MIDDLE, BOTTOM)	Use inside TD to vertically align the text or data within table cells.	Default is middle.	<TD VALIGN=BOTTOM>
TH, TR, TD NOWRAP	Use inside TR, TH, or TD to indicate that text inside cells should not be wrapped.	Can force very large cells to be created.	<TH NOWRAP>

Table 2.10

Netscape Extensions for Table Alignment Options

Tag or Option	Function	Comments	Examples
CAPTION ALIGN = (BOTTOM, TOP)	Use to specify where caption should be placed.	Default puts caption on top.	<CAPTION ALIGN= BOTTOM "Tablename">
TD VALIGN = (TOP, MIDDLE, BOTTOM)	Use inside TD to vertically align the text or data within table cells.	Default is middle.	<TD VALIGN=BOTTOM>

Because alignment is a crucial issue in setting up tables, both the HTML 3.0 proposals and Netscape offer special alignment options. They are summarized in Table 2.9 and Table 2.10, respectively.

New List Features

HTML 3.0 implements a few minor enhancements to HTML list structures. Figure 2.28 shows you how to apply these new features and Table 2.11 summarizes them. The <ALIGN>, <CLEAR>, and <NOWRAP> features described in the previous section are available with all lists in HTML 3.0. You can attach a list header to a list by using the new tags <LH> and </LH> to enclose header text, as illustrated in the example.

```
<OL>
<LH>New features of lists in HTML3.0</LH>
<LI> Sequence numbering control
<LI> List header tags
</OL>
```

Ordered Lists: You can use a new sequence number option to indicate the beginning number for an ordered list—for example, <OL SEQNUM=15> would start the automatic numbering with 15 instead of the default 1. You can use the new <CONTINUE> option to have the browser continue numbering a list starting from the place the last ordered list left off—for example <OL CONTINUE>. Use the new list header tag to mark a title or caption for a list as illustrated next. The list header is available for all HTML list types. Use the <COMPACT> option inside the list tag to direct the browser to try to put items as close together vertically as possible. A new feature called *style sheets* (described in a later part of this section) will eventually allow you to control the kind of numbering in ordered lists—for example, use of Roman numerals or lower-case letters. Figure 2.28 shows what you would need to type to use these new list features.

Unordered Lists: A new <PLAIN> feature allows you to create unordered lists without the default bullets—<UL PLAIN>. Because this kind of unordered list duplicates the visual appearance of <MENU> and <DIRECTORY> lists, the HTML 3.0 proposals have rendered obsolete these two list formats from HTML 2.0.

Additional new features access inline images or standardized dingbats to serve as the item markers in the list. For example, <UL SRC=Check.gif> would use an image called check.gif as the marker instead of bullets and the tag <UL DINGBAT=FOLDER> would use a standard folder dingbat (dingbat is a printer's term for a typographic symbol usually used for decoration or emphasis). HTML 3.0 will offer a standard set of dingbats. As with ordered lists, <COMPACT> can be used to compress the vertical space between list items. Consult Figure 2.28 for illustrations of these new unordered list features.

```
<OL COMPACT>
<B><LH>New features of lists in HTML 3.0</LH></B>
<LI> Sequence numbering control
<LI> List header tags
</OL>

<OL CONTINUE >
<B><LH>This is new list header tag</LH></B>
<LI>Because of the CONTINUE option
<LI>This list starts with the number 3
<LI>The previous list stopped with number 2
</OL>

<OL SEQNUM=11>
<LH> <B> This demonstrates the sequence option</B>
<LI>Because of the SEQNUM=11 option
<LI>This list starts with the number 11 </OL>

<UL>
<LI> This demonstrates regular unordered list
<LI> Each item starts with bullet </UL>

<UL PLAIN>
<LI> This demonstrates use of PLAIN option
<LI> Each item starts with no bullet </UL>
```

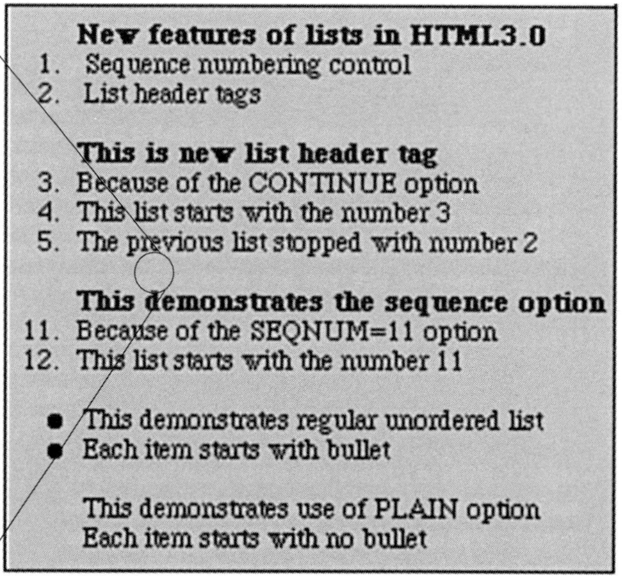

New features of lists in HTML3.0
1. Sequence numbering control
2. List header tags

This is new list header tag
3. Because of the CONTINUE option
4. This list starts with the number 3
5. The previous list stopped with number 2

This demonstrates the sequence option
11. Because of the SEQNUM=11 option
12. This list starts with the number 11

● This demonstrates regular unordered list
● Each item starts with bullet

This demonstrates use of PLAIN option
Each item starts with no bullet

Figure 2.28:
New list features in HTML 3.0.

Netscape Enhancements: Netscape offers some enhancements that are not in the official HTML 3.0 proposals, although they might someday be incorporated. Figure 2.29 illustrates the use of these features and Table 2.12 summarizes their use. In ordered lists you can specify the kind of numbering to be used with the <TYPE=> option. The choices are A (capital letters); a (lowercase letters); I (large Roman numerals); i (small Roman numerals); and 1 (normal Arabic numerals)—for example, <UL=I> would cause the items in the list to be numbered sequentially with Roman numerals.

You indicate the sequence starting point with the property <START>—for example, <OL START=5>. This would cause a numbered list to start with 5 instead of the default 1. Notice that this tag's name differs from the <SEQNUM> proposed for the HTML 3.0 specifications. Also, the sequence and the current number can be changed on the fly by putting the property <TYPE> or <START> into any <LI> tag. In Figure 2.29 the sequence changes numbering conventions to letters after the list item with the <LI TYPE= *tag*>.

In unordered lists, you can specify the kind of item marker to be used with the <TYPE=> property. The choices include disc, circle, or square—for example, <UL> Type=square>. As with ordered lists, the marker being used can be changed in midprocess by inserting a <TYPE=> property in a <LI> tag. Figure 2.29 shows what you would type to activate this feature.

```
<OL TYPE=A START= 5>
<LH> <B>Netscape[sp]s special options for ordered
 lists</B>
<LI> The TYPE= A option uses capital letters
<LI> The other options include
<LI> a= small letters. I= Roman num
<LI> i= small Roman. 1= Arabic num
<LI> The START= option works like the SEQNUM=
<LI> In this capital letter situation it starts with
 "E"
</OL>

<UL TYPE=square>
<LH> <B>Netscape[sp]s special options for unordered
 lists</B>
<LI> The TYPE= square option uses squares
<LI> The other options include
<LI> TYPE= disc and TYPE=circle </UL>
```

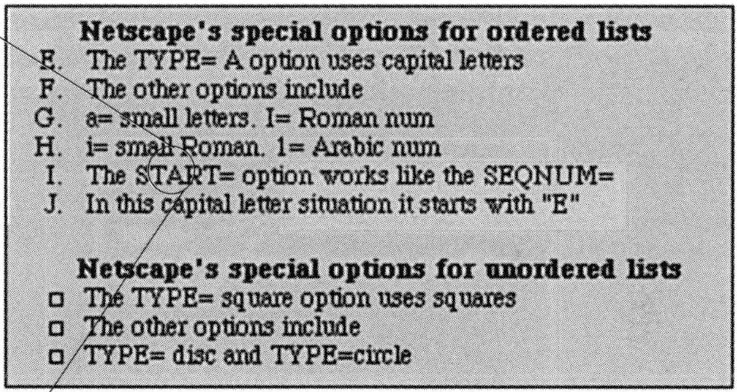

Netscape's special options for ordered lists
E.   The TYPE= A option uses capital letters
F.   The other options include
G.   a= small letters. I= Roman num
H.   i= small Roman. 1= Arabic num
I.   The START= option works like the SEQNUM=
J.   In this capital letter situation it starts with "E"

Netscape's special options for unordered lists
□ The TYPE= square option uses squares
□ The other options include
□ TYPE= disc and TYPE=circle

Figure 2.29:
New list features in Netscape.

Table 2.11

HTML 3.0 List Features

Tag or Option	Function	Comments	Examples
<LH> </LH>	List header. Use as title for list.	Applies to all kinds of lists.	<LH>List Header</LH>
COMPACT	Compact the vertical space between list items.	Operates as an option for all lists.	<OL COMPACT> <UL COMPACT>
CONTINUE	Used on ordered lists <OL>. Continue numbering from last ordered list.	Default is starting over with 1.	<OL CONTINUE>
SEQNUM=n	Use on ordered lists <OL>. n indicates the number to start with.	Default is 1.	<OL SEQNUM=10>
PLAIN	Used for unordered lists <UL> to indicate no bullet marks next to list items.	Default issues bullets.	<UL PLAIN>
SRC=URI	Use an image instead of normal bullet marker.	URI is pointer to the image.	<UL SRC=/imgs/star.gif>
DINGBAT=URI	Use special HTML 3.0 dingbats as markers of each item.	Standard dingbats are provided in HTML 3.0.	<UL DINGBAT=URI>

Table 2.12

Netscape List Features

Tag or Option	Function	Comments	Examples
TYPE=(A, a, I, i, 1)	Use the type to define numbering convention for ordered lists.	A = uppercase letters a = lowercase letters I = Roman numerals i = small Roman numerals 1 = Arabic numerals	<OL TYPE=1>

Tag or Option	Function	Comments	Examples
TYPE=(SQUARE, CIRCLE, DISC)	Used for unordered lists to define marker type.	Default is disc. Can change in mid-process by using in one of the <UL> items <UL TYPE=SQUARE>.	<LI TYPE=DISC>
START=n	Use to indicate the starting number in an ordered list.	Default is 1. Same as SEQNUM.	<OL START=5>

Customizing Horizontal Rules

HTML 3.0 enables you to use the <ALIGN> function with horizontal rules. In addition, Netscape offers several enhancements to the <HR> tag that are not yet in the HTML 3.0 official proposals. A <WIDTH> property allows you to specify how much of the window should be occupied by the line. It can be specified in percentages or pixels—for example,

<HR ALIGN=Center WIDTH=50%> would create a centered horizontal line that occupies 50 percent of the window. You can use the <SIZE> property to control the thickness of the line—for example, <HR SIZE=10> would create a 10-pixel-thick line across the screen. By default Netscape draws a shaded line; the <NOSHADE> property creates a solid line. Figure 2.30 illustrates use of the features described in this section and Tables 2.12 and 2.13 summarize their syntax.

```
<H4> This horizontal rule has a size of six pixels,
  a width of 50% of the window, and is aligned
  in the center.</H4>
<HR SIZE=6 WIDTH=50% CENTER>

<H4> This horizontal rule has a size of two pixels,
  a width of 200 pixels, is aligned on right
  margin, and is not shaded.</H4>
<HR SIZE=2 WIDTH=200 NOSHADE ALIGN=RIGHT>
```

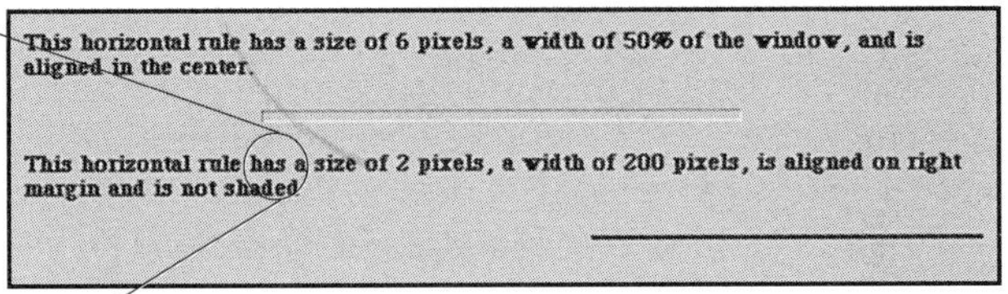

This horizontal rule has a size of 6 pixels, a width of 50% of the window, and is aligned in the center.

This horizontal rule has a size of 2 pixels, a width of 200 pixels, is aligned on right margin and is not shaded.

Figure 2.30:
Netscape's horizontal rule features.

Table 2.13

Horizontal Rule Features in HTML 3.0

Tag or Option	Function	Comments	Examples
<HR WIDTH=*n*%>	Width size can be specified in percentage only.	Use WIDTH to indicate how far across the window the horizontal rule should go. Default is 100 percent.	<HR WIDTH=100%>

Table 2.14

Netscape Horizontal Rule Features

Tag or Option	Function	Comments	Examples
<HR WIDTH=*n*%>	Options size can be specified in percentage or pixels.	Use WIDTH to indicate how far across the window the horizontal rule should go. Default is 100 percent.	<HR WIDTH=100%>
<HR SIZE=*n*>	Use SIZE to indicate the thickness of the horizontal line in pixels.	Default is 1 pixel.	<HR SIZE=10>
<HR NOSHADE>	Use NOSHADE to draw solid lines.	Default is shaded line.	<HR NOSHADE>

Blockquote, Address, Notes, and Footnotes

Minor enhancements are added to the blockquote, address, and preformat styles, such as allowing use of the <ALIGN CLEAR> and <NOWRAP> format control options. New notes and footnote styles have been added. Table 2.15 summarizes these new features. HTML 3.0 shortens the tags for blockquote to <BQ> and </BQ> from <BLOCKQUOTE> used in earlier versions of HTML. In addition, you can use the new <CREDIT> and </CREDIT> tags to enclose an attribution of the source of the blockquote within the blockquote. In Figure 2.31, the quote is attributed to Samuel Taylor Coleridge.

HTML 3.0 introduces a new style called Note to be used for warnings, asides, or other sidebars. You can implement it with the <NOTE> and </NOTE> tags. The proposals call for this kind of text to be formatted in a special way to attract attention. Notes can include images (for example, stop signs) by using the <SRC> image call within the tag—<NOTE src=stopsign.gif>. The Web page shown in Figure 2.31 makes use of the <NOTE> tag.

The new footnote style is indicated with the <FN> and </FN> styles. As an author, you will be able to include footnotes attached to particular text. Each footnote must be given a unique identifying name and the word or phrase to be linked to the footnote must be enclosed in anchor tags pointing to the footnote—<A href=#fn1>text to have footnote attached </A>. *Fn1* is an arbitrary name; you could use anything that started with a letter. Anchor tags are explained in more detail in Chapter 3. Elsewhere in the document you must mark up

the text that serves as the footnote. It is given an ID that corresponds to the ID referenced in the text—in this example, *fn1*. In Figure 2.31 the tags <FN ID="fn1"> and </FN> enclose the footnote text. The proposals suggest that Web browsers implement footnotes as popup notes. Figure 2.31 shows what a popup footnote might look like. These enhancements make academic or scientific articles better suited for formatting as Web documents.

```
Many on the Web are searching for Xanadu, the place
described by Coleridge:<BR>
<BQ>
Weave a circle round heim thrice,
And close your eyes with hold dread,
For he on honey-dew hath fed,
And drank the milk of Paradise<BR>
<CREDIT>Samuel Taylor Coleridge, Kubla Kahn</CREDIT>
</BQ>

<NOTE> Be careful about searching for things that
 you cannot find. <A  HREF="#fn1">Coleridge</A>
 was not a happy person.</NOTE>

<FN ID="fn1">Debates have raged for years on the
 relationship of mental illness and productiv
 ity of authors.</FN>
```

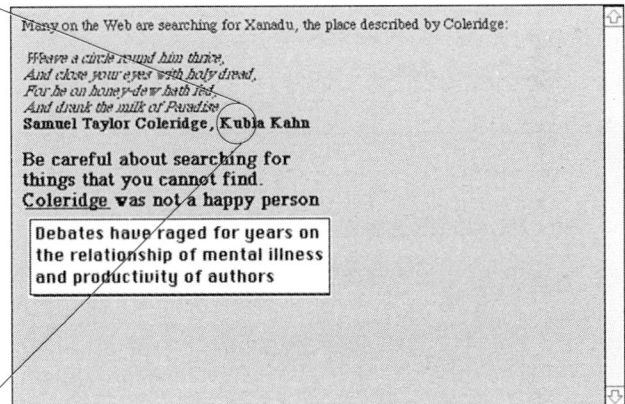

Figure 2.31:
HTML3.0 blockquote, source, note, and footnote features.

Table 2.15

HTML 3.0 Blockquote, Note, Footnote Features

Tag or Option	Function	Comments
<BQ> </BQ>	New name for blockquote tag from earlier HTML versions.	Old name will still be recognized for backwards compatibility.
<CREDIT> </CREDIT>	Use within blockquotes to mark up the source of the quote.	Optional.
<NOTE> </NOTE>	Use to mark up text that should be emphasized as a warning or sidebar.	Optionally a call to an inline image can be included with <NOTE src=yourimage.gif>.
"FN id=fn1" footnote text "/FN"	Use to designate a footnote to be attached to some text.	Use an anchor tag at the text to indicate which footnote to reference. "A HREF= #fn1"text to be footnoted "/A"

New Character Style Tags

HTML 3.0 implements a number of new physical and logical font styles. Table 2.16 summarizes all of these new tags. New physical tags allow you to indicate subscript <SUB>, super-scripts <SUP>, and strikethru <S> text. Strikethrough is used in editing to place a horizontal rule through words but leave them visible to allow readers to see what changes have been made ~~like this~~. New logical styles allow you to indicate the functions of text, which browsers may represent in a variety of ways. The styles include definition, quote, author, person, acronym, abbreviation, and inserted and deleted text. Remember, logical styles often stress identification of the functions of text rather than visual differences.

New physical style tags of <BIG> and <SMALL> allow you to directly control font size without changing header tags as was necessary in earlier versions of HTML. The <BIG> tag causes any enclosed text to be rendered larger than sur-rounding text; the <SMALL> tag causes any enclosed text to be rendered smaller than surrounding text. Figure 2.32 shows an example of this control of font size.

Netscape implemented its own version of size tags that gives even more control. You can use a <FONT> tag with a SIZE= option to control size. The valid numbers are 1 through 7. Three is the default size. Thus a tag <FONT SIZE=5> would make text two steps larger relative to the base. The tag </FONT> is the closing tag. The size of letters can be changed even in the middle of words. Figure 2.32 shows examples of how to use this tag.

```
<H3>Netscape[sp]s tags for controlling font sizes
      </H3>
The word <BIG> big </BIG> is rendered larger than
           surrounding text.<P><HR>

<H3>Netscape's tags for controlling font sizes
   </H3>
<FONT SIZE = 1> C <FONT SIZE = 2>h <FONT SIZE = 3>a
<FONT SIZE =4> <FONT SIZE = 5>n <FONT SIZE =
6>g<FONT SIZE = 7>e <BR>
<FONT SIZE = 2>Small
<FONT SIZE = 4>Medium
<FONT SIZE = 7>Large<BR>
<FONT SIZE = 3>Remember to change text back to
  normal size.
```

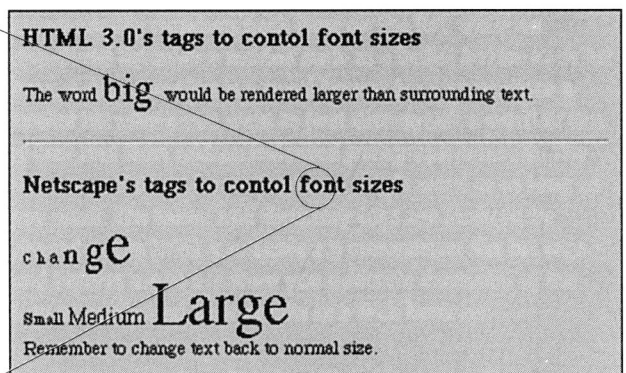

Figure 2.32:
How HTML 3.0 and Netscape control font size.

Table 2.16

HTML3.0 Physical and Logical Font Styles

Tag or Option	Function	Comments
Physical Styles		
<S> </S>	Strikethrough	Used in legal and editing work
	Subscript	Text is shifted down and usually reduced in size
	Superscript	Text is shifted up and usually reduced in size
<BIG> </BIG>	Make enclosed text larger than surrounding text	
<SMALL> </SMALL>	Make enclosed text smaller than surrounding text	

continues

Table 2.16

Continued

Tag or Option	Function	Comments
Logical Styles		
<DFN> </DFN>	Definition—the defining instance of a term	
<Q> </Q>	Enclosed text treated as quote with quotation marks	
<AUTHOR> </AUTHOR>	Enclosed is author of text	
<PERSON> </PERSON>	Enclosed is a person's name	
<ACRONYM> </ACRONYM>	Acronym	
<ABBREV> </ABBREV>	Abbreviation	
<INS> </INS>	Inserted text	In editing markup it is often shown as bold or in a different color
<DELETE> </DELETE>	Deleted text	In editing markup it is often shown as strikethru or in a different color
Netscape Enhancements		
<FONT SIZE=5>	Use the Font tag with size= option to declare a font size	Options: 1-7. The current base is 3
</FONT>		

Mathematical Expressions

Mathematical expressions have always been difficult to represent in plain text because of their unusual symbols and the critical importance of relative placement. HTML 3.0 institutes a special mathematics tag for enclosing these expressions. Standard conventions derived from the UNIX text formatting program LaTeX govern the way the expressions are indicated. For example, the following expression indicates the integral from a to b of f(x) over 1+x:

```
<MATH>&int;_a_^b^{f(x)<over>1+x} dx</MATH>
```

HTML 3.0 compliant Web browsers will graphically present the expression in a proper way. Because mathematical markup is a technical subject beyond the scope of this book, readers who want further details can consult the online references for the HTML 3.0 proposals on rendering mathematical expressions at http://www.hpl.hp.co.uk/people/dsr/HTML/maths.HTML.

Other New Features

HTML 3.0 implements several new tags and structures that allow you to designate functional subsections of your documents. Eventually, these will be linked to author-created style sheets, which will give you more control over how browsers render your documents. For example, you would be able to indicate that all text marked up as BQ (blockquotes) be rendered in a certain font, font size, and paragraph spacing. The style feature is still far from agreement even on the official proposal, so you will not be able to use it for a while.

<DIV> tag and <CLASS> property

You will be able to use a <DIV> tag and <CLASS> property to designate functional parts of your documents such as the abstract or bibliography. You can pick any names you want for the <CLASS> terms. The short example that follows shows how you could indicate a section as an abstract. Eventually, you will be able to create a style sheet that tells Web browsers how to visually represent each section—for example, you might decide that the abstract should be rendered in italic style text and the bibliography should be rendered in a smaller font than the document's body.

```
<DIV CLASS=abstract>
<P>Abstract:  The author explains the opportunities
  and limitations of HTML3.0 </DIV>
```

Many scientific documents use section headings to clarify structural relationships. For example, sections are typically given sequential numbers and might be numbered 1, 2, 2.1, 2.2, 3, 3.1, and so on. HTML 3.0. provides a cleaner way to indicate logical structure of the document using the new <CLASS> property you add to your headings—for example, <H2 CLASS=Section> *some text* </H2>. The word "section"

could be anything you want; you are merely using it to identify other parts of the document that should be considered part of the same set of elements. You would place a similar indication in each logical heading tag throughout the document for those parts of the text you wanted to consider one of the *sections*. In your style sheet, you would be able to indicate that the class of *sections* should be treated as logical divisions; the browser would then automatically number each heading identified as a section sequentially in accordance with whatever numbering system you chose—for example, Arabic or Roman numerals. Each section has been assigned a particular class definition (in this example, "section").

Other tags allow you modify the automatic numbering; for example, placing a <SKIP> property in the tag <H2 SKIP> would cause the enclosed heading not to be numbered and <H2 SEQNUM=6> (sequence number) would allow you to arbitrarily change the number sequence so that the enclosed heading would have the number you chose, not the next one in the automatic numbering.

<REL> and <LINK> Tags

The <HEAD> section is expanded to allow authors to introduce linkage information and other *meta information* about the documents that can be used by servers and browsers. Up until now, the <TITLE> was the main element of the head section. In HTML 3.0, other information such as indications of documents related to the current one can be included. For example, the style sheet feature alluded to earlier will use a new <LINK> tag placed in the head section to identify the network address of the style document to govern the rendering of sections of a document. Thus one style sheet could be used by many documents. You use a <LINK> tag to indicate the reference document that contains the style sheet that is needed to interpret the currently loading document.

In the example that follows, REL stands for the relationship to the current document and HREF stands for hypertext reference to the location of the document. (See Chapter 3 for more details on links.) This sample line included in the head section would cause the browser to fetch the style document and use it to decide about visual representation of the document currently loading. See the reference section for pointers to additional information about style sheets.

```
<LINK REL=StyleSheet HREF=teststyle.dsssl>
```

<META> Tag

A new <META> tag included in the head section can indicate meta-information—that is, supplemental information about the document that informs servers set up to initiate special processes. For example, meta information might include an indication that the server should initiate a special animation process. Meta-information might include the expiration date of a document. Once these become more common, servers and browsers can be customized to respond appropriately. In this example the HTTP-EQUIV indicates a class of information (expiration date) and the CONTENT indicates the date. This information could be used to warn the user about outdated information or to automatically update the document. The META tag is still highly tentative and can't be used until appropriate server capabilities are defined. One day, it may become an important tool for Web authors. See the reference section for pointers to additional information.

```
<META HTTP-EQUIV=Expires CONTENT="04 June 1995">
```

Table 2.17

HTML 3.0 Miscellaneous Features: Mathematical Expressions, Special Symbols, and Structural Indicators

Tag or Option	Function	Comments
$$	Indicates expressions to be displayed in mathematical notation.	Builds on UNIX LaTeX conventions for mathematical representation.
<DIV CLASS=*preface*>	DIV indicates major structural divisions of a document. Class names can be anything the author wants.	Once style sheet feature is implemented, the author will be able to indicate print attributes of each class.
<H2 CLASS= *section*>	Headings indicated with the same class names will be considered logically at the same level. Class names can be anything the author wants.	Eventually, style sheets will allow browsers to automatically number headings at same level.
<H2 SKIP>	SKIP allows author to deactivate automatic logical level numbering for particular heading.	Only relevant when automatic heading numbering has been activated with style sheets.

Tag or Option	Function	Comments
<H2 SEQNUM=*n*>	SEQNUM allows author to change the sequence of number to be applied to headings.	Only relevant when automatic heading numbering has been activated with style sheets.
<LINK REL=StyleSheet HREF=teststyle.dsssl>	Use in the head section to indicate documents linked to current document.	LINK may be the main mechanism for indicating style sheets. No closing tag necessary.
<META HTTP-EQUIV= Expires CONTENT= "04 June 1995">	Many different types of information can be included in META besides expiration date. Indicates information about a document that browsers and servers can use to set up special processes such as dynamic updating.	Dependent on clients and servers being specially configured to respond to the meta information. No closing tag necessary. Netscape has implemented some META features in version 1.1.

Many features described in this table are very tentative at press time. You will not be able to use them until Web design committees define them more explicitly.

Using HTML Editors and Converters

HTML editors and HTML converters facilitate the process of formatting your text for Web documents. Editors and templates have built-in access to HTML syntax. Typically, you simply select the text to be formatted, and then click a menu option to choose a style tag; the program inserts the proper prefix and suffix tags. Many word processor and layout programs are expected to include HTML formatting options in upcoming software updates. Online services such as CompuServe will also be offering HTML editors as part of their Web services. Examples of HTML editors for the Macintosh include BBEdit, HTML Editor, Simple HTML Editor, and Arachnid. Examples of editors for Windows include SoftQuad HoTMetal, HTML Assistant, Microsoft Internet Assistant, and Quarterdeck WebAuthor. X Windows examples include ASHE, City University HTML Editor, and tkHTML.

You must realize, however, that these templates and editors are not magic. They cannot add formatting possibilities that standard HTML cannot display. For example, in most word processors you can easily create text with mixed styles and sizes of fonts on single lines. You can create exotic spacing of text. Most likely this fancy formatting cannot be rendered in HTML. The HTML template will have to eliminate the special formatting. In order to excel at Web design, you need to understand the fundamentals of HTML source code so you will know what is possible and impossible.

The reference list gives you online addresses for information about editors and where you can download specific editors for a variety of platforms.

Information about HTML Editors and Templates

- *Stanford Yahoo site information about editors*

`http://www.yahoo.com/Computers/World_Wide_Web/`
`HTML_Editors`

- *NCGA index of HTML editors*

`http://union.ncsa.uiuc.edu/HyperNews/get/www/HTML/`
`editors.HTML`

- *WWW—tools for Web providers*

`http://www.w3.org/hypertext/WWW/Tools/`

- *Other lists of editors and filters to convert formats to HTML*

`http://www.ncsa.uiuc.edu/SDG/Software/Mosaic/Docs/`
`faq-software`

`http://www.utirc.utoronto.ca/HTMLdocs/`
`intro_tools.HTML`

Sample List of Specific Editors

- *HTML editor for the Macintosh*

`http://dragon.acadiau.ca:1667/~giles/HTML_Editor`

- *Simple HTML editor for Macintosh (SHE)*

`http://dewey.lib.ncsu.edu/staff/morgan/simple.html`

- *HTML Writer (Windows)*

`http://www.et.byu.edu/~nosackk/html-writer/`
`index.html`

- *HyperEdit (Windows)*

`ftp://ftp.ncsa.uiuc.edu/PC/Mosaic/util/hypedit.zip`

- *HotMetel editor for Windows*

`http://www.sq.com/`

- *A simple HTML editor (ASHE) X Windows (UNIX)*

`ftp://ftp.cs.rpi.edu/pub/puninj/ASHE`

- *tkHTML (UNIX)*

`http://alfred1.u.washington.edu:8080/~roland/`
`tkHTML.html`

HTML converters (also called filters) take a slightly different approach than the editors. They assume you already have produced some material and attempt to automate the process of converting to HTML format. They make guesses about how a document formatted by a particular application—for example, a word processing, page layout, or spreadsheet—should be converted. For example, word processor "styles" such as "head1" are automatically assigned HTML header tags. Tables are converted into a HTML style called "preformatted" (or in HTML 3.0 into a format called "table") that preserves the spacing of the table. Footnotes are automatically converted into HTML lists. Usually you can create a "map" of the relationship between styles in your original document and HTML styles.

These converters don't work for everyone. Their success depends on the amount of consistent structure you use in your work. Highly structured writing with logical header categorizations translate with fewer problems than a more freeform composition. Usually, you must go back in and clean up errors. Most of the converters allow for customization in which you can create a mapping table that tells the converter what word processor styles to convert into what HTML format indicators, but again they can't do magic. The following reference list provides pointers to general information about converters and filters and where you can download specific ones.

Information about HTML Converters and Filters

- *WWW index of converters*
`http://www.w3.org/hypertext/WWW/Tools/Filters.HTML`

- *Yahoo information about converters*
`http://www.yahoo.com/Computers/World_Wide_Web/`
`HTML_Converters`

Summary

This chapter has introduced the basic HTML tools that control visual appearance of Web pages. In this chapter you have learned the following:

- The basic structure of HTML
- The steps for creating an HTML document
- All HTML tags for text formatting and syntax necessary to apply them
- The process by which Web protocols such as HTML change

- New HTML 3.0 tags and structures and the syntax necessary to apply them

Now your task is to get creative with these and push their possibilities as far as you can. The most intriguing capabilities are still yet to come. You can create HTML documents that allow a user to click hyperlinked text or images on-screen in order to access resources anywhere in the world. The next chapter shows you how to use HTML to turn your Web pages into interactive hypermedia documents.

Chapter 3

Creating Hyperlinks

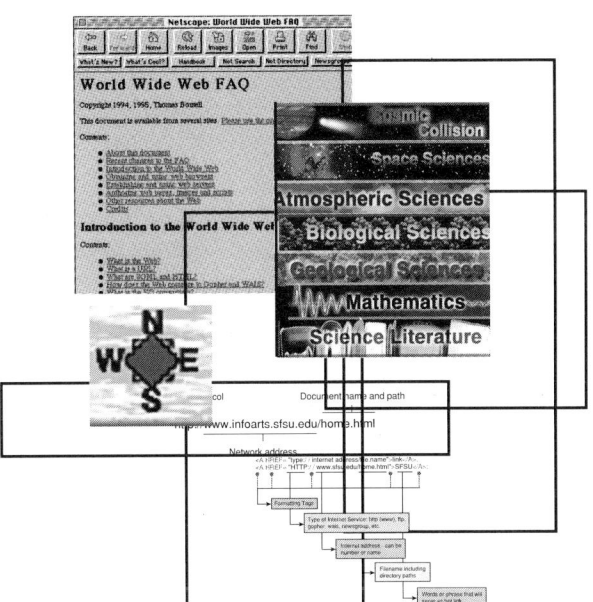

HTML does much more than just identify your document's parts. Its other major purpose is providing you with the means to create interactive hypermedia. *Hypermedia* combines multimedia resources—graphics, sound, and video—with *hypertext*, a nonlinear way of reading textual information. In a hypertext document, important words or phrases can be emphasized. The keywords, called *links,* are underlined and, depending on your browser, may appear in a different color. Graphics can be used as links to access more information, too; these usually appear with a border around the graphic. Links are also commonly known as *hyperlinks* or *hotlinks.* Links can act as pointers to more information on that specific subject. When you click your mouse on a link, you'll be ushered to a related or more detailed Web document. You might click on additional links that take you much further away from your original document, or you could return to your starting point and explore in a different direction.

HTML relies on its markup tags to accomplish this inter-activity. In this chapter you will learn how to define your link with the correct tag and include the URL (Uniform Resource Locator) of the linked resource. URLs are the Web's notation for identifying the location of a Web resource. You'll learn more about them later in this chapter. You'll also learn about how links can access other Internet resources, such as FTP or Gopher sites. Finally, you'll analyze the role links play in how you design your Web site.

Arranging Active Hyperlinks

Why are hyperlinks useful? Structuring your site to include hyperlinks lets your Web readers follow their interests and inquiries wherever they lead. Including links to additional related information makes it easier for your audience to conduct further research. There are also more practical reasons: breaking your documents into shorter, independent segments makes them more readable and decreases the time readers must wait for segments to load from the network.

Many users of the Web don't necessarily need to know how links work. If they see a link that interests them, they can just click to follow it. But you will certainly benefit from an understanding of the underlying processes. Knowing the ins and outs of linking will help you troubleshoot problems that crop up in links you author, keep a lookout for typos when typing in URLs, and strategize about the most appealing and effective ways to set up your site's linking structure.

After the user clicks on a link, the Web browser sends a request to the Internet-connected *server* (sometimes called the *host*) computer indicated in the link for the specific information. The request can be for text, image, sound, or digital video. This request is broken into packets with embedded addresses and is forwarded to the right place. Once the destination computer receives the message, it locates the resources in its local storage, analyzes their format, prepares them in the right protocol so they can be correctly sent on the Internet, and sends them back to the requesting client computer. As the data is received, the Web browser presents the information on the local computer that made the original request in a format indicated by the original author.

The Web browser hides all the details of addressing the requests and responses, formatting them for the Internet, negotiating between computers, and presenting the infor-mation on the computer screen. The system works, like other Internet systems, because there are a set of conventions and protocols governing how requests and responses should be formatted and how the process of communication should proceed. These conventions include the HTML tags that designate hotlinks and the Uniform Resource Locator (URL) format for designating the address of resources and access method.

Figure 3.1 shows a typical example of the richness of links you can find on the Web. CartooNet is a resource for those who produce and love cartoons. Its link page includes pointers to galleries of cartoon shows, news of relevance to cartoonists, and information for those who want to buy and sell cartoons.

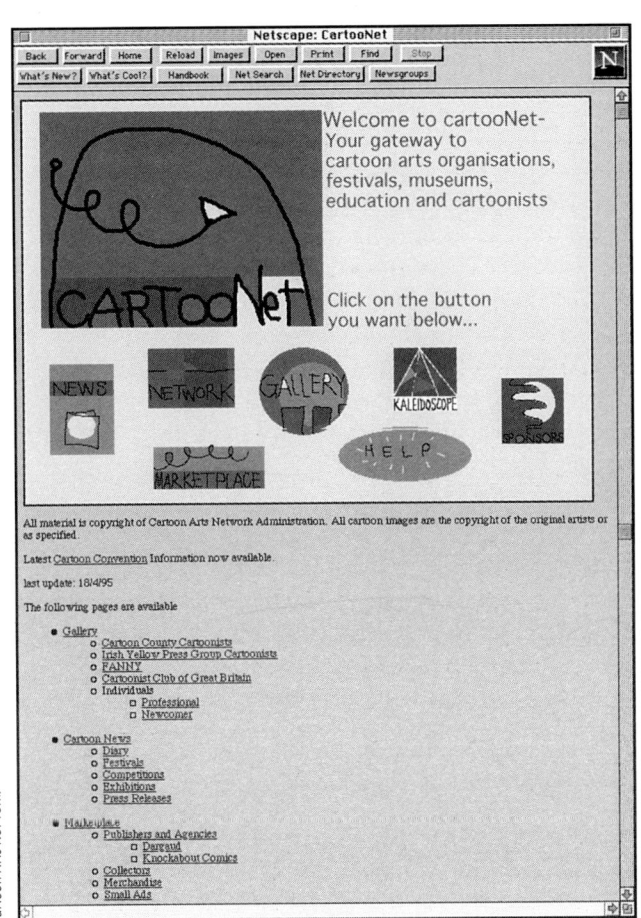

Figure 3.1:
CartooNet's page of links.
`http://www.pavilion.co.uk/cartoonet/`

Indicating Hotlinks in HTML Documents

You can designate any text or images on your pages as hotlinks. A link can point to particular sections in the very same document in which it appears, to other documents located on the same machine as the original, and to other resources located on any Internet-connected computer that has been set up as a server ready to accept Web requests from users with sufficient access permissions.

Basic Anchor Tags

Here is an example that shows the sections of a basic HTML link to a particular document:

```
<A HREF= "http://www.sfsu.edu /home.html" > SFSU</A>
```

Note that there are several parts to this formatting convention, which are illustrated in Figure 3.2. The link starts with the <A> attribute, which stands for *anchor*. Next comes the term *HREF*, which stands for hypertext reference. The <HREF> attribute is followed by the URL that indicates the address of the resource, which should be enclosed in beginning and ending quotes. The URL must be typed accurately—including matching the upper- and lowercase characters—in order for the URL to successfully link.

The next item is the text or image that will serve as the active link in the document and be highlighted in the browser. In this example, the link consists of the text SFSU (which, incidentally, stands for San Francisco State University). This text is all that the user will see; the URL does not appear as part of the Web page presented on the display. When the viewer clicks on these words or images, the Web browser application will go fetch the URL indicated and replace the

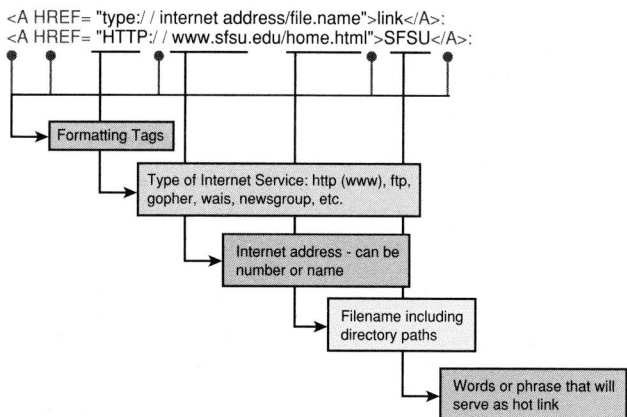

```
<A HREF= "type:/ / internet address/file.name">link</A>:
<A HREF= "HTTP:/ / www.sfsu.edu/home.html">SFSU</A>:
```

Formatting Tags

Type of Internet Service: http (www), ftp, gopher, wais, newsgroup, etc.

Internet address - can be number or name

Filename including directory paths

Words or phrase that will serve as hot link

Figure 3.2:
Standard sections included in URLs.

currently displayed document with the SFSU home page, which shows the Web resources available at that site. Finally, there is the closing tag indicated by the </A> symbol.

Figure 3.3 shows another example of a Web page full of links. The illustration is an excerpt from the hotlist to science resources offered by the Exploratorium Science Museum's Web server. This particular section of their list of links focuses on information related to the collision of the Shoemaker-Levy comet with the planet Jupiter. The illustration includes both the Web page users would see and the HTML document that set up the links.

Relative versus Absolute Pathnames

In some special situations you do not need to specify the whole network address of the link as illustrated previously. You can use a *relative* pathname if the link points to a

document or file that is located in the same directory as the document containing the link, or in one of its subdirectories. Without an *absolute* address indicated, browsers will construct a full address by using the stem of the current document.

For example, if one of the links on SFSU's home page pointed to another document called *Description.html* that was located in the same directory, you could use the following URL:

```
<A HREF= "Description.html" > Description of
  University</A>
```

The browser would construct the full address by extracting the stem http://www.sfsu.edu/ and adding the new part Description.html to assemble the total new URL: http://www.sfsu.edu/Description.html. Subdirectory relative addressing works similarly. For example, you could create a directory of images located in the same directory as the page with the links, which could be addressed with the following URL:

```
<A HREF= "pictures/campus.gif" > Image of Campus</A>
```

The browser would construct the full URL: http://www.sfsu.edu/pictures/campus.gif.

Relative addressing assists the development process if you are creating Web pages on a computer other than the one where they will ultimately end up. All the relative addresses will transfer without modification if you arrange for all the files to be located in the same directory or its subdirectories on the target computer. Relative addressing also makes your HTML code very portable. If you are designing on your local machine, porting to your server is a breeze. Otherwise, you could spend a lot of time relabeling all your links.

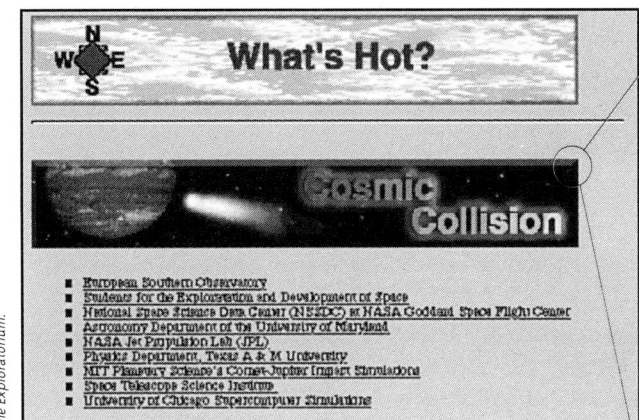

```
<TITLE>What's Hot?</TITLE>
<IMG ALIGN = bottom SRC = Whats_Hot.gif>
<HR> <P>
<IMG ALIGN = BOTTOM  SRC = CosmicCollision.gif>
<P> <UL>
<LI> <A HREF= "http://http.hq.eso.org/educnpubrelns/
     comet.html">European Southern Observatory</A>
<LI> <A HREF= "http://seds.lpl.arizona.edu/sl9/
     sl9.html">Students for the Exploratation and
     Development of Space</A>
<LI> <A HREF= "http://www.gsfc.nasa.gov/planetary/
     COMET.HTML">National Space Science Data Center
     (NSSDC) at NASA Goddard Space Flight Center</A>
<LI> <A HREF= "http://pdssbn.astro.umd.edu/c1993e/">
     Astronomy Department of the University of
     Maryland</A>
<LI> <A HREF= "http://newproducts.jpl.nasa.gov/sl9/
     sl9.html">NASA Jet Propulsion Lab (JPL)</A>
<LI> <A HREF= "http://info.cv.nrao.edu/staff/
     pmurphy/patsl9.html">Physics Department, Texas
     A & M University</A>
<LI> <A HREF= "http://www-erl.mit.edu/flolab/
     csl9press/csl9hj.html">MIT Planetary Science's
     Comet-Jupiter Impact Simulations</A>
<LI> <A HREF= "http://stsci.edu/top.html">Space
     Telescope Science Institute </A>
<LI> <A HREF= "http://pscinfo.psc.edu/research/
     user_research/mac_low/mac_low.html">University
     of Chicago Supercomputer Simulations</A>
</UL>
```

Figure 3.3:
Example of the Exploratorium's hotlist of links to Web resources and the HTML document that sets it up.
http://www.exploratorium.edu/floor/Hotlist.html

Links to a Particular Section of a Document

By default an HTML link will position the viewer at the beginning of a document. HTML also allows you to specify links to a particular section of a document rather just to its beginning. For example, you might want to point your readers to the exact place they can find certain information instead of having to scroll down many screens in a long document.

To accomplish this reference to particular sections, you must take two formatting actions:

1. First, you must indicate the location in your document that you want your readers to be able to jump to. You do this by creating an anchor label for that place. You place this targeted label text within an <A> tag, and use the <NAME> attribute to assign this keyword or name associated with that place in the text. You

enclose the text of your document, which you want to be located, with this label anchor and its closing tag. Your opening tag should look something like this: <A NAME= "*text*">. Your Web readers will not see these keywords; they function only to allow browsers to find the section they should scroll to when a link points to it.

2. Second, you must indicate the links that will access the sections of your document. You accomplish this by adding the pound sign (#) followed by the words or phrase that will serve as the indicator of the target section immediately after the URL inside the quotes.

Figure 3.4 shows a Web page with a table of contents of information about animals, with three sections identified with *NAME* anchors. The sections are arbitrarily named L1, L2, and L3. For example, the section about Elephants has the tag <A NAME="L1"> placed before the word *Elephants* which your readers will actually see. The top of the table of contents also has the section tag <A NAME="Tab"> placed before it because you want to allow readers to scroll easily back to the table of contents from each section. Your readers click on the topics that interest them and jump to that part of the document; they don't see the linking or the coding that takes them there.

As Figure 3.4 illustrates, you can use links to point to different sections in a single document. If you have a long HTML document, it's a good strategy to include at its beginning a table of contents with links to all the sections that follow. As described in the "Relative versus Absolute Pathnames" section, the URL for this kind of internal access is simplified.

In long documents you should provide a link within each section that leads back to the table of contents or initial welcoming page. This is necessary because other Web authors might create external links into a section of your document. For example, using the animal directory shown in Figure 3.4, another Web author with a page listing resources about gorillas might include a link in the document that points straight to your document's gorilla section. In a long document a Web navigator who arrived at your page that way would have no idea of how the currently viewed text relates to any larger scheme or context. Providing an obvious link in each section back to some orienting text, such as a table of contents or an opening page, is a useful navigational aid. It's also considered good etiquette by most Web designers.

The process for creating links to particular sections of external documents is similar. Your link reference, however, needs to include the whole absolute address of the URL in addition to the section reference. For example the reference to the Gorilla section might be indicated like this if it was located at the computer with the network address *www.sfsu.edu* in the directory *infoarts* in the document *animal.html*:

```
<A HREF= "http://www.sfsu.edu /infoarts/
  animal.html#L2" > Gorilla Information at
  SFSU</A>
```

For more practice with writing links, try the following short exercise. Figure 3.5 shows the way it would appear in a browser's window.

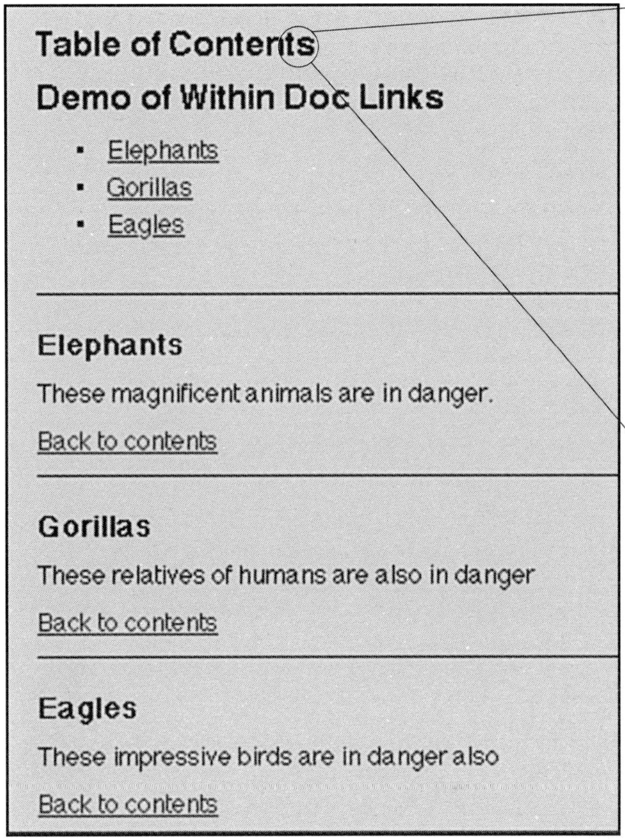

Table of Contents

Demo of Within Doc Links

- Elephants
- Gorillas
- Eagles

Elephants

These magnificent animals are in danger.

Back to contents

Gorillas

These relatives of humans are also in danger

Back to contents

Eagles

These impressive birds are in danger also

Back to contents

```
<TITLE>Demo of links to sections</TITLE>
<H2><A NAME="Tab">Table of Contents</A> <P>
 Demo of Within Doc Links</H2>
<UL>
<LI>
<LI><A HREF="#L1">Elephants</A>
<LI><A HREF="#L2">Gorillas</A>
<LI><A HREF="#L3">Eagles</A></UL><HR>

<A NAME="L1"><H3>Elephants</H3></A>
These magnificent animals are in danger.<P>
<A HREF=#Tab>Back to contents</A><HR>

<A NAME="L2"><H3>Gorillas</H3></A>
These relatives of humans are also in danger.<P>
<A HREF=#Tab>Back to contents</A><HR>

<A NAME="L3"><H3>Eagles</H3></A>
These impressive birds are in danger also.<P>
<A HREF="#Tab">Back to contents</A><HR>
```

Figure 3.4:
Using links to jump between sections of a single document.

Exercise 3.1:

Adding hyperlinks to your HTML document

Step 1:

In this exercise, you'll create a couple of links to external documents as well as a link within the same document. Begin by entering the text and HTML structuring tags that identify this document as an HTML document and identify the title.

```
<HTML>
<HEAD>
<TITLE>Creation of Hyperlinks</TITLE>
</HEAD>
<BODY>
<H1>Table of Contents</H1>
<H2>Pointers to HTML Information</H2>
<UL>
<LI>A good place to start is NCSA's Primer on
  HTML<P>
<LI>You can also read the Official HTML
  Specifications.
</UL><P>
<H2>My Personal Notes</H2>
When the linking tags for this document are in
place, the first link in the section above will
cause the text <I>NCSA's Primer on HTML</I>  to
become an active link to that document located at
the Mosaic home site's location in Illinois.  Be
careful to type the line exactly; any misspellings,
extra spaces, changes of case or other errors will
cause links to fail. The second link to <I>Official
HTML Specifications</I> will take you to the
official specifications for HTML, located at the
W3 organization's server.</P>
Unlike the  earlier exercises in this book,  you
will need a live network connection to test this
```

```
exercise and follow the links to external documents.
Make sure your network connection is active.<P>
Back to Table of Contents.<P>
</BODY>
</HTML>
```

Step 2:

Next, you'll add the links described in the bulleted list. The URLs for these two links are provided here:

```
<LI>A good place to start is <A HREF= "http://
www.ncsa.uiuc.edu/demoweb/html-primer.html">
NCSA's Primer on HTML</A>
<LI>You can also read the <A HREF= "http://
www.w3.org/hypertext/WWW/MarkUp/
MarkUp.html">Official HTML Specifications.</A>
```

Step 3:

Now let's put in an internal link back to the top of the list of links so a reader can quickly get back to our table of contents. Surround the last line of text in the body of your document with anchor tags as follows:

```
<A HREF=#Top>Back to Table of Contents</A> <P>
```

The reader will only see the words *Back to Table of Contents.*

Step 4:

This link to the table of contents will not work unless we put a NAME anchor at the place we want to scroll back to. Position the cursor after the <H1> tag near the top of your document. Enter the <A NAME> tag as follows:

```
<H1><A NAME="Top">Table of Contents</A></H1>
```

Step 5:

Save your document as an ASCII text file. Use .html (if you're using a Macintosh or .htm for a DOS/ Windows platform) for the filename's suffix. Here is what the source code for your final document should look like:

```
<HTML>
<HEAD>
<TITLE>Creation of Hyperlinks</TITLE>
</HEAD>
<BODY>
<H1><A NAME="Top">Table of Contents</A></H1>
<H2>Pointers to HTML Information</H2>
<UL>
<LI>A good place to start is <A HREF= "http://
 www.ncsa.uiuc.edu/demoweb/html-primer.html">
 NCSA's Primer on HTML</A>
<LI>You can also read the <A HREF= "http://
 www.w3.org/hypertext/WWW/MarkUp/
 MarkUp.html">Official HTML Specifications.</A>
</UL><P>
<H2>My Personal Notes</H2>
When the linking tags for this document are in
place, the first link in the section above will
cause the text <I>NCSA's Primer on HTML</I>  to
become an active link to that document located at
the Mosaic home site's location in Illinois.  Be
careful to type the line exactly; any misspellings,
extra spaces, changes of case or other errors will
cause links to fail. The second link to <I>Official
HTML Specifications</I> will take you to the
official specifications for HTML, located at the
W3 organization's server.</P>
Unlike the  earlier exercises in this book, you will
need a live network connection to test this exercise
and follow the links to external documents. Make
sure your network connection is active.<P>
<A HREF=#Top>Back to Table of Contents</A><P>
</BODY>
</HTML>
```

Step 7:

Don't try the links out yet. Make sure you haven't made any typographical errors, and confirm that all the opening and closing tags are included where necessary.

Step 8:

Click on the "Back to Table of Contents" link. Your browser's window should take you back to the top of your document.

Step 9:

Now try clicking on the other links you wrote. Your browser should fetch the files indicated from the specified servers when you click on either of the two external links. (For this to work, your Internet connection must be active.)

Figure 3.6 presents another illustration of links used to refer to internal sections of a document. The document illustrated is excerpted from the World Wide Web Frequently Asked Questions (FAQ) Web page. This document is a popular resource for Web readers trying to learn how the Web works. It consists of a table of contents at the top, with each entry hotlinked to the relevant sections farther down.

Follow the link labeled "Authoring Web pages, images and scripts" and you'll jump to a later section of the same document. If you look at the HTML coding for this link, you'll see the URL consists of only the anchor name:

```
<A HREF="#authoring">Authoring Web pages, images and
  scripts</A>
```

Clicking the link takes you to the screen shown in Figure 3.7. Look at the HTML coding for this heading and you'll see the anchor name that makes this internal link possible:

```
<H2><A NAME="authoring">Authoring  pages, images and
  scripts</A></H2>
```

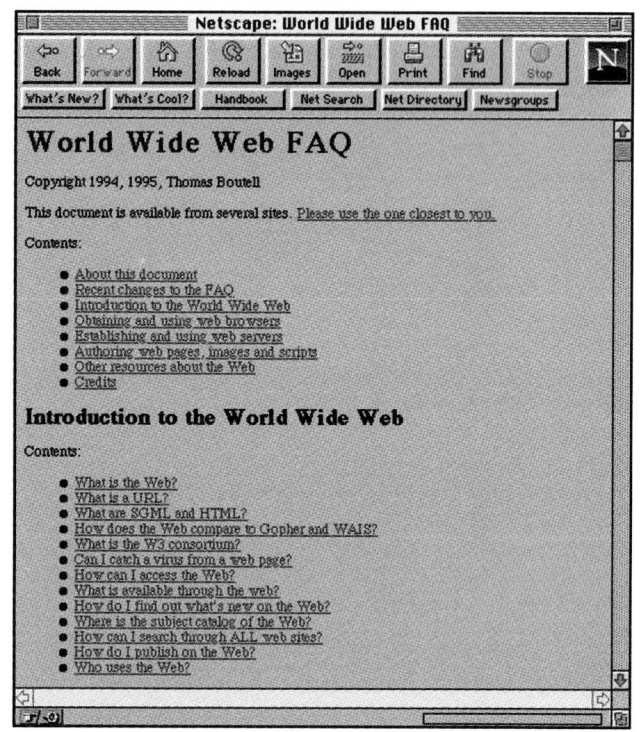

Thomas Boutell.

Figure 3.6:
WWW FAQ Web page illustrating the use of a table of contents with internal links.
`http://sunsite.unc.edu/boutell/faq/www_faq.html`

Each item in the table links to a later section of the document using the `<HREF = # name>` tag. In this example the contents entry "Information about this document" links to a section that the author named "meta-info". That later section (part of which is illustrated) starts with the tag `<A NAME="meta-info">` .

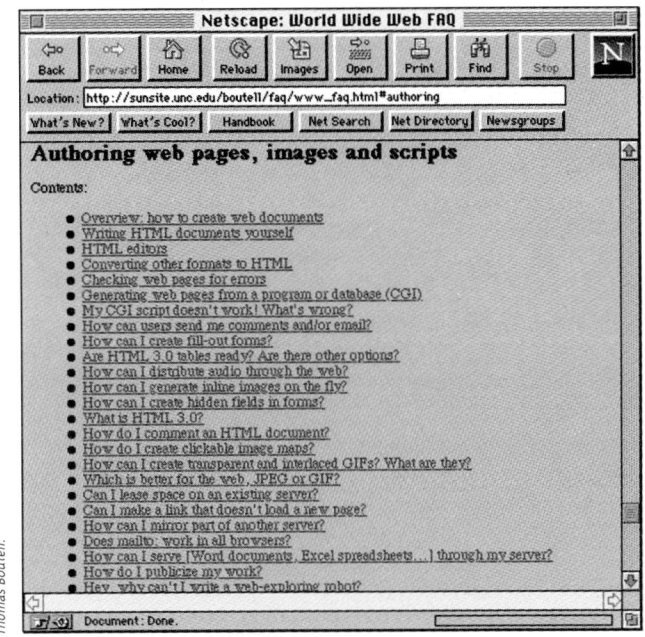

Figure 3.7:
Jumping to an anchor within a single document.
`http://sunsite.unc.edu/boutell/faq/`
`www_faq.html#authoring`

Understanding Uniform Resource Locators (URLs)

We've seen a few URLs in action up to this point, but we haven't really examined the different parts that constitute them. The first section of a URL, called the *scheme* or *protocol,* identifies the type of Internet resource that's being requested—for example, a WWW (http), FTP, or Gopher

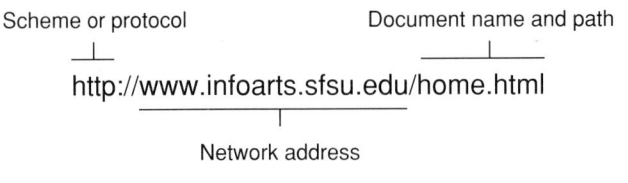

Scheme or protocol   Document name and path

http://www.infoarts.sfsu.edu/home.html

Network address

Figure 3.8:
Components of URLs.

document. The Web client needs to know this so it can use the proper protocols to request the document. It also needs this information so it can apply the correct processing methods to handle the incoming data as it is received. You must type the symbols :// after the resource indicator.

The second section, the *path name,* indicates the network address of the machine that the resource resides on. This could be the standard Internet number address (for example, 130.212.13.61) or the name (www.infoarts.sfsu.edu). These two representations are synonymous; special servers called *Domain Name Servers* (DNS) take in the text name address and convert it to the number address that the Internet actually needs to transmit information. Many of you are already quite familiar with these from your experience with other Internet services such as e-mail.

An optional part of the address allows specification of the Internet port that the machine will use for access. Ports are virtual addresses created by UNIX to allow several services to run on the same physical machine. Often this can be omitted because the ports are standardized for particular Internet services—for example, World Wide Web accesses usually come in on port :80 and Gopher comes in on port :70. It would be essential to include if the server were using a nonstandard port

The third section indicates the directory path in which the document resides. The fourth section indicates the name of the particular document being accessed. Finally, a fifth optional section could indicate the specific anchor section tag to go to in the document accessed, beginning with a # symbol as described earlier in this chapter.

You will find URLs easy to work with as you grow familiar with their use. As you continue to work and design on the Web, you will probably amass quite a collection of URLs—your friends' home pages, "cool sites" that others have recommended, and sites related to your various projects. Since these can be awkward to remember and type correctly, you might want to take advantage of your Web browser's "bookmark" (Netscape) or "hotlist" (Mosaic) feature, which lets you save the URL of any document you're viewing to a personal reference list. When you type in a URL you must specify it exactly; even one letter, space, or slash out of place will result in failure to link to the resource. Bookmarks or personal hotlists are therefore a real timesaver in terms of getting the addresses right. The references list several online resources for more information on URLs.

Resources Related to URLs (Uniform Resource Locators)

- *URLs and The Names and Addresses of WWW objects (W3 Organization guides)*
`http://www.w3.org/hypertext/WWW/Addressing/`
`Addressing.html`

- *NCSA's primer on URLs (Mosaic home site)*
`http://www.ncsa.uiuc.edu/demoweb/url-primer.html`

- *Netspace's Guide to URLs (Comprehensive guide)*
`http://www.netspace.org/users/dwb/url-guide.html`

URLs and missing resources

Many of you may have experienced the problem of URLs that point to empty Cyberspace. Trying to make a link, you get back error messages such as "can't find document". What's going on?

As the Web grows older, some links are going "stale." Links can fail for a variety of reasons—for example, the resource could have been deleted, renamed, or moved to another directory; the machine on which it resides could have been renamed or decommissioned; or the resource could have been moved to another location. Because there is no central authority supervising the resources or their naming, there is no way to let users know about the changes.

The Web community is working on a solution called the Universal Resource Name (URN). This convention will identify Web resources by a unique ID name assigned to them. All links will refer to the name, not to the specific machine, directory path, and file as is now common. When a link is attempted, the computer will access a lookup table that will translate the name into the specific address information. The advantage of this system is that should the resource get changed, renamed, or moved, only the lookup table entry would need to be changed.

Until this scheme is implemented, however, it is essential that you be extremely careful in your use of URLs. Check their accuracy. Unfortunately, even some of the URLs listed in this book might be inaccurate when you read them, even though they were accurate at the time of publication.

Different Kinds of URLs

The number of Web servers available is growing exponentially, but the Internet contains many riches in addition to Web sites. In a stroke of design genius, the original creators of Web protocols made it very easy for Web browsers to access other Internet services such as FTP, E-mail, Gopher, Telnet, and Usenet newsgroups. These resources become part of the information access you can offer your Web visitors and the URL becomes the magic gateway to them all.

HTTP

The basic Web protocol for exchanging information is http (Hypertext Transfer Protocol). You have seen the http specification in the URLs described previously. Web information that has been prepared in accordance with Web conventions and placed on a Web server can be accessed with this protocol and needs the http in the URL to get to it. Http consists of four simple actions:

1. A client opens a connection to a server.
2. Client requests a particular document.
3. The server answers the request.
4. The connection is closed.

FTP

FTP (file transfer protocol) is an Internet protocol that allows users to remotely access files on other computers. That means that, with a password, one can sign onto a computer, navigate the directories, and request that the distant computer send a file to the requesting computer. In anonymous FTP, system operators specially designate some *public* files so that anyone on the Internet can access the files without a password. Significant worldwide archives of information were made available via FTP long before the Web was created.

Many Web sites include pointers to FTP resources as part of the information they offer. You can use pointers when you want to make large files such as images, documents, or actual executable programs available to users. Some of you may have downloaded the browser you use via FTP. Many of the image, sound, and digital video archives available on the Web are actually FTP archives.

Basic FTP can be difficult to work with because you must remember special commands and syntax and it is difficult to navigate through a remote directory structure if you don't know it well. The Web seamlessly integrates FTP access into its graphical user interface. Once a user clicks on a URL that points to a FTP resource, the browser displays generic folder icons to indicate the directory structure. Once users find the file they want, clicking on it automatically activates the FTP commands to download the file into the user's computer. The users need know nothing about FTP. The URL for FTP access is very similar to the normal Web URL except that the http is replaced with *FTP*. The following example would function as a pointer in your Web page to Boat's image archive:

```
<A HREF= "ftp://boat tivoli.com/pub/boats/"> Boat
  Image Archives</A>
```

Quick primer on compression and ASCII encoding

When Web servers send large media or program files to a browser application, they are actually using FTP Internet conventions. The user is usually shielded from the details. As a Web developer, however, you may need to know more than the casual user—both because you may need FTP to access programs and resources that you will use in building your site, and also because you may need to know how to make large files available to users as part of what your site offers. There are two aspects of Internet file transmissions that you need to understand: ASCII encoding and compression.

ASCII Encoding: The Internet has been known to mangle media and program files that are not formatted correctly for transmission. Internet conventions originally assumed that communications would be in text format. Computer text is stored in accordance with the ASCII convention. In this convention, all the standard characters are represented in the first 7 of the 8 bits that make up a byte of computer information. The last bit is not significant for storing regular text. Early Internet protocols used this fact to speed communications by throwing away the unused bit. Unfortunately, image, sound, and application files do use every bit, including the eighth bit. Discarding it will totally disrupt the integrity of the files.

Formats called Binhex and Uuencode were developed to address the problem by encoding 8 bit information into 7 bits before sending and decoding back to 8 bits on the other end. .Hqx at the end of a file's name means that it was encoded using Binhex format, and .uu at the end means uuencode was used. Programs are available for all platforms to accomplish encoding and decoding including StuffIt,

Binhex, and UUlite for the Mac; Binhex.com and Udecode for DOS machines; and Hexbin, Uuencode, and Uudecode for UNIX machines.

Compression: Media and application files can be enormous and take a long time to transmit on the Net. Researchers have developed a variety of compression algorithms that help solve this problem by reducing the size of files without losing any information. Compressors use a variety of mathematical approaches to extract unused bits of information in order to fit files into smaller spaces. For example, image files often contain long runs of repetitive data to represent solid blocks of color. A technique called run length encoding uses this fact to reduce file size by storing information about the number of repeating patterns rather than every included bit of information.

As with encoding, one needs a program to compress before sending and decompress after reception. There are a great variety of formats and programs that you might encounter. The extension at the end of a file indicates the format and program used for compression. Here are some examples: On the Mac there is StuffIt (.sit and .sea), compact pro (.cpt), and diskdoubler (.dd). On DOS machines there is Pkzip.exe (.zip), Zoo.exe (.zoo), and Arc.exe (.arc). On UNIX machines there is compress,(.Z) gnu compress (.gz), and tar (.tar). On the receiving end, you need a program that can decompress. Occasionally, you need a program that can decompress the format created on another platform.

Deciding when and how to apply compression: Trying to automate the process, Web browsers scan the extension at the end of files they download and then launch helper programs to decode and/or decompress the files. So if the Web does decompression and decoding automatically, why do you need to know this? You must make decisions about your files. Should you apply compression? What coding and compression formats should you use? What choices will ensure that the file will be usable by the largest possible audiences?

Remember that users will not be able to use the files you offer unless they have the proper helper application that knows how to work with the format you choose. You can accomplish broad use by selecting formats that are widely used and for which helper applications are commonly available. You also face a perplexing decision in regard to compression. Is the time saved by sending a compressed file worth the extra time it requires on the user's side to wait while the browser launches and applies a decompression helper application to the data? We will revisit this question of time tradeoffs many times.

Gopher

For the years proceeding the development of the Web, *Gopher* was the major user-friendly Internet service. It used easily navigated, text-based menu structures as the major interface method and it automatically took care of details needed to access other related network services such as FTP, Telnet, and Netfind. That is, the resources available were presented in a numbered lists. The user made choices by typing the desired number, which either brought forth other nested menus or the desired document. Many locations in the world established Gopher servers full of information resources that were open to any Internet user.

Many Gopher servers offer information not available on the Web. You can easily provide links for your Web readers to these resources because Web protocols seamlessly integrate access. Once a user clicks on a URL that points to a Gopher resource, the browser displays generic folder icons to indicate the directory structure. Users can point and click to navigate this visual representation of the Gopher structure. Here is an example of a URL that points to a Gopher site called UCSB Music Gopher site, which provides information on music history and theory:

```
<A HREF= "gopher://UCSbuxa.UCSb.edu:3001/11/.Arts/
  .Music">UCSB Music Gopher site </A>
```

Telnet

Telnet is another long standing Internet information service. Telnet lets a user actually log on to a remote computer. Many sites, including many library catalogs, were organized to allow users without accounts to log on as guests and use specified resources. Web protocols incorporate access to Telnet resources within browser interfaces. The following example shows the URL to access Melvyl, the University of California at Berkeley's library information system:

```
<A HREF= "telnet:// melvyl.ucop.edu"> Telnet to UC
  Berkeley's Library </A>
```

Note that Telnet access requires the user to have a special helper program such as NCSA's shareware Telnet available. When the browser sees a reference to Telnet in the URL, it automatically opens the helper program's window and initiates a Telnet session. See Chapter 4 for more information about helper programs.

Usenet (Newsgroups)

The Usenet is another Internet resource containing information often not available on the Web, which you can make available in your site. As with FTP, Web protocols allow you to make the Usenet easily accessible. Usenet is an international system of newsgroups in which Internet users maintain ongoing asynchronous discussions on various topics. Asynchronous means that the newsgroups are run like bulletin boards, to and from which users can post or receive messages at any time. At last count there were over 12,000 topic groups. These range from technical topics such as graphics and sound formats to highly specialized academic discussion groups such as Egyptian archaeology. They also include topical groups focused on topics such as AIDS to idiosyncratic informal groups such as alt.kill.Barney. Although the quality of discussion in the groups varies greatly, significant information resources are available.

You use a slightly modified URL to create links to newsgroups. The following link would access the newsgroup on Internet announcements including new Web sites:

```
<A HREF= "news: comp.infosystems.announce"> News of
  new sites </A>
```

Note that use of the News link presupposes that the users have a newsgroup service as part of their Internet service and that the preferences on their browsers have been configured to point to the Internet address of the news server.

Mailto

E-mail is the most widely used Internet service. Web protocols allow you to incorporate e-mail as one of the services offered by your pages via the *mailto* URL type. For example, many Web sites, in an attempt to strengthen their design, include a request for comments and feedback via an e-mail link. Also evolving standards of Web etiquette request creators of Web pages to list their e-mail address link on the page for Web readers' information.

When users click on a URL containing an e-mail link, most contemporary browsers open up a special e-mail composition window in which users can edit their messages, and add a subject line. When done, the user chooses the send option and the message is on its way, provided the user's Internet connection contains access to a mail server. The example that follows shows a pointer to the e-mail address of the Webstrina (Web Master) of San Francisco State University's Web site:

```
<A HREF= "mailto: webstrina@sfsu.edu"> Send Comments
  on SFSU's Web Site  </A>
```

HTML 3.0 New Linking Tag

The HTML 3.0 specifications propose one new feature related to linking. A new property called *ID* will become available to use for internal linking. It will replace the NAME tag described previously, although browsers are expected to continue to support the NAME tag for some time.

You can make almost any HTML element into an internal anchor by adding the ID property within its tag. For example, a list or a header could become a location that could be scrolled to when a proper HREF tag is used to reference it. The examples that follow show an ordered list tag and a header tag with the added ID property and the corresponding HREF tags that scroll to those elements. As with the NAME tag, you can give any name you want to any ID location as long as it is unique within the document. Clicking on the words *Go to list 1* would scroll the document to the beginning of that list.

```
<OL ID="list1">....</OL>        <A HREF=#list1>
  Go to list 1</A>
<H3 ID= "Dogs">....</H3>        <A HREF=#Dogs>
  Go to Dogs section</A>
```

Chapter 2's section on HTML 3.0 introduced the new footnote feature, which uses the ID property to identify the actual footnote text that would appear when a user clicks on text marked up with a footnote tag. The ID property will offer considerable flexibility into the way you can arrange internal links.

Designing for Information

Links are a tremendous tool. They offer you great flexibility in creating interactive documents. However, there are millions of information structures that can be built from links. This capability confronts you with the challenge of *information design*.

- What is the underlying structure of the information you are going to offer?
- What kind of inquiry or navigation process do you want to support?
- When should links lead to local resources and when to resources elsewhere on the Web?
- What points should you consider in selecting words or images to use as the hotlinks?

These are not easy questions to answer. Researchers world-wide are investigating the processes people use in inquiry and the most effective ways to organize information to support those processes. There are journals and professional societies focused specifically on hypertext and hypermedia. Your Web design work can help define new approaches.

Some analysts are upset with the tendency of many Web authors to create lists of links without much structure. For example, many home pages include hotlists, which often seem assembled in hodgepodge fashion without any attempt at adding organizational structures such as categories to help the Web navigator.

The Exploratorium hotlist, part of which was presented in Figure 3.3, offers an excellent example of useful categorization. The section illustrated focuses on information related to the cosmic collision. The Exploratorium, however, is attempting to offer a comprehensive list of Web links to a wide variety of topics relevant to science education in addition to the collision of the comet with Jupiter.

Their site designers faced several typical information design questions regarding the presentation of links: What conceptual boundaries should they use to demarcate what should be included in their site? What topic headings should they use to divide up the information? What navigational aids such as section graphic headers should they use to help Web readers keep track of where they have been and where they might go? Information design often challenges developers to create usable, appealing ways to divide up complex information spaces. The Exploratorium's Web designers decided to use seven major categories. They also decided to use large text within background inline image boxes referring to the topic

The Exploratorium.

Figure 3.9:
Categories (and associated graphics) used to delineate sections of Exploratorium's hotlist.

indicated as they major graphic aid for navigation. For example, the section graphic for "Biological Sciences" includes a background graphic of a DNA molecule. These graphics are used to make obvious the major divisions in the master list of hotlinks.

The Exploratorium's hotlist of links is much too large to present here. To illustrate the solution they developed to categorization and user navigation, Figure 3.9 presents a collage of the section graphics they used, which have been extracted from the list. Each of these appears in the hotlist followed by the hotlinks related to the topic represented.

Indications of previously browsed resources

Hypermedia users can easily get lost. For example, they lose track of what they have already seen. Developing aids for navigators is a major item on many researchers' agendas.

Many Web browsers implement a primitive form of navigational aid; they use conventions to differentiate resources that have already been pursued from those that have not. For example, previous use might be indicated by a different colored text or a broken underline depending on what other conventions are used to indicate potential links. A browser keeps a record of all the recent URLs accessed with a specified recent time span and uses that information to render previously pursued hotlinks differently from those that have never been looked at. Mosaic even can dim the color of the link depending on how much time has elapsed since a user last accessed it.

As a Web designer, you have no control over how different browsers will indicate previously visited resources. Nonetheless, you must be aware of this feature in order to ensure that other formatting you introduce does not interact negatively with these built-in conventions.

Quick Guide to Linkage Structures

What linkage structures are you going to use? The question cannot be answered without detailed knowledge of the goals and content of the site you are creating. The structure must

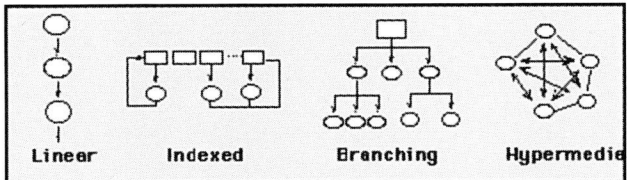

Figure 3.10:
Varieties of linkage structures.

and content of the site you are creating. The structure must fit the site. Still, there are some classic patterns of interactivity that you can use as starting points**. Figure 3.10 shows a diagrammatic summary of some of these structures.

The four diagrams in Figure 3.10 each represent a different model for structuring the presentation of information. Links are used differently in each of these. Realize that these models can be combined in a great variety of ways.

- In the *linear* structure, links are used to create traditional information patterns such as you would find in a conventional essay. Each section leads to the next in the sequence determined by the author. These are useful for situations in which presentation of information is "staged"—that is, each presentation relies on the reader having already been through prior Web pages before dealing with the current one. Many stories fit this model.

**For more details, see my paper "The Aesthetics and Practice of Interactive Design" in the Siggraph94 Visual Proceedings —ACM, Chicago, 1994. This paper describes the theoretical bases of interactivity, an analysis of different kinds of interactive events, guidelines for designing interactivity, and future developments. The paper is available at the Web location http://userwww.sfsu.edu/~swilson.

- The *indexed* structure provides a main home page with accessible sections listed as you would find in a table of contents. Each section can be randomly accessed, but then the user must return to the index. Encyclopedias are good examples of this model—each entry can be read in any order. The index serves as the critical navigational center.

- The *branching* structure provides a series of choices at each level as the user moves through. Previous choices determine the options that are offered at the next level. This organization can be useful because the user is shielded from details until they are necessary. The many geographically based indexes on the Web provide examples of this structure. Typically the user is confronted with a map of the world. Clicking on an area brings up a more detailed map of countries; additional clicking brings up a list of cities and ultimately the available resources related to that city. Other kinds of indexes are arranged similarly — for example, music archives organized by increasingly finer distinctions of musical types.

- *Hypermedia* structures provide the user access to most sections at all times. These systems attempt to avoid hierarchical organizational structures such as those discussed in the branching model. They attempt to make available the full range of choices at every location. For example, some of the experimental online galleries encourage Web visitors to jump from section to section without necessarily going back to an index. The Web has been optimized for Hypermedia structures. In part the Web gets its name from the fact that a diagram of hypermedia paths of inquiry would resemble a web more than a line.

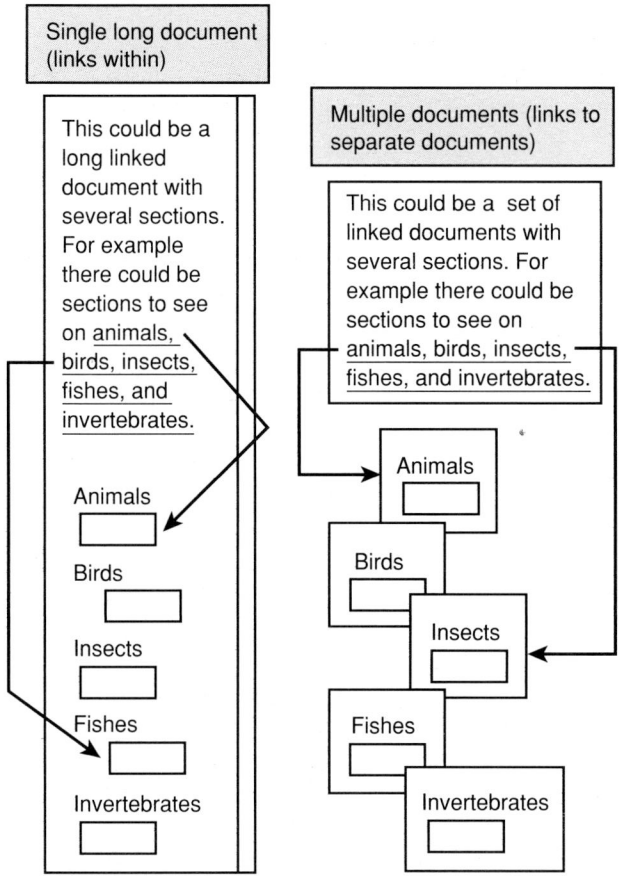

Single long document (links within)

This could be a long linked document with several sections. For example there could be sections to see on animals, birds, insects, fishes, and invertebrates.

Animals

Birds

Insects

Fishes

Invertebrates

Multiple documents (links to separate documents)

This could be a set of linked documents with several sections. For example there could be sections to see on animals, birds, insects, fishes, and invertebrates.

Animals

Birds

Insects

Fishes

Invertebrates

Figure 3.11:
Design decisions in organizing linked resources.

There is no single correct solution for how information should be presented. Asking questions about information structures related to your own site and others that you see is a critical step in perfecting your Web design work.

Let's assume you have a complex document full of information. You have some choices of how to organize the information. You could arrange it as a set of interlinked, separately named documents or as a single, complex document with the internal links described previously. Figure 3.11 shows the two arrangements. There are visual, network, and information management implications of what you choose.

Here are some questions to ask as you go about information design for the sites you work with. Can the separate sections stand alone conceptually? Is it important to show the document embedded in its larger context? Is it important to encourage scrolling to other parts of the document? Visually, would the material look stronger as a separate document?

Linking for Quicker Access

Access time varies in the two arrangements described in Figure 3.11. Each access to another document takes more time than access to part of a document that is already loaded. Is the value to be gained by treating the sections as separate worth the added time for additional link accesses? The decision is really a tradeoff. Loading the original document will take longer for a complex, multisection document than for short, single section documents. Will your readers have the patience to wait while a very complex document takes time to load?

Web access takes too long!

Accessing resources over the Web is not like retrieving a file from your local hard disk. Web resources can take a long time to arrive. Waiting time is one of the most frequent complaints made by Web users. The time can vary for many reasons: the size of the file, the number of inline images, the nature of the Web client, the bandwidth of the user's connection, Internet traffic, and the computing load on the computer where the particular resource resides. Sensitivity to the user's waiting time is an important design issue.

Short Attention Span Surfing

Links can be tremendously alluring. You've probably experienced this situation in your own Web surfing. You're following a browsing path and you arrive at a page full of links that look interesting but really are not related to your research topic at hand. Often you click on one of the new links and you're off somewhere else. You can even forget what you were originally looking for and how you got to where you are.

Of course, technically you can always get back. Your Web client maintains a history list that you can access to backtrack. But mentally it can be difficult. The inviting links on the Web pages that point to new resources located at other sites allow quick pursuit of many ideas; they also can be distracting and disruptive of some kinds of inquiries.

As a Web designer, you are challenged to offer rich links but also hold on to your Web readers. Remember a link can transport them away with a click and they may never come back. Some Web designers are using external links very carefully. For example, they restrict the places in which external links are offered or copy external resources to local hard disks so that users will stay in the local system as they view that resource. Managing external links becomes part of your information design challenge.

Designing a site

In many places in this book (here and in later chapters), I offer brief "makeover" exercises of a site to illustrate Web design principles. All the makeovers focus on a real site, the Conceptual Design/ Information Arts (CD/IA) program at San Francisco State University, where I teach. The faculty in this program had created preliminary versions of a Web site they wanted to offer.

Improving the design of a site goes beyond manipulating text and graphics. In order to make informed decisions about design, you need to understand what you hope to accomplish in your Web site and who you hope to reach. Our example site, which focuses on the relationships of art, technology, and the larger culture, had several purposes. These included providing information to current and prospective students, showcasing student and faculty art and research, identifying Web resources related to its focus, and creating a Web "presence." Improving its information design was undertaken with those purposes in mind. Even though this is an academic site, you will find that the principles apply to a wide range of sites, including businesses, not-for-profits, entertainment, and research settings.

Exercise 3.2:

Makeover of a site's use of links

Hyperlinks tend to serve two major purposes in any site—navigating through the information available at the local site and pointing to relevant resources located anywhere on the Internet. Let's take a look at this site's original links. Figure 3.12 shows an early version of this site's home page.

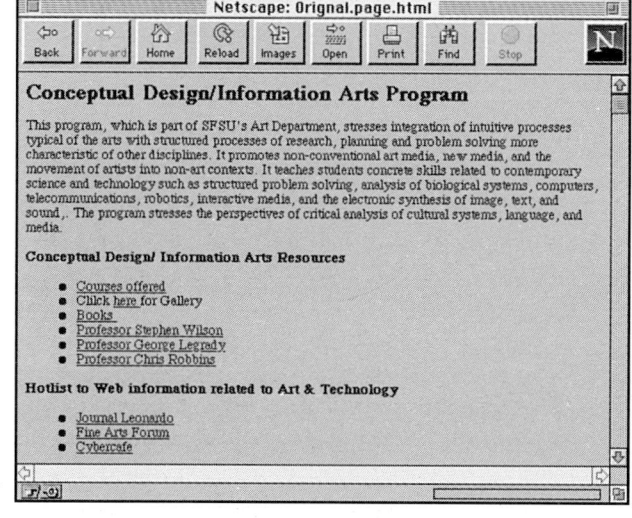

Stephen Wilson.

Figure 3.12:
Original version of Conceptual Design/ Information Arts site.

Step 1:

Fixing errors in the ways links are indicated. You can see some common errors in the list of links listed in the original page. The link for *books* does not provide nearly enough information for a Web visitor. What books? The site meant to offer links to course reading lists. We changed it to more explicitly name the resource that was being linked to. The code for that item could be changed to:

```
<LI> <A HREF = #Read>Conceptual Design Course
   Reading Lists</A>
```

The item for the link to the Gallery in the list also shows another common problem of using meaningless words like *here* as anchors. The anchor phrases should be meaningful. Also the word *gallery* does not really provide enough information. We change the anchor link to refer to a meaningful phrase and we add a bit more information. The example that follows shows the original and the revised item in the list.

```
Original:  <LI> Click <A HREF = #Gallery> here </A>
   for Gallery
Revised: <LI> <A HREF = #Gallery> Experimental Web
   Art Gallery </A>
```

Step 2:

Using links to let Web visitors decide if they want more information. The original Web page goes into too much detail in its first paragraph. People who are just browsing the site may not want this much information. Also, this first material assumes that the Web visitor already knows a lot.

We revise the first text to be shorter and more appropriate for new visitors. We use the Header, DL, and EM tags to make a short, visually appealing initial description to the site. We offer more details as a navigational option through a link to another more elaborated document as the first option in a list of links that follows (illustrated in Step 3). The source code for the initial description would be revised like this:

```
<DL>
<H2> Conceptual Design/Information Arts</H2>
<H3><B><EM><DT> An arts program that explores the
 relationship
<DD>of art, science, technology and culture </EM>
</B></H3>
<DD><H5>-Located at San Francisco State University
</H5>
</DL>
<HR SIZE=5>
```

Step 3:

Making clear the logical structure of the site. The list of links in the original is not organized in accordance with a clear logical pattern and it does not take advantage of conceptual layering. The short link text fragments do not give enough information for the readers to decide if they want more on any given topic.

As a solution we organize the material available in the site into logical sections and give the Web readers more information related to each topic section. We use DL list structure to present the major sections and the descriptive material that is part of each. The code for the first two subsections in the main list would look like this:

```
<DL>
<H3>
<DT><A HREF= "Description.html">Description of
 Program and Courses </A></H3>
<DD>Purpose of the program; Descriptions of courses;
 Requirements for admission and graduation
</DL>

<DL>
<H3>
<DT><A HREF= "Research.html">Research Materials in
 Information Arts/ Conceptual Design</A></H3>
<DD>Bibliographies in Art & Technology;   Course
 syllabi; Faculty papers
</DL>
```

Step 4:

Breaking up the information offered into several subdocuments. In the original, all local information is offered in one document. All subsections are part of the same document referenced by internal hyperlinks. The course listings section starts right after the index section. Web readers would need to wait for the whole document to download even though they might be interested in only part of it.

To fix that, we need to break the information into logical HTML subdocuments, each of which can be loaded independently. We make the initial index short and sweet. You can see in the source code listed in step 3 that each topical section leads to another HTML document, not to part of the original document as was originally the case.

Step 5:

Increasing the ease of navigation around the site. Navigation around the site is not as easy as it might be. Each section offers a link back to the top but nothing else. Cross navigation will be especially important if the site is separated into sections.

As a solution we created a hyperlink index at the bottom of each section that allows navigation back to the top or to the other main sections. The same index appears in all subdocuments in order to capitalize on user familiarization with the pattern. We use a table structure to format the index, illustrated at the bottom of Figure 3.13. Its code looks like this:

```
<TABLE BORDER=2 WIDTH=90%>
<TR>
<TH  COLSPAN=5> <A HREF= "Index.html"> Conceptual
  Design/Information Arts Index</A>
<TR> <TH> <A HREF= "Des.html"> Description</A>
<TH> <A HREF= "Research.html"> Research</A>
<TH> <A HREF= "Gallery.html"> Gallery</A>
<TH> <A HREF= "Hopage.html"> Fac&Stud Info</A>
<TH> <A HREF= "Links.html"> Links</A>
</TABLE>
```

Figure 3.13 shows the same site modified with many of these improvements. It shows the new main index with links to topical subsections. The detailed paragraph has been moved to the Description subsection. The bottom of Figure 3.13 shows a link table, which will appear at the bottom of all pages. This allows the Web visitor to instantly navigate to the top of index or to any of the other main subsections. The information structure of the site is clearer, it is easier to get around, and the page is visually more interesting.

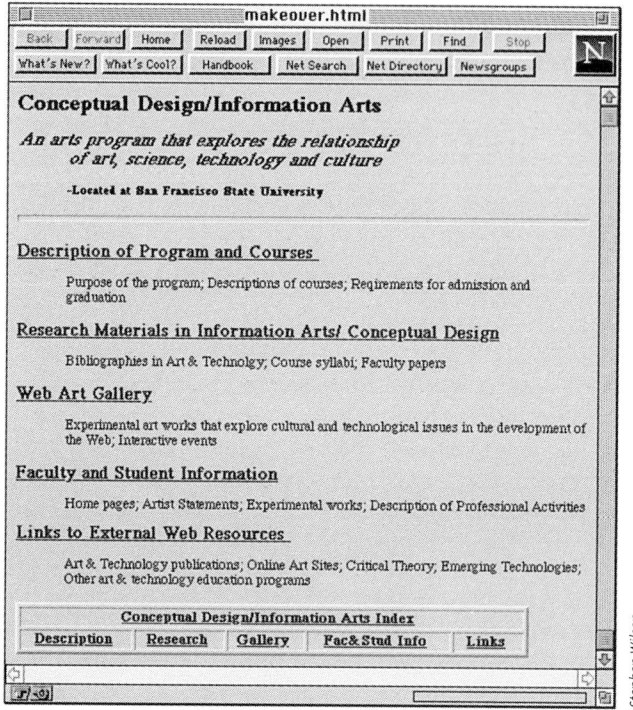

Stephen Wilson.

Figure 3.13:
Revised version of Conceptual Design/ Information Arts index.

Note that revisions proposed for this site use a fairly conventional hierarchical information structure with heavy reliance on indexes for navigation. Some involved with the site have suggested that there are more experimental or poetic structures that might be more appropriate for a site focused on conceptual and experimental arts. Do not assume that the classic index style presented here is the only way to organize information.

Summary: Links as Cyberspace

The ability to transcend physical space is one of core features of Cyberspace-based science fiction. With hypermedia links, the World Wide Web begins to make these fantasies real. Sometimes in the midst of a Web browsing session, I sit back and think about all the physical places I have been to with my links. Geographical distance is made irrelevant. It is awe-inspiring. Even more remarkable is the elegant simplicity and easy authoring of the HTML hyperlink system.

One of the things Web surfers are most interested to link to is the Internet's rich collection of image resources. The next chapter shows you what you need to know to start incorporating images as part of your Web pages.

Chapter 4

Working with Images

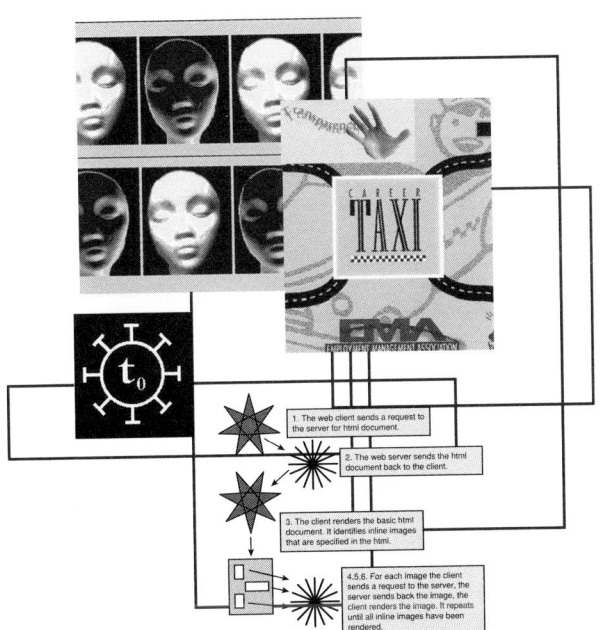

The visual richness of the Web is attracting millions of new users to the Internet. Its images welcome visitors who otherwise might be uncomfortable with computer networks and offer a kind of information that is difficult to convey in words. Almost all Web pages include graphics. You will find many reasons to include graphics in your pages—setting the tone for your site, explaining complex concepts simply through illustration, and creating visual embellishment for your textual information, among others.

Graphics are amazingly easy to incorporate in your Web pages. This chapter will teach you how to work with Web graphics, explain what graphics formats are used, describe helper applications that are used for working with them, and present new developments in HTML 3.0 that will add to the Web's graphics capabilities. It will also help you design your graphics to respond to the Web's specific requirements and show you techniques for creating exciting visual effects.

Understanding Graphics File Formats

Many of you may have worked with computer graphics for years. Although you may be quite expert in working with them, you may feel your technical understanding of how computer graphics actually function and how formats differ is a bit shaky. Let's take a break for a short refresher course because this technical information will help you make more knowledgeable decisions about what formats to use in your Web offerings.

Graphic formats are conventions by which the visual information of an image is represented by the digital values that computers can deal with. There are two major categories of computer-based artwork: *bitmapped* (or *raster-based)* and *object-oriented* (or *vector-based*) graphics.

Bitmapped Graphics

Bitmapped graphics treat images as a matrix of dots, or picture elements called *pixels*. Examples of bitmapped graphics include the images that come from paint, image processing, scanning, and video capture applications. Bitmapped images are well suited for representing the continuous variations of tone typical of photographic or video imagery. Some standard file formats for bitmapped graphics include GIF (short for Graphics Interchange Format), JPEG, TIFF (cross-platform), PCX and BMP (for PCs), and x-bmp (UNIX format).

Some file formats differ in terms of how many colors they can assign to each pixel. Because computers represent data using a binary system (1s and 0s), and computer memory is composed of bytes that each contain 8 digital bits of information, you can see that the greatest number of colors an 8-bit file format can contain is 2^8 or 256 colors. A black-and-white image requires only two values, and thus requires only one bit per pixel. On the higher end, a 24-bit color graphic requires 1 byte each for red, green, and blue values; it can contain up to 16.7 million possible colors but will require a great deal of storage space. Figure 4.1 shows how colors are represented in computer memory.

GIF, the first cross-platform standard for the Web, supported only 8-bit color. If you wanted to offer Web visitors 24-bit color, you had to use links to external graphics in formats such as JPEG and TIFF. Now that browsers are beginning to support JPEG even for inline images, this reason for using external images will become less important.

Object-Oriented (Vector-Based) Graphics

Object-oriented graphics (sometimes called vector-based graphics) are radically different from bitmapped graphics. Instead of storing the discrete color spots of the image, these programs store mathematical definitions of the objects that make up the image—for example, information about the shapes' or text segments' locations on the screen, dimensions, outline, the color of the internal fill, or relative positions. With object-oriented graphics, each element of the graphic maintains its structural integrity and can be edited, modified, or adjusted in relation to other objects. This

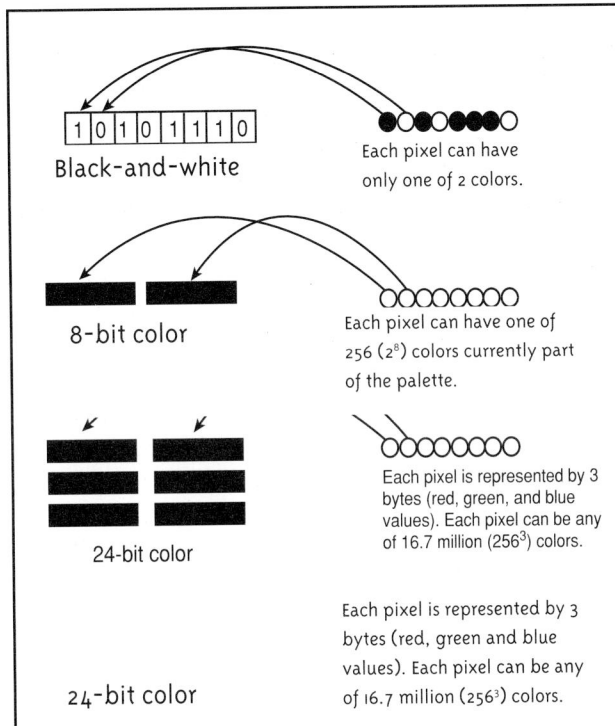

Black-and-white

Each pixel can have
only one of 2 colors.

8-bit color

Each pixel can have one of
256 (2^8) colors currently part
of the palette.

24-bit color

Each pixel is represented by 3
bytes (red, green, and blue
values). Each pixel can be any
of 16.7 million (256^3) colors.

24-bit color

Each pixel is represented by 3
bytes (red, green and blue
values). Each pixel can be any
of 16.7 million (256^3) colors.

Figure 4.1:
Representations of colors in computer memory bit patterns.

approach is ideal for drawing, illustration, CAD, and 3-D
modeling programs in which independent object creation
is a natural part of the process.

Think of object-oriented graphics as a collage layout in which
each object can be independently moved and adjusted;
bitmapped graphics are more like painting, where no change

is possible other than scraping off the paint or laying a new
layer on top. Vector formats have additional benefits: images
stored in vector formats are optimized for print purposes. If
you have a 600 dpi printer, you can print an object-oriented
graphic at the highest resolution—600 dpi. Some Web sites
that distribute graphics files intended for print purposes
therefore store their files in vector formats such as PostScript.
In addition, vector formats are memory-efficient ways of
storing information about 3-D environments and will become
more important in applications such as the Web-based
virtual reality systems, including VRML (discussed in Chapter
10). Examples of other object-oriented file formats include
PICT and 3-D modeling and CAD formats such as CGM and
DXF.

Figure 4.2 illustrates some of the differences between
bitmapped and objected-oriented graphics. Because each
graphic element in an object-oriented graphic maintains its
independence, moved objects do not affect any underlying
objects. In bitmapped graphics the whole image is represented as a pattern of pixels so that graphic elements cannot
be edited and moved independently of other parts of the
image. Cutting something away leaves only the background
underneath, not the original image.

Note: For more details on how computer graphics
work, see my previous books *Multimedia Design
with HyperCard* (Prentice Hall, 1991) or *Using
Computers to Create Art* (Prentice Hall, 1986).

Object Graphics

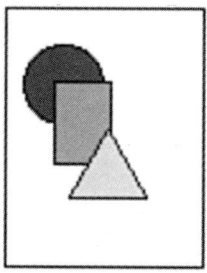 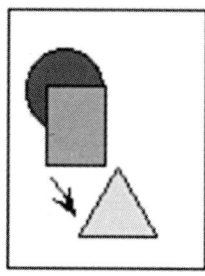

Bitmapped Graphics

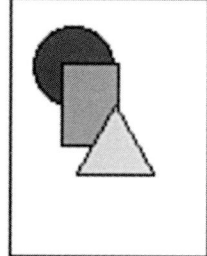 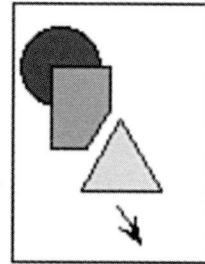

Figure 4.2:
Object versus bitmapped graphics.

Compression

Even within the bitmapped and object-oriented approaches, there are variations in formats. For example, even though GIF and JPEG are both bitmapped formats, one of their most important differences is compression. Compression is important because it reduces file sizes and hence transmission time on the network. GIF uses a simple *lossless* algorithm that allows all the information in the file to be totally reconstructed upon decompression. This is a sophisticated mathematical algorithm that restores the value for each pixel to its original value on decompression. JPEG uses a *lossy* algorithm, in which some of the information, less essential for visual perception, is discarded for the sake of achieving high levels of compression. Upon decompression, the original values of the pixels cannot be totally reconstructed—hence the name *lossy.*

Deciding Which File Format to Use

So now graphics formats may be less of a mystery. But still, how do you decide when to use each format? Is anything lost in translation from one to the other?

This question will probably come to mind every time you decide to use an external graphic. For example, high-resolution TIFF images lose some information going into other formats. Obviously, a 24-bit image with millions of colors loses some clarity if you convert it to a 256-color, 8-bit GIF format image. Graphic converters try to calculate the best 256-color palette they can to represent the full color range; they use a process called *dithering*, in which the colors of adjacent dots are altered to approximate the missing colors. Because each format handles these processes differently, you'll want to be careful about graphic conversions if, for example, your files will represent an art gallery or museum's Web site and quality is the prime consideration.

Translation from object-oriented into bitmapped formats means that the individual objects lose their integrity. The image will no longer have components that can be independently modified and moved. The representation on the screen may accurately portray the image but underlying information is gone. Translation requires that the receiving format do the best it can to preserve the shape information, and details can get lost or slightly distorted. But in many situations, this will not matter because all the user wants is an accurate visual portrayal, not a file that can still be manipulated in the creator program. Again, you'll have to consider what's the most important factor for you.

Whether you're creating an inline or external image, choosing a cross-platform graphic format is the most practical decision. You'll have the largest possible audience that can see your image because standard Web clients are most likely to be preconfigured to process those formats and to have an appropriate helper application.

GIF and JPEG are currently your best choices for formats and are the most frequently used graphics file formats you'll find on the Web. More details about these formats are given in the next sections.

GIF—Graphics Interchange Format

GIF (pronounced "jif") was originally developed to facilitate cross-platform graphics for file transfers on CompuServe, which makes it well suited to meet the demands of image distribution on networks. GIF is a 8-bit, 256 color, bitmapped format. It stores data about the color of each pixel in the image in a straightforward process. A color palette of colors used is stored with the image. 24-bit images saved in GIF format must be dithered down to an 8-bit representation. Some limited lossless compression is used in converting to GIF format.

History of GIF format

The users of services such as CompuServe faced the same dilemma that confronted Web developers—namely, how to allow users with various kinds of computers to work with resources developed on other kinds of computers. GIF was the format developed to serve as the lingua franca of micro-computer graphics. Converters were written for each kind of computer (for example, Apple II, Atari, Commodore, IBM, Macintosh, Amiga, UNIX, X Windows) that would convert native format graphics into this universal format. Similarly the converters would be able to receive GIF images and convert them back into formats native to the particular computer. Developers wrote these programs and offered them freely as freeware or shareware.

There is some confusion about the legal status of GIF because UNISYS holds a patent governing the compression routine that is part of the format. It has implemented a royalty requirement for developers of programs that use GIF (for example, most Web clients). Users of these programs will not need to pay a royalty. It is unclear how the Web community will respond. Some new format may replace GIF as the most common standard, such as GIF24 under development. For now you can continue to use GIF, but monitor future developments carefully.

JPEG—Joint Photographic Experts Group Format

JPEG is a format devised by a group called the Joint Photographic Experts Group that came together to devise a compression scheme uniquely suited to reducing the file sizes of computer-generated images. They also had the goal of creating a cross-platform standard.

JPEG takes advantage of human perceptual characteristics to discard less essential information and hence reduce file sizes. Examples include the eye's low awareness of some subtleties of color and brightness changes. It works with 24-bit color and is especially suited for naturalistic images where there are continuous tone changes in grayscale or color.

JPEG is a "lossy" system in which some information is lost in absolute terms. That is, one could not totally reconstruct the original image data from the compression. Nonetheless, because the method that it uses to compress discards information that research has shown to be less essential for human visual perception, it has achieved a notable reputation for high quality images and high levels of compression.

It is less suitable for images with few colors, sharp edges, line drawings, or synthetic computer graphic illustrations because the tonal variations that it works with are missing. Also, it is not as quick as some other compression schemes because it requires sophisticated calculations. Although it was supposed to be standardized, some variation has resulted from the ways different software and hardware companies have implemented it. A new cross-platform JFIF (JPEG file interchange format) standard has been developed, which ensures that all computers will be able to use its files. Most contemporary applications generate JPEG files that conform to the JFIF format.

How do you decide between GIF and JPEG? If your image is full color with subtle tonal variations, use JPEG. If it is an illustration or computer graphic with few, well-delineated colors, GIF will work well. But if you use a format that is not well suited for the particular image, your file can be larger than is necessary. For example, a high-quality JPEG version of a line drawing will most often be larger than a GIF version of the same image. Table 4.1 summarizes some of the basic characteristics of each format.

Table 4.1

Summary of Differences between GIF and JPEG Formats

	GIF	JPEG (JFIF)
Color depth	8 bit or less	8 bit, 24 bit
Image type best handled	Line drawing, synthetic computer graphics	Naturalistic, full tonal range, photolike, scanned images.
Compression	Moderate levels of *lossless* compression that loses no information	High levels of compression that uses a *lossy* approach that discards some information. Optimized to preserve information critical for visual perception.
Time for display	Fast	Some decompression time required, which slows down transfer.

Computer industry approaches to cross-platform graphics

The computer industry has identified cross-platform accessibility of graphics as a priority. For example, Common Ground and Acrobat are two systems that will allow users on multiple platforms to view richly formatted graphics and text even though the receiver does not have the originating applications. In these schemes the publisher translates the original file into a file formatted in one of these exchange formats. Receivers need only a free or inexpensive reader application that allows them to see the material in much of its original glory.

Similarly, both Microsoft (in OLE technology—object linking and embedding) and Apple (in Open Documents) are working on new approaches to making files flexibly interoperate with a multitude of possible applications that can manipulate them. You can expect that, with appropriate further development, these approaches will be called into service to enable publishers and readers to solve the cross-platform rendering problem on the Web.

What follows are online references that offer more information about computer graphics formats.

General Information about Computer Graphics Formats

- *Usenet computer graphics group (FAQ) frequently asked questions covering topics such as formats, how-to questions, and sources of additional information*

`http://www.cis.ohio-state.edu/hypertext/faq/`
`usenet/graphics/faq/faq.html`

- *SIGGRAPH International Computer Graphics Organization site with a variety of resources on technical and design issues in computer graphics*

`http://www.siggraph.org/`

- *Virtual library computer graphics site with pointers to bibliographies and other information resources on computer graphics*

`http://www.dataspace.com/WWW/vlib/comp-`
`graphics.html`

Inline versus External Images

The images you view with your Web browser fall into two general categories: *inline images*, which can be displayed directly on a Web page, and *external images*, which you must download separately and usually access through a link. Depending on the format of the graphics and the particular browser you are using, you may need a helper application to view external images.

You'll see helper applications discussed later in this chapter and again in the next two chapters on sound and video. As you'll discover, to use the full multimedia potential of the Web you may need to install and configure several helper programs to handle different multimedia file formats. Graphics are the only form of Web multimedia that give you an option for avoiding helper programs—that is, if you stick to using only inline images. All graphical browsers let you display inline images. Because you can't be sure what helper programs your audience has and is using, why not hedge your bets and stick with inline images? Well, as we discuss in detail next, only a limited number of file formats are suitable for inline images—GIF, JPEG, and (for some browsers) XBM. External images let you use other graphics formats that give you many more options for color use and compression. You can also use external graphics to make large graphics (over 30K) available on your Web site without causing your page to take forever to load. Figure 4.3 shows a high-resolution satellite image of the world's weather displayed on the Web at MSU's weather map server, through a helper application. Figure 4.4 shows an inline image from Ylem's Art on the Edge site.

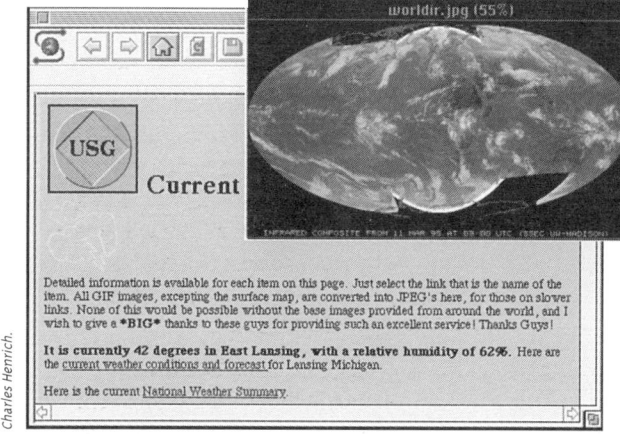

Figure 4.3:

Example of external image displayed in viewer window.
```
From the weather map server at http://
rs560.cl.msu.edu/weather/getmegif.html
```

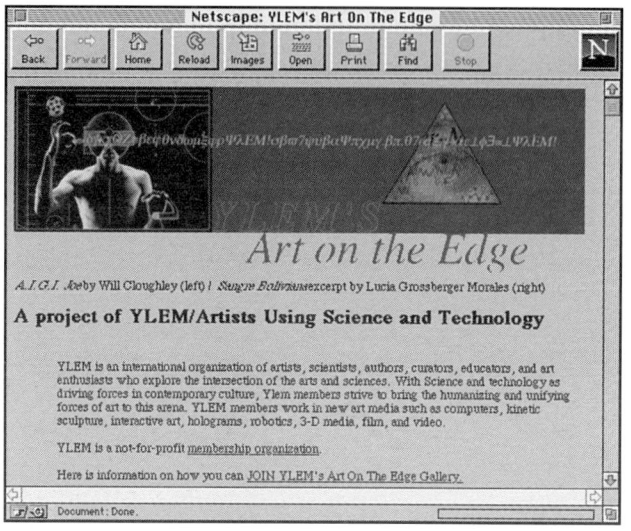

Figure 4.4:

Inline image from YLEM's Art on the Edge site.
```
http://www.exploratorium.edu/Ylem/ylemhome.html
```

The Pros and Cons

You should consider several factors before choosing to make your graphics inline or external, including the quality of the image, the integration of the image with the basic Web page, the time to load, and the image viewing control given to the viewer.

Table 4.2 compares some of the relative advantages and disadvantages of using external and inline graphics.

We'll return to the issues of formats, helper applications, and access time later in this chapter.

Table 4.2

Side-by-Side Comparison of Inline and External Graphics

Design Factor	Advantages of Inline Graphics	Advantages of External Graphics
Integration with main HTML presentation	Yes, because graphics appear alongside text and other elements on the page.	No, because external graphics must appear in a separate window.
Extent of user control over appearance	Author has some control over the format of presentation, such as relation to other elements. Guaranteed viewing (unless the user deactivates automatic image loading).	External windows give users more control over size, location, etc. of image windows.
Available graphic formats	Standard format (GIF) available in all clients and other formats (XBM and JPEG) available on many clients.	Can use any format supported by users' helper applications.
User access to graphic resources	In some browsers (for example, Netscape) image can be saved via a special "save image to disk" command. In other browsers (for example, Mosaic) the image can be saved only via screen capture software.	Files can be saved for later manipulation or viewing. Allows you to give users access to higher-resolution images (for example, 300 dpi) that could be on high-resolution printers.
Access time	Browser will automatically load each image. User does not need to wait for external helper application to launch and decode image.	Gives users a decision about whether to load an image or just save it to disk (with its associated time requirements).

HTML Tags for Incorporating Graphics

The HTML code for including an image in your Web document is fairly simple. The basic inline image tag is

```
<IMG  SRC = "image.GIF">
```

The <IMG> prefix tells the client to display the indicated graphic resource, if it is capable of doing so; as you'll see, nongraphical browsers must simply print the word "[IMAGE]" on the screen instead of rendering the graphic itself unless alternative text is specified. The <SRC=> indicates the URL or filename (if it is a local resource). The URL should be enclosed in quotes. Use this tag with a properly defined URL pointing to a GIF or JPEG image and you've got yourself an inline image. No closing tag is needed for <IMG>.

You can even include images that reside on other host computers, as long as you know the path to the directory that contains the desired image. Your <IMG> tag should reference the full URL for the image, like so:

```
<IMG  SRC = "http://www.host.com/directory
  image.GIF">
```

Figure 4.5 shows an example of a signature inline image at the FineArt Forum's home page. The code line that accesses this image is simply <IMG SRC="faf.gif">.

You're not limited to using one inline image to a line. Most browsers will place as many images as possible on a line, provided no paragraph or break tags separate the inline image tags. One way to think of these elements is as letters

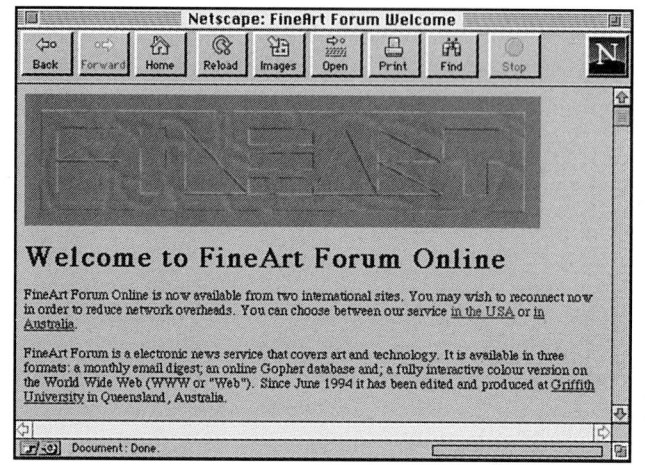

Figure 4.5:
Anatomy of tag for an inline image at Fine Arts Forum.
Fine Arts Forum is at http://www.msstate.edu/
Fineart_Online/home.html

or typographic characters that happen to be graphics. If you want images to appear on different lines, then you must use <BR> or <P> tags just as you would with text. This multi-image capability gives you great flexibility in formatting Web pages. Figure 4.6 shows a display that takes advantage of this feature.

Figure 4.6:
Multiple inline images on a line.

Optional Attributes

There are three optional attributes that you can include with the <IMG> tag:

- An alignment indication (*<ALIGN=>*) that shows how the image should be aligned with adjacent text. This attribute can take three possible values: *TOP*, *MIDDLE*, or *BOTTOM*.

- An alternative text indication (<ALT=>) that indicates text to be displayed so the page will make sense to people whose browsers cannot display images or who chose to disable image loading. Including <ALT> code shows consideration for readers who use Lynx or another nongraphical browser. The alternate text will also be important for browsers that try to service the visually

disabled because future systems will speak screen text. **Note that not every browser supports the <ALT> attribute yet.**

- An imagemap indication (*<ISMAP=>*) that tells browsers to jump to a different Web location when the user clicks the mouse on an indicated "hot spot." This advanced capability is discussed in greater detail in Chapter 7. Here's an example that incorporates all three attributes:

```
<IMG ALIGN = top    ALT= "text"  SRC = "image.GIF"
   ISMAP>
```

Figures 4.7a and 4.7b show an example of one site with images loaded and with <ALT> text displayed instead.

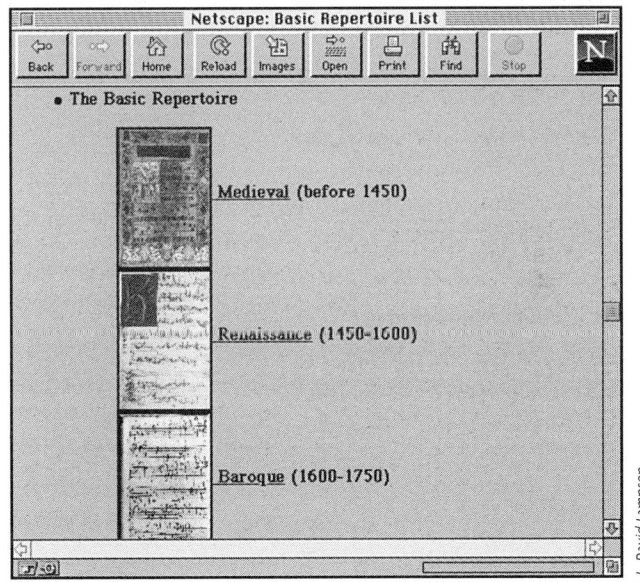

Figure 4.7a:
Images loaded at the Classical Repertoire site.
`http://www.webcom.com/~music/rep/top.html`

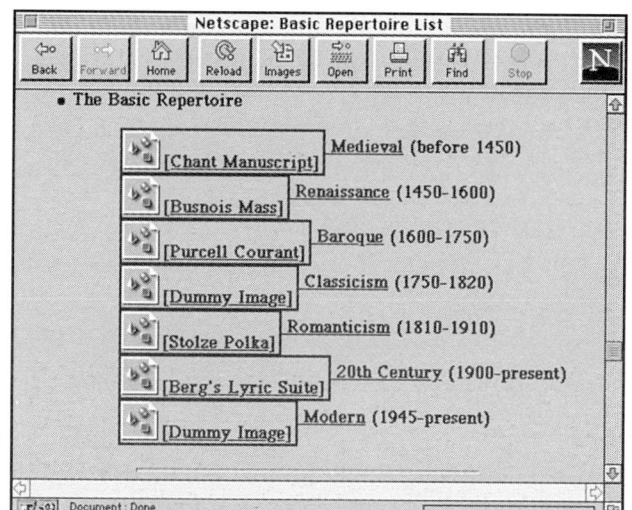

Figure 4.7b:
The Classical Repertoire site with images disabled.

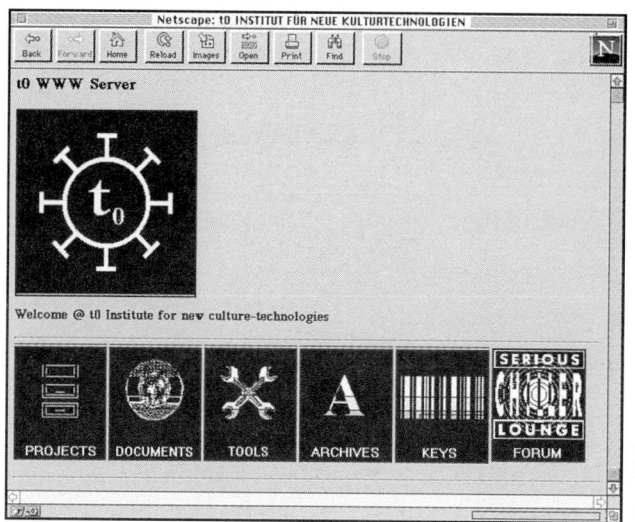

Figure 4.8:
Institute for New Culture Technology's use of inline images as links.
`http://kernighan.imc.akh-wien.ac.at/t0/t0/`

Using Images as Hyperlinks

Images can serve as hotlinks to other resources with appropriate linking tags affixed. There are a lot of exciting possibilities for making use of images in this way. Some experimental sites use only inline images as their index, a very visually appealing way of presenting straightforward information. Figures 4.8 and 4.9 offer examples of indexes of links built from inline images.

To make an image into a hotlink, you only need to surround your image tag with the opening and closing link tags described in the last chapter. The syntax can get a little bit confusing because there will need to be two URLs—one for accessing the image and another for the destination of the link. As an example, take a look at the following HTML source code for the linked image in Figure 4.9.

```
<A HREF="tribe_links/index.html">
<IMG ALIGN=LEFT WIDTH=43 HEIGHT=175
  SRC="gifs/border.gif" ALT="Tribal Links">
```

The vertical jungle image on the left side accesses the index for the site. The <HREF> part of the tag identifies the HTML document to be linked to. The <SRC> part of the line indicates that the "gifs/border.gif" image is the active link. Just as most Web clients distinguish hotlinked text by rendering it in a different color or with an underline, a hotlinked image is distinguished as a link with a colored border.

Copyright 1995 Rainforest Action Network.

Figure 4.9:
Rainforest Action Network's use of inline images as links.

You can also create links to jump to external image files. This is a good strategy if you want to offer users access to many high-resolution images or if you want to avoid cluttering up your pages with large image files that take a long time to load. Then, only those who have high-speed connections or users who actively choose to endure longer access times will choose to follow your link. You can easily accomplish this kind of hyperlink by using the <A HREF> tag, which was discussed in Chapter 3. The only difference here is that the URL you specify is a path to a graphics files instead of an HTML file. For example, Figure 4.10 illustrates an image archive in a site called "Travels with Samantha" that presents photo-documentation of a trip across North America. The Web visitor is invited to click on any of the thumbnail images to access larger, high-resolution versions of the photos. Here is the source code showing how the thumbnail image of bears fighting is linked to a related high-resolution JPEG file:

```
<A HREF="final-photos/bear-fight.jpg">
  <IMG  SRC="final-photos/bear-fight.gif"></A>
```

Because the JPEG image is an external graphic, it will be displayed in a separate window if you follow this link.

Philip Greenspun (philg@mit.ed).

Figure 4.10:
Inline images used as links to external images, from Travels with Samantha.
```
http://www-swiss.ai.mit.edu/samantha/travels-with-
samantha.html
```

Exercise 4.1:

Adding internal and external links to images for a Web document

Step 1:

For the inline image part of this exercise you must have a graphics file in your local directory in a graphics format that your Web browser can understand, such as GIF or JPEG format. There are several ways to obtain or create this file. You can use any standard graphics program, such as Photoshop, which offers JPEG or GIF as one of its output formats. You can either create a new graphic or convert another file. Save your file in GIF or JPEG format and name it *Exercise.GIF* or *Exercise.JPEG* as appropriate. Your Web browser will use the file's extension to determine how to display the image.

Alternatively, you could download an image from one of the Web documents or image archives listed in this book. The later section on "Obtaining Images for Your Pages" points to online sources of images.

Once you've obtained your sample image, place it in the same directory or folder as the HTML document you're creating for this exercise.

Step 2:

Using your word processor, type the basic HTML document we'll use as the basis for this example:

```
<HTML>
<HEAD> <TITLE> "Image Use on the Web"</TITLE>
</HEAD>
<BODY>
<H3> Using Images on the Web </H3>
```

```
My image.<P>
Surprises can be dangerous.<P>
</BODY>
</HTML>
```

Step 3:

We're going to add our inline image immediately following the <H3> header. Make sure that the text you enter for the <IMG SRC=> pathname matches the graphic's filename and extension exactly. In our example, we now have a line of code that reads as follows:

```
<IMG SRC= "Exercise.GIF">  My image.<P>
```

(This will cause your inline image and the text "My image." to appear on the same line. If you want your text to start on a new line, enter a <P> tag after the <IMG> tag.)

Step 4:

Next, let's create a reference to an external image. You'll need the absolute pathname for the URL of an image that's already on the Web. For this exercise, try the following URL to point your readers to a surprise image. The code you enter should look like the following:

```
<A HREF= http://gto.ncsa.uiuc.edu/pingleto/herps/
images/cobra.gif> Surprises can be dangerous <A>
<P>
```

Step 5:

Save your document as an ASCII text file. Use .html (if you're using a Macintosh or .htm for a DOS/Windows platform) for the filename's suffix. Here is what the source code for your final document should look like:

```
<HTML>
<HEAD>  <TITLE> "Image Use on the Web"</TITLE>
</HEAD>
<BODY>
<H3> Using Images on the Web  </H3>.
<IMG SRC= "Exercise.GIF">  My image.<P>
<A HREF= http://gto.ncsa.uiuc.edu/pingleto/herps/
  images/cobra.gif> Surprises can be dangerous <A>
  <P>
</BODY>
</HTML>
```

Step 6:

Activate the browser and use the "Open Local" or "Open File" option to access the file you have just created.

Troubleshoot the inline image, if necessary. If your browser window shows a generic image icon instead of your image, there are several things you can check. First, make sure your browser's autoload images option is activated—otherwise, it will ignore inline images. If you need to correct this, adjust it and reload your HTML document. Second, check that your image is in GIF or JPEG format, is named in your HTML document exactly as it is on your hard disk, and the pathname is accurate. (If your graphic is located in the same directory folder as your HTML document, it's OK to use the relative pathname.)

Step 7:

Before you try the external link, make sure you haven't made any typographical errors, and confirm that all the opening and closing tags are included where necessary. You will need a live network connection to actually test the external image link.

Step 8:

Observe how your browser draws your inline image, and note how long it takes to load. Now try clicking on the external link. Your browser should fetch the file when you click the external link. See Figure 4.11.

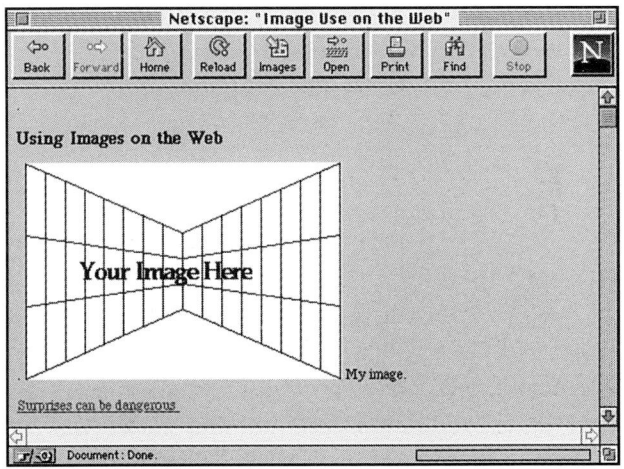

Figure 4.11:
Adding image links to your Web page.

HTML 3.0, Netscape Extensions, and the Future of Web Graphics

The Web community is actively working to increase HTML's capabilities with images in the proposed HTML 3.0 specifications related to graphics. Netscape Communications has also introduced some additional graphic capabilities beyond those in the official proposals, which only your Netscape-using audience will be able to see. You can do the following:

- Lay out text and graphics more precisely on your Web pages.

- Specify border characteristics.

- Explicitly designate image height and width.

- Control the color and pattern of backgrounds.

- Use a new flexible <FIGURE> graphic element.

- Use graphic elements in HTML structures, including horizontal rules and lists, where they could not previously be used.

- Incorporate a static <BANNER> capability that will draw a graphic header, such as a logo, on a set of your pages.

Tables 4.4 and 4.5 at the end of this section summarize the tags and syntax that control these capabilities.

These extensions greatly expand your visual control over inline images and create fascinating design and art opportunities. They overcome some of the troubling HTML image-manipulation shortcomings. However, because they are not yet part of the international HTML standards, they will appear as you intend only if your audience is using either a browser that has implemented the HTML 3.0 proposals or Netscape (for the special Netscape extensions). Although Netscape is currently the most widely used Web browser out there, you need to consider what other browsers your specific audience may be using. As a Web designer, you need to address these challenges: Do you use these capabilities and risk many users not seeing your work correctly or do you go ahead and use them because they offer the most advanced design

capabilities available? The call is up to you. Let's take a look at what these extensions can do. The following reference list includes the Web locations where the HTML 3.0 proposals and Netscape's special extensions are described in more detail.

Pointers to HTML 3.0 and Netscape's Extensions to HTML

- *Information on the HTML 3.0 Proposals*
```
http://www.w3.org/hypertext/WWW/MarkUp/html3/
Contents.html
```

- *Information on Netscape Extensions to HTML*
```
http://www.netscape.com/assist/net_sites/
html_extensions.html
```

- *Validation Service that Detemines Whether Your Source Code Meets Various Levels of Specifications Including HTML 3.0*
```
http://www.halsoft.com/html-val-svc/
```

Horizontal Alignment Options

With HTML 2.0, you are limited to aligning your images along the left-hand margin. Any text that follows cannot wrap around the image; if the text extends beyond one line, it may be broken, as shown in Figure 4.12. If your text is longer than a single line, the text wraps below the image onto the next line rather than immediately on the side of the image where you might have preferred it.

Because graphic designers and desktop publishers have had access to programs with more advanced image alignment and text wraparound capabilities for years, the market has demanded improving these HTML capabilities as well.

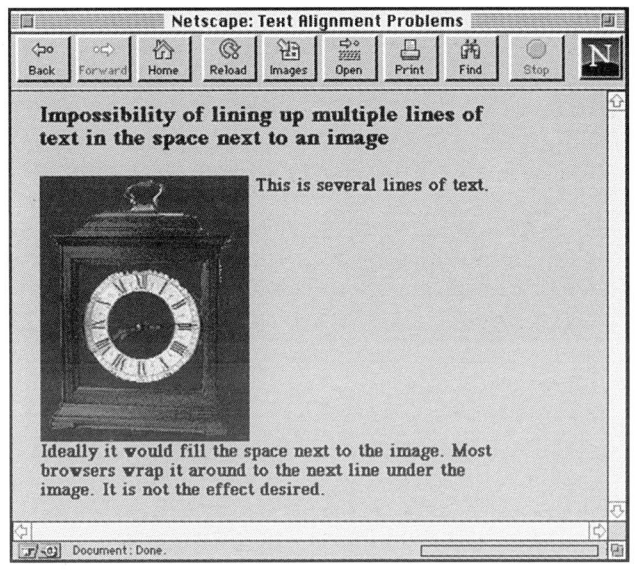

Figure 4.12:

Text wrapping below an inline image instead of running around it.

HTML 3.0 and Netscape's extensions allow you to align images in the center and on the right in addition to the left of the browser window. Right and left alignment will by default line the images up with the edge of the text in the window, which includes a slight margin from the window border. If you want them to line up on the window border, you can use the <BLEEDLEFT> and <BLEEDRIGHT> options instead.

These extensions also allow you flexibility in positioning text next to images. To implement these features, you include an <ALIGN> attribute in your <IMG> tag and you can then expect that the text *will* wrap around the image, as shown in the top half of Figure 4.13. The source code for the first image is as follows:

```
<IMG ALIGN=LEFT SRC="smask.GIF">
```

Without the <ALIGN> attribute, you'll get something like the figure in the bottom half of Figure 4.13. The source code for the second image is simply:

```
<IMG SRC="smask.GIF">
```

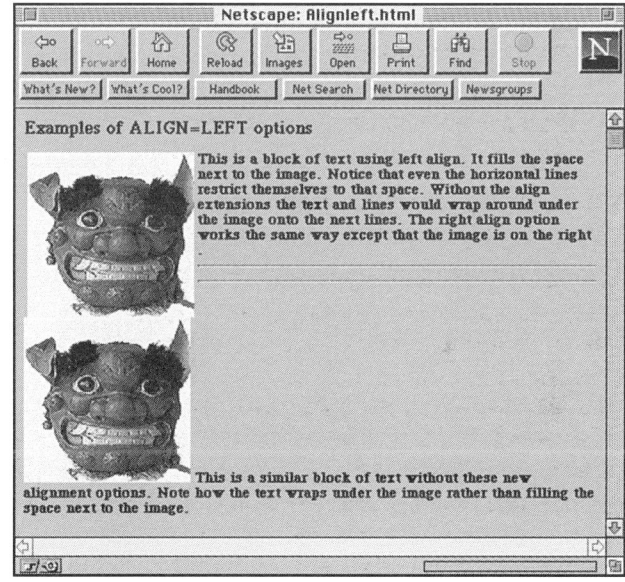

Figure 4.13:

The <ALIGN=LEFT> attribute.

Before the HTML 3.0 official proposals were developed, Netscape introduced the <CENTER> tag that accomplished the same function as the <ALIGN=CENTER> property that was added inside of other tags. The <CENTER> tag uses different syntax. Instead of being incorporated into the <IMG> tag, it stands alone before the elements you want centered and requires a closing tag. Netscape is likely to support both syntaxes even after the official specifications are ratified. The example that follows shows both syntaxes.

Official HTML 3.0 Proposals:

```
<IMG SRC=image.GIF ALIGN=CENTER>
```

Netscape Extensions:

```
<CENTER> <IMG SRC="image.GIF"> <CENTER>
```

You can also control the distance from the image that text or other elements will appear with Netscape's <HSPACE> and <VSPACE> options. Note these are *not* part of the official HTML 3.0 proposals. The <HSPACE> indicates the number of pixels the browser should introduce between the image and any text or images aligned on its right or left sides. <VSPACE> determines the number of pixels that should separate the image from elements located either above or below it. Note that the text in Figure 4.13 begins immediately next to the right side of the image, creating a crowded feeling. Figure 4.14 shows the image that would result from using the tag that follows, which would create a 30-pixel horizontal margin.

```
<IMG SRC="smask.gif" ALIGN=LEFT HSPACE = 30>
```

Because the align left and right options supersede standard HTML's rigid line-based layout in which only one line of text can appear next to images, you must explicitly indicate where you want the next line of text to follow. Do you want it to appear on the side of the image or start below on the next line?

Figure 4.14:
Using Netscape's <HSPACE> attribute.

As a result, you need new commands to tell the browser where you really want to put text. HTML 3.0 allows you to add the <CLEAR> option to HTML tags such as headers, <P> and <BR>. <CLEAR=LEFT> will find the next available free space on the left margin; <CLEAR=RIGHT> finds the next available space on the right margin; and <CLEAR=ALL> will place the text below all elements on either margin. The example shows part of the source code that would produce Figure 4.15. Because the image is aligned left, all text appears next to it until there is a <BR> tag with a <CLEAR=ALL> property.

```
<IMG SRC="arrowup.gif"  ALIGN=LEFT>
<H4>This text appears right next to the
  image....option.
<BR CLEAR=ALL>
This text appears below the image because ....
  document.  </H4>
```

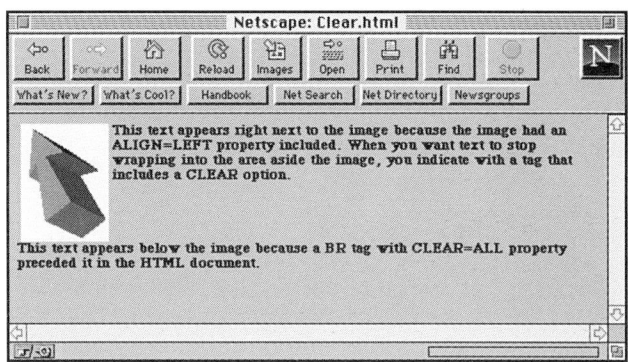

Figure 4.15:
Using the <CLEAR> attribute.

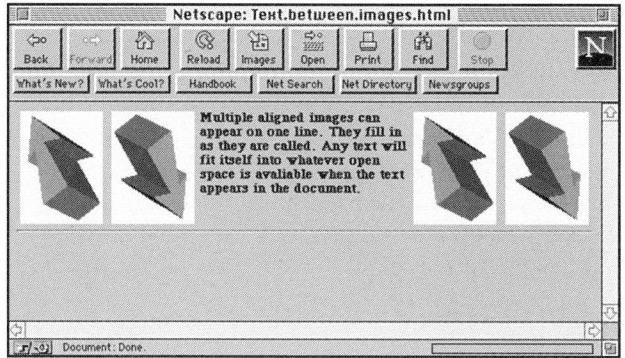

Figure 4.16:
Using the <ALIGN> option to place multiple images and text on a line.

You can also use the <CLEAR> option to position images in relation to each other. Browsers will continue to position inline images on the same line next to each other as long as there is space.

You can use the align options to create many kinds of visual special effects. The order in which your <IMG> and text tags appear in your HTML document becomes critical. Once an image is called with an <ALIGN=RIGHT> or <LEFT> option, any following text will fill in next to it unless you use a tag with a <CLEAR> attribute. By ordering your calls of text and <IMG> tags, you can create a variety of layouts.

Figure 4.16 shows the placement of several images on the same line with a box of text located in the space between the images. Two images are aligned on the left and two on the right. The following text fills in the space between. The example shows part of the source code that produced that image.

```
<IMG ALIGN=LEFT  SRC ="arrowup.gif"> <IMG ALIGN=LEFT
 SRC = "arrowdown.gif">
<IMG ALIGN=RIGHT  SRC ="arrowdown.gif">
 <IMG ALIGN=RIGHT SRC ="arrowup.gif">
<H4>Multiple aligned images ..... document.</H4>
<BR CLEAR=ALL>
<HR>
```

The align option opens up many kinds of additional layout possibilities. Figure 4.17 gives a hint of what you can do. It illustrates how you could create a stair-step layout. By interleaving <IMG> tags and text, you create this effect because the text will fill in whatever space is available when it is called. The amount of space keeps changing because new images are placed after each line of text, so it is hard to predict what the resulting display would look like on different browsers and different screen views. The example that follows shows key parts of the source code that would create Figure 4.17. Note that the Netscape <HSPACE> commands will not work on other browsers and the text would crowd the images more than in the figure.

```
<IMG ALIGN= LEFT  SRC ="arrowup.gif" HSPACE=4>
A stair step can be created by interleaving image
  and text.
<IMG ALIGN= LEFT  SRC ="arrowup.gif" HSPACE=4>
Each time the text will fill in the next available
  space.
<IMG ALIGN= LEFT  SRC ="arrowup.gif" HSPACE=4>
It takes some experimentation to get the display
<IMG ALIGN= LEFT  SRC ="arrowup.gif" HSPACE=4>
to look just like you would like.
<IMG ALIGN= LEFT  SRC ="arrowup.gif" HSPACE=4>
It can look interesting.
<IMG ALIGN= LEFT  SRC ="arrowup.gif">
<BR CLEAR=ALL>   <HR>
```

What size is the user's browser window?

Note that the display in Figure 4.17 could appear very differently if users resized their screen to a smaller or much larger view. Web documents that incorporate inline images placed anywhere other than on the left margin are subject to this kind of potentially disrupted display. Images and text can be wrapped in unanticipated and sometimes unappealing ways. Although there is no way to guard against all eventualities, many Web page creators build their pages using the default browser size for 13-inch monitors (approximately 470 pixels across) as a target size.

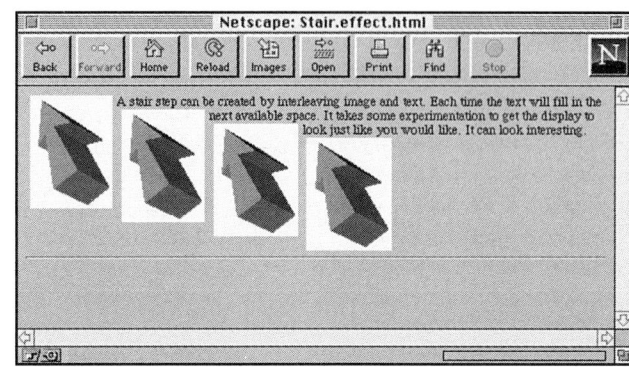

Figure 4.17:
Using the <ALIGN> option to create a stair-step layout.

Recognize that these are only a small sample of the possibilities; you can discover more by experimenting with various combinations of multiple image calls interleaved with text and visiting as many other sites as you can.

Also realize that there may be some layouts of images that cannot easily be achieved even with the new align features. Also, until the new HTML 3.0 standards are widespread, you might want to implement layouts that will work on browsers that only recognize HTML 2.0 or that don't rely on the Netscape enhancements. By judiciously using the <PRE> tag, you can force alignments of images by incorporating a fixed amount of blank text between images. The <PRE> tag forces a browser to render the blanks and thus separate the images. For example, the following line would align several images on a line with blank spaces between them.

```
<PRE>
<IMG SRC="im.GIF">  <IMG SRC="im.GIF">  <IMG SRC="image.GIF">
</PRE>
```

Vertical Alignment

Netscape also introduces other vertical alignment options that correct some of the limitations of HTML 2.0. As we've mentioned, HTML always allowed top, middle, and bottom alignment options that controlled where images lined up vertically in relation to text. Netscape adds other options, including texttop, absmiddle (absolute middle), baseline, and absbottom (absolute bottom). These are not yet part of official HTML 3.0 proposals. Where might you use these additional options? When a single line contains several images of different sizes, the net effect may not be quite what you expected. These options allow you to specify exactly what you intend—for example, align the top of the next image with the top of the basic text line, with the top of the tallest image on the line, or align the bottom with the absolute bottom of the lowest image in the line.

Figure 4.18 shows how images aligned with some of these options would appear. Here is how the source code for these five images appears:

```
<IMG SRC="arrowup.GIF"   ALIGN=BOTTOM> (Image 1)
<IMG SRC="arrowdown.GIF"  ALIGN=MIDDLE>(Image 2)
<IMG SRC="arrowup.GIF"   ALIGN=TEXTTOP>(Image 3)
<IMG SRC="arrowdown.GIF"  ALIGN=ABSMIDDLE>(Image 4)
<IMG SRC="arrowdown.GIF"  ALIGN=BOTTOM> (Image 5)
```

Image 1 aligns with the bottom of the preceding text. Image 2 aligns with the middle of the preceding image. Image 3 aligns with the top of the text on the line. Image 4 aligns with the absolute middle of the vertical space occupied by all images and text. Image 5 aligns with the bottom of the text.

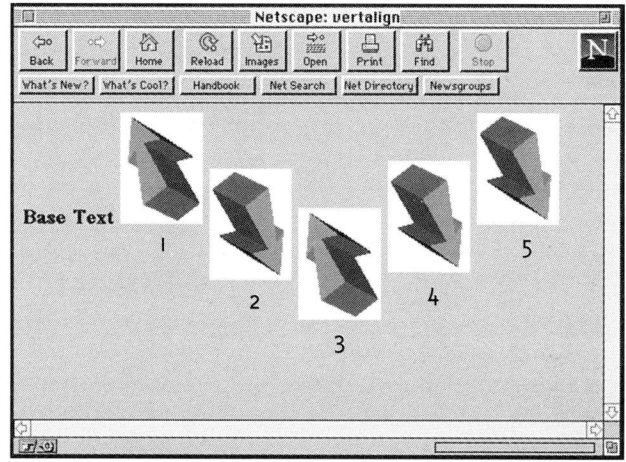

Figure 4.18:
Using Netscape's vertical <ALIGN> options.

Border Option

Netscape introduces options not included in HTML 3.0 proposals that invite you to control the borders on your images. The <BORDER=> option specifies in pixels a border around the image. The example shows parts of the source code that generates Figure 4.19:

```
<IMG ALIGN=TOP SRC="smask.in.gif" BORDER=4>
<IMG ALIGN=TOP SRC="smask.in.gif" BORDER=10>
<IMG ALIGN=TOP SRC="smask.in.gif" BORDER=20>
```

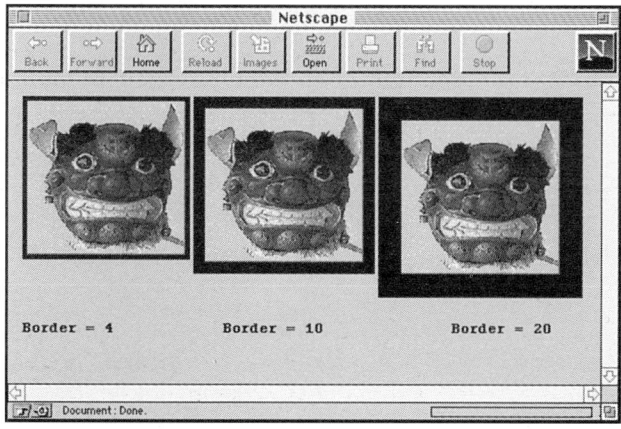

Figure 4.19:
Using the <BORDER> attribute.

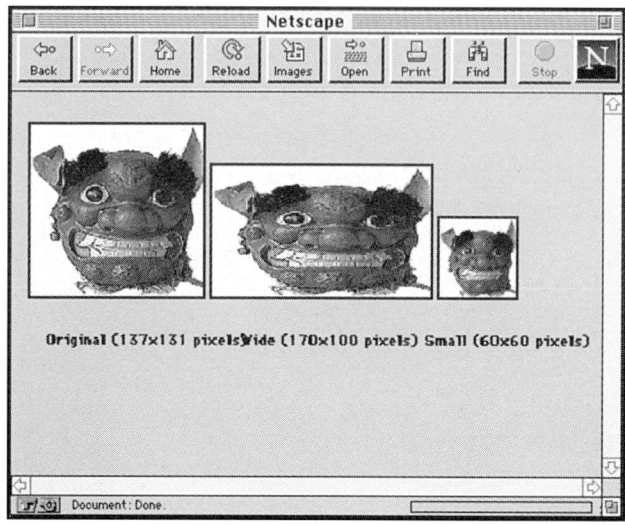

Figure 4.20:
Using the <WIDTH> and <HEIGHT> attributes options to size
images.

Size Option

HTML 3.0 and Netscape allow you to scale and distort images
on the fly. You can use the <WIDTH=> and <HEIGHT=> options
to specify any pixel dimensions you want for your image. The
example that follows shows key parts of the source code that
generate Figure 4.20's display of the same image rendered at
three sizes. If you do not include both width and height
indications, most browsers will proportionately scale the
other dimension so that the image maintains the same
proportional relationship of height to width as the original.
The default unit used by the size tags is pixels; you can
change the unit to *en spaces* (the printer's term for the space
occupied by the letter *n* in the current font) by including a
<UNITS=en> option within the <IMG> tag.

```
<IMG SRC="smask.gif" BORDER=2>
<IMG SRC ="smask.gif" WIDTH=170 HEIGHT=100 BORDER=2>
<IMG SRC ="smask.gif" WIDTH=60 HEIGHT=60 BORDER=2>
```

Low-Resolution Image Loading

Netscape offers a special enhancement—not yet included in
the HTML 3.0 proposals—that allows you to load a small, low-
resolution image before the full-resolution one. This image
will load very quickly and thus make the wait for the full-
resolution image more tolerable to viewers. The option to
accomplish this is a special <LOWSRC> attribute included
in the basic <IMG> tag. You can find more information at

http://www.netscape.com/people/hagan/html/images.html.
Here's an example of the syntax used to produce this effect:

```
<IMG LOWSRC="lowres.jpg" SRC="fullres.jpg">
```

Backgrounds

HTML 3.0 and Netscape allow you to create a background
color or pattern for your Web page through HTML tags. You
accomplish this by adding the <BACKGROUND> property to
the <BODY> tag. You can use any inline image to tile a
background pattern; the browser will tile the image repeat-
edly to fill the browser window. In addition, Netscape adds
features, not yet in the official HTML 3.0 proposals, which
allow you to specify RGB values to color the background and
to change the text color of standard text, links, and visited
links. RGB refers to the standard computer color-naming
system that specifies values for the **r**ed, **g**reen, and **b**lue
components of each pixel.

Figure 4.21 shows a sample page from the *Netscape Enhanced
Hall of Shame* site with an inline image used for a background. The example shows the part of the source code that
generates the background. The tag for incorporating this
inline image is

```
<BODY BACKGROUND="../images/texture1.gif">
```

The designer of this page used a small gray box with the
script words *Hall of Shame* superimposed as the core image
for the background. Figure 4.21b shows the basic image used
to create the background. You can see that the browser
repeated it in a tile format necessary to fill the window.

Using a Netscape enhancement, you can also designate
solid colors for your backgrounds by using the <BGCOLOR=>
attribute. You indicate your desired colors using hexadecimal

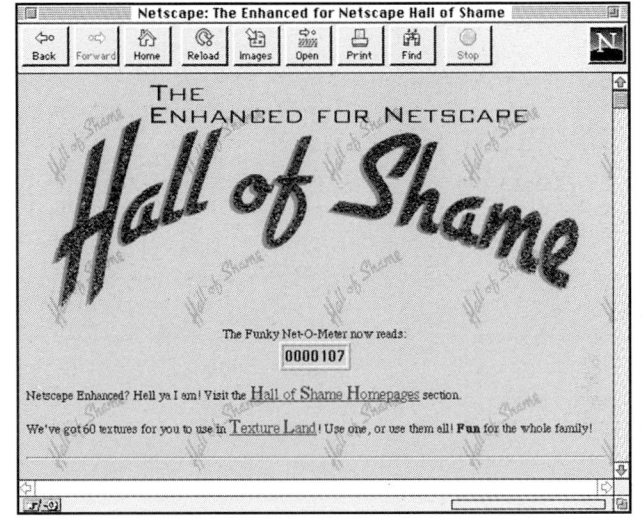

Chris Pearce (yyz@europa.com).

Figure 4.21a:
*The <BACKGROUND> property as used by Netscape Enhanced Hall
of Shame.*
```
http://meat.europa.com/netbin/netscape.htm
```

Chris Pearce.

Figure 4.21b:
*The image used as the background tile in the Netscape Enhanced
Hall of Shame.*

notation, a number system often used in the computer world, which is built around the base 16. This code would generate a solid magenta background:

```
<BODY BGCOLOR="#FF00FF">
```

Even before computers, the theatrical lighting profession and video industry used RGB systems to specify colors. Projected light is mixed by adding different intensities of red, green, and blue light. Color video screens similarly build colors by controlling the intensities used to illuminate the red, green, and blue phosphors of the screen. The computer world adapted this system as a way to specify the color of pixels exactly by designating colors by their components of red, green, and blue. In a full 16.7-million, 24-bit color system, each color component is represented by one byte and can have any of 256 values of red, green, and blue. You can exactly specify a color by indicating the relative intensity of each. For example, a color composed of equal portions of red and blue and no green would appear as some shade of magenta (Red=255; Green=0; Blue=255)

For technical reasons related to the binary nature of computer memory and information processing, a base 16 system is deemed a useful way to represent these values. Our normal number system is a base 10 system in which there are 10 symbols (0-9) and relative position is used to indicate multiples of 10 (423 means 4 hundreds, 2 tens, and 3 ones). Hexadecimal works logically the same way except that it uses positions to indicate multiples of 16, not 10. Because it needs 16 symbols, it needs numerals beyond the normal 0-9. Letters are used for other values, as indicated here:

0=0	4=4	8=8	C=12
1=1	5=5	9=9	D=13
2=2	6=6	A=10	E=14
3=3	7=7	B=11	F=15

The hexadecimal value *A* equals 10 in the decimal system. Similarly the hexadecimal value *5B* equals 91 in decimal (5 x 16 + 11). Until you get used to it this system can be confusing; the hexadecimal value 32 stands not for 3 tens and 2 ones, but rather for the decimal value 50 (3 x 16 + 2) even though it looks like normal 32. For more details on the hexadecimal system and its origins, see my book *Using Computers to Create Art* (Prentice Hall, 1986) or any introduction to computer graphics. Some computer graphics applications such as xv for UNIX will show you the RGB hexadecimal values directly by clicking on a color. PC and Mac applications such as Photoshop show you the relative RGB values but indicate them in decimal rather than hexadecimal notation.

A <BGCOLOR> designation is composed of a triplet of hexadecimal values. In the previous example, FF (255) is the red value, 00 is the green value, and FF (255) is the blue value. After you have some experience with the RGB system, you will find it easy to *mix* your own colors digitally. The reference list that follows points to the background color site that provides the codes for many useful colors by name and displays their hexadecimal equivalents. Also, you can experiment by creating HTML pages that include the <BODY BGCOLOR= "#*rrggbb*"> tag, which your browser will render in color. Table 4.3 presents the codes for some common colors. You can mix millions of combinations.

Table 4.3

Hexadecimal Equivalents of Some Example Colors

Intense Red FF0000	Intense Green 00FF00	Intense Blue 0000FF
Pink FF8888	Light Green 88FF88	Light Blue8888FF
White FFFFFF	Medium Gray 888888	Black 000000
Cyan 00FFFF	Magenta FF00FF	Yellow FFFF00

Information about Backgrounds and Background Colors

- *Netscape's information about the use of backgrounds*
http://home.netscape.com/assist/net_sites/bg/index.html

- *Web site that translates colors into hexadecimal values*
http://www.infi.net/wwwimages/colorindex.html

- *Netscape's sample textures that can be used as background images*
http://home.netscape.com/assist/net_sites/bg/backgrounds.html

- *Hall of Shame's textures that can be used as backgrounds*
http://www.europa.com/~yyz/textures/textures.html

- *Kai's Power Tips site's archive of background textures*
http://the-tech.mit.edu/KPT/bgs.html

Because the <BACKGROUND> property allows radical alterations of color, Netscape's specifications also allow you to indicate the color of normal text, links, and visited links so that text will not get lost in the background. This is accomplished by adding attributes that identify the desired color in the same hexadecimal notation. For example, this source code would render normal text in green, links in blue, and visited links in red:

```
<BODY BACKGROUND="sample.gif" TEXT="#00FF00"
LINK="#0000
FF" VLINK="#FF0000">
```

Beware of some design traps when using backgrounds. Overly complex backgrounds can confuse your Web readers and make it difficult to read the foreground text and images. Changing the expected color of links and text can additionally perplex your readers because many have come to rely on the conventions. Because any background image must be downloaded and tiled before anything else can appear, your Web visitor's waiting time increases. Web readers who have disabled image loading will not see your background image. In your Web surfing, search for sites where the background enhances the appeal and effectiveness and for those where backgrounds detract.

Design excesses and the Netscape Enhanced Hall of Shame

Netscape's and HTML 3.0's extensions greatly increase your repertoire of design possibilities, but they are a double-edged sword. If they are not used with care, they can create Web displays that are garish, confusing, and embarrassing in their excess. Figure 4.21a is drawn from the Netscape Enhanced Hall of Shame. This site is a humorous commentary on the design dangers. Its creators have used many Netscape extensions in extreme fashion. The site is alive with blinking, fonts changing sizes, and images aligned here, there, and everywhere. The site also provides links to other sites that are judged to have badly used the extensions. The site also questions the rush to use new non-standard features that may not be available to all Web users, a design issue discussed throughout this book.

Figures

HTML 3.0 offers a new inline image capability beyond the <IMG> tag called *figures*. The <FIG> tag allows some important new features including incorporating optional captions, overlays, credits, and descriptive text. Regular HTML tags can be applied to the text elements to control their style. Other HTML elements will by default flow around the figure unless the new <NOFLOW> property is added to <FIG> tag.

Figures are still in the proposal stage so you will need to determine if your current browser has the feature before you can experiment with it. Similarly, you will also need to ascertain how widespread the capability is before you incorporate it as part of your public Web pages. Here is an example of the syntax for using the new feature:

```
<FIG HREF="baseimage.GIF">
<OVERLAY HREF="superimpose.GIF">
<CAPTION> A New Figure Image </CAPTION>
<P>Text to accompany the image
<CREDIT>Author's Name</CREDIT>
</FIG>
```

The overlay image would appear on top of the base image. The example shows local file URLs; you can use any images located anywhere on the Web by using URLs showing the full network address. The use of graphic overlays can significantly shorten downloading time. Once a base image is downloaded, it will be kept in the cache and can quickly be redrawn if the same image is reused on other pages. Only new overlays would need to be accessed.

Figures also allow Web designers to designate <SHAPE> hot-zones in the figure and the URL that should be accessed when a user clicks on each area. Previously a similar capability required use of the <IMAGEMAP> structure, which necessitated specially configuring the server to respond appropriately. This new <SHAPE> feature greatly simplifies the authoring of images with active areas and is discussed in more detail in Chapter 7.

Use of Inline Images in Horizontal Rules and Unordered Lists

HTML 3.0 will let you use of inline images in place of the standard horizontal rules. You will only need to include a <SRC=> attribute inside the <HR> tag, as shown in the example.

```
<HR SRC="longimage.GIF">
```

Similarly you will be able to use inline images to replace the bullet markers for list items. You will need only to indicate a <SRC=> attribute inside the UL tag, as shown in the example:

```
<UL SRC="funnymarker.GIF">
```

Banners

The HTML 3.0 specifications will enable a new <BANNER> structure, which will allow for the appearance of standard graphic and text elements on all pages that share the same <BANNER> definition. For example, you would be able to create a logo and standard link buttons that would appear on every page in the set. This part of the specifications is still in the development stage at press time so details and sample syntax are not available.

Table 4.4

HTML 3.0 Inline Image Features

Tag or Option	Function	Comments
<ALIGN=*option*>	Specifies horizontal alignment of image. Enables wraparound text. Property included inside <IMG> tag.	Options include <RIGHT>, <LEFT>, <CENTER>, <BLEEDRIGHT>, <BLEEDLEFT>, <JUSTIFY>.
<WIDTH= *n*> <HEIGHT= *n*> <UNITS=*option*>	Allows arbitrary resizing of inline images. Default unit is pixel. Can also be specified in en units. Properties included inside <IMG> tag.	If only one dimension is given, browsers will automatically calculate the other dimension to maintain original proportions.
<BACKGROUND= (IMAGE)>	Specifies the URL of an image to be used as the background for browser window. Property included inside <BODY> tag.	Browsers will repeatedly tile the image in order to fill the window.
<FIG> </FIG>	Specifies a new figure structure.	Similar to the <IMG> tag but with new capabilites. Not yet widely implemented.
<OVERLAY= *URL*>	Specifies the URL of an image to be rendered on top of a figure. Must be enclosed within <FIG> structure.	Optional. Not yet widely implemented.
<CAPTION></CAPTION>	Tags to enclose text to serve as a caption for figure.	Optional. Not yet widely implemented.
<CREDIT> </CREDIT>	Tags to enclose text to serve as a credit for figure. Must be enclosed within <FIG> structure.	Optional. Not yet widely implemented.
<BANNER>	Specifies a static set of images and text that will appear on a set of pages.	Still tentative.

Table 4.5

Netscape Inline Image Features (Not Yet Included in Formal HTML 3.0 Proposals)

Tag or Option	Function	Comments
<CENTER></CENTER>	Centers the image. These are standalone tags that enclose <IMG> structure.	Netscape syntax prior to official HTML 3.0 proposals.
<HSPACE=n VSPACE=n>	Specifies the horizontal (<HSPACE>) or vertical (<VSPACE>) pixel distance to be inserted between the image and any other elements placed nearby. Property included inside <IMG> tag.	
<BORDER=n>	Specifies the width of the border enclosing an inline image in pixels. Property included inside <IMG> tag.	
<BGCOLOR= "#$rrbbgg$">	Specifies a solid color to be used for background. Property included inside <BODY> tag.	Color must be specified by using hexadecimal values between 00 and FF for red, green, and blue.
<TEXT="#$rrggbb$"> <LINK="#$rrggbb$"> <VLINK="#$rrggbb$">	<TEXT> indicates the color for normal text. <LINK>specifies color for links. <VLINK> specifies color of already visited links. Properties included inside <BODY> tag.	Color must be specified by using hexadecimal values between 00 and FF for red, green, and blue.
<LOWSRC= *image*>	Calls for a low-resolution version of picture to load before the high-resolution version. Property included inside basic <IMG> tag.	Typically is a very small file-size image so it will load quickly.

Helper/Viewer Applications

So how do Web browsers display external graphics? In a brilliant design move, the developers of the Web protocols made the Web extensible. Without predetermining what specific formats it should handle, they built in a general capability for the Web protocol to transmit and potentially interpret any kind of files including media. To accomplish this, they specified that clients be able to call on "helper" or "viewer" applications (also called *helper apps*) to display or process files that the protocol does not intrinsically understand. This means that as long as the proper helper applications are configured, Web browsers can potentially handle any file format available now or in the future.

Even though you have surfed the Net, many of you might never have checked out the helper configuration files of your Web client. They come with default settings that may have worked for you without intervention. Also, new versions of browsers such as Netscape increasingly incorporate the ability to handle the JPEG graphic formats that used to require a helper app to view. Figure 4.22 shows the configuration files of a Mac Mosaic browser. Other browsers will contain similar files. These files map the type of files, using extensions such as GIF, AU, or WAVE, that might be encountered with the helper applications that can handle them.

The helper application process works as follows:

1. Each server has a configuration map that tells it how to handle certain kinds of files (usually called MIME types).

2. It determines the nature of the file being requested by a Web reader by inspecting the extension name at the end of the file—for example, "imagename.jpg" is a graphics file in JPEG compressed format.

3. When you make contact and request a certain resource, the server uses its configuration map to determine the proper protocol to use in sending the file. Internet transmission protocols can mangle image, sound, or program files if they assume the files are text because text is sent by a different protocol. Part of the information in an image file will be lost if it is sent this way.

4. When your browser receives the file, it inspects the extension to see what kind of file it is. It then checks its own configuration map to see what helper application is set up to handle that kind of file.

5. The Web browser then launches the appropriate helper application, which opens the file in a separate window associated with that application. If no helper application is defined, the browser will offer you the option of saving the file or defining the new helper application.

6. You can typically use the application to manipulate the image in a variety of ways. For example, most graphic helper applications can scale the image, convert its formats, crop it, and allow you to save it to a permanent file or discard it.

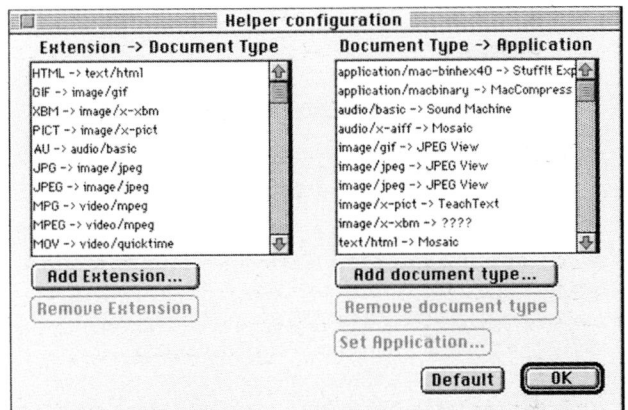

Figure 4.22:
Helper configuration map in Mosaic.

7. You can choose to leave the external window open or shut it, but you must click back in the browser window to return to the standard WWW interface.

Because these helper apps are the environments in which Web readers will view your images, you should be aware of how these helper applications work. How will the graphics appear in different browsers with different helper apps? What options do these applications provide the user? In order to think about these questions, let's take a look at a sample helper graphics application.

GIFConverter is one of the most common helper applications available on the Macintosh. It allows WWW browsers to open several graphic formats including JPEG, GIF, TIFF, PostScript EPSF, and PICT among others. It also allows the user to save images in any of these formats, and thus act as a converter between formats.

Figure 4.23 shows Mosaic's view of a Web page from the "Visible Human Project" and a GIFConverter window that has opened to view an external JPEG image from the site. The figure also shows one pull-down menu from GIFConverter's menubar to show some of the kinds of manipulations that are available. Figure 4.24 shows the window opened by LView, a graphic helper application for Windows. It is displaying a JPEG image of a Balinese dancer from the Smithsonian's archive of high-resolution anthropological images. In addition to providing a viewer, graphic helper apps offer a wide variety of capabilities such as scaling, cropping, rotating, changing color depth, adjusting palettes, and setting compression levels. These manipulations are useful tools for working on your images before placing them on the Web.

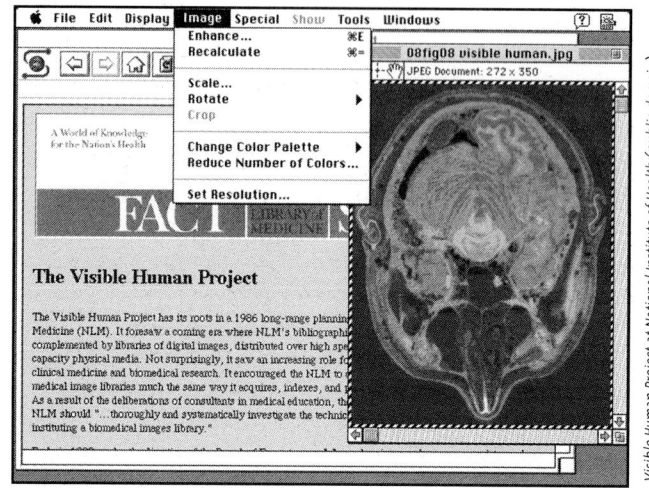

Visible Human Project at National Institute of Health (public domain).

Figure 4.23:
GIFConverter, a Macintosh helper application for viewing external images.

Image from Visible Human Project at http://
www.nlm.nih.gov/factsheets.dir/visible_human.html

Smithsonian Collection (public domain).

Figure 4.24:
LView, a Windows helper application for viewing external images.
```
Image from Smithsonian collection at http://
sunsite.unc.edu:80/pub/multimedia/pictures/
smithsonian/jpeg/new-photo-uploads/BALI.JPG
```

Some Sample Helper Applications for Graphics

Many different helper applications for displaying and manipulating external images are available for all platforms. The following are some current popular helper applications and Net locations for downloading them. There are others available at the Mosaic FTP site (ftp://ftp.ncsa.uiuc.edu/Mosaic/) .

Macintosh:

- **GIFConverter.** A shareware program that lets you display images and work in many different formats, including GIF, TIFF, RIFF, PICT, JPEG (JFIF), MacPaint, and Thunderscan.
- **JPEGView.** Shareware program for working with graphics. Works with JPEG, PICT, GIF, TIFF, and BMP formats.

Both are available for downloading at ftp://ftp.ncsa.uiuc.edu/Mosaic/Mac/Helpers.

DOS/Windows:

- **Lview Pro.** A shareware program that can display GIF, TIFF, JPEG, PCX, BMP, and Targa graphics. Available for downloading at ftp://ftp.ncsa.uiuc.edu/Mosaic/Windows/viewers/lview31.zip.

UNIX:

- **xv.** A shareware program that can display GIF, TIFF, JPEG, Sun raster, and XBMP formats. Available for downloading at ftp://ftp.cis.upenn.edu/pub/xv.

Implementing Transparency and Interleaving Special Effects

Normally inline images completely obscure the background over which they appear. Also they typically are drawn on the page starting at the top and moving down one line at a time until they fill their full rectangle. Web developers have created techniques by which you can make your images appear transparent and by which you can use an "interleaving" process to change the way the images are drawn on the page as they are downloaded.

Transparency

Inline images usually appear in a rectangle that completely obscures the background color of the Web window. Sometimes they include their own color background. Wouldn't it be great if inline images could appear to float on your Web page without this box? They can if you know how.

Some varieties of GIF formatted images allow you to declare one color as a transparency passthrough color. In the cinema and video industry this is called a *key*. Every pixel that has that color value is rendered transparent. On Web clients this means that the background gray (or whatever background color or image has been chosen) shows through. In this amazing effect the image seems to float on the screen. Figure 4.25 illustrates some images in which their background boxes have disappeared.

Figure 4.25:
Transparent image.

Transparency is not achieved with an HTML tag. You must prepare your source images in a special way in order to achieve this transparency. There are several steps:

1. Decide what color will be transparent and clean up your image so that one particular color is used only for the parts of your image that you want to be transparent. Otherwise, parts of your image that happen to be that color will vanish into transparency. You will need to use a color touch-up program such as Adobe Photoshop to manipulate these colors.

   One way to do this is to isolate an image from its background. Using a program such as Photoshop, you select all of the background area and fill it with a solid block of your transparency color. You can also create special effects by introducing the transparency color inside your image to add to the floating effect.

2. Make sure that the GIF image is stored in GIF89a format, which supports transparency. All current shareware graphic helper apps, such as those listed in the section on helper apps, give you this option.

3. Use one of the special transparency shareware or freeware programs—such as giftrans, a freeware UNIX program—to format the image with the target color declared as transparent. Store the image in GIF format.

Most Web clients will now treat the target color as transparent and the image will appear to float above the Web page. The reference list that follows provides pointers to information about creating transparent images on most platforms and to the programs that let you designate the transparency color.

Interleaving

Browsers typically draw inline images by filling in the image's rectangle one line at a time starting at the top. A few inline images, however, seem to resolve into existence, starting with the whole image filling the rectangle with blocky low resolution. As the data loads, you can see the image transform itself from an unfocused image into a clean image.

Many viewers prefer this method of image loading because it gives them an quick sense of the image before they have waited for the whole loading process.

You can incorporate this feature into your images. Several GIF converter shareware programs, listed at the end of this section, offer an option of saving images in the "interleaved" format.

If your Web audience has one of the Web clients that support this capability to progressively display images, it will see your interleaved images appear in this special way. Current versions of Netscape have the capability and other browsers are in the process of incorporating it. Even if your Web audience does not have a browser with this capability, it will still be able see the image, although without the progressive revelation.

Several Web sites offer additional information about these transparency and interleaving techniques, and shareware programs to prepare images are available for downloading.

Pointers to Transparency and Interleaving Techniques

- *Yahoo reference list to information sources*
`http://www.yahoo.com/Computers/World_Wide_Web/`
`Programming/Transparent_Images/`

- *Transparent Background Images Information Page*
`http://melmac.corp.harris.com/`
`transparent_images.html`

- *Macintosh "Transparency" shareware program to create transparent GIF images*
`ftp://ftp.med.cornell.edu/pub/aarong/transparency/`

- *Windows "Lview Pro" shareware program to create transparent GIF images*
`ftp://oak.oakland.edu/SimTel/win3/graphics/`
`lviewp1b.zip`

- *Windows & UNIX "giftrans" shareware programs to create transparent and interleaved GIF images*
`http://melmac.corp.harris.com/transparent_images.html`

- *Windows & UNIX "giftool" shareware programs to create transparent and interleaved GIF images*
`http://www.homepages.com/tools/`

Keeping Viewer Needs in Mind

Loading graphics on the Web is much more time-consuming than loading text. Large images or multiple images seem to take forever. Depending on how busy the Internet is, the load on the particular server containing the documents, the speed of the browser, and so on, users can feel as though they spend all their time waiting for images to display. For this reason, most Web browsers let users disable or delay the loading of inline images.

You must balance your desire to include inline images against the cost of user time. You should be able to justify the use of each image you include on your Web documents. If you must make large graphic files available, you should make them external graphics (with an indication of the graphic's file size). Many users have reported that they routinely turn off the inline image access because they are unwilling to wait for many images to load. How successful is a visually exquisite Web document with many inline images if users ignore them? Figure 4.26 shows the image-control options in Mosaic.

Figure 4.27 shows the steps in the process of loading an inline image after the user has clicked the mouse to request the HTML page that contains the image.

Obviously there are plenty of steps in the inline process that consume time. The following sections include tips for minimizing your audience's waiting time.

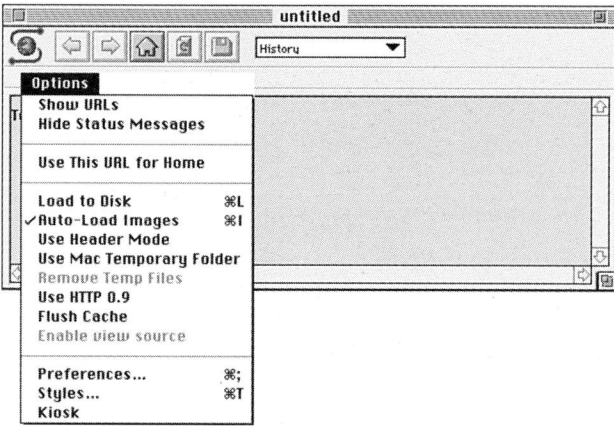

Figure 4.26:
Mosaic's settings for disabling or delaying the loading of inline images.

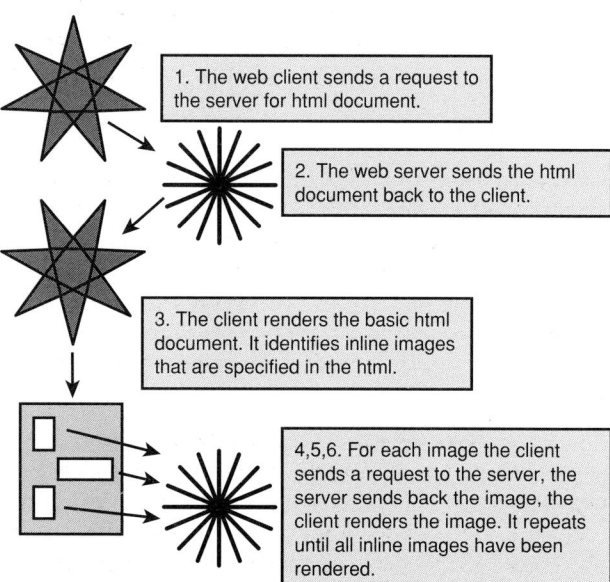

1. The web client sends a request to the server for html document.

2. The web server sends the html document back to the client.

3. The client renders the basic html document. It identifies inline images that are specified in the html.

4,5,6. For each image the client sends a request to the server, the server sends back the image, the client renders the image. It repeats until all inline images have been rendered.

Figure 4.27:
Time-consuming steps in accessing inline images.

Offer the User a Choice

With external images, users have a choice about whether they will access any particular graphic resource. Many archives of images give the viewer information about file size as an aid in decisions about whether to download. Figure 4.28 shows a listing of insect drawings from an archive at the University of Illinois with this kind of information. Inline images don't offer that choice except for configuring your browser to turn off image loading. Some sites have begun to offer alternative HTML pages that omit inline images. For example, Figure 4.29 shows a page from Stanford Student Radio Station KDZU's hot and cool list of Web resources, which offers five versions of the same list—with few, some, or many inline images. It warns the reader about the time load.

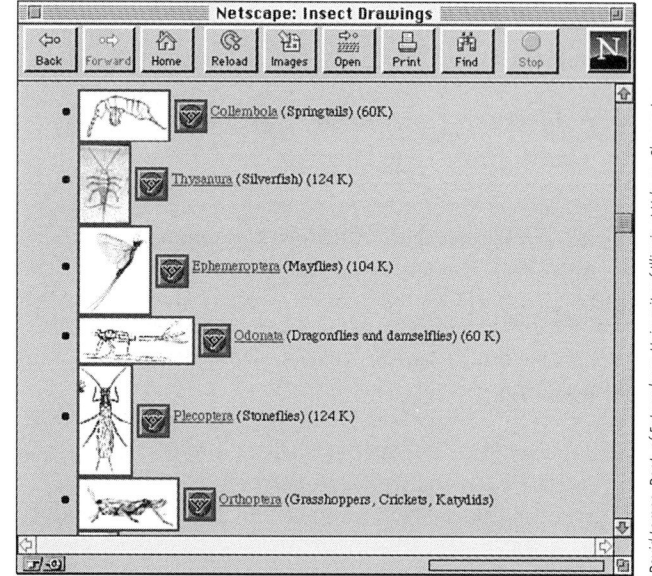

David Lampe, Dept. of Entomology, University of Illinois at Urbana-Champaign.

Figure 4.28:
A Web page of insect drawings that offers users file size information from a University of Illinois archive.
`http://www.life.uiuc.edu/Entomology/insectgifs.html`

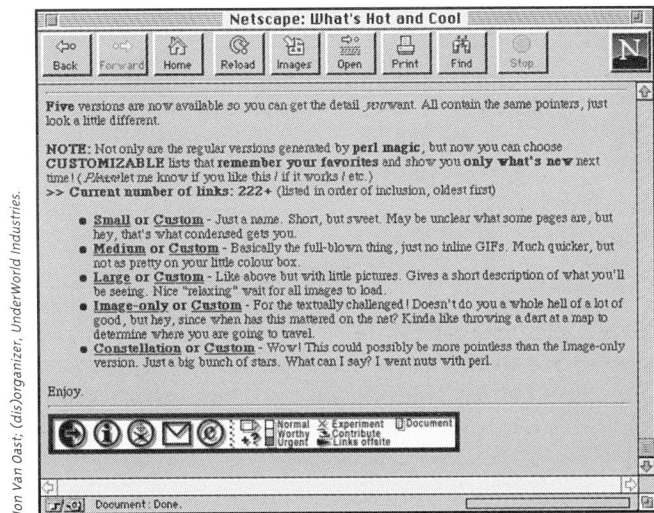

Jon Van Oast; (dis)organizer, UnderWorld Industries.

Figure 4.29:
Options offered by KDZU's Web site based on image loading requirements.
`http://kzsu.stanford.edu/uwi/reviews.html`

Minimize the Size of Images

Large images take more time than small images because they take the server more time to access and take more time to transmit over the Internet. You can strive to minimize the size of the images you transmit. Remember that a 50 percent reduction on each dimension of a rectangular image actually reduces the file to 25 percent on average of its original size, as illustrated in Figure 4.30.

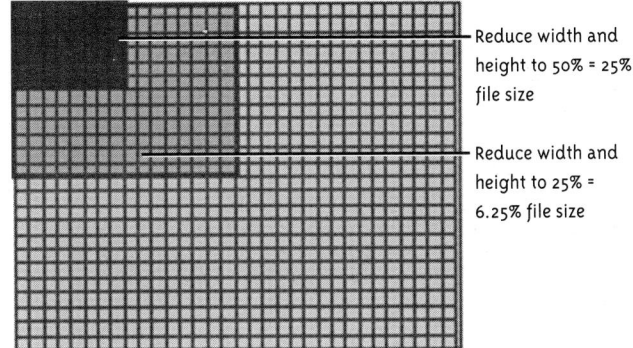

Reduce width and height to 50% = 25% file size

Reduce width and height to 25% = 6.25% file size

Figure 4.30:
Relationship of file-size reduction to height and width reductions.

There are other ways to reduce the size of an image file. You can crop the image to exclude any extraneous material. How many colors are really used in your graphic? You may be able to reduce the file format from 8 bits (256 colors) to 4 bits (16 colors). Consider the amount of compression offered by the different graphics file formats.

Reduced image size does not necessarily need to result in visual impoverishment. Carefully placed small images can have a profound effect. Images, such as long, narrow horizontal forms, which vary from the conventional aspect ratios we've been accustomed to by photography and television, can have much impact for their size. Also, reduced color images can be stylistically appealing in a minimalist sense.

Figure 4.31 shows one way of using multiple small images to create a visual display that fills window space in an interesting way. Each line of the source code consists of multiple <IMG> tags with calls to the same set of images. Browsers will place them next to each other until they run up against the window border.

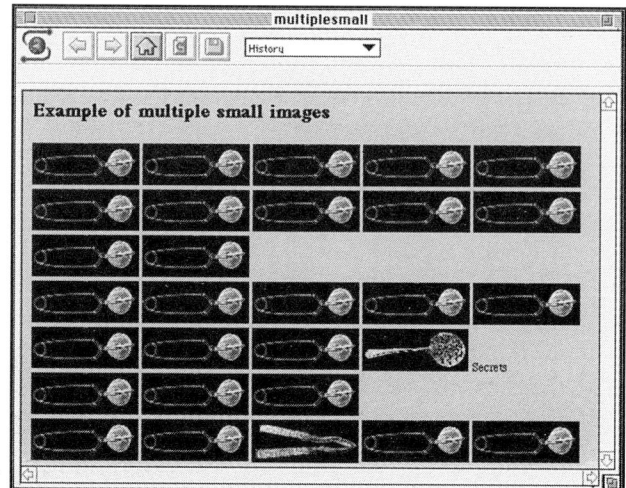

Stephen Wilson.

Figure 4.31:
Visual experimentation with small images.

B. David Cronshaw; TV Net.

Figure 4.32:
A composite image from TVNet.
`http://tvnet.com/TVnet.html`

Saving Time with Composite Images

Note that while small images save time at the transmission step, they do not save time at the accessing step. Three small images will take just as much time for access (connection, inquiry, and server getting ready to send image) as would three large images.

Composite images are a way to save time at these access points. If the page can be designed so that one larger image looks like it is several separate small images, time will be saved. Even though the larger image will take more time to transmit than one smaller image, it will take less time than requesting the several small images that make part of it. Only one access request, connection, and server preparation will be required.

Many composite images you encounter on the Web also serve as hotlinked *imagemaps*. In addition to displaying images that look like they are made of several smaller images, imagemaps also serve as sophisticated hyperlinks, which can determine where the Web visitor has clicked and respond differently. Chapter 7 explains imagemaps in more detail. Even when you are not creating imagemaps, however, composite images can save downloading time. Figure 4.32 happens to be an imagemap, but it is illustrated here to show the visual possibilities of composite images.

Repeating Images

Most browsers keep a cache of recently loaded resources including inline images. Repeated use of the same image can happen very quickly because the browser skips all the steps of making external requests, access, and transmission times. Intriguing visual displays can be created by judicious use of repeated forms, as illustrated in Figure 4.33.

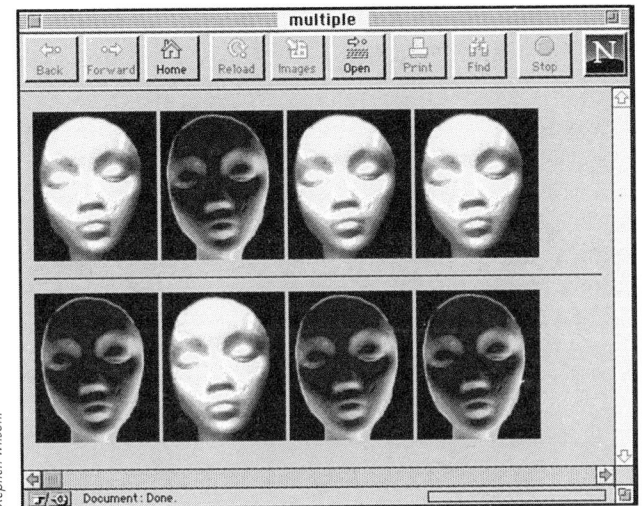

Stephen Wilson.

Figure 4.33:
Repeated images.

Users with Text-Only Browsers

In the midst of the thrill of offering hypermedia on the Web, it is easy to forget some realities that may confront some segments of your audience. Some will be using systems that lack the high bandwidth connection to the Internet necessary for multimedia access (or they may have chosen to disable the image access in order to accelerate access). Some in the Windows and UNIX worlds might be using computers without sound presentation capabilities. Some may use text-based Web browsers such as Lynx that allow users to access the Web and its hypertext features via terminal emulation. What should you do about them?

One approach is to design Web documents so that they work well for both users with state-of-the-art systems and for those who are restricted to text-only systems. For example, you can design captions of images and the text that surrounds them to convey a sense of the image even for someone using a browser that cannot display images. Some Web sites provide text alternatives to key images; Figure 4.34 shows an example from the White House's home page that provides a link to a textual version of the page.

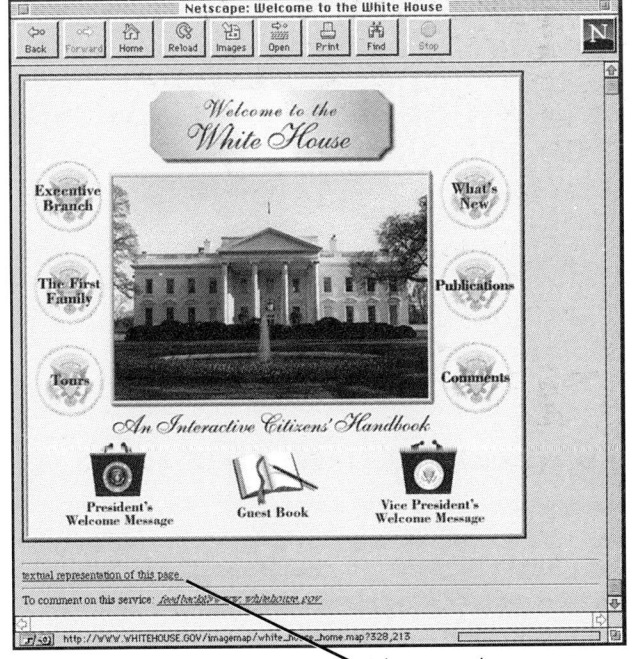

Internet Services at the White House.

Link to text-only page

Figure 4.34:
White House Web page with a link to nongraphical alternative for readers using text-only Web clients.
http://www.whitehouse.gov

Unequal access

Some feel that Web authors need to be extremely sensitive to issues of privilege and unequal distribution of computing access and do what they can to be sure that their productions do not exclude certain classes of users. (See the Web page of the Computer Professionals for Social Responsibility organization for more information about these concerns: http://cpsr.org/home.)

Design Opportunities with Web Graphics

Inline images can be used in a variety of ways. They can be used as initial signature graphics, category indexes, navigational aids, link mechanisms, and as the core subject matter of a site. The images can be in any form—for example, photographic, drawn, cartoons, or computer-generated imagery.

Obtaining Images for Your Pages

How do you use graphics in your Web pages if you do not have drawing programs or image-capture software? The Web makes it easy. Many sites offer online archives of images in a variety of fields such as photography, art, scientific illustration, nature, entertainment, travel, and computer graphics. Many of these sites include public domain images generously offered for free downloading and use. The reference list presents some well-known archives. Just point your Web browser toward the URLs listed in the reference list that follows and navigate through the indexes to find images related to topics that interest you.

Once you have accessed an external image, you can use the display window's file menu to save the image to your local hard disk. If the image is opened in a browser's window, be sure to use the *Save Source* option instead of *Save Text*. Also, be sure to attach the extension at the end of the name that indicates the format of the image—for example JPEG or GIF.

Pointers to Image Archives on the Web

- *Computers:Multimedia:Pictures Archive (Index of Archives)*
`http://www.yahoo.com/Computers/Multimedia/`
`Pictures/Archives/`

- *HTTP—Image Archive—ACM-UIUC (variety of topics)*
`http://www.acm.uiuc.edu:80/rml/Gifs/`

- *UK Image Archive (variety of topics)*
`http://www.comlab.ox.ac.uk/archive/images.html`

- *Smithsonian Image Archive (science, anthropology, history)*
`http://sunsite.unc.edu/pub/multimedia/pictures/`
`smithsonian`

Icons

- *Network Services WWW Icons and Logos*
`http://www-ns.rutgers.edu/doc-images`

- *Icon Browser—Large Collection*
`http://www.di.unipi.it/iconbrowser/icons.html`

- *Searchable Directory Index of Icons*
`http://www.bsdi.com/icons/AIcons/`

Signature Images

Many Web sites include an initial inline image at the beginning of their home pages, as a kind of welcoming emblem or symbol for the resource. Including a starting inline image at the top of a Web page is a very widespread practice. Because first impressions count for so much, you should plan your initial inline image with great care if you decide to use one. The image should immediately communicate some essential qualities of the site, but also contain elements that intrigue and invite the Web visitor to go deeper. Figure 4.35 shows the signature image of the Sundance Film Festival site.

Time to load is an especially important consideration with the first image. Many visitors will be just surfing around. One sure way to turn them off is to hit them with a huge signature graphic that takes a very long time to load. Your challenge here is to create engaging signature graphics that are also small and quick to load. After visitors have committed to your site, you can assume they might be more willing to receive larger images.

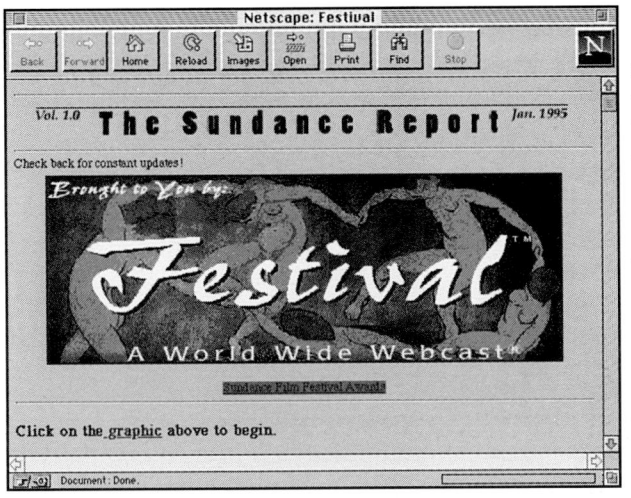

Reprinted by permission of the Sundance Institute. Site maintained by Christian Gaines with the technical assistance of Jim Carlson.

Figure 4.35:
Signature image from the Sundance Film Festival site.
`http://www.interport.net:80/festival/`
`sundance festival`

Dangers of relying only on signature inline images

Text-based browsers will ignore these inline images. Also, many users turn off image loading in order to accelerate access. Thus, you must be careful not to totally rely on the beginning image as the information on your first page because these users will see nothing when the page loads.

Page Dividers and Category Markers

Many sites use inline images as category markers and page dividers. One technique uses a repeating inline image to divide sections. These clarify divisions in the information structure and add visual interest to pages that can often be very long. Uncle Bob's children's site, illustrated in Figure 4.36, uses lines of smiling faces throughout the document to divide sections.

Lines of smiling faces

Bob Allison.

Figure 4.36:
Uncle Bob's children's site uses inline images as section dividers.
`http://gagme.wwa.com/~boba/kids.html`

You can also use inline images to augment site indexes. Many Web sites include a list of hyperlinks (using any of the HTML list structures) at the beginning indicating the various sections Web visitors can link to. Adding a small image to

each item in the list can give readers more information about the sections and also visually enrich the index page. Furthermore, you can integrate your site presentation and assist user navigation by using larger versions of the small index images as signatures for each section. Figure 4.37 shows the visual index page from a Japanese site called the "Atom home page."

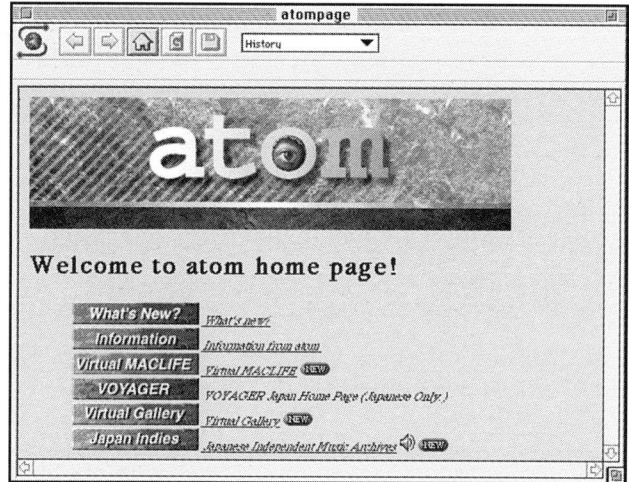

Atomu Suematsu.

Figure 4.37:
Inline images enhancing index at Atom site.
`http://www.atom.co.jp/`

Navigational Aids

Some sites use inline images as navigational aids by creating sets of images that reappear in each section. These images, serving as familiar road signs to guide users, function as shortcut hyperlinks to the main destination pages in a site.

Figure 4.38 shows three examples of inline image sets used as navigational aids.

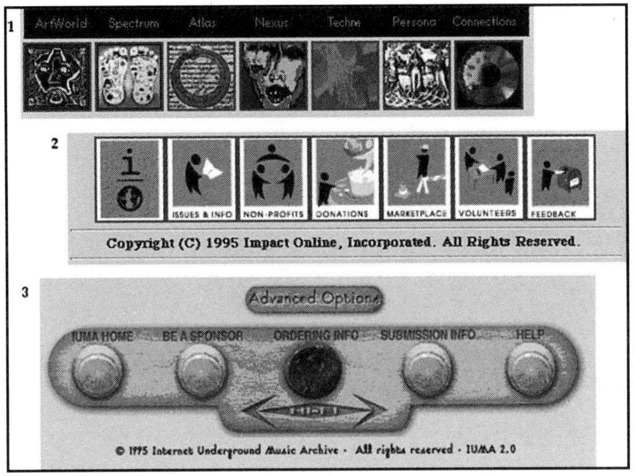

Figure 4.38
Inline images used as navigational maps.
From three sites:
(1) Anima—`http://www.wimsey.com/anima/ANIMAhome.html`
(2) Impact Online—`http://www.webcom.com/~iol`
(3) Internet Underground Music Archive—
    `http://www.iuma.com/`

Coordinated Image Sets

Many highly acclaimed sites use a coordinated approach to inline images. The images in each section are designed to coordinate images in other sections. They repeat formal arrangements, stylistic choices such as color, and graphic components. The content of each graphic conveys information about what can be found in the section and ties the section to other sections. The coordination helps to keep users from the feeling of hypermedia vertigo that is common in moving around Web sites. Figures 4.39a and 4.39b show two of the coordinated graphics from several sections of the WorldCam online movie information site.

Guidelines for External Images

What design guidelines apply to using external images on the Web? Choose carefully between inline and external images, using external only if the size, resolution, or color of the image warrants the special treatment. Choose the external image format carefully, matching the format to the nature of your image. Be sensitive to user downloading time by offering thumbnail previews and warnings about file size. Figure 4.40 shows the downloading time warning posted by the California Museum of Photography for users with slow connections.

Be sensitive to user computing circumstance—for example, by considering what helper applications users are likely to have and paying attention to image size.

These guidelines all deal with the special circumstances of offering external images on the Web. But they miss the most important element, the compelling nature of the image itself. The guidelines for achieving that excellence are the same as they would be for images that have nothing to do with the Web.

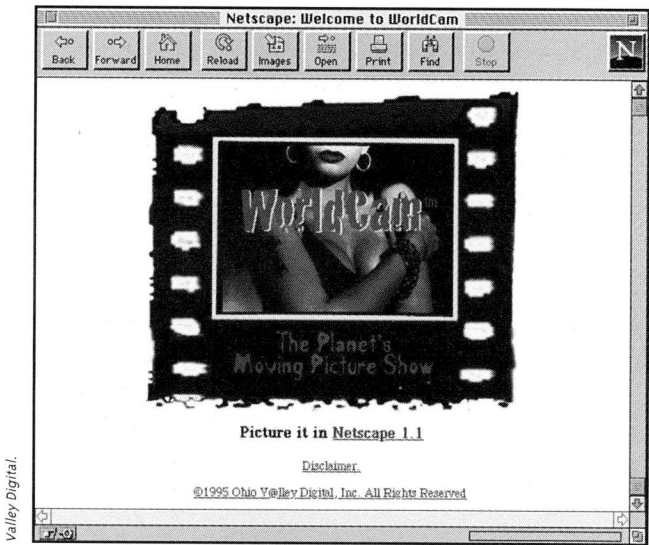

Figures 4.39a and 4.39b:
Inline images found in the sections of the WorldCam site.
`http://www.ovd.com/`

Exercise 4.2 steps you through the process of adding graphics to your site based on the site's content.

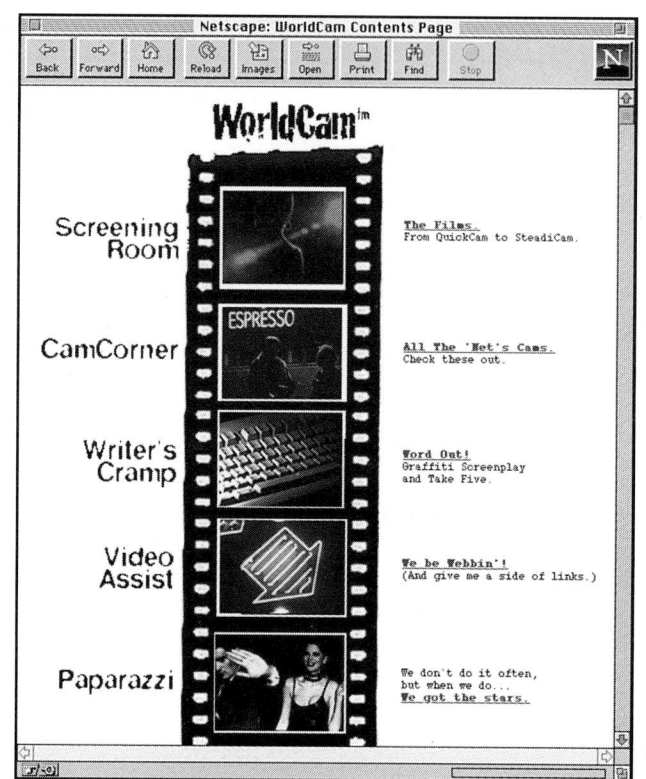

University of California, Riverside/ Museum of Photography.

> **University of California, Riverside**
>
> **California Museum of Photography**
>
> **Continue with graphic presentation, or switch to text?**
>
> **AVISO:** If you have a slower SLIP or PPP connection to the Internet, you might want to use just text lines and choose to download selected photographs.
>
> - Continue with GRAPHIC PRESENTATION
>
> - Switch to just TEXT DESCRIPTIONS
>
> **NETWORK EXHIBITIONS**

Figure 4.40:
California Museum of Photography warning to users with slow connections.
`http://cmp1.ucr.edu/`

Exercise 4.2:

Adding graphics based on a site's content

This exercise continues the revisions to the Conceptual Design site introduced in Exercise 3.2 in Chapter 3. Because this site advertises an art program, the creators were interested in adding intriguing and informative graphics to their pages. We'll walk you through some of steps used in creating the graphics for this site. Figure 4.41 shows the result.

Step 1:

The site needed a signature graphic. A 3-D display of key concept words was created with a 3-D modeling program and saved in GIF format. This image conveyed the site's interest in cultural analysis and the use of contemporary tools. We rendered the graphic transparent by processing it with the Transparency program for the Macintosh. Minimizing file sizes was a major consideration in all the images, so we kept all images relatively small and simple. This image occupied 8K.

Step 2:

In order to better use the full width of the window, we placed the graphics and Introductory text into a borderless table. The table allows predictable control of placement and easy alignment. The Align left option also could have been used to accomplish the placement of text next to the image. We used actual HTML text—instead of incorporating the text into the image—so that text-only browsers and users that had deactivated image loading would still get the information. The table has one row of two side-by-side cells. Here is the source code that creates the top image and text:

```
<TABLE>
<TR>
<TD><IMG SRC="4words.trans.gif ALT= "Art,
 Technology, Theory, Research" width=200>
<TD>
<DL>
<H2> Conceptual Design/Information Arts</H2>
<H4><B><EM>An arts program that explores the
 relationship of art, science, technology
 and culture </EM></B>
 </H4>
<H5>-Located at San Francisco State University</H5>
<TABLE border> <TR> <TD><A HREF=
 "textonly.html">Click for text only version</A>
 </TABLE>
</DL>
</TABLE>
```

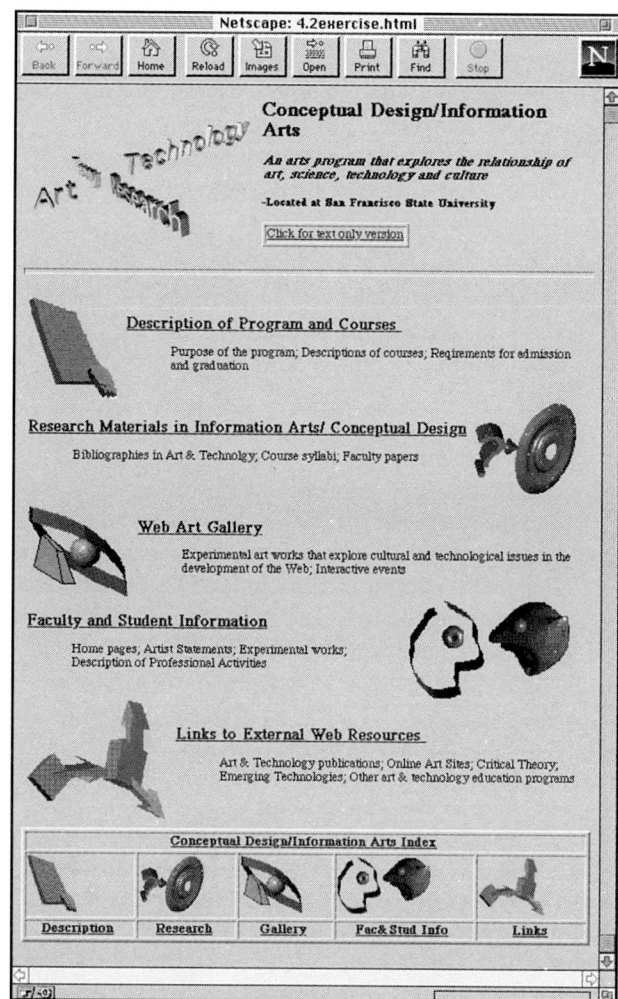

Stephen Wilson.

Figure 4.41:
Sprucing up a text-only Web site.

Step 3:

We indicated <ALT> text so that the keywords of the image will display for those without graphics. We provided a link to a text-only version for Web visitors who want that. Visually we placed that link inside a one-cell table in order to take visual advantage of table borders. It was a table within a table.

Step 4:

We added a small index graphic for each of the main sections that readers could link to. To maintain consistency, these were also created in a 3-D modeling program and rendered in similar colors to the main signature graphic. Each symbolically referred to the topic of its section. These images will be used again as the signatures for the pages of each section that the user might link to. Again, to control alignment, we used the table structure. Each section consists of a two-cell table containing the image and HTML formatted link text. This index will make perfect sense even if Web visitors have deactivated image loading.

To increase the visual interest, we alternated the horizontal placement of images and text for each section. This was easily accomplished by switching the placement of the <IMG> tag and HTML text in the first and second cell of the table that makes up each section. Note that in some situations a totally standardized left-margin placement of the images might be more desirable. Each image was made transparent and very small to speed downloading. Each image is approximately 4K. Here is the code for the first section on "Description of Program." The code for all the other sections is structurally the same except for the switch of image and text between the cells.

```
<TABLE>
<TR>
<TD>
<IMG SRC="descr.GIF">
<TD>
<DL><H3>
<DT><A HREF= "Description.html">Description of
 Program and Courses </A></H3>
<DD>Purpose of the program; Descriptions of courses;
 Requirements for admission and graduation
</DL>
</TABLE>
```

Step 5:

Originally the page had a table at the bottom that served as a general, quick hypertext index for Web users. This link table, which appears at the bottom of every section, allowed Web users instant access to all sections and to the introductory index page. We added the section images to the table to make it visually more interesting and reinforce its navigational structure. We used the height property inside of the <IMG> tag to decrease the size of the images. Because these are the same GIFs as used in the index, they were loaded from the cache and required no extra network access time. The graphics were easily added to the original table by adding another row to the table that consists only of the GIF images. Here is the code for the index table:

```
<TABLE BORDER=2 WIDTH=100%>
<TR>
<TH COLSPAN=5> <A HREF= "Index.html"> Conceptual
 Design/Information Arts Index</A>

<TR> <TD> <IMG SRC= "descr.GIF" Height=50> <TD>
 <IMG SRC= "res.GIF" Height=50> <TD> <IMG SRC=
 "gallery.GIF" Height=50> <TD> <IMG SRC=
 "facinfo.GIF" Height=50> <TD> <IMG SRC= "links.GIF"
 Height=50> </TR>

<TR> <TH> <A HREF= "descr.html"> Description</A>
 <TH> <A HREF= "Research.html"> Research</A> <TH>
 <A HREF= "Gallery.html"> Gallery</A> <TH>  <A HREF=
 "Hopage.html"> Fac&Stud Info</A> <TH>  <A HREF=
 "Links.html"> Links</A></TR>
</TABLE>
```

The graphics on this page served several purposes. They made the site visually more intriguing and reinforced the information design of the site. Because they were very small files, they accomplished a lot without making the user wait forever.

Summary

My best advice for working with Web graphics is to study as many Web and non-Web images as you can. Note the ones that inspire and excite you and see if there is something you can learn from how they accomplish their effects. Read what you can of theory and technique. Experiment with your own Web offerings and solicit honest response. Revise and try again.

The next chapter continues our tour of media by exploring Web sound. Its strategy is the same as this chapter's—assessing the special opportunities and possibilities of working with one of the exciting media formats on the Web.

Chapter 5

Working with Sound on the Web

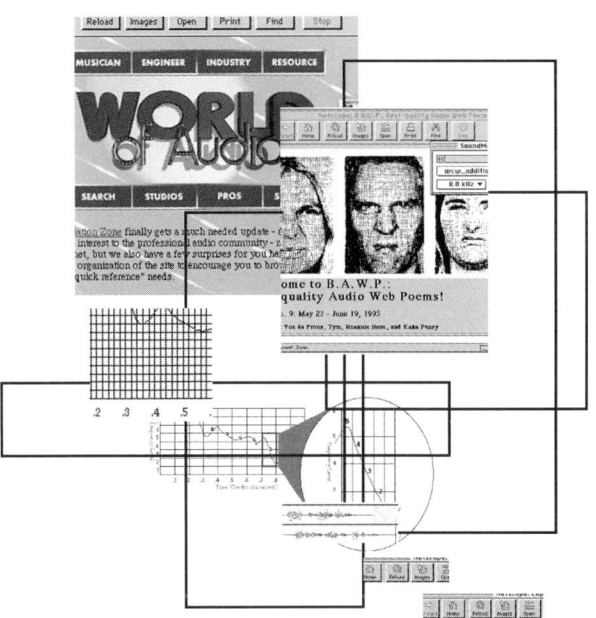

Sound fills a space like text and image cannot. Speech can convey the sense of a person that is missing from text. Music can draw on centuries of cultural references. The richness of sound is part of the vitality of the Web and its growing appeal.

There are many reasons you might want to use sounds in your Web pages. You might want to offer resources that are intrinsically sound-based, such as music, speeches, drama, spoken poetry, or sound art. You might want to annotate other Web resources with your own spoken commentary. Experimenters are exploring a wide variety of unusual sounds such as clocks ticking, synthesizers speaking, and the wind blowing.

There are many user-friendly computer sound tools that make it possible for you to work with sound even if you have a limited understanding of the technical basics. As a Web author, however, you will need to know as much as you can because it will help you ensure that your sounds work well on the Web. You'll need to choose appropriate cross-platform sound formats, understand which helper applications can convert or support these formats, prepare your sounds in the most appropriate format, and anticipate future Web sound developments.

From the user's perspective, accessing sounds is much like accessing external images: your browser must know how to interpret the file format in order to know how to deal with it. Users will need to use a helper application to play back your sounds and their Web browser will need to be configured to find the helper application when sound files are downloaded. When your browser accesses a sound resource (indicated by the extension on the filename), it launches the application and offers an external window that allows you to play the sound or manipulate it in other ways. There is no standard inline sound option that automatically loads sound with the basic HTML page, although some developers are working on that capability. (For example, see the description of Real-Audio in Chapter 10.)

You don't have to learn any new HTML codes to work with sounds. You add links to sounds with the same anchor tags you use with external images, as you saw in Chapter 4. In order to offer a sound, you need to capture it with sound digitizing hardware or download a file from an existing source such as a CD-ROM of sound clips or an online sound archive. Next, you'll need to convert your sound to a format that most Web visitors are likely to have. Once you've converted it, you use the anchor linking tags to let your Web readers access the sound. The source code that follows shows an example:

```
<A HREF="dogbark.AU"> Hear my dog bark </A>
```

(The AU at the end of the filename is the extension for the UNIX μLaw sound format that has become standard on the Web. The μLaw format has become standard because it was available early on all platforms and because it can produce smaller file sizes than other formats such as WAV or SND.)

Figure 5.1 shows a Web page from the Kraftwerk site. Kraftwerk is a European band famous for their experimental music. They offer samples from several of their albums. Here is the HTML coding for accessing a sound clip from their work "Technopop":

```
<A HREF= "http://www.cs.umu.se/studenter/kraftwerk/
Audio/techno_excerpt.au"> Technopop -
Demoversion 1983 (au-format) - 4.0 MB  </A>
```

The site lists the format and length of the sound so that Web users can decide whether they want to download it—a good Web etiquette practice.

By now you already know enough to create a Web page with sound resources. In Exercise 5.1, you will create a Web page with a link to a sound of the noises elephants make. We give the URL for finding this sound resource online, and the reference list at the end of the exercise offers pointers to some additional Web sound archives in case you want to experiment further. In this exercise you will just create a link to the sound rather than actually placing it on your local hard disk. Later, you will learn how you can download the sound to make it a local resource.

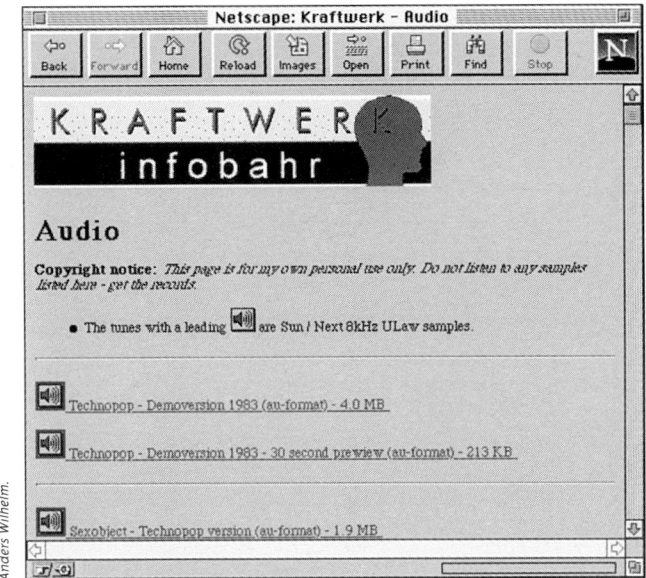

Anders Wilhelm.

Figure 5.1:
Kraftwerk offers access to samples of their music.
`http://www.cs.umu.se/studenter/kraftwerk/Audio/`
`audio_kraftwerk.html`

Exercise 5.1:

Use a link to place a sound on your page; then test it with a browser

Step 1:

Launch your Web browser and establish a live connection to the Internet. Point your browser toward the ACM sound archive at http://www.acm.uiuc.edu/rml/Sounds/.

Step 2:

You will see a set of generic folders listing various kinds of sounds. Open the folder called "Sound Effects," which contains the sounds we want to use in this exercise. You will see a long list of sounds. Each item gives a short name of the sound, its length in bytes, the date it was entered in the archive, and a link to the sound. Most of the sounds are in AU format.

Step 3:

To create your links, you need to know the exact URL of the sounds. We are going to use the sound called "elephant sound." The URL for our elephant sound is http://www.acm.uiuc.edu/rml/Sounds/Sound_effects/elephant.au. (Most browsers will display the URL of a potential link as you move your cursor over it. For example, Netscape shows it on the bottom below the horizontal scroll bar.) Move the mouse pointer over the elephant sound entry and you will see its address. You can also set your browser to view the source code for this Web page; this will enable you to see all the URLs embedded in link tags in the document.

Step 4:

Now it's time to create your Web page. First enter the text and HTML tags for this example as follows:

```
<HTML>
<HEAD><TITLE>Elephant Sounds</TITLE></HEAD><BODY>
<H2>Listen to elephant trumpet sounds.</H2>
<HR>
<DL>
<DT> Accessing sounds on the Web
<DD>Here is what an elephant sounds like. (8176
 bytes - AU format)
```

```
</DL>
</BODY>
</HTML>
```

Step 5:

The only code that we are adding is the link for the sound. Change your text to read as follows:

```
Here is what an <A HREF= "http://www.acm.uiuc.edu
rml/Sounds/Sound_effects/elephant.au">elephant
</A>sounds like. (8176 bytes — AU format)
```

Step 6:

Save your document as an ASCII text file. Use .html (if you're using a Macintosh or UNIX or .htm for a DOS/Windows platform) for the filename's suffix. Here is what the source code for your final document should look like:

```
<HTML>
<HEAD><TITLE>Elephant Sounds</TITLE></HEAD>
<BODY>
<H2>Listen to elephant trumpet sounds.</H2>
<HR>
<DL>
<DT> Accessing sounds on the Web
<DD>Here is what an <A HREF= "http://
www.acm.uiuc.edu/rml/Sounds/Sound_effects/
elephant.au">elephant</A>sounds like. (8176
bytes — AU format)
</DL>
</BODY>
</HTML>
```

Step 7:

Activate your Internet connection if you went offline after viewing the Sound Effects site.

Step 8:

Access this new page you have created using the Open Local or Open File option. Your Web page should look similar to Figure 5.2. The word *elephant* should be highlighted as a link.

Step 9:

Click the link. Your browser will load the sound file into its cache. Your browser should then open a sound helper application and offer a sound control window that will let you play the indicated sound.

Troubleshooting sound links

What if the sound doesn't link successfully and the sound doesn't play? There are several things to check: Is your link correctly formatted and does the URL of the sound link exactly match the example? Remember wrong case, extra spaces, and misplaced slashes will all cause the link to fail. Also check the configuration file of your browser. Web browsers rely on the MIME convention that tells them what helper application should be used for files of certain types with certain extensions. Make sure that the configuration file shows that sound files with the AU extension should be linked to an appropriate helper application for your platform. Also make sure that your browser is configured for a sound helper application and that the application is present on your hard disk.

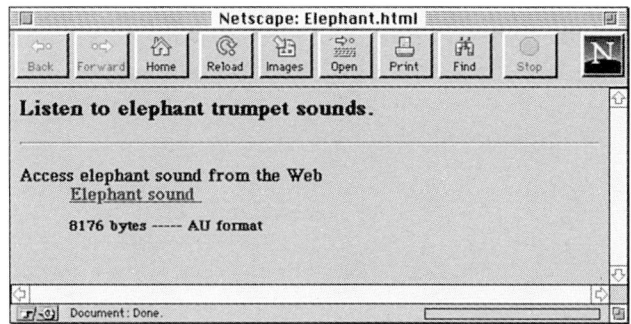

Figure 5.2:
Creating a Web page to access external sounds.

A Quick Primer on Computer Sound Technology

How do computers record, generate, and control sound? Although a full explanation is not feasible here, this section offers a brief introduction to synthesized and sampled sound. Readers should consult the references listed in the pointer sidebar for computer-mediated sound for more details on computer sound technology. Figure 5.3 shows screen shots from the World of Audio, one of the many sites offering technical information to sound producers.

Pointers to Sound Archives

- *Index to Sites with Audio Clips at Northwestern U. (sources in voice, music, and other sounds)*
`http://www.eecs.nwu.edu/~jmyers/other-sounds.html`

- *International movie sounds*
`http://sunsite.sut.ac.jp/Multimed/Sounds/Movies`

- *Yahoo sound index*
`http://www.yahoo.com/Computers/Multimedia/Sound/`

- *WWW Virtual Library index of audio archives*
`http://www.comlab.ox.ac.uk/archive/audio.html`

- *Netherlands Sound Archive*
`http://pmwww.cs.vu.nl/archive/sounds-html/index.html`

Pointers to Information about Computer-Mediated Sound

- *IRCAM (Institut de Recherche et Coordination Acoustique/Musique)*
`http://www.ircam.fr/`

- *Computer music tutorial (UC Santa Barbara)*
`http://www.ccmrc.ucsb.edu/htmls/tutorial/tutorial.html`

- *Electronic and computer music faq*
`http://www.cis.ohio-state.edu/hypertext/faq/usenet/music/netjam-faq/faq.html`

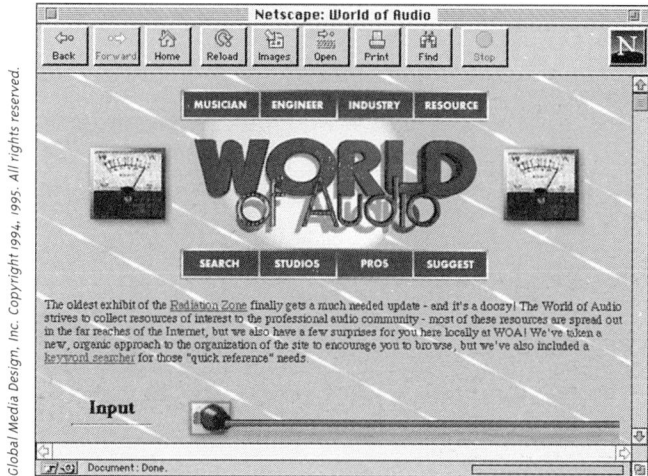

Figure 5.3:
World of Audio site; offering technical information to sound producers.
`http://www.magicnet.net/rz/world_of_audio/woa.html`

It's possible to work with computer sound without knowing much on the technical side. User-friendly sound manipulation programs allow you to record and alter sounds on your computer and make them available on your Web pages. As you start to experiment, however, you will realize you need more than a basic understanding. You will need to make decisions about formats and you may want to manipulate sound in ways that are not standard. Furthermore, researchers are actively trying to expand the Web's capabilities with sound via innovations such as new formats and real-time interactive sound. The more you know, the better able you will be to take advantage of these new developments.

Advent of Computer Sound

Contemporary computer and electronic technology have accelerated the development of technologically based sound. There are now sophisticated techniques for sound synthesis and digital recording. The visionary collaboration of sound artists and equipment manufacturers to develop MIDI (Musical Interface for Digital Instruments) standards ensured worldwide compatibility among equipment and software and brought prices down. Samplers are now a vibrant part of the world music community. Increasingly, computers are being produced with built-in sound capabilities.

Macintoshes and some UNIX machines such as Suns and HPs always had sound capability and now Windows and UNIX platforms are beginning to arrive with sound technology as standard equipment. Inexpensive software for digital sound manipulation is available on all platforms.

The widening access to sound technology has opened digital sound as a potential art and communication form for increasing numbers of participants. For example, synthesizers and sequencing software enable even individuals without the physical coordination to play traditional instruments to work with sound in sophisticated ways. High-quality sound digitizers and sound-editing software offer capabilities that were available only in specialized, expensive sound studios a few years ago.

Synthesized Sound

Computer sound falls roughly into two major categories: synthesized and sampled. Synthesized sound depends on electronic components to generate synthetically systematic variations in voltages that drive speakers to create sound. The components are organized to give control over features of sound such as frequency (pitch), amplitude (loudness), waveshape, sound envelopes, and other characteristics that help define the differences among sounds. Internal computer sound chips, sound boards, and special external devices such as synthesizers are constructed to give the user control over the generation of sound.

Contemporary electronic musicians rely on the MIDI standard to orchestrate communication between computers and sound generators. The MIDI standard covers both the nature of hardware connections and the software conventions for representing sounds. A MIDI file contains a sequence of indications for the timing of notes being turned off and on, indications of which synthetic instrument should sound each note, and control of other effects. If the MIDI file and the instrument conform to the right standard, the file can be played on many different instruments and be manipulated with any MIDI software. Also, the file takes little storage space because it indicates only abstract instructions about notes rather than the actual digitized recording. Figure 5.4 shows a schematic representation of the synthesis of complex sounds from simpler wave forms.

Online Resources for MIDI Information

- *MIDI home page*
`http://www.eeb.ele.tue.nl/midi/index.html`

- *Introduction to MIDI*
`http://www.eeb.ele.tue.nl/midi/intro.html`

- *MIDI Farm*
`http://www.midifarm.com`

- *MIDILink Musician's Network*
`http://www.midilink.com/users/midilink/`

- *World of audio MIDI info*
`http://www.magicnet.net/rz/world_of_audio/`
`midi_pg.html`

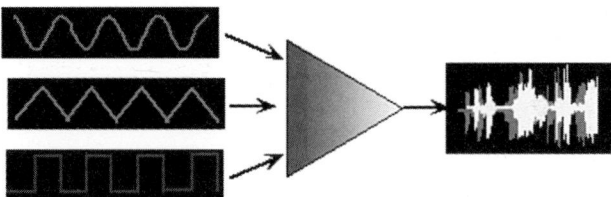

Figure 5.4:
Synthesized sound.

Sampled Sound

Sampling is the name given to digital recording. A sound is converted by sampling electronics into a digital form that the computer can understand and store. All information inside a computer must ultimately be stored in memory as discrete values. Naturally occurring sound such as speech and vibrating materials, however, can be characterized as *analog* events. This means the sounds are continuously varying in their qualities. Frequencies do not usually change abruptly in discrete jumps. Sampling converts this continuous wave into the discrete values that will represent it in computer memory and processing.

In sampling, an electronic component called an *analog-to-digital converter* reads in the sound flow (represented electrically as changing voltages) and periodically converts the voltage at each instant into a discrete value. The process of taking these sequential readings is the sampling process. The accuracy with which the discrete values can faithfully represent the changing flow of the sound is directly related to how often this sampling occurs. *Sampling rate* is the term used to describe how many examples of frequencies are recorded in a unit of time—for example, a second. The higher the sampling rate, the more subtleties of change can be captured.

The number of bits of computer memory given to each sample can affect the accuracy of the sampled sound. Allowing two bytes of memory (16 bits or 65,536 possible values) instead of one byte (8 bits or 256 possible values) means that more subtlety of variation can be captured. Audio CDs typically use 16-bit resolution. The experimental site called the World of Audio (illustrated in Figure 5.3) offers a "Bandwidth Listening Room" in which you can hear the effects of various sampling rates, bit resolutions, and compression schemes on samples of sound.

Figure 5.5 shows a schematic representation of a sound wave varying over time. It illustrates the advantage of increasing the sampling rate. In the large graph a frequency sample is taken every tenth of a second. The frequency value of the sound wave must be represented by one number for each unit of time. (For the sake of illustration, the frequency levels in the illustration are represented as simple numbers.) The bold numbers next to the curve are the sample values. You can see that in some time segments, that one number does not do a very good job of representing the changing frequencies. For instance, the time period between .7 and .8 is best represented by the value 3 even though the frequency varies around that value significantly.

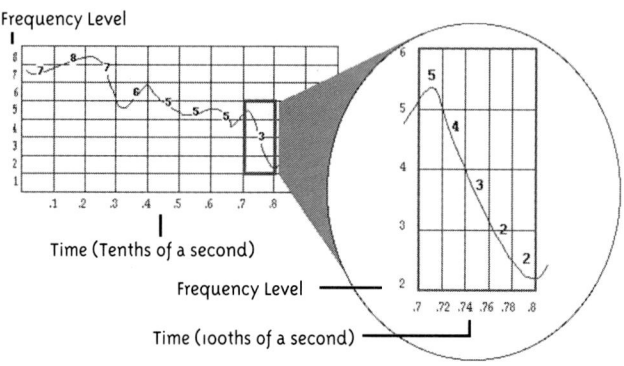

Figure 5.5:
The effects of increasing sampling rate.

The small blow-up graph shows the advantage of multiplying the sampling rate by 5. Assuming that frequency samples were taken every .02 of a second, you can see that the sound will be represented by the sample values 5, 4, 3, 2, 2 instead of just by 3. This set of values is a more accurate representation of the sound's frequency change over time. In the computer graphics world, screen resolution offers a good analogy. A computer screen that can only display 320 x 240 pixels is not going to be able to show as fine detail as the same size screen displaying 640 x 480 pixels.

As you create sounds for the Web you will often need to make decisions about sampling rates. You can see that increasing the sampling rate increases the accuracy of the digital representation of the sound. Unfortunately, it also increases the storage space and downloading time for your files.

Figure 5.6 shows another way you can increase the fidelity of your sampled sounds—increasing the resolution of each sample. If you use 8-bit sampling, each sample can assume only 1 of 256 values. 16-bit sampling allows each sample to assume any of 65,536 values. Because of the binary nature of computer memory, using 16 bits instead of 8 bits actually multiplies the number of gradations by a factor of 256. Since it would be difficult to display this level of detail in the figure, the blow-up box shows the results of merely doubling the resolution for representing frequency levels. More of the changing wave form can be represented because there are finer gradations available for representing the best values in each time sample. The values extend from 2 to 8 instead of 2 to 5 as in the previous example. One analogy in the computer graphics world is numbers of colors possible per pixel. A system capable of showing 16.7 million colors can portray much more subtlety of image than one only capable of 256 colors.

Deciding on the resolution of your sampled sound is another decision you will need to make as you work with sound. Again there is a trade-off of accuracy versus storage because file sizes will be doubled with 16-bit resolution.

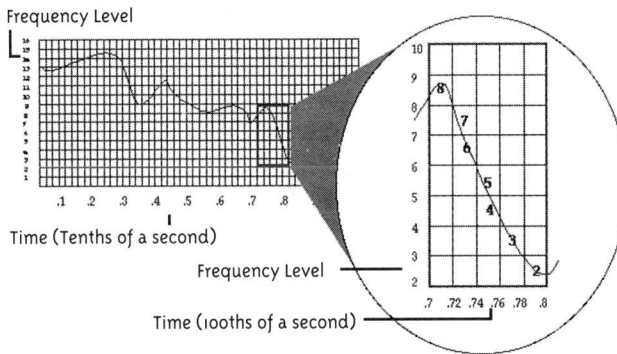

Figure 5.6:
The effects of increasing bit resolution.

Most computers on the market that are equipped with sound come with rudimentary sound sampling capabilities. They allow users to input sound that is digitally sampled and stored. Most have a sound chip for output that can create simple synthesized sounds or play back sampled sounds stored in the computers' memories. Most of these sound chips have the ability to generate higher quality sound than is apparent when heard on the low quality small speakers inside computers. Redirecting the sound signal to an external amplifier and good speakers offers a decent quality sound. Those who want even more sophisticated sound capabilities must buy special sound boards or external devices (usually linked by MIDI to the computer).

Although they differ in some details, all digitized formats fundamentally enact the same process of storing samples that some sound capture hardware has extracted from a changing sound signal. Most also offer similar kinds of choices about sampling rates, bit resolution, channels of sound to be used (stereo or mono), and compression, which will be discussed in sections that follow. Although there is significant debate about the differences among them in technical details of how they actually arrange files and their sampling and compression algorithms, these discussions are not feasible here and will not impact your sound work on the Web now. They may become more important as new proposals for Web sound are promoted. Interested readers can consult the sources in the reference list that follows for more details.

Information on Audio File Formats

- *FAQ on sound formats*
`http://www.cis.ohio-state.edu/hypertext/faq/`
`usenet/audio-fmts/top.html`

- *MIT information on sound formats*
`http://tns-www.lcs.mit.edu/vs/audiofile.html`

- *Sigsound computing & sound*
`gopher://gopher.acm.org/`
`11the_files.sig_forums.sigsound`

Choosing a Sound Format for Web Publishing

You must make several decisions before you put sounds on your Web pages. Should you publish in MIDI format or in a digitized format? If you choose digitized sound, which specific file format should you use? How should you juggle the trade-offs among sound quality, availability on different platforms, file sizes, and transmission times?

Digitized (Sampled) Sound Formats

Many computers are well-equipped to handle sampled sound, but as a Web publisher you'll face the dilemma of addressing diverse computing platforms. Each computing platform has its own native sound file formats. For example, Audio Interchange File Format (AIFF) is in common use on the Macintosh, WAVE (WAV) is in use on Windows machines, μlaw format sound (AU) is used on UNIX machines. (There are several variants on the AU formatted sounds including μLaw, a-law, 8-bit linear, and 16-bit linear encodings. I refer to the whole family as μLaw.) Other sound file formats are in use in each environment, but these are the most common.

There are two sound formats competing for honors as the cross-platform standard. The UNIX sound format (μLaw, indicated with the extension .AU) has been the most popular sound format in the Web community to date. Thus, Web sound composers in Macintosh and Windows environments usually use helper applications to convert the standard sound formats in their environments into the AU audio format. AU format may become even more important in the future because developers are working to include built-in AU sound capability in new browsers.

Recently, MPEG audio has also been proposed as another cross-platform standard (MPEG audio is related to MPEG video, which is discussed in the next chapter). Because MPEG audio takes much computing power to convert other formats and its helper applications are not yet widely distributed, it is not yet a popular cross-platform standard.

Decisions about Sampling and Bit Resolution

No matter what format you decide on, you will have to make decisions about sound parameters such as sampling rate, bit resolution, and number of channels (mono vs. stereo). All sound editing and manipulation programs for the various platforms will enable you to set these parameters. What sampling rates does the computer sound input hardware and software support? Common rates are 5khz, 8khz, 11khz, 22khz, and 44khz. Khz stands for kilohertz or thousands of variations (samples) per second. Remember, the higher the sampling rate, the higher the quality of the sound. Higher sampling rates also mean bigger file sizes and consequently longer transmission times over the Internet.

The bit resolution of the sampling represents a similar decision. Most sound software will allow the user to decide how much memory is allocated to each sample and hence the subtlety of information that can be reflected in each sample. Two customary settings are 8-bit and 16-bit (CD quality).

Sound creators may also need to make a decision about whether the sound should be sampled in monophonic, stereo, or even more channels. There are the familiar file size/ transmission time trade-offs—16-bit files take double the storage as 8-bit and stereo takes double the size of mono.

The probable sound capabilities to be expected in your audience's computers also sets a limit: 44khz sampling rates can be equivalent to CD quality sound but many computers lack the capability to play back this kind of sound file at its full quality. Some sound types can benefit more from higher sampling rates—for example, speech is often quite clear at 11khz sampling rates whereas music benefits more from 22khz rates or higher. Similarly some receiving platforms will lack the capability to play the higher resolutions and/or stereo. You face tough decisions: Do you offer the highest quality sound (with its attendant increase in file sizes and transmission times) even though many users' systems cannot play it in its full glory? Or do you compromise and offer some lesser quality that will be faster to download and be the best that many systems can process anyway?

Compression

Several ingenious compression algorithms have been developed that can reduce sound file sizes significantly while minimizing quality loss. These schemes take advantage of the unique characteristics of sampled sound to effectively compress while losing the least information possible—for example, the ear's insensitivity to certain frequencies. Because the file sizes end up smaller, the transmission times are shorter.

There are different compression techniques developed to apply to the sound formats on the different platforms. In the Macintosh world, the operating system supports MACE compression on AIFF files. Window's WAVE files are typically compressed with ADPCM (Advanced Digital Pulse Code Modulation) technique. A related ADPCM technique is used with UNIX sound files. Almost all sound editing and helper programs offer access to the standard compression options for the platform they run on.

Should you compress? How much compression should you apply? Choosing to compress has both advantages and disadvantages: Compression reduces file sizes and transmission time. But compression also places an extra decompression time load on the helper application that plays the sound at the user's end. Ultimately, the most important question is sound richness. Although high quality compression loses relatively little information, it does lose some such as fidelity in high frequency ranges or the amount of noise introduced. Higher levels of compression sacrifice more quality. Judging from the preponderance of non-compressed sounds available on the Web, many Web sound designers seem to be opting not to compress. The section that follows on helpers will return to these questions of sound parameter and compression choices.

The newly developed cross platform MPEG2 standard includes sound compression as a basic feature and combines high compression rates with high quality sound. It makes extraordinary demands on computing resources to create, convert, or to play it. Software-only MPEG sound players can be very slow. As discussed in Chapter 6 on video, new hardware MPEG chips and boards are becoming available that can accelerate MPEG processing enormously and that ultimately may make MPEG the sound format of choice. Even now, because of the advantages of MPEG sound, many Web sound archives such as the Internet Underground Music

Archive are beginning to offer their sounds in this format. Figure 5.7 shows a page from their Experimental music section. Each band's excerpt is available in either AU or MPEG2 format via the buttons underneath the band's picture. For more information on MPEG audio consult the MPEG FAQ located at http://www.cs.tu-berlin.de/phade/mpegfaq/index.html.

Lawrence A. Rubin—Internet Underground Music Archive.

Figure 5.7:
Internet Underground Music Archive's options for sound formats.
http://www.iuma.com/IUMA-2.0/olas/genre/EX_001.html

MIDI Format

Even though MIDI is the world standard for professional electronic music, this format is not a practical Web choice at this time for several reasons. First, MIDI does not work for non-musical sounds such as speech. Second, helper applications capable of playing MIDI files are not widely available.

Finally, the receiver must have a MIDI instrument or a sound board with MIDI capability as part of the basic equipment connected to the computer, but few non-professional musicians have computer systems that meet this requirement.

This situation may be changing, however. Many of the sound boards being sold for IBM-compatible computers now include a MIDI capability as part of their basic function. Also, QuickTime 2.0 for the Macintosh, Apple's multimedia system extension, includes MIDI simulation using the Macintosh's internal sound chip. There already is an international file format standard for MIDI files called "General MIDI" that will ensure that MIDI files played on different instruments and boards will sound somewhat similar. Although MIDI-formatted sound files may be an option for Web publishers some time in the future or for special limited audiences of receivers already prepared to play MIDI files, the number of Web navigators ready for MIDI is currently too small to count on. The references point to online resources with more information about MIDI.

Pointers to Archives of MIDI Files

- *Index to MIDI archives*
  `http://datura.cerl.uiuc.edu/netStuff/midi/midi.archives.html`

- *Music and MIDI sites page*
  `http://www.iquest.com:80/~diac/diac-jumps.html`

- *World of Audio MIDI info*
  `http://www.magicnet.net/rz/world_of_audio/midi_pg.html`

- *Classical Music MIDI archives*
  `http://www.hk.net/~prs/midi.html`

Helper Applications

Currently all Web sound is made possible through helper applications. No user can hear sounds from the Web without them. No Web author can offer μLaw-formatted sounds without them. No matter where you obtain your sounds—recording them yourself, getting them from FTP archives, from "clip sound" collections—the odds are that you'll probably need a helper application to convert formats.

These extraordinary sound helper programs serve multiple purposes. These are the programs browsers execute to play sounds downloaded from the Web. They do much more than just play the sounds. Typically they let the users control playback, convert a wide array of sound formats, and save sounds to the local hard disk. These programs are also critical to Web designers. Some allow you to record and convert sounds. You can set the sound parameters discussed previously, such as sampling rate, resolution, and compression. The conversion function is critical to preparing sounds for the Web; you can transform sounds created in your platform's native formats into many other formats including μLaw. Almost all sound helper applications will offer these core features. They differ primarily in their capability to work with less popular formats and in allowing you to set more exotic sound parameters, which are not used by most Web authors. Here are the most frequently used sound helper programs.

Macintosh Helper Applications

- SoundMachine: Opens, plays, and records files in AIFF, System 7 Sound, and AU Available for downloading at ftp://ftp.utexas.edu/pub/mac/sound/soundmachine-21.hqx

- SoundApp: Opens, plays, and can convert sound files in AIFF, Soundedit, System 7 Sound, Quicktime sound tracks, and UNIX AU (all variants), Windows WAVE, Sound Blaster VOC, MOD, Amiga IFF, Sound Designer II. Available for downloading at ftp://ftp.utexas.edu/pub/mac/sound/soundapp-151.hqx

- MPEG Audio for Macintosh 0.3.1: Plays MPEG 2 Audio files. Available for downloading at ftp://ftp.utexas.edu/pub/mac/sound/mpeg-audio-for-mac-031-fat.hqx

- MPEG CD: Plays MPEG 2 Audio files . Available at ftp://ftp.iuma.com/audio_utils/mpeg_players/Macintosh/

DOS/Windows Helper Applications

- WHAM (Wave Hold and Multiply): Plays, records, and converts sounds in WAV, VOC, IFF, AIFF, AU, raw formats. Available for downloading at ftp://gatekeeper.dec.com/pub/micro/msdos/win3/sounds/wham133.zip

- WPLANY (Will Play Any): Plays files in WAV, VOC, IFF, AU, raw formats. Available for downloading at ftp://ncsa.uiuc.edu/Mosaic/Windows/viewers/wplny09b.zip

- NAPLAYER (Netscape Audio Player): Plays sounds in AU and AIFF formats. Comes bundled with Netscape Navigator 1.1 or later. Information available at http://home.netscape.com/newsref/ref/winaudio.html

- MPGAUDIO: Plays sounds in MPEG2 formats. Available for downloading at ftp://ftp.iuma.com/audio_utils/mpeg_players/Windows/

- MPEGWIN: Plays sounds in MPEG2 format. Available for downloading at ftp://gatekeeper.dec.com/pub/micro/msdos/win3/desktop/mpegwin.zip

UNIX Helper Applications

- XPLAY: X-Windows application that plays a variety of sound formats. Available at ftp://ftp.ai.mit.edu/pub/xplay/

- AUDIOFILE: X-Windows application that plays a variety of sound formats. Available at ftp://ftp.dec.com/pub/DEC/AF

- SOUND TOOLS (sox): Translates sound files and performs effects on AU, AIFF, VOC (Windows), WAV files. Available a ftp://ftp.iuma.com/audio_utils/converters/source/sox-10.11.tar.Z

- MAPLAY: Plays sounds in MPEG2 format. Available at ftp://ftp.iuma.com/audio_utils/mpeg_players/Workstations/

To illustrate the functions of sound helper apps, Figure 5.8 shows a screen shot of SoundMachine for the Macintosh opening a sound artist's extension of a William Carlos Williams poem from the BAWP archive (Best-quality Audio Web Poems). The sound control dialog box, which simulates tape player controls, allows the user to execute functions such as start, stop, fast forward, fast reverse, loop, and provides information about the sound sample. Figure 5.9 shows the control window from the Windows WHAM sound helper application. It displays the sound wave of the sound being worked on and offers options similar to SoundMachine.

Exercise 5.2 walks you through the steps to convert a sound from native format to the Web standard AU format. It uses the sound helper app SoundApp for the Macintosh to illustrate, but the steps you'd follow are similar with sound helper applications on any platform.

Lee Markosian.

Figure 5.8:

SoundMachine sound helper application playing sound from BAWP poetry archive.

http://www.cs.brown.edu/fun/bawp/

Exercise 5.2:

Converting a sound to AU format using a helper application

Step 1:

First you'll need a sound to work with. This could be a sound you record or that you obtain from archives or other sources. For the sake of this exercise, we will assume the sound is in native format for the platform you are working with (AIFF for the Macintosh in this example or WAV for Windows if you work on PCs). For convenience let's call it Test.AIFF.

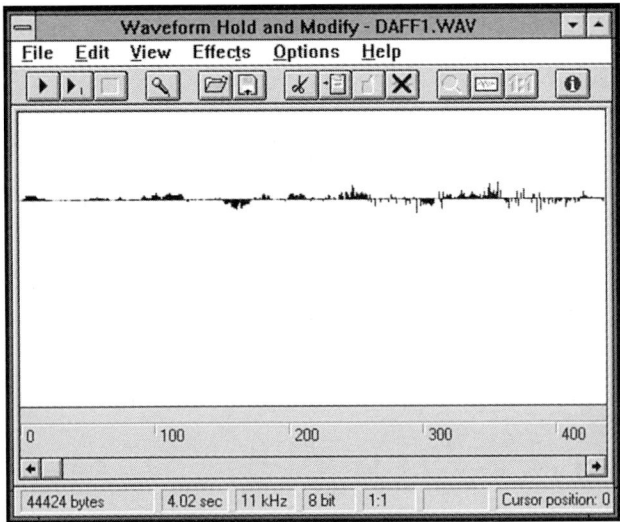

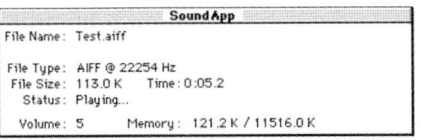

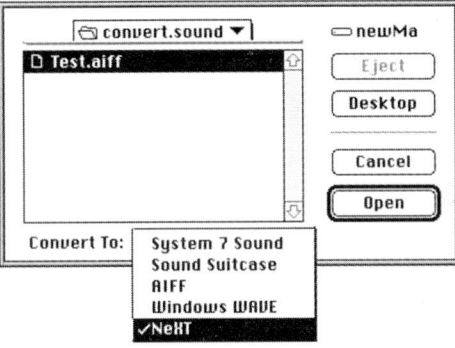

Figure 5.9:
Controls window from WHAM, a sound helper application for
Windows.

Figure 5.10:
Using SoundApp to convert an AIFF sound to AU format.

Step 2:

Launch your sound helper app. In SoundApp, choose Open from the File menu and open your original sound file. SoundApp plays the sound and opens a dialog box like the one in the top of Figure 5.10, with information about the format of the file, its sampling rate, and its length.

Step 3:

You are now ready to convert your sound's format. Choose Convert from the File menu. Pointing to the "Convert to" popup menu opens a list of the possible formats. Choose NeXT to convert to the UNIX μLaw format. (It is just a SoundApp quirk that the name of one particular UNIX machine is listed instead of a more generic indication of μLaw

format.) The sound will then be saved in the indicated folder with the .AU extension automatically added.

Step 4:

This sound is now ready to be offered to the Web via the linking tags described earlier in Exercise 5.1.

Producing Your Own Web Sounds

You have seen how easy it is to convert sounds into Web format. But the Web sounds will only be as good as the originals you produce. You must strive to make the sound production and recording as sonically and electronically clean as is feasible with the level of production you can support. For example, if you are producing speech, you should record it with a good microphone in a quiet space with appropriate acoustic characteristics. In situations where there are spatially dispersed sound sources, you should use multiple microphones. For all kinds of sound, you should record the original sound using as high a quality tape recorder as you can afford rather than recording directly into the computer where you will be subject to spurious computer sounds. Pay attention to background sounds; without special attention, it is easy to be unaware of sounds that will plague you on playback. When digitizing, use a direct cable between your recorder's output and the computer's input instead of a microphone and the tape player's speaker.

After the sound is digitized, you can still improve it. There are sound editing and manipulation programs that enable you to adjust sounds in ways beyond the capabilities of the sound helper apps. Examples of these programs include Audioshop and SoundEdit16 for the Macintosh and Wave and Sound Forge for Windows. These programs give you access to tools that used to be available only to professional sound engineers, such as cutting and pasting, mixing of sound sources, noise reduction, equalization, volume boosting, and special effects. Some of these tools, such as the ability to cut out unnecessary blank spaces, are very useful in preparing Web sounds to be as compact as possible. Although it is impossible to fully discuss these programs here, I mention them because they may be unfamiliar resources to readers who are newly becoming involved with computer sound. Figure 5.11 shows some of SoundEdit16's capabilities. The left side shows the pull-down menu of special effects available and the right side shows the mixing window in which the two sounds can be combined with any combination of relative volumes and timing.

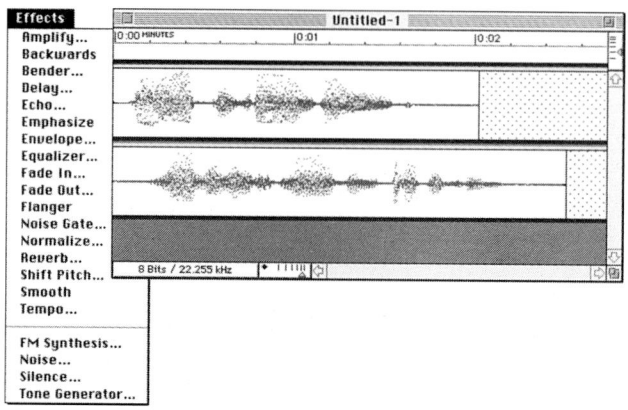

Figure 5.11:
Special effects and mixing options available in SoundEdit16.

Keeping Viewers' Time in Mind

You face a time-to-download problem with sound just as you do with external images. Sound files can be enormous in size. For example, 30 seconds of high quality, uncompressed digitized sound might occupy approximately 1,320,000 bytes. Your Web audience thus can be confronted with a significant wait as the process of accessing, receiving, and playing a sound unfolds.

Addressing this transmission time issue is essential to keep in mind when publishing sound on the Web. You can take certain steps:

- Make sure the sound is cut to the most essential elements. Do not include unnecessary silences or portions.

- Consider breaking up the sound into smaller sections so that can each be accessed separately.

- Describe the sound file thoroughly in the link text so readers can decide if they want to access the file.

- Notify your audience about the size of the file as part of its link information. Consider offering smaller excerpts and previews that linkers can access in the process of deciding if they want the whole file.

Figure 5.12 shows a listing from the "Exposure" section of the Virtual Radio site, which offers samples from a great variety of bands. Each listing includes file size information so Web readers can decide if they want to wait.

You can do even more. You can give choices among excerpts and whole sounds with file sizes and formats listed. You can give as much text description as possible about what the linker is going to get. Figure 5.13 shows a Web page from the Alt.Music site. This site allows Web visitors to listen to songs from the bands it features. This page shows the song Peresoso from the band Devics. It lets Web visitors choose snippets instead of whole songs if they want.

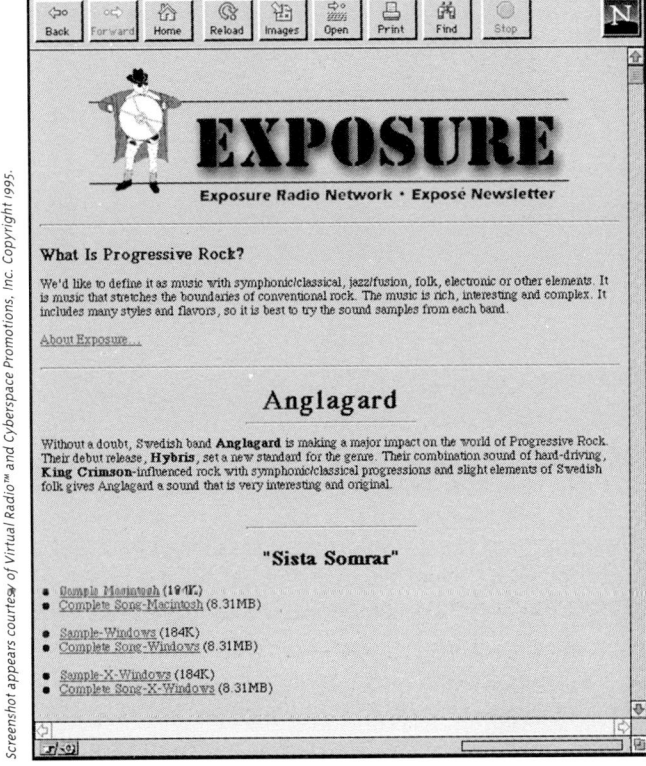

Screenshot appears courtesy of Virtual Radio™ and Cyberspace Promotions, Inc. Copyright 1995.

Figure 5.12:
Sound file size information offered to potential linkers by the Virtual Radio site.
`http://www.microserve.net:80/vradio/VR/html/nv/`
`exposure/exposure.html`

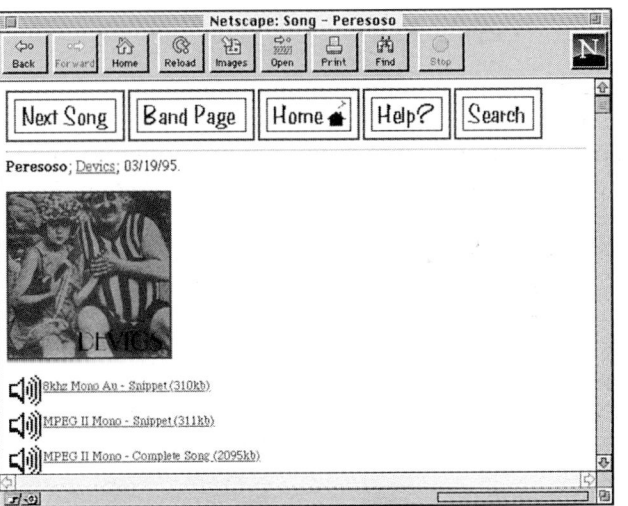

Gavin Jeffries (Alt. Music).

Figure 5.13:
Options offered by the Alt.Music site in accessing samples of music from bands.
`http://www.xmission.com/~adm/bands/devics/`
`peresos.html`

Considering Users without Sound Access

Web navigators who are using text-only browsers will not be able to hear the sounds as part of their Web browsing. Even some of those who can use graphic browsers may lack sound generation capability—for example, those working on some varieties of Windows/DOS and UNIX machines.

How can you be imaginative in finding new ways to communicate information that would be transmitted by sound? Missing an opportunity to enrich their offerings, many sound sites totally ignore visual communication. Many of these sites consist mostly of text listing the sounds and maybe one signature graphic. Others, for example home pages for rock bands, often include supplementary material like album covers, pictures of the performers, images from the locale of the band, and background images related to the music. These sites have a life even for Web visitors who do not listen to the sounds. Figure 5.14 presents a Web page from the Cavestar site created by a California composer/producer of experimental music, which includes rich graphic and textual resources in addition to samples of the sounds.

Sounds Available on the Web

Here are some questions to think about as you plan the sound resources you want to place on the Web:

- Are there similar works already available?
- What other sounds are available?

- What contexts are they offered in?
- What uses for sound are other Web sites exploring that might be useful to you?

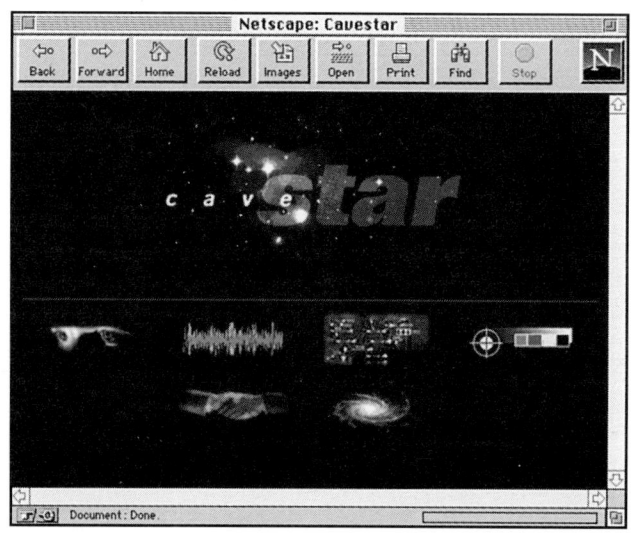

Kevin Crosslin.

Figure 5.14:
Web page from the Cavestar site that offers supplemental visual information.
`http://www.primenet.com/-cavesta/menu.html`

As stressed often in this book, research is one of the most important actions you can take as a Web designer. This section offers a mini-survey of sound sources to help you start thinking about your potential sound work. Consult Appendix A, "Research and Publicizing Yourself on the Web," for information that will help you conduct more thorough research into Web sites that are using sound in ways related to your goals.

Sounds on the Web are available both in sites specially focused on sound and as part of the general information offered by sites not especially focused on sound—for example, an executive's speech about a new product. The archives focused explicitly on sound are easy to find because there are excellent indexes at sites such as Yahoo. Web sites that use sound clips more casually, as just another kind of informational resource, are harder to seek out. Yet, this use of sound is one of the most interesting applications of sound on the Web. It adds to the variety of a Web page and offers an often unexpected resource. Be expansive in your own thinking about sound. Consider its use even if you did not originally consider sound part of your work.

Let's take a look at some of the sound archives available on the Web. They present sound resources in spoken word, music, non-human sounds, and experimental work.

Spoken Word Resources

This category ranges from recordings of speeches, radio programs, movie and television soundtracks, to storytelling, theater, poetry, and work by sound artists. For example, Internet Talk Radio is exploring the feasibility of radio-like programming on the Internet. The G. Robert Vincent Voice Library at Michigan State University, a very extensive voice recording archive, makes part of its collection available. This valuable resource is the largest academic voice library in the United States with over 50,000 persons recorded over a period of 100 years. It is one of those resources many might not find except for Web access.

Harper Audio, another unique voice resource, presents 10-minute readings from famous literature. They faced the common Web dilemma of how to protect their intellectual property. Their site posts a warning to Web visitors.

Figure 5.15 presents a Web page from another spoken word sound site—the Library of Congress' "Nation's Forum" archive with speeches from early 20th century public figures.

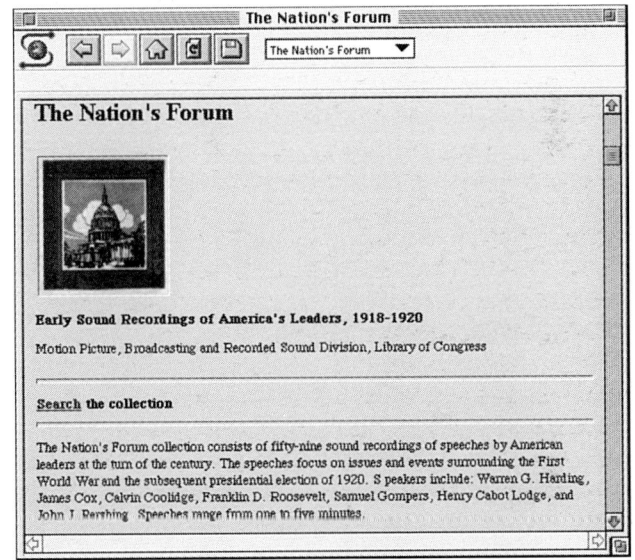

American Memory Project, Library of Congress. Web site realized by Dean Wilder, Jane Bossert, and Ed Paton (public domain).

Figure 5.15:
Nation's Forum archive of speeches by historical figures around 1900.
`http://rs6.loc.gov/nfhome.html`

Music Resources

The Web offers up the world's variety of music including such offerings as marching bands, classical performances, popular, jazz, folk, world beat, experimental contemporary music, and the national traditions of many countries. The international nature of the Web creates a rich opportunity for people to become familiar with musical genres that they might not encounter in any other way. Figure 5.16 shows one example of a specialized Web music resource, the home page from the marching band archive.

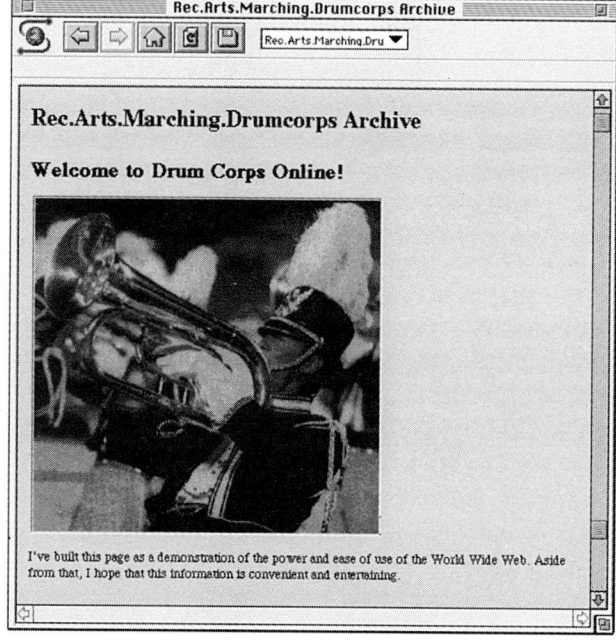

Figure 5.16:
Marching band achive.
`http://lal.cs.byu.edu/dci/dci.html`

Many sites are establishing clear musical identities. For example, the Internet Underground Music Archive (illustrated in Figure 5.1) presents bands from all over the world with a wide range of genres, ranging from easy listening and rock to blues and hard-core industrial. They proudly declare their intention to explore the new Web-created opportunities for artists to publicize their music: "IUMA has put songs by more than 300 independent, unsigned artists online, enabling world-wide distribution of their music to an estimated 30 million people. IUMA is leading the drive toward artist-compensated, high-fidelity, online music distribution."

Other Web sites offer similar access to wide ranging contemporary music, including the Kosmic Free Music Foundation (Figure 5.17). Learning about these music resources can be useful because you might want to include access to some of their sound resources in your pages and because they may give you new musical ideas to explore if you are planning on creating music oriented resources for your own site.

Experimental Sound Resources

The Web also offers non-traditional sounds and experimental sound work. For example, the University of North Carolina's SunSite site offers an archive of miscellaneous sounds such as Monty Python clips, phonemes, screams, whales, and Chinese music.

Experimental sound work takes a great variety of forms. Some is spoken word and some is music—for example, some contemporary bands listed in the Internet Underground Music Archive cross over into what is commonly called sound art. You can learn more by studying sound artists such as John Cage, who explored the boundaries between speech, music, and noise. (Net information on Cage is available at

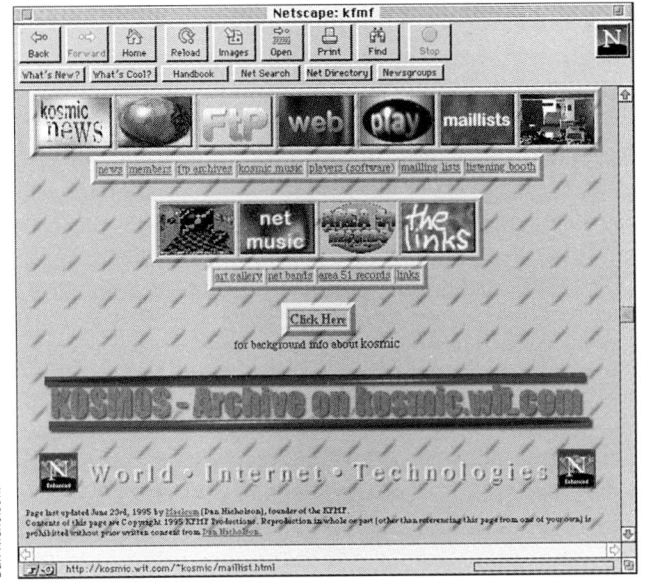

Dan Nicholson.

Figure 5.17:
Kosmic Free Music Foundation.
`http://kosmic.wit.com/~kosmic/`

`http://www.emf.net/~mal/cage.html`.) Other Web sound experiments include interactive speech synthesizers, online talk radio, and automatic "genetic" music generation.

Figure 5.18 shows a Web page from the Genetic Music site. The statement that follows explains their approach to algorithmic music generation:

> This is an experiment in trying to evolve programs that write "music." It uses genetic programming to evolve expressions for note length, amplitude, frequency, duration and the spacing between notes.

It plays music for users who can then VOTE! for the different sounds produced. Using the votes received, the program generates a new set of sounds by crossover and mutation from the current generation.

Experimental sound sites can be provocative sources in your own sound design. You might want to incorporate links to the sounds in your own pages and they can stimulate new ideas to expand the ways you think about Web sound.

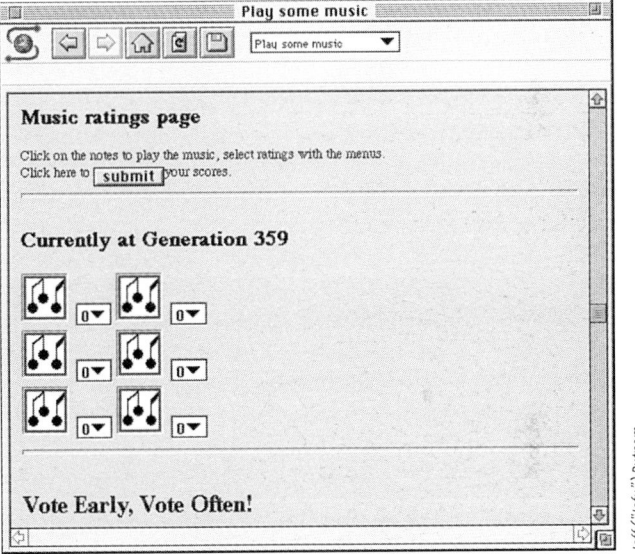

Jeff ("Jefu") Putnam.

Figure 5.18:
Genetic Music site.
`http://nmt.edu/~jefu/notes/notes.html`

Summary

As you can see, there are important design decisions involved in successfully incorporating music and sound into your Web documents. Sound files can take a long time to transmit and can frustrate users. You must carefully consider the purpose behind adding sounds: Why is sound appropriate? Could text serve just as well? Is the sound as condensed as possible? Is it technically well-produced? How does it work with the text and images on the site?

The sound arts community has built up considerable technical expertise. Draw on this resource. For example, many spoken sound files now becoming available on the Web are created in ad hoc fashion while the Web author sits in front of the computer. This approach may be satisfactory for many purposes, but you do have other options. Sound media producers in radio, cinema, and video pay much attention to the choice of speaker (for example, gender, age, sonic qualities of the voice), the flow of diction, the prosody, the script, and the technical details of production.

You must make your sound work as strong as it can be. Listen to the sounds around you with fresh ears. Study and listen to the sound work of sound artists in the traditions that interest you. Read sound history, criticism, and theory. The Web can provide you access to much of this information. Make the sounds you offer on the Web as engaging and effective as you can.

In the next chapter, we look at digital video. Web video generates even more excitement than sound. Some even think it may ultimately replace TV as we know it now. You will see that with some experimentation and effort you will be able to offer video resources almost as easily as sound. Chapter 6 shows you how.

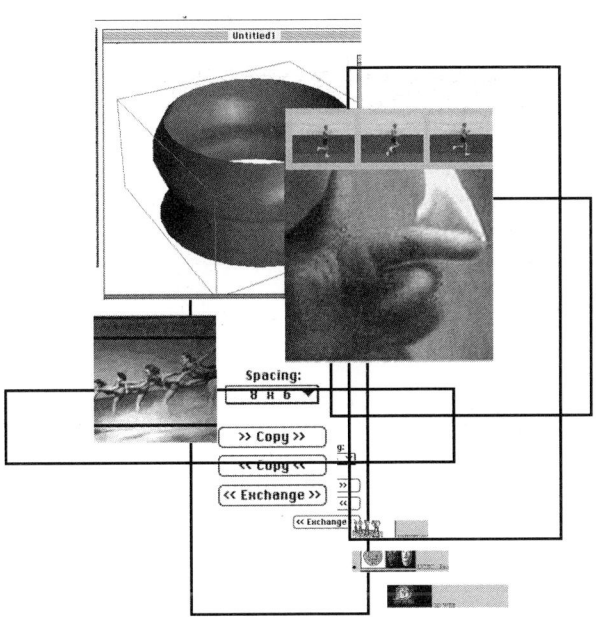

Chapter 6

Working with Video

Video and cinema are art forms unique to the 20th century. More than any other media, they offer the possibility of simulating lifelike action. In fact, early in the days of cinema, audience members reportedly ran screaming from the theaters in fear of the moving images. The Web promises another profound revolution: it will allow you to make your video easily available to an international audience.

In this chapter, you learn some technical basics about how digital video works, how to format video for Web distribution, how to use helper applications that work with video, how to create HTML documents to make video available on Web pages, and how to design and produce your video offerings so they will be engaging for your Web audience.

The HTML coding for offering video uses the same anchor tags to create links that you saw with image and sound. For example, the following line would offer a link to the video of a skyline image of San Francisco if it were located in the same folder as the HTML page containing this reference:

```
<A HREF="skyline.MPG"> See video of San Francisco
skyline</A>
```

The *.MPG* at the end of the filename indicates that it is an MPEG video file. For this to work you would need a digital video file formatted in a file type that Web browsers can understand. Web browsers rely on the file's extension to determine the format. In this example, the video was formatted in the MPEG (Motion Picture Experts Group) format, a common one for distribution of video on the Web. Your Web audience would need an appropriate helper application to work with their browsers to actually play the video. The browser would interpret the extension, check its configuration file for what helper application could play that kind of file, and then launch the helper application and load the MPEG file. It would open the video in a separate window. Figure 6.1a

shows a Web document with a link to a video clip, and Figure 6.1b shows a helper application displaying that video clip. The video, created by a French animator, is of an animated fly-by of a fractal-generated river valley.

Exercise 6.1 shows you how easy it is to add video links to a Web page. Since we haven't yet discussed details of capturing video and formatting it for the Web, we'll use links that point to video that exists already on the Web. For this exercise, I'll provide a pointer to a video resource on the Web. You can search in the video archives listed in a later section called "Obtaining Video from the Web" if you want to experiment with other videos.

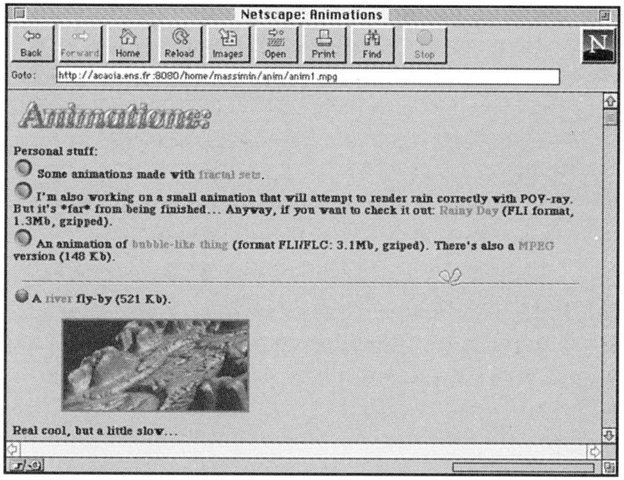

Figure 6.1a:
A link to a video file.
```
http://acacia.ens.fr:8080/home/massimin/anim/
anim.ang.html
```

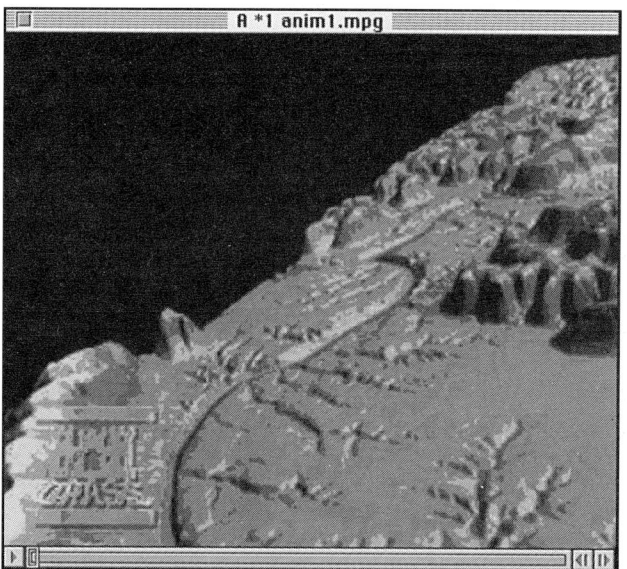

Figure 6.1b:
Choosing the link opens a video helper application.

Exercise 6.1:

Adding a video link to an HTML document

Step 1:

To create a working link of this exercise you must have a video file in your local directory in a video format that your Web browser can understand, such as MPEG or QuickTime. The later section on "Obtaining Video from the Web" points to online sources of images.

Once you've obtained your sample video file, place it in the same directory or folder as the HTML document you're creating for this exercise.

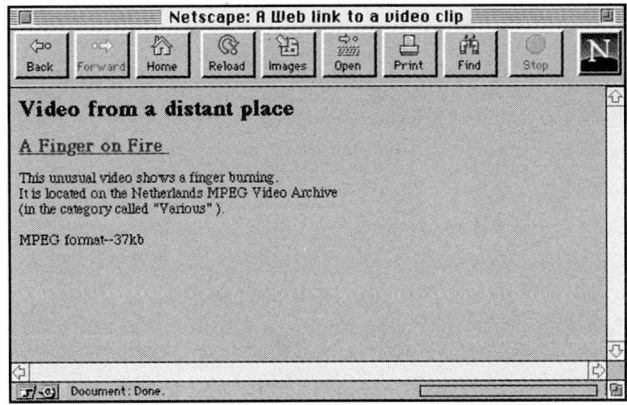

Figure 6.2a:
Adding a video link to a Web page.

Step 2:

Using your word processor, type the HTML document we'll use as the basis for this example:

```
<HTML>
<HEAD>
<TITLE> A Web link to a video clip </TITLE>
</HEAD>
<BODY>
<H2>Video from a distant place</H2>
<H3>A Finger on Fire</H3><P>
This unusual video shows a finger burning. <BR>
It is located on the Netherlands MPEG Video Archive
<BR>
(in the category called "Various" ).<P>
MPEG format—37kb
</BODY>
</HTML>
```

Step 3:

We're going to make the words "A Finger on Fire" the link to our video file. You'll need the absolute pathname for the URL of a video that's already on the Web. For this exercise, try the following URL to point your readers to an unusual video that shows a finger burning. Make sure that the text you enter in the anchor tag matches the video's filename and pathname exactly. In this example, you now have a line of code that reads as follows:

```
<H3><A HREF= http://www.eeb.ele.tue.nl:8080/mpeg/
movies/various/firefing.mpg> A Finger on Fire </A>
</H3><P>
```

Step 4:

Save your document as an ASCII text file. Use .html (if you're using a Macintosh or .htm for a DOS/Windows platform) for the filename's suffix. Here is what the source code for your final document should look like:

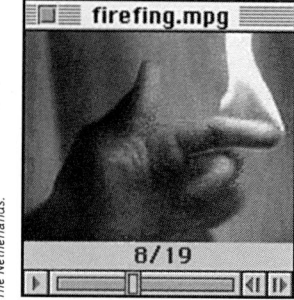

Heini Withagen Eindhoven. University of Technology, The Netherlands.

Figure 6.2b:

The movie shown in this exercise is "A Finger on Fire."
`http://www.eeb.ele.tue.nl:8080/mpeg/movies/various/firefing.mpg`

```
<HTML>
<HEAD>
<TITLE> A Web link to a video clip </TITLE>
</HEAD>
<BODY>
<H2>Video from a distant place</H2>
<H3><A HREF= http://www.eeb.ele.tue.nl:8080/mpeg/
movies/various/firefing.mpg> A Finger on Fire </A>
</H3><P>
This unusual video shows a finger burning. <BR>
It is located on the Netherlands MPEG Video Archive
<BR>
(in the category called "Various" ).<P>
MPEG format—37kb
</BODY>
</HTML>
```

Step 5:

Activate the browser and use the "Open Local" or "Open File" option to access the file you have just created. Click on your new video link. If you have

the appropriate helper application and your browser is configured correctly, the video will load and play in a helper window.

What Is Digital Video Technology, and How Does It Work?

Before you include movie clips on your Web pages, you'll need a basic understanding of how it should be prepared and how computers store and display video. As a Web designer, it is to your advantage to understand as much as you can about how digital video works, because this knowledge will help you make the best decisions about producing your video and formatting it for the Web. It will also help you understand future video-related innovations that are likely to come from the research community.

The amount of information contained in a video clip is enormous. Full-motion video, produced in accordance with the international NTSC standard, displays 30 images a second. For a one-minute video, that's 1,800 images—and we haven't even accounted for any audio resources yet!

Why do videos flash so many images each second? Video (and film) relies on a perceptual characteristic of the brain and eye called *persistence of vision*. Persistence of vision keeps an afterimage on the retina for a fraction of a second after it is gone, tricking the brain into seeing continuous motion. For example, the global standard for 16mm cinema

Jessica Hodgins and the Animation Lab graphics, Visualization and Usability Center; Georgia Institute of Technology.

Figure 6.3:
Persistence of vision illustrated by an animation of running.
`http://www.cc.gatech.edu/gvu/animation/research/runner.html`

presents the eye with 24 discrete image frames (frames is the name given to the discrete images that fills the screen) per second. Normal NTSC video (the National Television Standards Committee video signal convention used in the United States and Japan) presents the eye with 30 frames per second to accomplish the same effect. The PAL standard video (used in Europe and other parts of the world) presents 25 frames per second.

Figure 6.3 illustrates the phenomenon of persistence of vision. It shows shots from an animated sequence of a runner produced by the animation lab at Georgia Tech. Each discrete visual image shows the body in a particular configuration; if the images come quickly enough, the runner seems to move smoothly.

Storing all these frames of visual information in digitized format consumes enormous amounts of computer memory and processing time. A single uncompressed, 24-bit, full-color, 640 x 480 digitized screen image would take up 921,600 bytes of memory. A second's worth of video would require 30 of these, or 27,648,000 bytes of memory. Sound would require additional memory.

Your computer must work very quickly to convert this flow of information from analog to digital form and store it correctly. Contemporary developments in video capture, compression, and display, however, have finally made digital video a reality for everyday computers. Macintosh AV, Windows Multimedia, and some video-ready workstations (for example, SGI "Indys") now come with video digitizing capability built in. Video boards can be inexpensively purchased for those PCs that don't have the capability.

Contemporary analog-to-digital converters allow digital video systems to capture up to the full 30 frames of information (actually 60 half frames called *fields*) every second. Compression hardware such as C-cube MPEG compression chips and software such as QuickTime for the Mac and Windows VFW manages to compress this data flow by up to a factor of 200 in order to reduce the amount of information to be stored and processed. However, many inexpensive systems still cannot keep up with this rate of processing and compression at full screen resolution. Many digital video systems function at full data rate only if the video capture window is reduced to a smaller size—for example 320 x 240 pixels. Remember that reduction of each dimension by

50 percent reduces the total amount of information to be stored to 25 percent on average. A later section will show other ways of minimizing the digitizing load, such as reducing the frame rate, reducing the quality of the image, or changing the compression method used. All methods, however, involve some compromises of quality.

Figure 6.4 shows a screen shot of a video resource on the Web called Splash. It is a computer animation that simulates a drop of water hitting the surface of a liquid. It illustrates the typical small size that many Web movies must use in order to keep their file sizes down.

Splash—a simulation of water droplets, by Bill Knight and Bob Clark of the Hewlett-Packard Co, Corvallis Oregon.

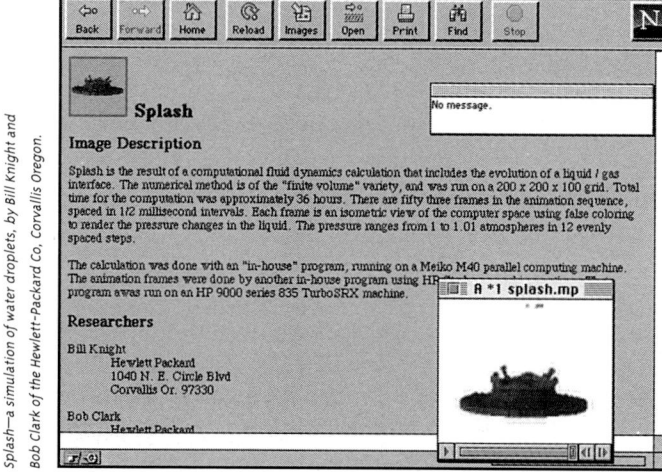

Figure 6.4:
Splash playing in a small window.
http://www.ncsa.uiuc.edu/SDG/DigitalGallery/
SPLASH.html

Choosing a Format for Publishing Movies on the Web

In this section, you'll discover:

- How does video compression work?
- What digital video formats are available for different platforms?
- What formats are the best for presenting video on the Web?

Each computing platform has its own native file and compression formats for storing digital video. The ones you're most likely to see used on the Web—and that you'll want to choose for yourself—are called MPEG, QuickTime, and Video for Windows. All of these formats are scalable. This means that even if the original movie was created on a high-end machine at 30 frames per second, the movie will still play on a slower, low-end machine. The slower machine will play it at a slower rate, dropping frames to keep the sound and image somewhat synchronized.

Frame Differencing (or Interframe Compression)

All video compression formats (QuickTime, MPEG, and Video for Windows) make use of a technique called *frame differencing*. To achieve high levels of compression and maintain quality, frame differencing must build on unique features of the information that makes up the moving image. It uses the fact that adjacent frames in a stream of images are very similar to each other with relatively small changes. It stores only the information that differentiates one frame from the previous one and discards the redundant information. In decompression, the processor reconstructs each frame by using the difference information. The video compression routines also take advantage of knowledge about what kinds of motion and image change the eye is especially sensitive to and then throw away the less essential details.

In many videos, the backgrounds stay relatively constant and only moving parts of the foreground image change. Figure 6.5 illustrates the way frame differencing would work with a real video sequence. The video sequence illustrated is an America Newsreel clip of historical cinema documenting a Florida water-skiing extravaganza (probably from the '50s) drawn from the OnDemand Stock Footage Server collection of National Archives cinema.

The background scene is similar from frame to frame. Frame differencing would determine certain frames to be *key frames* and store only those in their entirety. For each frame in between, only the information that changes is stored (for example, the water skiers). This technique is called *interframe coding*. Upon decompression, the video sequence would be reconstructed by drawing the key frames and then using the change information to fill in the missing frames.

In absolute terms, some information is lost in this compression/decompression, although high-quality compressors preserve most of the visually essential information.

MPEG

MPEG format uses lossy compression of individual frames and interframe encoding of changes among frames while minimally affecting image quality. MPEG was developed by an international group of experts in digital video called the Motion Picture Expert Group (hence the name of the format), which was convened specifically to develop cross platform, digital video compression standards and techniques. They developed approaches that have achieved international notoriety for their ability to achieve very high levels of compression while preserving image and motion quality. They submitted the standard to the International Standards Organization (ISO) and MPEG1 is now a widely used standard. The digital video community is currently working on MPEG2, the next standard, which promises even higher quality and more compression. An even newer standard called MPEG4 is on the drawing board.

Figure 6.5:
Frame differencing compression technique applied to a water-skiing sequence.
`http://www.footage.net:2900/OnDemand/`

Compression and quality come at a cost. The algorithms that analyze each frame and calculate the differences are quite complex and require considerable computing power. Slow CPUs take a long time to encode and decode and even relatively fast CPUs cannot process MPEG in real time. Companies such as C-cube, IBM, and Compression Labs have developed specialized MPEG encoder and decoder chips that accelerate the process greatly and add-on boards are now available for all platforms. Some analysts believe MPEG decoding will become a standard part of future computer systems.

Because of its combination of quality and compression, MPEG has become the *de facto* standard for digital video transmitted on the Web, with shareware MPEG players available for all platforms. If your speed requirements for coding and decoding are moderate, these software-only MPEG compressors and decompressors can do the job, although they do have some limitations. Some current MPEG helper apps cannot yet encode MPEG sound along with images, which results in silent movies. But the new MPEG boards based on the encoder chips will accelerate the process and make sound interleaving possible. Interested readers should consult the sources in the following sidebar "Pointers to MPEG Information" for more technical details about MPEG.

Pointers to MPEG Information

- *Web FAQ on MPEG*
`http://www.cs.tu-berlin.de/-phade/mpegfaq/`
`index.html`

- *MPEG Info Enterprise Integration Technologies (EIT)*
`http://www.eit.com/techinfo/mpeg/mpeg.html`

- *MPEG FAQ (frequently asked questions)*
`http://www.crs4.it/~luigi/MPEG/mpegfaq2.html`

`http://www.cis.ohio-state.edu/hypertext/faq/`
`usenet/mpeg-faq/top.html`

- *How to make MPEG movies*
`http://www.arc.umn.edu/GVL/Software/mpeg.html`

- *Yahoo MPEG pointers*
`http://www.yahoo.com/Computers/Multimedia/Movies/`
`Technical_Information/MPEG_Technical_Information/`

QuickTime

QuickTime, the Macintosh's format for digital video, includes several features. It provides an open architecture so it can play video stored in a variety of compression formats. (These are called *codecs*—derived from the words *compression* and *deco*mpression.) It also provides a standard interface to users for controlling recording and playback, and for making technical decisions about the trade-offs of image quality, frame rates, and amount of compression to be applied. QuickTime also lets you play digital movies on any machine that has appropriate QuickTime code available. Although originally designed for the Macintosh as part of its operating system, QuickTime players are now available for Windows and UNIX machines (access locations are presented in the list that follows).

Because of the unique way Macintosh computers set up files with separate data and resource forks, QuickTime movies destined for cross-platform presentation need to be *flattened*. Most applications that allow QuickTime movie

Slider-frame selection

Single step forward and backward

Play button

Sound level

Resize playback window

Figure 6.6:
Example of QuickTime display window with playback options.

creation, such as Fusion Recorder, offer this flattening option as part of the file saving process. QuickTime files created on other platforms, such as SGI machines, don't have this problem because their file systems don't have this dual structure. QuickTime movie files are much larger than equivalent MPEG files but they code and decode much faster on low-end hardware.

Figure 6.6 shows a basic QuickTime playback window with buttons for play, single step forward and reverse, and sound level functions. The slider shows the position of the current frame and allows the user to access particular points in the video.

Video for Windows

Microsoft Windows offers its own standard video format called Video For Windows (VFW) that's similar to QuickTime. It creates files with the extension AVI.

Converting to File Formats Appropriate for the Web

Currently MPEG is the most common cross-platform Web video format and until recently almost all video resources on the Web were offered in MPEG. Because MPEG players were available for all platforms, Web video producers converted their native video files to MPEG unless they knew that large segments of their specific target audience used QuickTime or VFW. Your safest bet is to use MPEG.

The situation is in flux, however. QuickTime players have become available for Windows and UNIX machines and thus it is a candidate to be a cross-platform standard. Increasingly you see Web video archives that offer both QuickTime and MPEG versions. QuickTime's advantage is that it takes less time to code and decode; its disadvantage is that it generates larger files that take more time to download. At the same time MPEG hardware decoders are becoming less expensive and more widespread. You will need to monitor these developments closely in order to make the best decisions in the future.

Helper Applications

When your readers activate links to your digital video files, their Web browsers must activate a helper application that can play that file. Many of the applications that convert video formats double as video players. The list that follows shows the most common video helper applications for different platforms and where you can download them.

Macintosh

- Sparkle: Plays and converts MPEG and QuickTime files. Available for downloading at ftp://ftp.ncsa.uiuc.edu/Mosaic/Mac/Helpers

- SimplePlayer: Plays QuickTime files. Available at http:/
  /quicktime.apple.com/

Windows

- MPEGPLAY: Plays and converts MPEG files. Available for
  downloading at ftp://ftp.ncsa.uiuc.edu/Mosaic/
  Windows/viewers/mpegw32e.zip
- VTMotion Scalable MPEG Player: Plays MPEG files.
  Available at ftp://gatekeeper.dec.com/pub/micro/
  msdos/win3/desktop/mpegxing.zip
- Windows QuickTime Player: Plays QuickTime movies.
  Available at http://www.ncsa.uiuc.edu/SDG/Software/
  WinMosaic/QTini.html
- Windows AVI to QuickTime Converter: Converts AVI
  Windows video to QuickTime. Available at ftp://
  sumex-aim.stanford.edu/info-mac/grf/util/avi-to-qt-
  converter.hqx

UNIX

- MPEG Player: Plays MPEG files. Available at ftp://tr-
  ftp.CS.Berkeley.EDU/pub/multimedia/mpeg
- Xplay Gizmo: Plays MPEG files. Available at ftp://
  ftp.ncsa.uiuc.edu/Mosaic/Unix/viewers/xplaygizmo/
- Xanim: Plays QuickTime and AVI files. Available at
  http://www.portal.com/podlipec/home.html

Figure 6.7 illustrates Sparkle for the Macintosh. This helper
app works with browsers to display MPEG files. It allows users
to control movies with a playback slider, to step through
them by single frames, speed them up and slow them down,
convert between QuickTime and MPEG, and to save the files
to local hard disks. Figure 6.8 illustrates MPEGPLAY for
Windows. It offers similar controls for playback and converts
between AVI and MPEG.

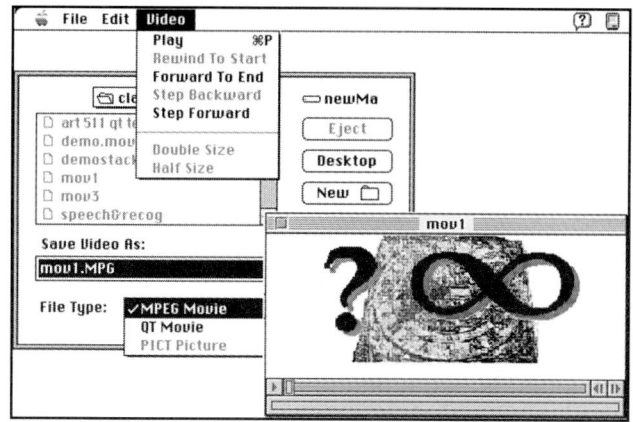

Figure 6.7:
Interface screen from Sparkle, an MPEG helper application for the
Macintosh.

Figure 6.8:
Interface screen from MPEGPLAY for Windows.

Preparing Digital Video for the Web

How are you going to produce your video for the Web? There are many easy ways to obtain, create, and edit digital video. There are archives of video for downloading; inexpensive programs and hardware for digitizing either live or taped video; animation, morphing, 3-D modeling, and presentation programs for creating computer movies; and editing and manipulation programs for cleaning up the video and adding special effects. Digital video is an exciting field for experimentation and the Web is a great place to distribute your work.

Obtaining Video Clips

Even if you don't want to produce video yourself, you can still offer your Web audience video by finding relevant clips in online archives. There are archives of video on a great variety of topics including movies and TV; science topics such as zoology, astronomy, or physics; historical films; travel, sports, and hobbies; computer animations; and experimental multimedia art. You can provide a real service for your Web visitors by identifying and offering links to video relevant to your topic. As will be explained in the section on design, it is important that you provide descriptive text, format, and size information along with the links so your readers can decide whether they really want to wait for the download time. The list that follows provides pointers to some well-known Web video archives that offer diverse videos in a variety of fields. These videos come from a variety of sources: individuals who want to share video they have created, documentation of research projects, companies offering teasers for their products and services, educational videos, and clips from television or movie sources.

Sources of MPEG Movies

- *American Memory Collection (early historical movies)*
`http://lcweb2.loc.gov/papr/mpixhome.html`

- *MPEG Movie Archive (various topics)*
`http://w3.eeb.ele.tue.nl/mpeg/index.html`

- *MPEG Movie Directory (various topics)*
`http://www.acm.uiuc.edu/rml/MPEG/`

- *Multimedia archive at SunSITE U.S.A. (various topics)*
`http://sunsite.unc.edu/pub/multimedia/`

- *Multimedia archive at Leeds University, U.K. (various topics)*
`http://cbl.leeds.ac.uk/mm/default.html`

- *QuickTime Movies (various topics)*
`gopher://info.asu.edu/11/other/misc/movies`

- *HollyWeb (Clips from movies and television)*
`http://www.ingress.com/users/spease/hw/hollyweb.html`

- *Thant's Animation Index*
`http://mambo.ucsc.edu/psl/thant/thant.html`

- *Fractal Movie Archive*
`http://www.cnam.fr/fractals/anim.html`

- *Science movies*
`http://www.ncsa.uiuc.edu/SDG/DigitalGallery/`

Producing Your Own "Live Action" Video

There are many reasons you might want to produce your own video—for example, teaching online illustrated lessons in education, demonstrating new products in business, communicating some aspect of research you are engaged in, explaining the joys of some hobby you are involved with, or experimenting with multimedia art. Cinema and video production is notorious for its complexity and expense. Hollywood productions cost millions of dollars per minute. Even industrial and educational video require sophisticated equipment and elaborate crews to produce. At the other end of the continuum is home video, which requires nothing beyond a video camera and a single camera person-writer-director-grip. Obviously, most Web publishers are not about to set up multimillion-dollar companies to produce their Web video. Nonetheless, Web publishers will want to achieve the highest production values possible within their budgets.

Luckily, contemporary technological advancements have made achievement of technical quality easier. Relatively inexpensive Hi-8 and Super-VHS cameras offer video capabilities that would have cost tens of thousands of dollars a few years ago. Analog and digital video editing systems allow control of sequencing that used to require expensive rentals of offline editing suites. The equipment manufacturers have started categorizing this new class of production as "prosumers"—that is, producers who are striving to surpass home-video consumer quality, but who are not quite at a professional level.

Producing video for the Web has many of the same requirements as non-Web video and cinema production. It must be as clean and technically polished as possible. You must attend to visual composition, continuity, pacing, lighting, sound recording, and editing. Obviously this book cannot deal with such a broad range of topics but there are online resources that provide information on cinema and video production for interested readers.

Resources Related to Cinema and Video Production

- *University of Michigan list of resources on film & video production*
  `http://http2.sils.umich.edu/Public/fvl/Resources.html#2.3`

- *Newsgroup on movie production*
  `news:rec.arts.movies.production`

- *Newsgroup on video production*
  `news:rec.video.production`

- *Filmmaker magazine (Print magazine oriented to independent filmmakers)*
  `http://found.cs.nyu.edu/CAT/affiliates/filmmaker/filmmaker.html`

- *WELL experimental video and film resources*
  `http://gopher.well.sf.ca.us:70/1/Art/Experimental.Film.and.Video`

Digitizing Video and Parameter Settings

After you have created your video, you must digitize it so it can be manipulated and transmitted on computer systems. To accomplish this, you need access to a system with the appropriate hardware and software to convert the video information as described previously. There are Mac AVs, Multimedia Windows machines, and video-ready Work-stations. There are also add-on video capture boards made by companies such as Creative Labs, Matrox, Spigot, Truevision, and VideoLogic.

Your parameter choices about the process of digitizing video are more complex than with still image and sound. Video makes high demands on a computer; it must convert the analog video and sound information into digital form, compress it, and store it to memory or the hard disk at a rate that keeps up with the constant flow of 30 frames every second. The processors in many older computers and hard disks not optimized for AV applications cannot keep up this rate of 30 full-frame images per second. There can be problems such as dropped frames and temporary loss of image-sound synchronization. Also, this much information consumes enormous disk memory space and must be compressed.
To address these limitations, you must make interrelated capture decisions about the frame rate, window size, and compression trade-offs in visual, sound, and motion fidelity versus file size.

You can reduce file sizes in several ways: reducing screen size, reducing frame rate, and/or increasing the amount of compression. Ideally, you should capture the video initially at the highest quality that your system and hard disk storage will allow—that is, the highest frame rate and visual quality. You can later make decisions to reduce size or quality if necessary. As you know by now, digital video files require enormous disk storage. For example, a QuickTime movie at 320 x 240 pixels and 30 frames per second will occupy approximately 1 MB per second. (The exact figure can fluctuate because different kinds of images and motion will compress with varying efficiency.)

Obviously, as you capture more and more video clips you can quickly fill up even very large hard disks. As a solution, you should estimate the probable final destination values that you desire for frame rate, screen size, and compression. You determine these by deciding how small of an image can still make your video understandable and enjoyable; how many frames per second will adequately portray the motion in your clip; and much compression-related image quality degradation you can tolerate. These determinations cannot be made in the abstract; experience will be essential in learning which settings are appropriate for various kinds of video. Unless you can afford a full professional digital video setup (such as Avid Suite Pro, Media 100 or Targa 2000), some compromise in quality is inevitable. Once you have made these determinations, you can set the capture parameters as slightly higher settings. This would leave some quality head room but also compress file sizes, even during the initial capture. If the original source material exists on tape, higher-quality captures can be redone if necessary.

Ultimately, however, your digital video will probably need to be compressed further. File size is a major consideration for transmitting any media on the Web, but is especially true of video. It is incumbent upon you to reduce file sizes wherever possible in consideration of your audience's concerns about transmission time.

All video capture software (for example, Video Fusion, Videoshop, and Premiere for the Mac and MediaMerge, MediaStudio and Premiere for Windows, and Digital Studio for SGI workstations) will allow you to adjust these various parameters. You can set frame size, frames per second, and extent of compression, as much as the limits of the hardware will allow. Surprisingly, some of the compromises are not as detrimental as you might think. For example, standard "full" motion, 30 frames per second (fps) video is not required to transmit the important elements of feel and meaning in many video sequences. Slower frame rates can work quite well and sometimes even add visual interest. Popular frame rates for delivering video over the Web are usually between 10-15 fpp in MPEG format and are often acceptable at 320 x 240.

Aspect ratios for digital video

You can set your video window frame sizes to be any ratio you want but certain proportions (4 units wide to 3 units high) are preferred because they adhere to television standards. If you know the material will never be converted to standard video, you can ignore this ratio and create the video in any size you wish. Realize, however, that other sizes will violate audience expectations.

Figure 6.9 illustrates the kind of settings you can make in video capture and movie creation software. It shows the standard dialog box available in QuickTime-based applications. Choices must be made about the compressor to be used, the visual quality of the compression, the frames per second to be recorded, and the frequency with which key frames are recorded. All choices involve trade-offs between quality of the video and file size.

Computer-Generated Animation

Computers offer you another option for making video besides capturing real action. Perhaps you're interested in computer animations, like those you see in television commercials? Then the world of computer graphics is open to you. You can use computer animation tools to create *synthetic productions*—that is, images generated by computer processing rather than recorded by a camera. It's similar to the difference between digitally recorded sound and MIDI synthesizer sound.

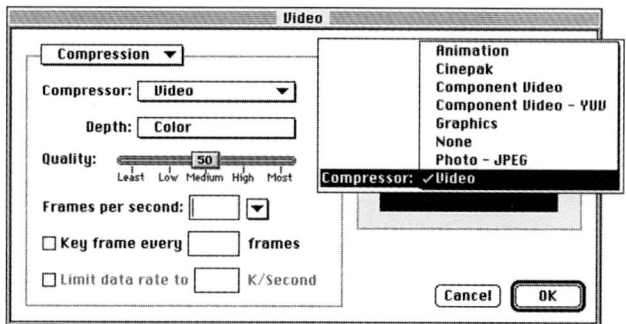

Figure 6.9:
Video digitizing decisions offered in QuickTime.

A variety of software types can produce computer-synthetic motion sequences. Animation programs allow explicit control of movement of computer objects on the screen (for example, Director, Multimedia Toolbook, Cast, and MediaShop). Some 3-D modeling programs allow animations of 3-D objects in time (for example, 3-D studio, Electric Image, Crystal Topas, Infini-D, and workstation software from Alias, SoftImage, and Wavefront). Morphing programs allow the animated transformations of one image into another (for example, Morph, Elastic Image, and Digital Morph). Presentation software (such as Powerpoint) allow you to save your slide shows in digital video format.

A treasure house of computer animation software has been developed for all platforms. This synthetic imagery has an advantage over captured video in that it is already available in digital form, requiring only conversion to an appropriate file format for the Web.

Figure 6.10 shows a sample screen from Director, a 2-D animation and authoring application that allows you to use a timeline "score" to control the movement and timing of images, sound, movies, and text on the screen. (All of these elements are called "cast" members.) The grid in the image is the score, which shows which cast members are visible at all points in time. Depending on the platform you are working on, you can create QuickTime or AVI movies of your animations. Figure 6.11 shows a sample screen from Infini-D, which is a 3-D modeling and animation program. The windows shown allow you to create synthetic 3-D shapes, apply textures to their surfaces, animate them in 3-D space, and create digital video of the animations. Figure 6.12 shows a screen from Morph, a program which creates a smooth animated digital video of the transition from your source to

your target image. Figure 6.13 shows the selection page from the UCSC computer graphics & animation home page that contains links to many different kinds of computer animations. The Web offers you a huge new audience for any animations you create in these kind of applications.

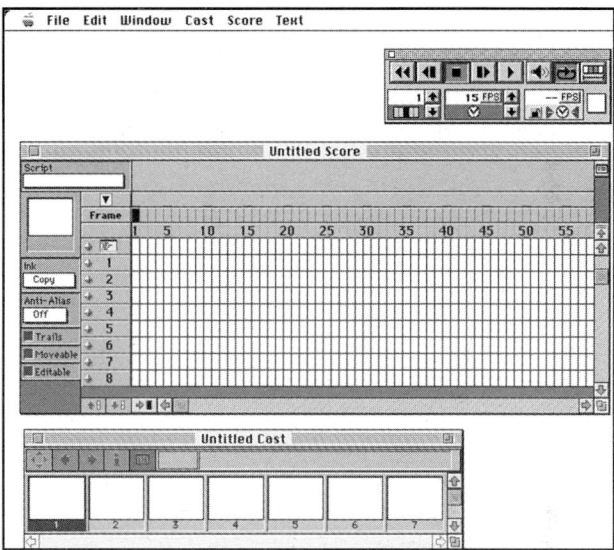

Figure 6.10:
Control windows from Director, a 2-D animation program.

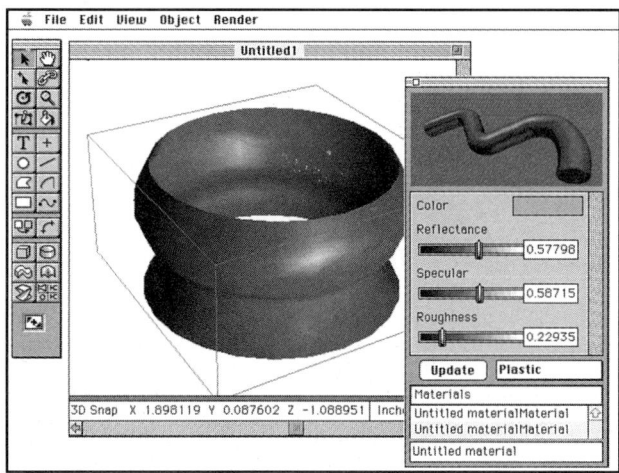

Figure 6.11:
Control windows from Infini-D, a 3-D modeling and animation program.

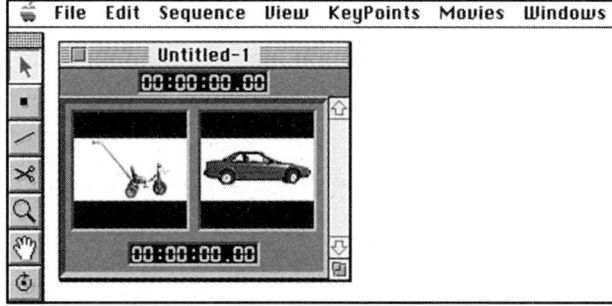

Figure 6.12:
Control windows from Morph, a morphing program.

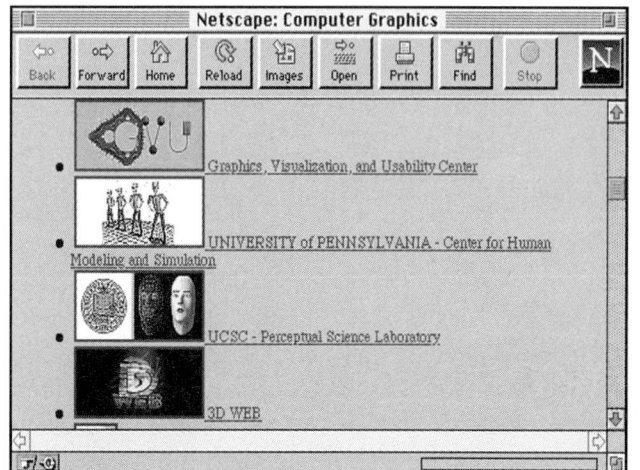

Figure 6.13:
UCSC computer graphics & animation home page.
`http://mambo.ucsc.edu/psl/cg.html`

Digital Video Editing and Manipulation Programs

No matter how you created your video—through capture or synthetic generation—you may want to edit it or add various effects before you offer it on the Web. For example, you might want cut out unnecessary sections or reduce frame rates to minimize file sizes, composite images and sounds from different sources, or add effects such as superimpositions and transitions between scenes. The video helper apps generally don't do much more than play video and convert formats. There are many excellent digital video editing and manipulation programs, however, that allow editing control and special effect treatments that would have cost hundreds of thousands of dollars only a few years ago (such as Premiere, AfterEffects, and MediaPro).

As an introduction to these capabilities, this section offers a brief outline of the kinds of capabilities offered by Premiere, which is available both for Macintosh and Windows computers. Other video manipulation applications offer similar features. Premiere allows you to do all of the following and more:

- Removal of unnecessary frames from video clips.

- Compositing of video by linking clips together from many sources.

- Changing the window size, window proportions, fps (frames per second), compression settings, and compression formats of video clips.

- Linking sound with video clips.

- Creation of titles.

- Setting the transition effects between clips.

- Overlaying video or sound in multiple layers.

- Changing the speed of segments.

- Adjusting visual characteristics of clips—for example, contrast, color balance, background color, and so on.

- Adjusting sound characteristics of clips—for example volume changes, reduction of noise.

- Application of exotic effects such as flying images, bending, multiplication, and so on.

Figure 6.14 shows the major construction window in Premiere. Track A and B show a timeline where various frames of the video are spread out. There is a barn door transition between them and the audio track is displayed in audio track B. Figures 6.15 and 6.16 show control windows for some of Premiere's special effects, a "Mesh Warp" filter that allows you to distort an image by moving control points, and the transitions selection box that shows a small sample of the visual effects that can be used in switches from one clip to another.

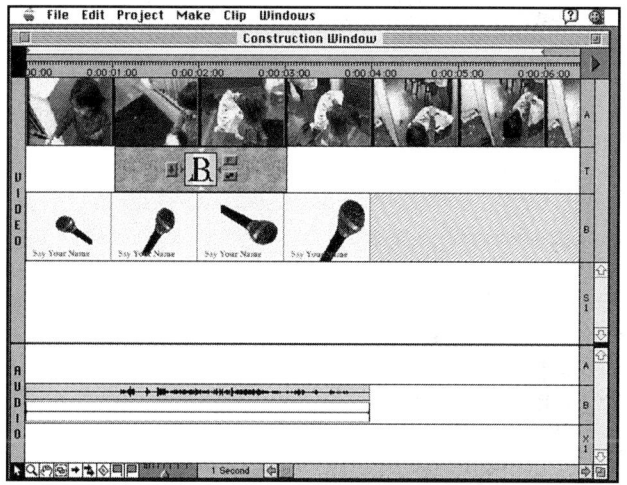

Figure 6.14:
Adobe Premiere's construction window.

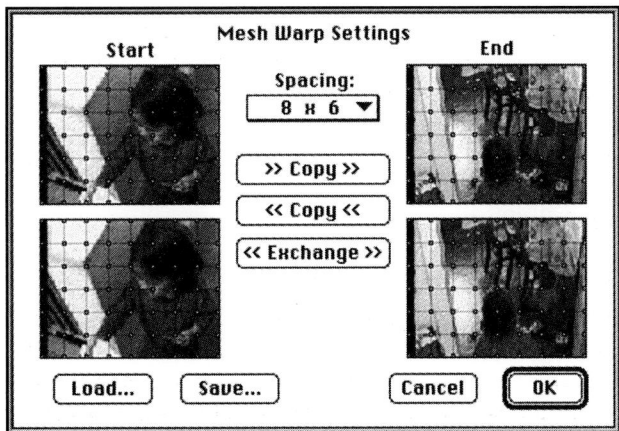

Figure 6.15:
Adobe Premiere's transitions mesh warp filter control box.

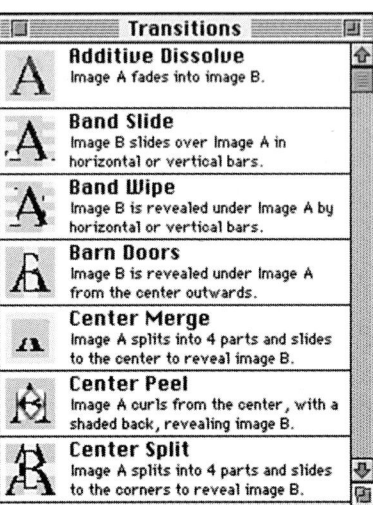

Figure 6.16:
Adobe Premiere's selection window.

Now you know most of what you need about the kinds of decisions to be made in creating digital video and formatting it for the Web. Exercise 6.2 walks you through the actual steps to change the format of a QuickTime movie into MPEG using the Sparkle helper app for the Macintosh. The steps would be similar on a Windows machine, although you would probably be converting from AVI into MPEG.

Exercise 6.2

Converting a QuickTime movie into MPEG format

Step 1:

First you must obtain a QuickTime (or AVI if you work on a Windows computer) movie to work with. You can generate it in any of the ways described previously. For this exercise, the movie is named info.mov. (Mov is the extension normally used for QuickTime.)

Step 2:

Launch the Sparkle helper application and open the QuickTime file from its file menu. The movie will appear in a display window with a playback controller beneath it.

Step 3:

Chose the Save as option from the file menu. A dialog box will open with a popup menu at its bottom for selecting file type. The MPEG format will be preselected as the default and the extension .MPG will be added to the file's name. Figure 6.17 illustrates this dialog box and popup menu.

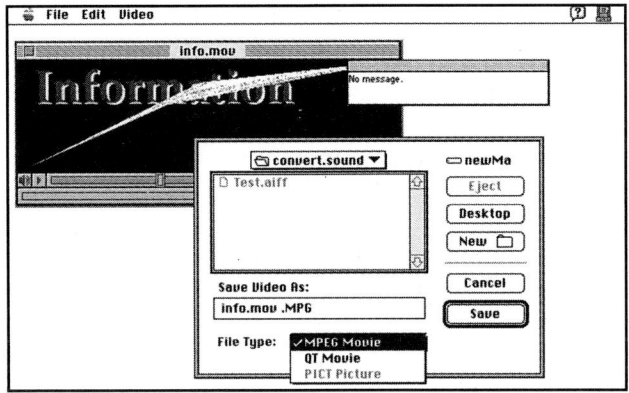

Figure 6.17:
Converting a QuickTime movie into MPEG format.

Step 4:

Click the OK button and a new version of your video will be saved in MPEG format, ready for distribution on the Web. (In the current version of Sparkle no sound can be included, although this may change in future versions when faster computers and MPEG chips become available.)

Keeping Viewer's Time in Mind

Did you think you had transmission time problems with images and sound? Digital video *really* taxes the Web. Digital video can take a very long time to transmit and open on the receiver's machine. Some of the largest files can even choke computers without sufficient memory and result in memory errors. It is not unusual to find digital video files of 4 or 5 megs.

What can you do to address the time problem? Motion segments should be carefully edited to eliminate unnecessary material, users should be advised about the file size of the videos they are about to access, files should be cut into multiple shorter segments if that is aesthetically possible, and users should be offered the option of accessing preview and summary clips first. All the file size reducing techniques described in the previous section on "Digitizing Video and Parameter Setting" should be judiciously used. It's considered good etiquette to include a warning about file size whenever you have links to video clips in your Web documents. Figure 6.18 shows a video selection page from the HotWired site, which provides descriptions and size indications to prospective linkers. This example shows a link to the Barbie Liberation Organization's nightly news video clip that gives information about their performance events to highlight this culture's attitudes toward gender.

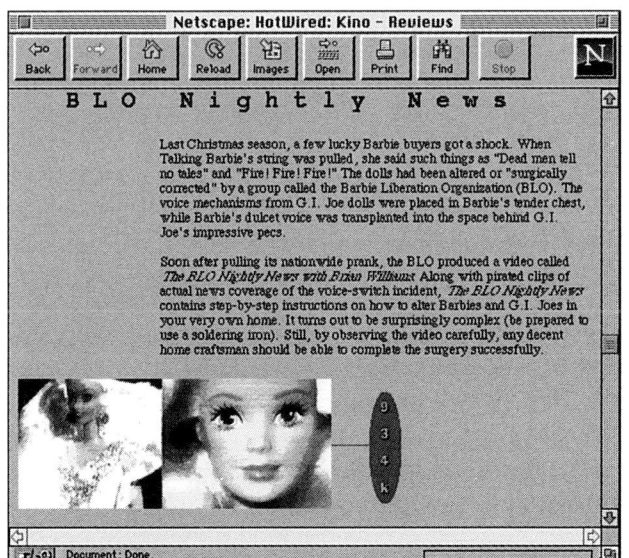

Figure 6.18:
HotWired video size notifications. Barbie liberation news clip.

`http://www.hotwired.com`

Considering Viewers without Digital Video Access

Many Web users lack the hardware and software capability for viewing digital video. Some will have only a rudimentary capability—for example, digital video might play slowly in very small windows. Again we face the now-familiar problem of how to address their computing situations.

As before, you can ignore this segment of your audience or design the information with alternatives for them. For example, you could offer composite stills for those with graphics but no digital video. Alternative text descriptions and summaries of the video can be offered for those with text-only access. Figures 6.19 and 6.20 show pages from Waxweb, a specially designed movie for the Web, which does attend to viewers with various kinds of access. Figure 6.19 shows the welcome page from the site and Figure 6.20 shows the page that users get when they pursue the "Burst" hypertext trail in the movie. Each scene in the sequence contains a small thumbnail image and text description of what all the links lead to.

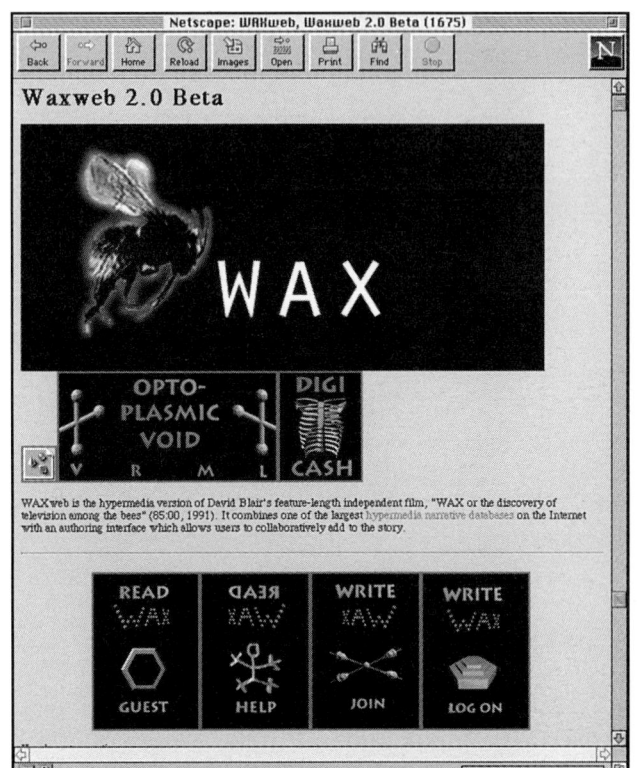

Figure 6.19:
Waxweb, a movie for the Web.

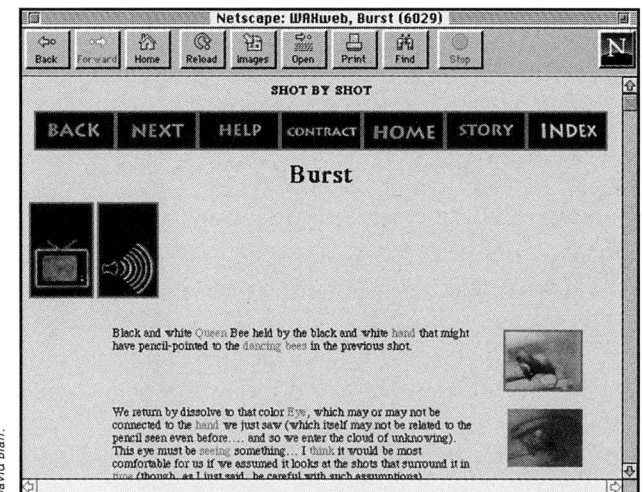

David Blair.

Figure 6.20:
Scene descriptions in the Burst page from Waxweb.

Design Opportunities with Digital Video

When you work with video you take on a significant challenge. You must juggle image, sound, motion, and time. Your audience has expectations shaped by years of television and movie watching. They have seen productions created by great talents and backed by extreme financial resources. Your productions will be viewed in this context. Yet, these challenges are great opportunities. Never before has there been such an instant showcase for new and fresh approaches as the Web. Your video must be as strong as you can make it.

Learning from Cinema and Video Traditions

There are almost as many approaches to cinema/ video as there are purposes for communication—for example, narrative, documentary, animation, experimental art, business presentation, and so on. Canons of practice can differ profoundly depending on genre—for example, exotic jumps in continuity or disjointed image composition that might be totally unacceptable in an educational film might be a major strength and point of interest in an experimental art film.

Even though you are working in new digital media, you can learn significantly from those who have worked in non-digital related media. Begin to study cinema and video from the perspective of a producer. In addition to just enjoying what you see, ask yourself these questions:

- What techniques do they use in telling stories, establishing mood, or conveying expository points?
- How do they establish continuity between scenes and use development over time to good advantage?
- How do they visually compose scenes to generate interest and communicate clearly?
- How do they interplay sound and image?
- How do they build the prior video experience of the audience?

Many theorists and practitioners have worked on these questions already. See the following online references in cinema and video studies that will be of use to those who want to understand some of this background.

References to Film and Video History and Theory

- *University of Michigan guide to film and video resources on the Web*
  `http://http2.sils.umich.edu/Public/fvl/film.html`

- *Cinema space for film studies and new media*
  `http://remarque.berkeley.edu:8001/~xcohen/`

- *Grafics—research group on the beginnings and the formation of the cinema and theatrical institutions*
  `http://grafics.histart.umontreal.ca/default-eng.html`

The relationship of cinema and video

This chapter has mostly referred to video. Yet, cinema is also an important source of history and techniques for Web video designers. Debate has long ranged about the implications of differences between cinema and video. For example, some analysts suggest that because cinema is usually seen in public, large-audience situations and video is seen in small, often private, viewing settings, the experiences can be psychologically quite different— for example, cinema was designed to play on the social interaction among audience members. Media theorist Marshall McLuhan expanded this theory to suggest that the cognitive activities required to construct a fast-changing projected electronic image (such as one sees on video or computer screens) make it different than the cool, high-resolution image of cinema.

Because of our exposure to cinema and television, works in video inevitably arouse certain associations for viewers. Video viewers interpret contemporary video works in light of all the television they saw growing up—for example, situation comedy, commercials, and TV news conventions. Cinema cannot help but suggest connections with Hollywood, celebrities, and the limits on morality and subject matter that are part of its history. Postmodern analysis and cultural theory suggest that the interaction of culture and media technology has grown so profound that it has become the major shaper of contemporary consciousness. For example, French theorist Jean Baudrillard asserts that we now live in "hyperreality" framed by media in which we react more to circulating media images than to any concrete reality. If you intend to work with digital video, you would be well advised to familiarize yourself with relevant theoretical and practical resources from this repertoire of ideas and strategies. For more information, see my article "Dark and Light Visions" available online at http://userwww.sfsu.edu/~swilson.

Pointers to Information on Marshall McLuhan and Baudrillard

- *McLuhan program at University of Toronto*
  `http://www.mcluhan.toronto.edu`

- *Carnegie Mellon English server on cultural theory (includes Baudrillard references)*
  `http://english-server.hss.cmu.edu/ctheory/CTHEORY.html`

- *Baudrillard online*
  `http://www.clas.ufl.edu/anthro/baud-online.html`

In addition to drawing on these historical sources, you can draw on more contemporary sources. Computer media have opened new fields of design in areas of computer graphics animation, games, special effects, and interactivity. The sources in the following reference sidebar point to information about computer animation and multimedia.

Information on Computer Animation, Computer Graphics, Games, and Multimedia

- *Yahoo computer graphics and animation resources*
`http://www.yahoo.com/Computers/Graphics/`

- *Gweb trade magazine on computer graphics*
`http://www.cinenet.net/GWEB/`

- *Computer graphics animation FAQ*
`http://www.cis.ohio-state.edu/hypertext/faq/`
`usenet/graphics/animation-faq/faq.html`

- *Multimedia institutes*
`http://www.yahoo.com/Computers/Multimedia/`
`Institutes/`

- *Virtual library on computer graphics*
`http://www.dataspace.com/WWW/vlib/`
`compgraphics.html`

- *Computer graphics FAQ*
`http://www.cis.ohio-state.edu/hypertext/faq/`
`usenet/graphics/faq/faq.html`

Technical Issues When Producing Video

How does one design strong video? All the equipment in the world does not guarantee results. Care, attention to detail, hard work, and artistic inspiration are always of value. Although a full discussion of video production techniques is outside the scope of this book, a few simple classic guidelines are presented here. Web authors need to attend to issues such as the following:

- Shots should be carefully composed with important subjects prominent and unnecessary visual material excluded.
- Camera angle and position should be selected to reinforce key ideas.
- Lighting should be sufficient and articulate with design purposes.
- Focus should be clean and sharp except where aesthetic purposes dictate otherwise.
- Cameras should be held stable.
- Sound should be as clean as possible with external microphones used when appropriate.
- Motion should be tracked carefully with zoom used only for specific purposes.
- Editing should be tight. Continuity in time should be matched carefully to aesthetic or communication purposes.

The traditional way of learning these principles is to study many film and video examples, looking for examples of strong and weak production techniques. Then you would make many small exercise videos that explore particular production issues that we could critique together. We would also address the special needs of Web video. Obviously that won't work here. Nonetheless, I can show you an example of that kind of production analysis, which will help you think about your own work.

Consider the classic water skiing video illustrated in Figure 6.5. If you haven't already played it on your computer, access it via your Web browser and watch it. Note that it is 537K, so it will take some time to load if you are on a slow link. Some of its compositional elements are worth noting. The subjects of interest are always kept in tight focus. The frame is usually composed so that the skiers fill the fore-ground rather than using more distant shots. The camera was mounted on a boat to keep up with the skiers and provide the same perspective without panning or zooming. The lighting was very clean (easy in this situation because the shot was taken in full sunlight).

Subject matter is also a critical consideration in video production. Even a technically excellent clip will not succeed if it is boring. Consider the subject matter in the skiing video. It works on one level just because the tricks the skiers do are exotic, visually enjoyable to watch, and demonstrate a fascinating level of physical skill. It had other appeals when it was originally produced. It was newsreel footage of a travel attraction filled with beautiful women in bathing suits in a faraway location (Florida) at a time when distant travel was not as easy as it is now. The video might not have the same appeal now for many audiences. Tastes have changed about what constitutes interesting travel attractions and there are new critical perspectives about watching women in bathing suits.

Special Issues in Web Video

Video on the Web makes its own special demands because of the need to reduce file sizes. Designing with these in mind will make your video work well on the Web.

- Size of windows: Compose your scenes so they are not too complex to work in small windows.
- Reduced frame rate: Try to create movement in your clips that does not rely on full 30 fps video. It should make sense and be appealing even if slower frame rates must be used.
- Compression reductions in visual quality: Compose your scenes to take into account the visual impact of compression. For example, simple backgrounds will compress cleaner than very busy backgrounds.
- Length of video: Short clips work best. If at all possible, compose your video so that it will make sense in short segments.
- Color vs. black-and-white: Black-and-white movies generally take less file space than color and sometimes can be clearer in highly compressed images. Consider black-and-white where possible.

Even more important, you should consider experimentation with the unique context of the Web. Ask yourself what kind of video could not exist in any other situation. For example, Waxweb (illustrated in Figure 6.19) is billed as the first movie produced explicitly for the Web. It is purposely produced in many small segments, takes advantage of the hypertext structure of the Web to offer many navigational paths, offers lots of information even to those without high bandwidth connections, uses a variety of media, encourages visitors' contributions, and presents an unorthodox artistic vision that might not get wide distribution in any other context.

The "Burning Man" event at the WELL's Telecircus site offers another example. This art/theater event, which takes place in the Nevada desert, creates an unusual visual spectacle of giant burning sculptures and performance events associated with them. Normally, very few people in the world would know about this event or get to experience any part of it. The creators created documentation of the event, which they made available on the Web. The videos they created are quite strange and beautiful. Figure 6.21 shows the Burning Man documentation from the Telecircus site on the WELL. Figure 6.22 shows the movie selection page and Figure 6.23 shows some scenes from their "Fireworks" video. Chapter 8, "Experimenting on the Web," discusses other video experiments on the Web, such as live feeds of unusual scenes and use of video in collaborative events.

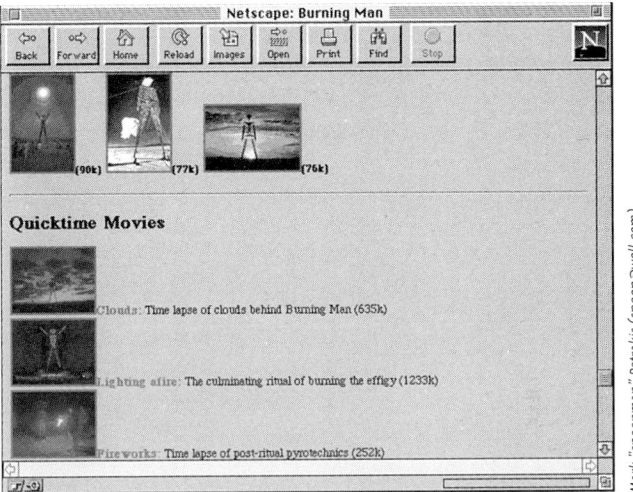

Figure 6.22:
Movie selection page from the Burning Man site.

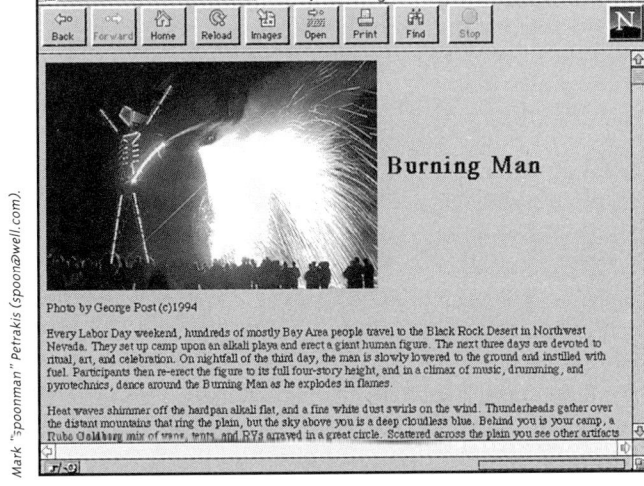

Figure 6.21:
Burning Man documentation from the Telecircus site on the WELL.

Mark "spoonman" Petrakis (spoon@well.com).

Figure 6.23:
Scenes from "Fireworks" movie documenting the Burning Man event.

Digital video via the Internet is an extraordinary development. It opens a window to future possibilities called *convergence*, in which computing, video, and communications technologies all begin to function together. Some analysts see this development as the dawning of new kinds of possibilities. For example, one day soon we may not have separate TVs, computers, and telephones. There may be only one device that simultaneously provides entertainment, education, international communication, information, and processing. Much of the information will be in the form of video. The Web is a laboratory to explore these possibilities, and you can help shape its future.

Interactivity is an important part of this future scenario. The Web is already highly interactive with its easy links to so many kinds of information. Chapter 7 shows how you can enhance this interactivity even more by creating live imagemaps and fill-in forms.

Summary

You must strive to ensure that your video accomplishes your artistic or communicative purposes with as much power and technical polish as possible. In support of this goal you have learned how digital video works, how to format it correctly for the Web, and how to design with the Web context clearly in mind.

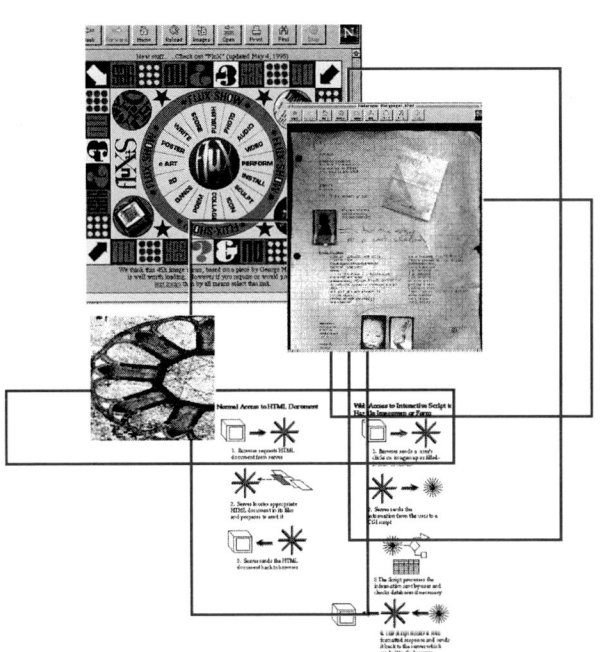

Chapter 7

Advanced
Interactive
Capabilities:
Imagemaps,
CGI Scripts,
and Fill-In
Forms

The Web is interactive at its heart; nothing happens unless the user clicks on hypermedia links. However, it has even more sophisticated interactive capabilities, including:

- Imagemaps—Clickable images that contain links to different locations depending on which "hot spot" or part of the image you click.
- Fill-in forms—On-screen worksheets that visitors can complete and submit.
- Indexes—Full-text searches of documents stored on your site.

Imagemaps and fill-in forms add truly interactive aspects to your Web documents. Through on-screen surveys, guestbooks, contest entries, and other forms, you can create a computer interface that responds to user commands. These are examples of *interactive events,* in which the user's input is required to accomplish a given task.

This chapter will give you a good understanding of how these exciting capabilities work by answering the following questions:

- How do you code your Web documents to include imagemaps and forms?
- What must you do at the server end to handle sophisticated interactions with users?
- How do you set up the hotzones in imagemaps to respond to user clicks?
- How do you write scripts that allow servers to respond to information users provide in forms?
- How do you design your Web pages to take best advantage of imagemaps and fill-in forms?

Basic Requirements for Implementation

Before you can make use of these advanced functions, you must establish that your Web browser and your server software are configured to access them. By now, most browsers do support forms, but not all browsers support them equally well. The server at which your site is based must be configured to access programs (usually called *gateway scripts*) conforming to the *Common Gateway Interface* (CGI) standard in order for you to include functions such as imagemaps, forms, or text searches in your Web documents. You should ask your system administrator or whoever operates your server software about what advanced functions are available to you.

But even if your server is equipped to deal with these capabilities, there still may be barriers to your ability to access them. You will need to learn how to create scripts to perform the actions you want, or discover where you can obtain such scripts. Reference lists later in this chapter list some online resources for obtaining this kind of help and Appendixes B and C provide details on setting up scripts. There are also a number of Usenet newsgroups where Web designers can post queries and exchange gateway scripts. Additionally, some Internet access providers consider these advanced functions a threat to server security or a burden on the server's load; as a result, they may restrict or prohibit user access for implementing forms and imagemaps in their Web pages. Again, you should get confirmation from your service provider or system administrator about what capabilities are available to you, the user.

Understanding the Process

A server calls on a gateway script to act based upon information that the user indicates in the browser. Here are the steps for what goes on behind-the-scenes in an interactive request:

1. The user clicks a button in a form, enters text into a box, or clicks an imagemap. The coding for all these functions includes a link to a URL that jumps to a gateway script.

2. The browser identifies the appropriate URL attached to that link, notes that it is a gateway script, and sends a message to the server requesting the next document. It includes the supplementary information (sometimes called the arguments) such as the text from the form or the coordinates of a mouse click in an imagemap.

3. The server receives the message and finds the support script or program that is indicated to handle the supplementary information coming with the request.

4. The support script processes the supplementary information. It may need to call on additional files to complete the processing—for example, a file that contains a database or a file that maps certain parts of the imagemap to certain actions.

5. The script generates an appropriate response in HTML format and sends it back to the main server software.

6. The server sends the generated document back to the requester.

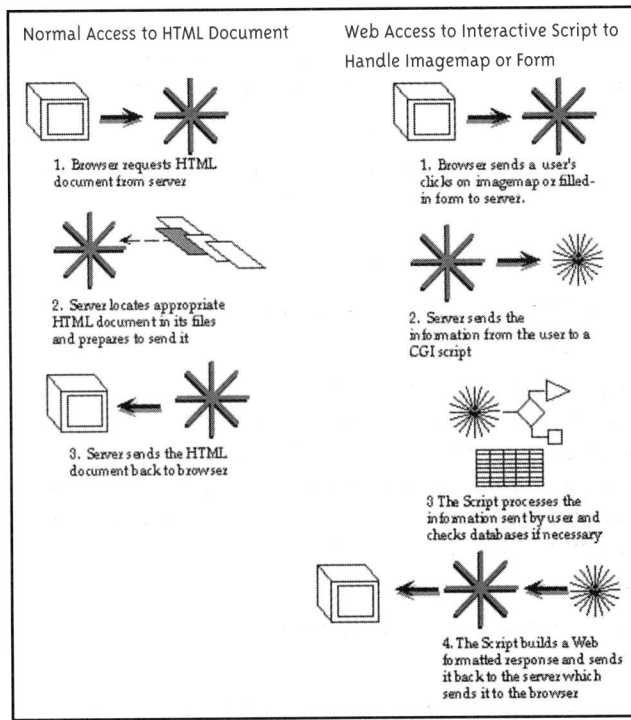

Figure 7.1:
Comparing steps in simple HTML requests versus interactive requests.

You can use almost any programming language to write your gateway scripts, provided of course that it's one supported by your server software. UNIX shell commands and perl, for example, are commonly used to create scripts. If you have some kind of programming or scripting background, this programming will not be a major problem for you. Even if you have no scripting or programming background, developers have refined user-friendly scripting languages such as HyperCard and AppleScript in the Macintosh world and Visual Basic in the Windows world that will allow you to create the response scripts. With any script, however, you will need the cooperation of the server systems operator to install the scripts in the right place (usually a directory called the cgi-bin directory in UNIX systems) and to set the system configuration files to find them.

What Is CGI (Common Gateway Interface)?

In the early days of the Web, developers who wanted to build interactive events constructed the support programs in whatever style or language they wanted. Others used programs and services already in existence, such as WAIS (Wide Area Information Services). The kinds of interfaces between these programs and the servers they worked with proliferated, creating the potential for many conflicts. With the introduction of the CGI standard, the Web community attempted to introduce some standardization into the methods servers and external programs and scripts would use to communicate. The CGI standard was developed by a collaboration of many of the developers of the first Web servers. A goal was to make the programming easier without stymieing the creativity of developers. This standard governs such things as what kind of information the servers will send to external programs (for example, what variables will be used to send the user's clicks in an imagemap) and how the external programs must format the information (for example, the headers attached to files) that the programs send back to the servers.

Imagemap, forms, and index handling programs now mostly assume the CGI convention. Several of the examples of methods for creating interactive imagemaps and forms (illustrated in Appendices B and C) will make use of CGI concepts. The sections that follow give a brief introduction to the CGI specifications. You can consult the reference list that follows for more online resources on CGI.

Pointers to Information on Common Gateway Interface (CGI)

* *Yahoo index of information on CGI*
```
http://www.yahoo.com/Computers/World_Wide_Web/
CGI___Common_Gateway_Interface/
```

* *NCSA (Mosaic home site) information resources on CGI*
```
http://hoohoo.ncsa.uiuc.edu/cgi/overview.html
```

* *FAQ (frequently asked questions) on CGI*
```
http://www.halcyon.com/hedlund/cgi-faq/faq.html
```

* *Examples of CGI Scripts and mini-tutorials (UNIX)*
```
http://hoohoo.ncsa.uiuc.edu/cgi/forms.html
```

```
http://hoohoo.ncsa.uiuc.edu/docs/setup/admin/
  script-data/GetScripts.html
```

```
http://www.catt.ncsu.edu/users/bex/www/tutor/
  index.html
```

```
http://hoohoo.ncsa.uiuc.edu/cgi/examples.html
```

```
http://wsk.eit.com/wsk/dist/doc/libcgi/libcgi.html
```

- *Examples of CGI Scripts and mini-tutorials (Macintosh)*

`http://www.uwtc.washington.edu/computing/www/`
`lessons/`

`http://edb518ea.edb.utexas.edu/scripts/cgix/`
`cgix.html`

- *Examples of CGI Scripts and mini-tutorials (Windows)*

`http://www.city.net/win-httpd/httpddoc/wincgi.htm`

CGI Header Specifications

In order for your script to be read by browsers and by your server software, you'll need to format the header and data specifications for your script output to comply with the CGI standards. The header of the material your script sends to the server must contain several items. If these are not exactly specified, the server will return an error and not send your information back to the requester. Each item must be on a separate line followed by a carriage return and linefeed character. At the end you should insert two blank lines with carriage returns and linefeeds. The items include server software name and version number, status code, and content type. If the material points toward another URL, it should contain a location item. Here is an example:

```
HTTP/1.0 200 OK
Server: MacHTTP
MIME-Version: 1.0
Content-type: text/html
```

The first line includes standard status codes and explanations. The status codes are all three-digit codes. For example 200 = OK means a normal transaction and 320 means redirection (the client should fetch a new URL). You may have seen some of the error codes if you've ever had difficulty locating a specific URL; for example, 404 = URL not found. The second line lists the name and version of the server software being used. The third line tells which version of MIME is being used and the fourth line identifies the content-type in standard Internet MIME format. The fourth line would give the URL of the new document if redirection was called for. You can find the full list of status codes at http://www.w3.org/hypertext/WWW/Protocols/HTTP/HTRESP.html. Appendix C presents samples of scripts that generate Web pages with this header.

CGI Data Specifications: Building a Web Page to Send Back

Your script would then need to append any information you wanted to send back to the requester below the header. This information would need to be formatted with standard HTML markup tags. For example, it might start with this line:

```
<HTML><HEAD><TITLE> Response to request</TITLE>
</HEAD>
```

In essence your script would need to build an HTML page dynamically that the server will ultimately send back to a requester to be displayed by the Web browser. Exercise 7.1 shows more details of this process of creating the page to be sent back.

CGI Data Sent to Scripts

The CGI specifications also require the server to send information to scripts in standardized *environmental variables*. These contain information about the server and its software, the requester's computer, and the information sent from the user—for example the text the user typed on a fill-in form. Each variable is given a standardized name so all scripts can refer to the same variable. Here's a sample of some of the CGI environmental variables and a brief description of the information they contain. A full list of them can be found in the CGI specification Web page listed in the reference list. Exercise 7.1 and 7.2 and the scripts in Appendix C show more details of how you can use them.

- SERVER_SOFTWARE: The name and version of the information server software answering the request (and running the gateway). Format: name/version.

- SERVER_NAME: The server's hostname, DNS alias, or IP address as it would appear in self-referencing URLs.

- REQUEST_METHOD: The method with which the request was made. For HTTP, this is "GET", "POST", and so on.

- POST_ARGS: The data passed in when using the POST method.

- CLIENT_ADDRESS: The IP address or domain name of the client making the request.

We've just described how a program can be executed when a user activates a link containing a URL that points to a script. In order for your script to be read by browsers and by your server software, you'll need to format the header and data for your script output to comply with the CGI standards.

In your HTML documents, you include a link to a gateway script with the anchor tag. Exercise 7.1 walks you though the steps in setting up the anchor tag in a Web page that would

point to your script and shows how to create a simple CGI script. The exercise illustrates how the server can tell that the URL points to a script instead of just another HTML document. This simple script will send back a Web page that contains the current date and time and the IP address or name of the requester's computer.

CGI scripts must be written specifically for the platform they run on. For example, you will not be able to run a Visual Basic application on your UNIX Web server. Example 7.1a's sample script is an AppleScript based script that runs on a Macintosh in conjunction with a Macintosh Web server such as MacHTTP or WebSTAR. Example 7.1b shows you how to write a perl script to accomplish the same effect on a UNIX server. All Web designers can benefit from these exercises, however, because the functional steps are the same on all platforms even though the details differ.

Exercise 7.1a:

Creating a link to a CGI script on a Macintosh Web server and the script that services the request

Step 1:
Create a Web page with basic structural tags. Here is the example we'll use:

```
<HTML>
<HEAD>
<TITLE> A simple CGI script </TITLE>
</HEAD>
</BODY>
<H2> Demonstration of a Simple Script </H2>
```

```
This link will access a CGI script that will return
the current date and time and print out your
computer's domain name or IP address.
Tell me the date and time.
</BODY>
</HTML>
```

Step 2:

Add the link tag that points to the script. The link tag is the same as other link tags except that it points to a *script* or *program* rather than to a HTML document. Here is what your coding for this Web page might look like with the link to the script added:

```
<HTML>
<HEAD>
<TITLE> A simple CGI script </TITLE>
</HEAD>
</BODY>
<H2> Demonstration of a Simple Script </H2>
This link will access a CGI script that will return
the current date and time and print out your
computer's domain name or IP address.
<A HREF= "http://netaddress/directory/scripts/
  time.cgi"> Tell me the date and time </A>
</BODY>
</HTML>
```

Note that the URL ends with the standard suffix for CGI scripts, *.cgi*, not with *.html*. When a user activates this link, the server would *call* the script and wait for a returned answer. The script would have the responsibility of generating a properly formatted document to send back to the server and ultimately to the user.

Several requirements must be met to actually try out this script. You will need access to an Internet-connected, Apple events-capable Macintosh running Web server software such as MacHTTP or WebSTAR. You will need to set the configuration file of the server to know where the script is located. The address of the script illustrated in Step 2 would need to specifically point to this computer's Internet address. You'll have to use Apple's Script Editor or some other application capable of generating AppleScript programs to create the script.

When the script gets called, it will build a Web page consisting of a CGI header and text, coded in HTML, to print the current date and time and to echo back the requester's computer domain name or IP address.

Step 3:

Initialize variables and create a standard CGI header. First you must initialize some variables that will be needed for the final formatting of the CGI document to be sent back to the server. CGI scripts need carriage returns and linefeeds to end each line. The initialization creates an explicit variable called crlf that contains both of these. It also builds a standard CGI header as described in the previous section describing CGI headers. It puts that header into a variable called http_10_header. The AppleScript code looks like the sample that follows:

```
global lf
global crlf
global cr
global http_10_header
```

```
set lf to ASCII character (10)
set cr to return
set crlf to cr & lf
set http_10_header to "HTTP/1.0 200 OK" & crlf &
  "Server: MacHTTP" & crlf & "MIME-Version: 1.0" &
  crlf & "Content-type: text/html" & crlf & crlf
```

Step 4:

Wait for an Apple event and use the environmental variables sent from the server: The MacHTTP server sends an Apple event called *WWWΩsdoc*. This is the event that the script is waiting for. The server also sends arguments that include the environmental variables discussed in the previous section on CGI data sent by servers to scripts. This simple script makes use only of the user's Internet name or IP address (*client_address*). An imagemap or form handling script would also make extensive use of the environmental variable *post_args* that would contain all the information from the user. The code that follows shows the programming structure that waits for the Apple event and makes the arguments sent from the server into variables available to the program—for example, *addr* is assigned to *client_address*.

```
on «event WWWΩsdoc» path_args given  «class
addr»:client_address
............ (body to be added in step 5)
end «event WWWΩsdoc»
```

Step 5:

Build a Web page that shows the script's output. In this case, the page will display the current date and time and the user's computer's address. You must create a string of text including HTML tags to send back to the server. This is the same text you would enter if you were making an HTML document from scratch except it is all one continuous string. The CGI header is already in the variable *http_10_header* that will be sent back to the server. The AppleScript command (current date) generates a string containing the current date and time. The return command means that the AppleScript program sends this string of HTML text back to the server to be forwarded to the requester. The return structure is shown next in the context of the entire script:

```
global lf
global crlf
global cr
global http_10_header

set lf to ASCII character (10)
set cr to return
set crlf to cr & lf
set http_10_header to "HTTP/1.0 200 OK" & crlf &
  "Server: MacHTTP" & crlf & "MIME-Version: 1.0" &
  crlf & "Content-type: text/html" & crlf & crlf
on «event WWWΩsdoc» path_args given «class
addr»:client_address
return http_10_header & " <HTML><HEAD><TITLE> CGI
Response</TITLE> </HEAD><BODY><H3>
You are coming from" & client_address & "<HR> The
current date and time is: " & (current time) &"
</H3></BODY></HTML>"
end «event WWWΩsdoc»
```

Step 6:

View the output. This script dynamically generates a Web page and sends it back to the user. If you have a Macintosh-based Web server, you only need to place this script in the location that the server expects CGI scripts. Figure 7.2 shows a sample Web page generated from this script.

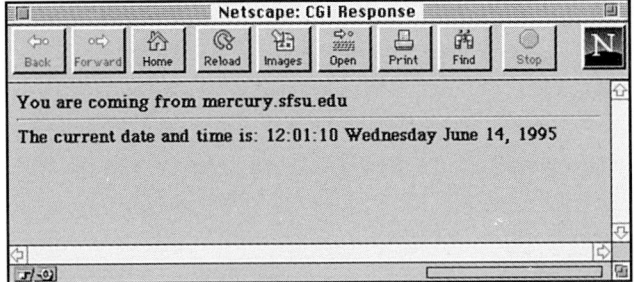

Figure 7.2:
Web page generated by script in Exercise 7.1a.

Exercise 7.1b shows you how to create a version of the script described in Exercise 7.1a that will run on a UNIX server. It is written in perl.

Exercise 7.1B:

Creating a link to a CGI script on a UNIX Web server and the script (written in perl) that services the request

Step 1:

Create a Web page with a link to the script. Your Web page to call the UNIX perl script can match the one shown in Exercise 7.1a.

```
<HTML>
<HEAD>
<TITLE> A simple CGI script </TITLE>
</HEAD>
```

```
</BODY>
<H2> Demonstration of a Simple Script </H2>
```

This link will access a CGI script that will return the current date and time and print out your computer's domain name or IP address.

```
<A HREF= "http://netaddress/directory/scripts/
time.cgi"> Tell me the date and time.</A>
</BODY>
</HTML>
```

Customarily, the script filename should end with the suffix *.cgi*.

Step 2:

Initialize variables and create a standard CGI header. Your script must generate a valid HTML document with a standard header to send back to the server. In this example, we want to send back the current date and time and echo back the user's address. We also need to create a standard Web header in conventional Web format. Our perl script creates a series of variables to hold the relevant information.

The first line defines what kind of interpreter you will be using and where it is. The second line assigns the CGI environmental variable *REMOTE_ADDR* that the server sent to the script to a variable named *$Address*. This contains the user's domain address. The third line creates a variable called *$Header* that will contain the properly formatted Web header. As in Step 3, it must contain one line identifying the HTTP format used and status code of the result, another line with the server name, and another line with the MIME type. Every line must end with a combined linefeed and carriage return.

The fourth line creates a variable called *$Date* that contains the current date and time. The example lines are illustrated here:

```
#!/opt/gnu/bin/perl

$Address = $ENV{"REMOTE_ADDR"};
$Header = "Content-type: text/html";
$Date = 'date';
```

Step 3:

Assemble the HTML document with the proper header and send it to the server. Your script must next actually generate a valid Web document with a standard header and send it to the server to send back to the browser. The first line that follows sends the header to the server. The second line creates part of the HTML document that contains the structural tags. The third line sends back the current date and time and the fourth echoes back the user's domain. The exit ends the script.

```
print "$Header\n\n";
print "<HTML><HEAD><TITLE>CGI RESPONSE
 </TITLE><H3>\n";
print "<P>You are coming from $Address<HR>\n";
print "<P>The Date and Time is: $Date </H3></BODY>
 </HTML>\n";
exit 0;
```

The characters "n" in the previous script generate a carriage return; two are required after a header.

Step 4:

That's it. The users receive a custom response to their links containing the current time and their addresses.

Working with Imagemaps

Imagemaps can serve double duty. The same images that visually delight and inform can also serve as front ends full of visual hot links leading to materials at your site. Your images can give viewers extra information about what to expect when they activate the links. Imagemaps can be straightforward visual indexes for some kinds of information—for example, geographic maps as gateways to information about the locations represented on the map. Figure 7.3 shows an example where places on San Francisco State University's campus map also link to information about those places.

Imagemaps can also provide a more metaphoric access—for example a symbolic collage of images suggesting more symbolic relationships between the images and the subjects to be accessed. Figure 7.4 shows Rob Hain's Web art event in which the user can pursue different paths. The image shows nine doors that lead to a page devoted to each of the muses. Also imagemaps allow a work-around for HTML's text style limitations. You can make an imagemap in which you use any kind of styled text you want to indicate links.

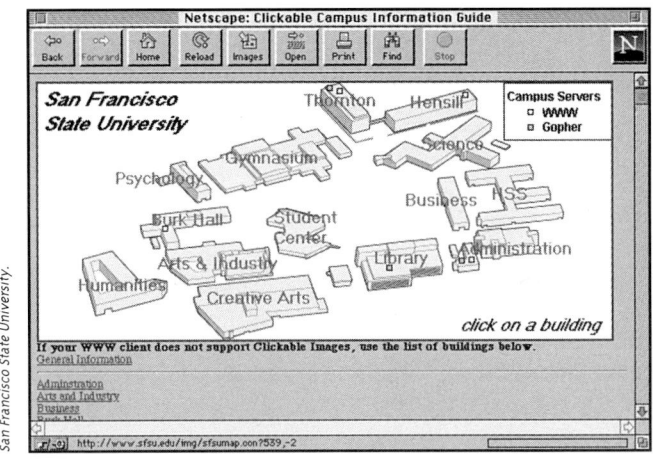

San Francisco State University.

Figure 7.3:
SFSU's interactive campus map.
`http://www.sfsu.edu/clickmap/sfsumap.htm`

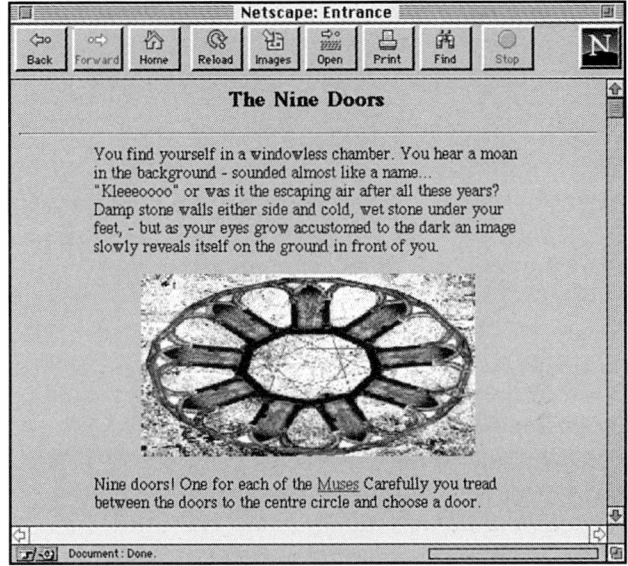

Rob Hain.

Figure 7.4:
Nine Doors to the Muses.
`http://www.scotborders.co.uk/musee/3doors.html`

How do you actually set up an imagemap? What are the steps? What do you need to know to make them work correctly?

There are five actions you must take to set up an imagemap:

- Deciding if an imagemap is appropriate
- Applying the <ISMAP> HTML tag
- Deciding where to place hot links
- Setting up a map file
- Arranging for the server to respond to imagemaps

Deciding if an Imagemap Is Appropriate

The first step in preparing an imagemap event is clarifying your reasons for making an image into an imagemap. How will an imagemap add value to your document—both visually and as an interface method? You will have much greater control over the design because you are not limited by HTML's limitations on text or image placement, but there are also technical considerations.

There may be some trade-offs you face in using an imagemap as opposed to single images. Although imagemaps are often a more intriguing interface than just using an array of more conventional images, they are more complex to set up and their processing can take a bit more time to complete because of the extra step of the server calling a script. Also, the Web readers get less information about the embedded links. Web browsers typically display the URL of a linked inline image as a user moves the mouse over the image. Moving a mouse over an imagemap, however, shows only the link to the URL of the script that will process the coordinates. An imagemap does not make clear to the user what URLs each section links to unless the designer somehow includes that information in the graphic image. Figure 7.5 shows a comparison of the same link information displayed via an imagemap and an array of small images. If your server setup allows them and there is no reason to make the embedded links obvious, imagemaps are generally preferable because of the greater visual control they give you.

Applying the <ISMAP> Tag

Identifying your image as an imagemap is the easiest part; just include the <ISMAP> attribute inside the <IMG> tag for your image. The URL in an <ISMAP> attribute points to a script that can handle the information about the coordinates of the mouse click. This alerts the browser that it should record and transmit the coordinates of where in the image a user has clicked the mouse. The example that follows shows an image tag with the <ISMAP> attribute.

```
<A HREF="/script.directory/imagemap">
<IMG SRC="choiceimage.GIF" ISMAP></A>
```

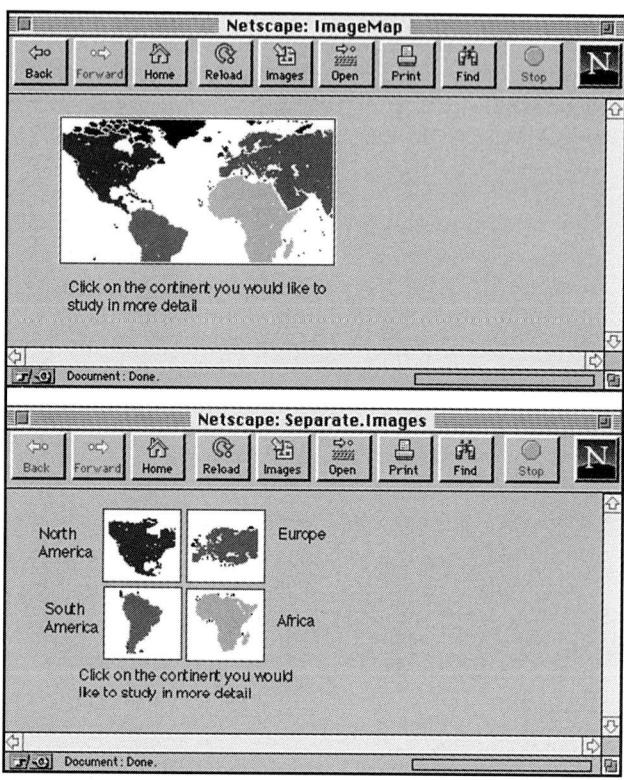

Figure 7.5:
Comparing an imagemap with multiple small image links.

Deciding What to Make a Hot Link

How do you decide what should be a hot link? For straight-forward informational events, the decision is fairly clear. There are discrete graphic components that each lead somewhere specific. Indeed, they are created to represent the resources they point at. For example, on the Berkeley "Subway" imagemap (Figure 7.6) each stop points to a Web resource. For more experimental applications of imagemaps the relationship between image and resource might not be so cut and dry. There might be symbolic or metaphoric connections, like in the Kids' Space site (Figure 7.7). Each item in the living room links to some resource, but the abstract imagery does not explicitly describe the destination. After you use the imagemap for a while the symbolic system becomes clearer.

Deciding Where to Place the Coordinates of Hot Areas in an Imagemap

Imagemaps use the Cartesian (or x,y) coordinate system to identify the location of the cursor where the user clicks. The browser determines the location relative to the origin of the imagemap image—for example, at a pixel located 100 pixels to the right and 50 pixels down from the corner—and sends these coordinates to the script indicated in the URL. Figure 7.8 shows a computer graphic Cartesian grid laid over a hypothetical imagemap. An invisible grid is mapped over the image. The grid is divided into equally spaced horizontal and vertical units. Each spot on the map has a coordinate address that is composed of its horizontal distance from the o horizontal axis (left side) and its vertical distance from the vertical o axis (top).

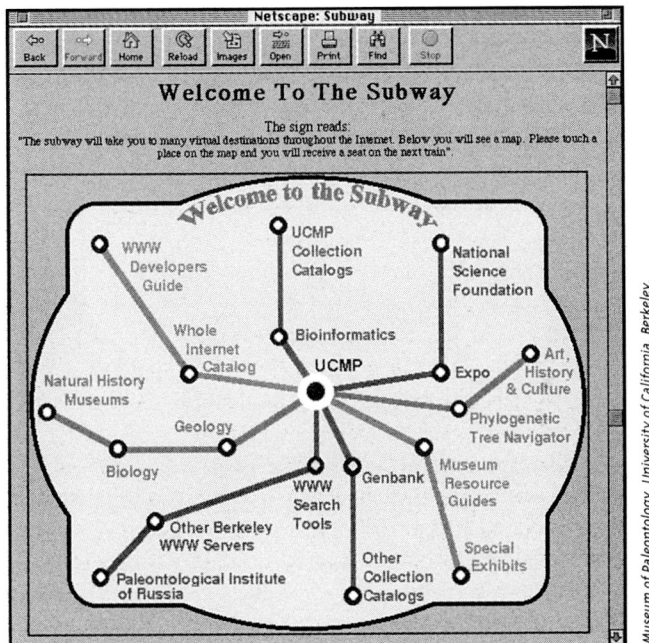

Figure 7.6:
Berkeley's subway map of Web resources.
`http://ucmp1.berkeley.edu/subway.html`

Figure 7.7:
Kids' Space imagemap.
`http://www.interport.net/kids-space/`

A quick primer on the coordinate system applied to computer graphics

In the two-dimensional version of the coordinate system, an imaginary grid is superimposed on a surface. A point of origin is declared and perpendicular axes are drawn through it. Each axis is imagined to be divided into equally spaced units.

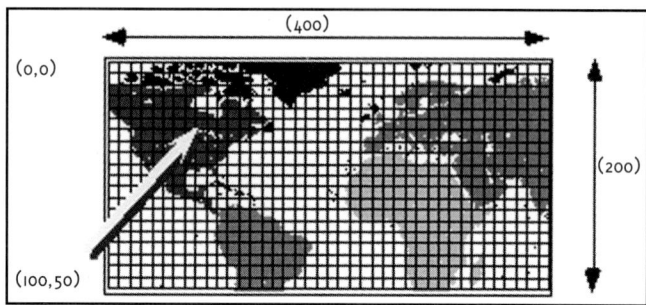

Figure 7.8:
Cartesian grid superimposed on image to identify location of mouse clicks.

All points are given values based on the number of units distant from o they are. Every point in space can then absolutely be identified by its horizontal and vertical position relative to the origin. Thus, a point might have the address (100,50) if it is 100 units right and 50 units down from the origin.

By convention the horizontal position is given first. The horizontal axis is often called the x axis and the vertical axis is called the y axis. The coordinates are consequently called the x,y coordinates. In classical Cartesian coordinate systems, such as you might have learned in geometry, units above the horizontal axis are considered positive and those below are negative. Computer graphics systems made a modification of this system in which the origin is at the top-left corner and positions below are indicated as positive numbers.

Browser software appends information about the coordinates onto the URL and sends it to the appropriate server. In this situation the URL cannot be an HTML page or media resource; it must be a script that knows what to do with the incoming coordinate information. For example the actual data sent to the server for the click in Figure 7.8 might look like this:

```
Net_address/map.script.cgi?100,50
```

This coordinate information will work only if you have already specified which areas will be the hot areas. Just as the browser software uses the coordinate system to locate the user clicks, the server software will use the system to identify what areas of the image are significant. Most commonly, the author does this by specifying boundaries surrounding the important graphic areas. You can specify these boundaries by identifying the coordinates of rectangles, polygons, and ovals that enclose the areas. For example, you specify a rectangle by indicating the coordinates of the upper-left and lower-right corners. In Cartesian coordinate space, only one rectangle can share these two corners. A polygon is specified by a list of the coordinates of all of its vertices. You identify a circle by specifying the coordinates of the center and the length of the radius (CERN system) or by specifying a pair of coordinates including the center and any edgepoint (NCSA system).

In designing an imagemap, you must determine this information about the elements of your image. Many graphics programs contain features that help you identify coordinates in your image. For example, the helper applications xv for UNIX systems, Adobe Photoshop for Mac or DOS/Windows platforms, and GIFConverter for the Macintosh will let you determine these coordinates. To accomplish this, you turn on the option to display coordinates, set the scale to pixels, and the coordinates of the mouse are continuously updated as you move the mouse around the image.

Setting Up a Map File

Ultimately the imagemap-handling script must assess whether the mouse click coordinates are inside one of the shapes defined as a hot area. Typically these scripts make use of supplementary *map files* that contain a list of the coordinates designating hot areas and the URLs that each links to. You must create this file by assembling the coordinates that describe the various shapes that bound the hot areas. There are special shareware programs that help you identify coordinates and create the map files, including:

- WebMap for the Macintosh (available at http://www.city.net/cnx/software/webmap.html)
- MapEdit for Windows (available at http://sunsite.unc.edu/boutell/mapedit/mapedit.html)
- MapMarker for UNIX systems (available at http://www.dl.ac.uk/CBMT/mapmarker/HOME.html)

Two different standards have been developed for how these files should be formatted. The CERN standard requires that each line of the file consist of the kind of shape, the coordinates of the shape placed in parenthesis, and then the URL. The NCSA convention specifies that each line should have the name of the shape, the URL, and then the coordinates without parenthesis separated by a blank space. The two conventions also differ in how they handle circles. CERN expects them specified by the coordinates of the center and a radius length; NCSA expects them specified by the coordinates of the center and any edgepoint. The list also needs a default URL for the situations in which the user clicks outside of any hot area; this default is essential for allowing your imagemap to respond no matter where the user clicks. You will need to ensure that you format your map file in whatever format the imagemap handling script you are using expects. This can be determined by checking the documentation.

Note that the Netsite 1.1N server from Netscape has implemented a much easier way to handle imagemaps; check with your system administrator or service provider to see if this is something you can take advantage of.

Figure 7.9 shows a world map image that can serve as an imagemap. The example that follows shows the map file that you would generate for that image in NCSA format. It also shows you what the file would look like in CERN format. Appendix B provides more details about setting up map files.

```
!— Map file for world map (in NCSA format)
default http://net.add/no.selection.html
rect http://net.add/NorAm.html 1,7 82,65
circ http://net.add/SouAm.html 74,89 100,140
rect http://net.add/Eur.html 125,4 165,45
poly http://net.add/Af.html 107,44 148,106 172,106
  187,72 164 44
```

```
!— Map file for world map (in CERN format)
default http://net.add/no.selection.html
rect   (1, 7)   (82, 65)      http://net.add/
  NorAm.html
circ   (94, 109)   20      http://net.add/SouAm.html
rect   (125,4)  (165, 45)  http://net.add/Eur.html
poly   (107,44) (148,106)  (172,106) (187,72) (164
  44)   http://net.add/Af.html
```

Arranging for the Server to Respond to Imagemaps

If you are not the systems administrator, you will need to work with that person to ensure you follow the correct conventions for your site to set up an imagemap response capability on your server:

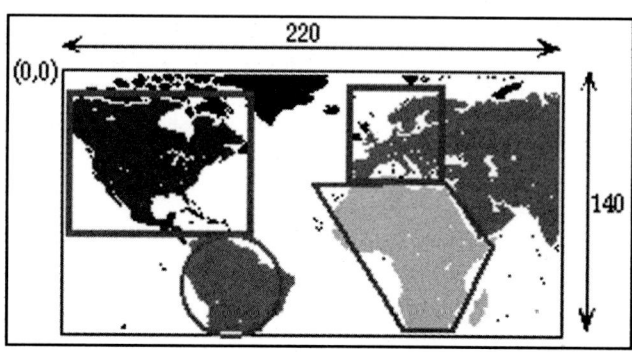

Figure 7.9:
Imagemap with boundary shapes indicated.

1. Obtain a current version of the server software that can respond to imagemaps—for example, version 1.05a or later of the NCSA UNIX server or HTTP 2.0 or later for the Macintosh.

2. Obtain one of the standard scripts that can respond to imagemap calls. (These are often distributed free with the server software.) Configure the script and place it in an appropriate directory.

3. Prepare the imagemap file that contains coordinates of the imaginary shapes that bound each hot area. Indicate the URL that should be fetched when a user clicks within any of these rectangles.

4. Set the configuration file of the server to know where to find the file that contains definitions of the hot link shapes.

5. Set up the links of the imagemap to point to the URL of the canned script that can handle imagemaps. The name of your file of hot areas will be part of that URL. This file is added after a $ in the URL. The example

shows what a reference to an imagemap script would look like. This appending of the specific map filename allows the same imagemap handling script to handle any number of different imagemaps just by changing the name of map file at the end.

```
<A HREF= Net_address/map.script.cgi$worldmapfile>
<IMG SRC=Worldmap.GIF ISMAP> </A>
```

The reference list that follows points to online references for learning about imagemaps and for obtaining canned imagemap handling scripts. Even though imagemaps are more complex than standard Web features, they can be easily mastered and become an important part of your repertoire.

Pointers to Imagemap Information, Examples, and Programs

- *Yahoo list of resources related to imagemaps*

```
http://www.yahoo.com/Computers/World_Wide_Web/
Programming/Imagemaps/
```

- *Instructions for setting up imagemaps for httpd (UNIX)*

```
http://hoohoo.ncsa.uiuc.edu/docs/setup/admin/
Imagemap.html
```

- *Imagemap tutorial (UNIX)*

```
http://wintermute.ncsa.uiuc.edu:8080/map-tutorial/
image-maps.html
```

- *Mac-imagemap.cgi canned program to run in conjunction with MacHTTP*

```
http://weyl.zib-berlin.de/imagemap/mac-
imagemap.html
```

The technical details of these arrangements will be different for Macintosh, Windows, and UNIX-based servers and even for different kinds of server software for the previous same platform. Luckily, the design principles will be very similar across platforms.

It is impossible within the scope of this book to tell you how to prepare scripts for every kind of server, but Appendix B gives more details on imagemap server scripts for popular server software packages. The tutorials listed in the previous reference list also provide additional server-specific information.

Imagemap Design Opportunities

What do you want to happen as the user clicks on various parts of your imagemap? Do you want to treat the imagemap as a sophisticated linking device by having a particular area to lead to a URL just like regular HTML links? This is such a common use that there are canned server scripts and programs to make these kind of imagemaps easy to implement.

But you can also put imagemaps to use in other ways that are not supported by canned programs. For example, I once created a Web art event that used imagemaps to ask Web visitors to indicate a preference for one of a few styles of information events—for example, linear, branching, or hypermedia structures by clicking on an imagemap with symbolic images representing these variations. After they clicked, the server sent back information about how many of the previous viewers shared their preferences and it listed the domain addresses of the last few Web visitors who had made that choice. This event worked because I wrote a script that took the coordinate information of their clicks, dynamically calculated the numbers of previous visitors who had made that choice, retrieved their domain addresses from the server's log, and then created an HTML document containing this information to send back to the client.

Mini-Gallery of Examples from the Web

Some of the most fascinating Web sites make use of imagemaps. Sometimes imagemaps are used for their unique power in organizing information. Sometimes they are used to get around HTML formatting limitations, to serve as indexes, or for expressive and experimental interactive purposes. In order to help you consider possible design opportunities, this section presents a mini-gallery of some notable examples of imagemaps.

Figure 7.10 shows the welcome page from the TeleCircus event, which showcases various artists' work, at the Well online service. This map is built out of images you can find in the various events and serves as an index. Clicking on one of the component images takes you to that section. The index map presented by the University of California (Berkeley) Museum of Paleontology uses historical photographs of reliefs on buildings at the 1893 Pan American Exposition to designate major categories of information (Figure 7.11).

Mark "Spoonman" Petrakis (spoona@well.com).

Figure 7.10:
TeleCircus at the WELL.
`http://www.well.com/cgi-bin/imagemap/tcircus1`

The Virtual Tourist (Figure 7.12) allows the user to find Web resources by clicking on a world map. Urban Diary, shown in Figure 7.13, is an experimental art event that is part of "The Place" online art gallery. It consists of active "diary pages" which contain elements that can be clicked for more elaboration.

Figure 7.11:

Museum of Paleontology.

`http://ucmp1.berkeley.edu/`

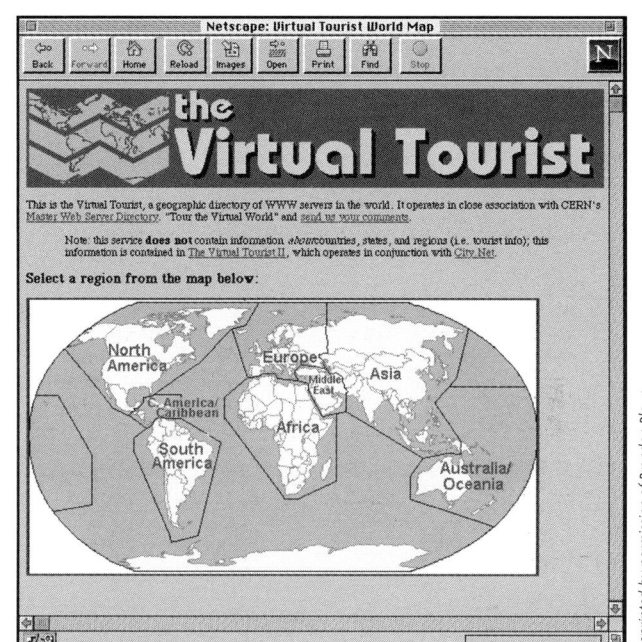

Figure 7.12:

Virtual tourist.

`http://wings.buffalo.edu/world`

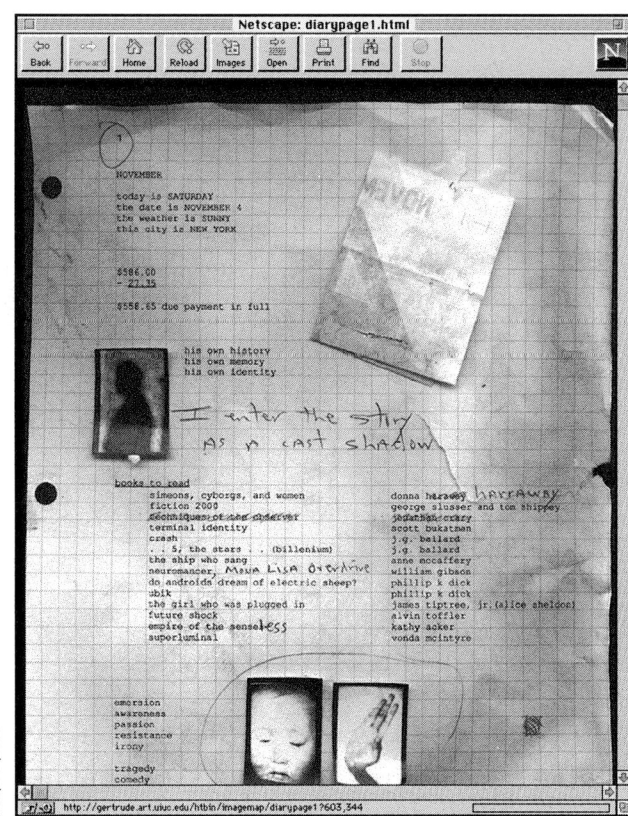

Joseph Squier.

Figure 7.13:

Urban diary.

```
http://gertrude.art.uiuc.edu/ludgate/the/place/
urban_diary/intro.html
```

Although imagemap designers vary in their approaches, there are some emerging principles to consider in your own work:

- Make the active areas clear graphically so a user knows where to click.
- Consider using text as part of the imagemap graphic to help clarify links.
- Use visual resources that the user will encounter later in the site or that are integrated with the subject matter of the site.
- Make sure that the amalgamated image works as well as its parts.
- Consider using metaphors in your image that the user is familiar with—for example, maps or buildings.
- Make your image as visually engaging as you can.

Working with Interactive Forms

Fill-in forms are another capability that greatly expand the Web's interactive capabilities. You can create events that ask users to choose options from pull-down menus, click on-screen buttons, or type text into entry fields. You can use radio buttons, checkboxes, and selection text fields to allow users to indicate the specific characteristics or nature of the information they want. Your program can then customize the response based on this information in order to create an event that users consider more appropriate or interesting.

Building this kind of site requires more than marking up an HTML document. You must arrange for your server to make use of the information the user has indicated. The authoring of an HTML page containing forms is relatively easy. Designing a form and the server scripts to respond to it, though, is a bigger challenge; you must carefully consider what information you will request from the user and what you will do with it. The following tasks come into play:

1. The server must be configured to receive the information from the form and send it to the proper program or script to respond.

2. A program must be written that contains the intelligence to receive the information and process it properly. Note that these programs will need to differ in accordance with the intended purpose of the form in the first place.

3. Many form-related events involve checking databases for information. The author will need to structure the database and establish it in a way that is tightly coupled with the program that will handle responses.

Designing and accomplishing these procedures are not trivial and certainly are more complex than the ease of creating a standard HTML page. The program and database must be designed with knowledge of the server environment in which it will run.

With forms, you can adapt some of the interface technologies that have become commonplace in interactive programs to the Web. You can use them to expand the ways that your Web events respond. You can use radio buttons, checkboxes, and selection text fields to allow users to specifically indicate their own characteristics or the nature of the information they want. Your program can then customize the response based on this information in order to create an event that users consider more appropriate or interesting.

For example, the Michigan State University weather map generating service, illustrated in Figure 7.14, asks the user to specify qualities of the map they would like to see, such as its format and the information it includes. A custom map is then generated and sent to the user.

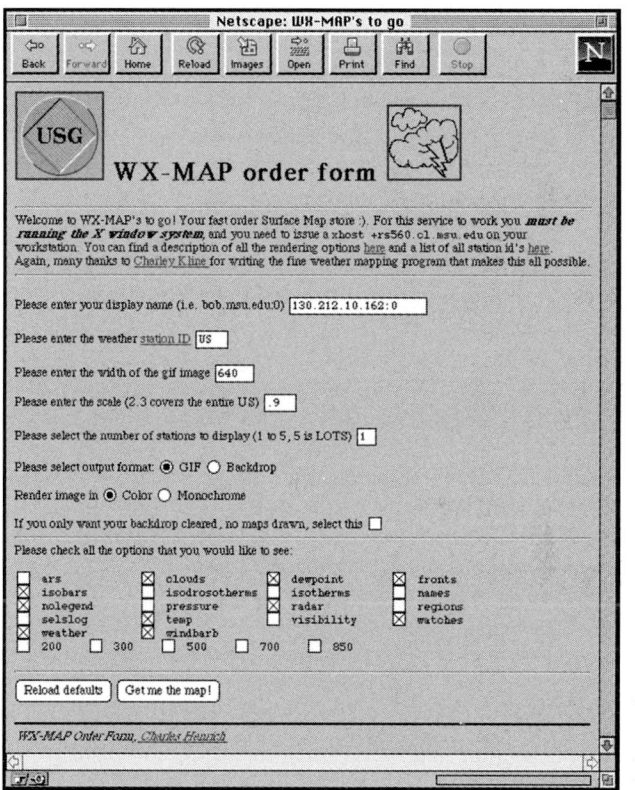

Figure 7.14:
Weather map request form from MSU.
`http://rs560.cl.msu.edu/weather/getmegif.html`

Text entry fields encourage even greater user participation. These fields can be used for many purposes—for example, recording the name and e-mail address of the user or specifying words that enable an interactive program to perform a function such as searching a database for information. Text fields can also be used for passwords and in commercial applications, for billing information such as credit card numbers (when appropriate security procedures are implemented).

Some experimental Web sites use forms to create accumulative databases that allow users to contribute text that then is available to subsequent users, in a sort of round-robin format. For example, the Confession Booth (Figure 7.15) allows the online visitor to use forms to choose the nature of the sin to be confessed to, to enter the confession, and to make selections in viewing others' sins.

Ultimately you must decide how forms relate to informational purposes. Does the presentation of selection interface features such as buttons and text fields enable you to accomplish your goals better or with more visual appeal? Do these capabilities enable you to create events that would be impossible in any other way on the Web? (For example, most checkbox or radio button array interfaces can be simulated with a list of more traditional hot links.) Are you willing to tackle the challenge of arranging a forms response system?

Understanding the Process

Forms, like imagemaps, use advanced HTML tags to create an interactive Web event that appears as an intrinsic part of the page. Users click on buttons, make selections from lists, and type into entry boxes. When done, they submit their responses. The URL for the form points not to an HTML

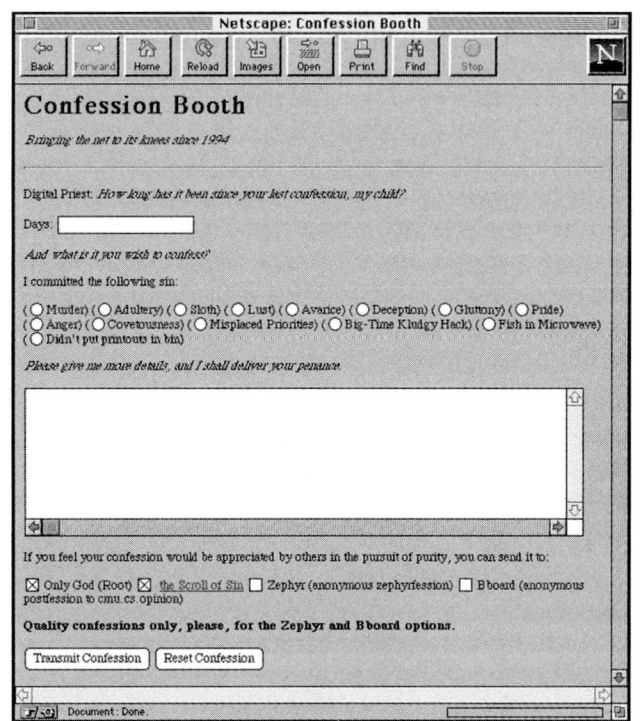

Figure 7.15:
Confession Booth: A Web event that accumulates user contributions.
`http://anther.learning.cs.cmu.edu/priest.html`

document, but rather to a script or program that you have designed to respond to the information the user has entered in the form.

The client sends along the URL appended with text that indicates the choices a user has made in the form. The CGI standard ensures that the text will be in a certain format. Your response program must parse this string of text to identify the relevant items and then do whatever you intended with this information. It must then send back some response to the server to be forwarded back to the user.

Appendix C provides more details about how the response programs and associated databases can be designed. The resources that follow provide information about enabling servers to respond to forms.

Pointers to Resources on How to Use Fill-In Forms

- *Yahoo's list of resources on forms*
`http://www.yahoo.com/Computers/World_Wide_Web/`
`Programming/Forms/`

- *Web communications tutorial on forms (UNIX)*
`http://webcom.com/html/tutor/forms/`

- *Carlos's forms tutorial for Macintosh*
`http://robot0.ge.uiuc.edu/~carlosp/cs317/cft.html`

- *Mosaic form support information (UNIX)*
`http://www.ncsa.uiuc.edu/SDG/Software/Mosaic/Docs/`
`fill-out-forms/overview.html`

- *Tutorial on using Mosaic and WAIS together (UNIX)*
`http://wintermute.ncsa.uiuc.edu:8080/wais-`
`tutorial/wais.html`

- *Digital Computer's form test site*
`http://www.research.digital.com/nsl/formtest/`
`home.html`

Overview of a Simple Form

As we take a look at the tags and options related to forms, I will also explain the interaction of these elements with other HTML formats and demonstrate ways to experiment with the layout possibilities. There is HTML code governing all of the following:

- The <FORM> tag, indicating that a document is a form and the <ACTION> attribute pointing to the script that will handle the form information.
- Text entry fields.
- Radio buttons and checkboxes.
- Passwords.

The text that is to be a form must be enclosed in a set of <FORM> tags—one at the beginning and one at the end. The beginning tag also includes an <ACTION> attribute that points to the URL of the supplementary program or script that will respond to the information provided in the form—for example, by retrieving information the user has requested. The beginning tag also must include a <METHOD> attribute that indicates the format that should be used to send the information back to the server. The <METHOD> options include <POST> and <GET>. Technically these two methods differ in how they pass information to the script and in the amount of information they can pass.

<GET> was the first style implemented on the Web in which the browser appended information to the end of the URL as one continuous string. <POST> sends the information in a separate block of data and identifies information linked to particular variables called *name-value pairs.* The methods differ in how much information they can send: <GET> is restricted in 4K whereas <POST>'s limit is 24K. <GET> and <POST> also differ in the way they handle non-text characters. <GET> sends the text as the user has typed it with special characters intact. <POST> "escapes" special characters, a

process in which they are encoded in their hexadecimal form in order to allow the transmittal of non-printing characters and to avoid ambiguities. For example, a space character (ASCII decimal 32, hexadecimal 20) will be sent as %20. In either case the responding program or script must be written to deal with the method that is specified. A following section presents examples of what the text sent to the server looks like. Figure 7.16 shows a simple form that asks for the user's name. The code follows:

```
<HTML>
<HEAD><TITLE>Basic Form Tags</TITLE></HEAD>
<BODY>
<H2>Basic FORM Tags</H2>
<HR>
<FORM METHOD="POST" ACTION="http://net-ad/
  form.response.cgi">
Please type your name<p>
<INPUT TYPE="text" NAME="who" SIZE="20" ><P>
</FORM>
<HR>
</BODY>
</HTML>
```

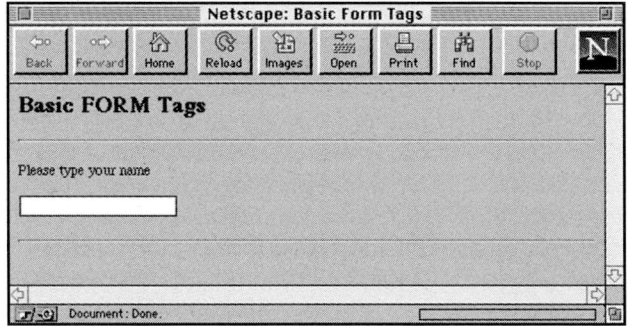

Figure 7.16:
Simple form request.

Text Entry Fields

HTML allows an array of text entry capabilities. Figure 7.17 illustrates several of these capabilities. This simple example form asks for the user's name, address, and telephone number. The code to create this form follows:

```
<HTML>
<HEAD><TITLE>Text Entry Forms Demo</TITLE></HEAD>
<BODY>
<H2>Demo of Basic Text Tags</H2>
<HR>
<FORM METHOD="POST" ACTION="http://net-ad/
  form.response.cgi">
Please Enter Basic Information<p>
Enter Name <INPUT TYPE="text" NAME="who" SIZE="20">
<P>
Enter Address<TEXTAREA NAME="address" ROWS=3
  COLS=40></TEXTAREA><P>
Enter Telephone # <INPUT TYPE="text" NAME="tel"
SIZE="12" MAXLENGTH="12"><P>
<INPUT TYPE="Submit" VALUE="Submit">
<INPUT TYPE="reset" VALUE="Reset">
</FORM>
<HR>
</BODY>
</HTML>
```

The initial <FORM> tag includes the <METHOD> and <ACTION> tags. The <ACTION>= tag is followed by a hypothetical URL (in quotes) to be linked to. The <METHOD>= tag is followed by the term <POST>, which is one of the options for information processing. The form is ended with a </FORM> tag. Note that the designation of a form with the form tag does not automatically result in any visual element on the client's window to separate the form from other text. If you wanted something explicit such as horizontal lines to set them off, you would need to explicitly indicate them.

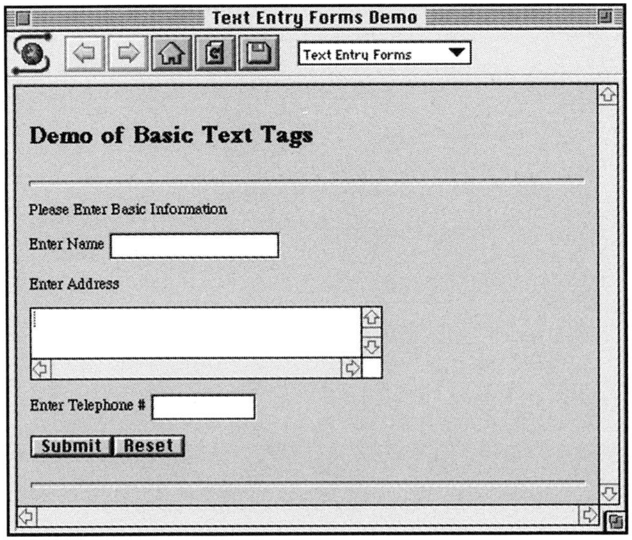

Figure 7.17:
Creating a simple form.

The example form provides the user with a default 20-character field. (The user could enter more than text but only 20 characters can be shown at a time.) In the <INPUT> tag, the <TYPE> attribute is set for "text", which tells the browser to set up to allow the user to type text from a keyboard. Other input types include selection devices such as buttons. The <NAME> attribute allows you to arbitrarily assign a label to the information entered. In this example, the user input will be known as "who". The server will eventually receive a string of text of all the information the user types. One element of that string will be something like the words "who=Joe Smith". The response program will need to be set up to look for the "who=" to match the field with text the user typed in this input area.

The request for an address is marked up by the tag <TEXTAREA>. This tag creates a special form of text entry field where the user can enter multiple lines of text. This new field also makes use of the <NAME> attribute and is labeled "address". You can specify the size of the field with the attributes <ROWS=> and <COLS=>. This example sets the field to measure 3 rows by 40 columns.

The last request asks for a telephone number, again using an <INPUT TYPE = "text"> field. The <NAME> tag gives it the label "tel" with <SIZE> attribute set to 12 characters. This field also uses the <MAXLENGTH> attribute, which sets the maximum of text characters that can be typed in. Twelve seems long enough to handle standard telephone numbers. At the end of the form are "submit" and "reset" buttons. They will be discussed in the next section.

Radio Buttons, Checkboxes, and Selections

Your fill-in forms can offer options for selecting items from a list. You can specify radio buttons, checkboxes, or scrolling text selection fields. Figure 7.18 presents an HTML document with these kinds of elements and the results in a browser. This example asks the readers for information about their favorite food, emotional and financial state, and their favorite sport. Here is the code that generates this form:

```
<HTML>
<HEAD><TITLE>Entry Forms Demo</TITLE></HEAD>
<BODY>
<HR>
<FORM METHOD="POST" ACTION="http://net-ad/
  form.response.cgi">
```

```
<DL>
<DT>Please Indicate your favorite food.
<DD><INPUT TYPE="radio" NAME="favfood"
 VALUE="pizza">Pizza
<DD><INPUT TYPE="radio" NAME="favfood"
 VALUE="hamburger">Hamburger
<DD><INPUT TYPE="radio" NAME="favfood" VALUE="ice
 cream">Ice cream</DL>
<HR>
<b>If you are happy, check here <INPUT
 TYPE="checkbox" NAME="emot" VALUE="happy"><BR>
If you are rich, check here <INPUT TYPE="checkbox"
 NAME="wealth" VALUE="rich"></b><BR>
<HR>
Please pick your favorite sport
<SELECT NAME="favsport" SIZE="3">
<OPTION SELECTED>Baseball
<OPTION>Football
<OPTION>Swimming
</SELECT><P>
<INPUT TYPE="reset" VALUE="Reset">
<INPUT TYPE="Submit" VALUE="Submit">
</FORM>
<HR>
</BODY>
</HTML>
```

Radio buttons are indicated with the <TYPE> attribute set to "radio". In this example survey about favorite foods, the user is asked to supply a value to the field "favfood" from a prepared list. The list was built by using the <VALUE> attribute in the <INPUT> tag; <VALUE> is assigned to various entries in the list—Pizza, Hamburger, and Ice cream—resulting in a list of choices with radio buttons when viewed in a Web browser.

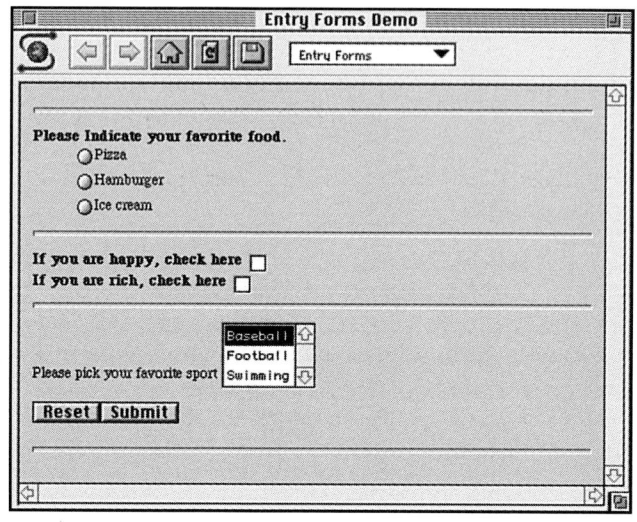

Figure 7.18:
Radio buttons, checkboxes, and text selection fields in a form.

```
<DL>
<DT>Please Indicate your favorite food. <DD>
 <INPUT TYPE="radio" NAME="favfood"
 VALUE="pizza">Pizza
<DD><INPUT TYPE="radio" NAME="favfood"
 VALUE="hamburger">Hamburger
<DD><INPUT TYPE="radio" NAME="favfood" VALUE="ice
 cream">Ice cream</DL>
```

Only one radio button can be selected from a list. Clicking one automatically deactivates any other. This behavior is like the radio buttons in old car radios—hence the name. Setting them all to have the same <NAME> makes them work as a set.

To illustrate how other HTML tags may be used with forms tags, the example puts the radio buttons in a definition list.

Remember that this structure creates a list with a line that is like a header and then subsequent items all indented. The list in enclosed with the <DL> tag at the beginning. The header line starts with the <DT> tag and each item in the list starts with a <DD> tag. The whole list is ended with the </DL> tag. This definition list structure results in each radio button being indented.

The next section of the display illustrates the checkbox toggle element. Checkboxes are indicated with the <TYPE> attribute set to "checkbox". In this example, the two checkboxes have <NAME> identifiers called "emot" and "wealth". Each one is also given a value with the <VALUE> attribute—"happy" and "rich" in this example. These will be the values that will be sent to the server if the user has checked the box; nothing will be sent if a box is not checked.

The final section illustrates a text selection field, which allows a user to select one line out of a scrolling list. (In a later example we'll look at how you can allow a user to select more than one line with use of the <MULTIPLE> option.) You indicate this kind of field with the </SELECT> tag. The example assigns its <NAME> as "favsport". You indicate each line in the field by putting the text to appear on a new line beginning with the tag <OPTION>; the whole structure is terminated after the last option in customary HTML style with a </SELECT> tag. The field can have as many lines as you want but you can determine the number of lines that the box will show at one time with the <SIZE> attribute. In this example, <SIZE> is set to "3"; the other options will be available via scrolling. If you want a default item preselected, you include the <SELECTED> attribute inside the <OPTION> tag. In the example, Baseball is the default selected item. Multiple defaults can be indicated by using the <SELECTED> tag after more than one <OPTION> tag. The browser will send all selected items forward to the server. The example shows the code to create this selection box.

```
<SELECT NAME="favsport" SIZE="3">
<OPTION SELECTED>Baseball
<OPTION>Football
<OPTION>Swimming
</SELECT>
```

At the end of the form are two special kinds of buttons—the submit and the reset buttons. All forms except those consisting of a single text entry field require a submit button. Clicking the submit button tells the client to send the information that is in the form to the server script at the URL listed at the beginning of the form HTML text (in this example, http://net-ad/form.response.cgi). With a single text entry field, pressing the Return or Enter key will transmit the information. The submit button is created with a special <INPUT TYPE="submit"> tag. The reset button will clear all entries back to their default values. Its tag is <INPUT TYPE="Reset">. The example shows this code:

```
<INPUT TYPE="reset" VALUE="Reset">
<INPUT TYPE="Submit" VALUE="Submit">
```

Setting Default and Hidden Responses

You can create a list of radio buttons or checkboxes with a default response already indicated. If you can anticipate your users' most likely choices, you can accommodate them by requiring less input on their end. In text entry fields you indicate a default response with a <VALUE> attribute in a text input field. Figure 7.19 shows the Web form that illustrates these features discussed in this section and the example that follows shows the code that generated the form.

```
<HTML><HEAD><TITLE>Forms Demo</TITLE></HEAD>
<BODY>
<H2>Demo of Defaults</H2>
<HR>
```

```
<FORM METHOD="POST" ACTION="http://net-ad/
  form.response.cgi">
<DL>
<DT>What do you prefer to eat?
<DD><INPUT TYPE="radio" NAME="favfood" VALUE="pizza"
  CHECKED>Pizza
<DD><INPUT TYPE="radio" NAME="favfood"
  VALUE="hamburger">Hamburger
<DD><INPUT TYPE="radio" NAME="favfood" VALUE="ice
  cream">Ice cream</DL>
<HR>
What do you prefer to drink?<br>
Juice <INPUT TYPE="checkbox" NAME="bev" VALUE=
  "juice""><BR>
Soda <INPUT TYPE="checkbox" NAME="bev" VALUE= "soda"
  CHECKED><BR>
<HR>
Which meal would you eat this?<BR>
<SELECT NAME="favmeal" SIZE="3" MULTIPLE>
<OPTION SELECTED> Breakfast
<OPTION>Lunch
<OPTION SELECTED>Dinner
</SELECT><P>
<INPUT TYPE="reset" VALUE="Reset">
<INPUT TYPE="Submit" VALUE="Submit">
</BODY>
</HTML>
```

Let's look at the method for indicating default text to show
up in a text entry field. The following code makes the word
"pizza" the default text in a text entry field. Of course, the
user could overwrite the given response.

```
<INPUT TYPE="text" NAME="food" VALUE="pizza"
  SIZE="20">
```

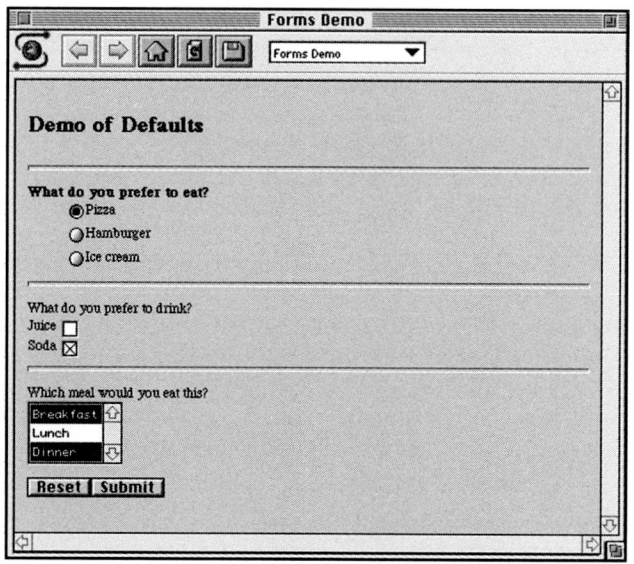

Figure 7.19:
Defaults and multiple choices.

You can preselect checkboxes and radio buttons by putting
the <CHECKED> attribute within the <INPUT> tag. For example
the following would result in the checkbox already clicked in
front of the option "soda".

```
<INPUT TYPE="checkbox" NAME="drink" VALUE="soda"
  CHECKED>
```

Text selection fields work in a similar way. Remember each
option is indicated on a separate line starting with the
<OPTION> tag. A default can be indicated by placing the
<SELECTED> attribute in the <OPTION> tag. The following text
selection list shows "Breakfast" as the default response.

```
<SELECT NAME="whichmeal" SIZE="3" MULTIPLE >
<OPTION SELECTED>Breakfast
<OPTION>Lunch
<OPTION>Dinner
</SELECT>
```

Text selection fields can be arranged to allow a user to select more than one line. This is accomplished by including the <MULTIPLE> tag in the line that defines the <SELECT> field. For example, the Select set of Breakfast, Lunch, and Dinner in the previous example includes the <MULTIPLE> tag to indicate this option. Figure 7.19 demonstrates all these default options and the <MULTIPLE> feature. The user has selected Breakfast and Dinner in the select field.

One additional feature that can be applied to input, selection, and text area fields is the <HIDDEN> tag. Any element with this tag will not visually appear on the page when the browser shows it. Although that option does not appear, its value will be sent to the server. For example, you might have several versions of the same form that appear in different situations; the hidden values would go along with the data and could be used by your script to respond differently.

Passwords

A user can be asked to type a password, typically to gain access to special resources. Commercial systems can use this to verify accounts and for billing of services. As with all forms features, a support script must be written to run in conjunction with the server to implement any checking functions. Figure 7.20 illustrates the HTML coding to set up a password and the example that follows shows the code that generated the form.

```
<HTML><HEAD><TITLE>Password Demo</TITLE></HEAD>
<BODY>
<H2>Demo of Password</H2>
<FORM>
```

```
Please type your password <INPUT TYPE="password"
NAME="userpasswd" SIZE="20" MAXLENGTH="20"><P>
<INPUT TYPE="reset" VALUE="Reset">
<INPUT TYPE="Submit" VALUE="Submit">
</FORM>
<HR>
</BODY>
</HTML>
```

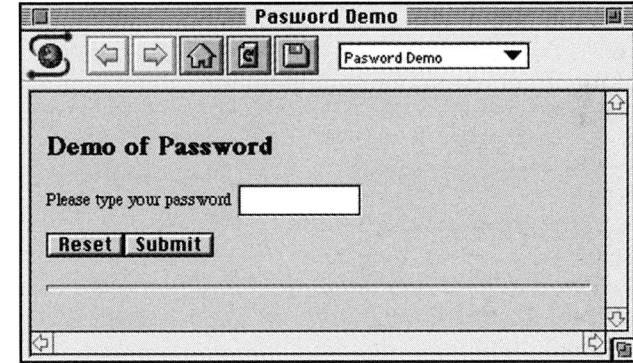

Figure 7.20:
Forms support for passwords.

Realize that this form-based password is not secure because Internet transmissions in general are subject to easy surveillance and manipulation. New systems to encrypt transmissions are being developed that will make secure Web communications possible. They are discussed more in Chapter 10. You should not rely on the password fill-in forms to protect sensitive information.

The password field looks like a regular text entry field. When the user types text, however, only asterisks appear. This approach provides a level of security so that no onlooker can see the text you enter on the screen.

Table 7.1

HTML Tags and Attributes for Fill-In Forms

Tag or Option	Function	Comments
<FORM> </FORM>	Encloses all the text and tags to be included in form.	Necessary for all forms.
ACTION= "*URL*" (Attribute included within initial FORM tag)	Indicates the URL of the server script that will process the information entered by the user.	CGI scripts typically end with .cgi suffix.
METHOD= " "(Attribute included within initial FORM tag)	Indicates the way the data is to be sent to the script.	Options include POST or GET.
<INPUT....>	Basic tag to set up a structure for user input.	Specific TYPE must be specified within the INPUT tag. No closing tag required.
TYPE= " "(Attribute included within INPUT tag)	Indicates the kind of input structure to be created.	Options include text, textarea, radio button, checkbox, password, submit, and reset. Submit sends the form's data to the server. Reset sets all values in the form to their default values. Password creates a text entry box that does hides the text that the user enters.
NAME= "*text*"(Attribute included within INPUT tag)	Indicates the variable or label to be attached to the information entered by the user.	Label is essential toscripts for identifying which responses go with which form element.
SIZE= "*n*" (Attribute included within INPUT tag)	Used to specify the size of text related entry fields.	Size indicates the number of visible character spaces shown for text entry fields. Size indicates number of visible lines to show for selection box entry structure. User can type more characters or scroll to more lines.
MAXLENGTH="*n*" (Attribute included within INPUT tag)	Sets the maximum number of characters that can be entered in text entry field.	Indicates the value to be sent to script if a checkbox or radiobutton is selected.
VALUE="*text*" (Attribute included within INPUT tag)	Indicates the default value of an input element.	Indicates the text to show up in a text entry field.
CHECKED (Attribute included within INPUT tag)	Indicates that a radio button or checkbox should be displayed as preselected or checked.	
ROWS=*n* COLS=*n* (Attribute included within TEXTAREA tag)	Indicates visible size of the textarea input element in rows and columns.	Additional lines can be accessed via scroll bars.
<SELECT> </SELECT>	Sets up a multiline text selection box.	

Tag or Option	Function	Comments
MULTIPLE (Attribute included within SELECT tag)	Indicates that the selection box should allow user to select multiple lines.	
<OPTION>	Indicates one line of text to be displayed in the selection box. Created with the SELECT structure.	Each OPTION is placed on its own line ended with carriage return.
SELECTED (Attribute included within OPTION tag)	Indicates that the option inside a selection box should show up preselected.	

What Does a Form Send to the Server?

Once the submit button is pressed, all the information of the form is consolidated and sent to the server. It is appended to the URL after a "?" symbol. Remember that the URL in a form is indicated in the <ACTION> tag in the original definition of the form. It must be sent to a script or program that has been written to extract the information that comes from the client. The programming is facilitated by the fact that this information is sent in a standard CGI format— for example, in a variable called the *Query_string*.

The browser accumulates the information in the form and sends each <NAME> value-pair set equal to the submitted user response assigned to it. The fields are separated with the "ε" symbol. The URL and attached *Query_string* for the example in Figure 7.19 would be the following:

```
http://net-ad/ form.response.cgi? favfood="pizza"
  &bev="soda"&favmeal="Breakfast"%20"Dinner"
```

If a checkbox or item is empty, a blank <NAME> value for that field will be sent. For example, if a user ignored an address text entry field and went on to fill out a field asking for a telephone number, the resulting *Query_string* might look like the following:

```
http://net-ad/ form.response.cgi?
who="Joe"%20"Smith"&address=&tel="415"%20"555"%20"5555"
```

Certain characters that a user types have to be "escaped" in order to keep a program from becoming confused. Because the $, +, and ε symbols are used as critical demarcations in the formatting, they need a special indication when users include them in their responses. Non-printing characters such as the space or linefeed similarly might be escaped. One approach sends the ASCII code for a character—for example, the space character is ASCII code 32 (decimal) and the question mark (?) is ASCII 63. Usually these characters are sent in the hexadecimal equivalent preceded by the % symbol—for example, space would be %20 and ? would be %3F. In the previous example you can see the %20 between the Joe and Smith. For more information on ASCII and hexadecimal numbers, consult any table of ASCII equivalents. You can find a listing of all the ASCII codes at http://www.infocom.net/~bbs/symbol.html.

Making the critical text legible and decoding these special characters are some of the more important tasks facing scripts that respond to forms. For example, your script might move through the text string received from the browser, converting every hexadecimal code back to its normal ASCII equivalents. This is such a common need that there are shareware scripts to accomplish it. The list that follows shows two examples of these scripts.

- Uncgi (a decoding front end for UNIX) available on the Web at http://www.hyperion.com/~koreth/uncgi.html)
- Decode OSAX (a scripting addition for Macintosh AppleScript programs) available at http://www.biap.com/machttp/tools/decode_url.hqx

Design Opportunities with Fill-In Forms

Form design doesn't end with preparing the form page itself—you must give equal weight to the script that responds and any support databases or information structures that are required.

Form scripts are even more open-ended than imagemap scripts. Because there are so many purposes you could have for a script, it can require some real detective work to find existing script resources that suit your purposes. If you want to provide advanced Web consulting, you'll probably want to learn how to create scripts yourself.

The design issues you face in designing fill-in forms really address broader issues in information and database design. You must ask yourself these questions:

- Is a form structure really necessary or would a set of simple links work just as well?
- What are the appropriate categories of information to request?
- Should information be requested via closed structures such as radio buttons, checkboxes, or text selection fields or via an open-ended structure such as text entry?

- If a closed structure is used, are all appropriate options included? Are the options exhaustive? What escape option, if any, is given for users who might not find any of the offered options appropriate?
- What kind of responses are to be expected within each category?
- How will the script respond to each category and to each response value in each category? How will it respond to free-form text?

Technically, you must make sure that all the components are tightly coupled. The HTML form must be clear to users and request the information you need. The script must be built on the knowledge of what labels will be assigned to each element of information and any databases that work with the script must be carefully designed so that information can be easily entered and retrieved in predictable ways. The dynamic response to users generated by the script must be clearly linked to the original form that originally requested the information. Information design of the total system is a critical step in creating a form and its associated scripts.

Exercise 7.2a shows you in detail a step-by-step example of the process of designing a form and the script to handle it. It is, however, only one of a multitude of possible uses for forms. Appendix C shows you two more examples of different systems.

This example is designed for a Macintosh system running a Web server such as MacHTTP or WebSTAR. It uses HyperCard as the environment for running the script that processes the form data sent from the user. Exercise 7.2b shows how to accomplish the same results using a perl script on a UNIX-based server. Although the details differ for other platforms and scripting environments, the functional steps are similar.

Exercise 7.2a:

Creating a password access system via a form sent to a Macintosh-based server

Step 1:

Analyze the information system. The first step in developing a forms-based information system is clarifying the goals of the system and the major functions it must accomplish. The system this exercise illustrates is a simple password access procedure. It offers a body of information only to those who have registered their name and password. When someone signs on, it asks if they previously registered. If they have, it asks them to type their password. It checks the password-name pair against its database of valid passwords. If there is a match, it sends the requested information back.

If they do not have a password, it offers the new user a chance to register name and password choice and then enters the information into its database. Some designers find flow charts a useful tool for representing systems such as this. Figure 7.21 shows the flowchart of the system.

Step 2:

Design the HTML form. The form must accomplish two major purposes: It must allow Web readers who have already registered to fill in their name and password so it can be checked against the database, and it must allow new visitors to register their name and password so they can have access. Figure 7.22 shows a form to request passwords or allow registration. Technically, the page contains two forms to accomplish these separate functions even

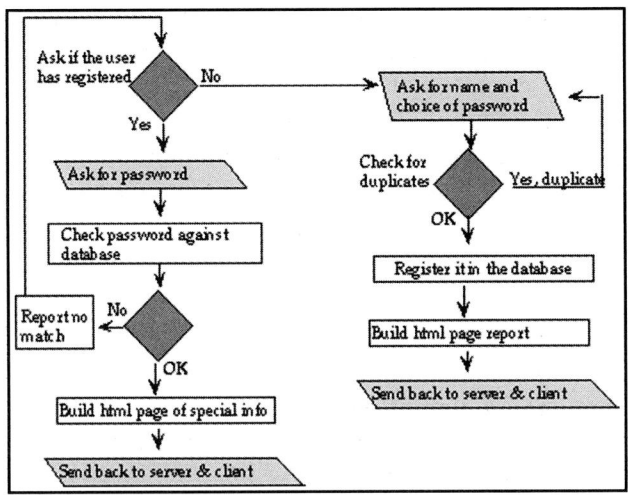

Figure 7.21:
Flowchart of system to check paswords or allow registration.

though it looks like a unified presentation to the user. The example that follows shows the HTML code you type to create this page.

```
<HTML><HEAD> <TITLE>Password Demo</TITLE></HEAD>
<BODY>
<H2>Demo of Special Resources Available via
  Passwords</H2>
<HR>
<FORM METHOD="POST" ACTION="http://net-ad/
  HyperCard.cgi$checkpass">
<H3>If you have a password, please sign in</H3><BR>
What is your loginname <INPUT TYPE="text" NAME="who"
  SIZE="20" MAXLENGTH="20"><BR>
What is your password <INPUT TYPE="password"
  NAME="passwd" SIZE="20" MAXLENGTH="20"><P>
<INPUT TYPE="Submit" VALUE="Submit">
```

```
<INPUT TYPE="reset" VALUE="Reset">
</FORM>
<HR>
<FORM METHOD="POST" ACTION="http://net-ad/
  HyperCard.cgi$newpass">
<H3>Register name and password to receive special
  access</H3><BR>
What do you want for loginname <INPUT TYPE="text"
  NAME="who" SIZE="20" MAXLENGTH="20"><BR>
What will be your password <INPUT TYPE="password"
  NAME="passwd" SIZE="20" MAXLENGTH="20"><p>
<INPUT TYPE="Submit" VALUE="Submit">
<INPUT TYPE="reset" VALUE="Reset">
</FORM>
<HR>
</BODY>
</HTML>
```

Note that the <ACTION> attribute in the two forms points to a program called HyperCard.cgi. In this example, we are using HyperCard as the form handling program. To comply with CGI practice we have renamed HyperCard on our hard disk to be HyperCard.cgi. Also note that the two <ACTION> statements differ slightly. The form for checking passwords has *$checkpass* attached to the end.

```
ACTION="http://net-ad/HyperCard.cgi$checkpass"
```

The form for registering a password has *$newpass* attached at the end.

```
ACTION="http://net-ad/HyperCard.cgi$newpass"
```

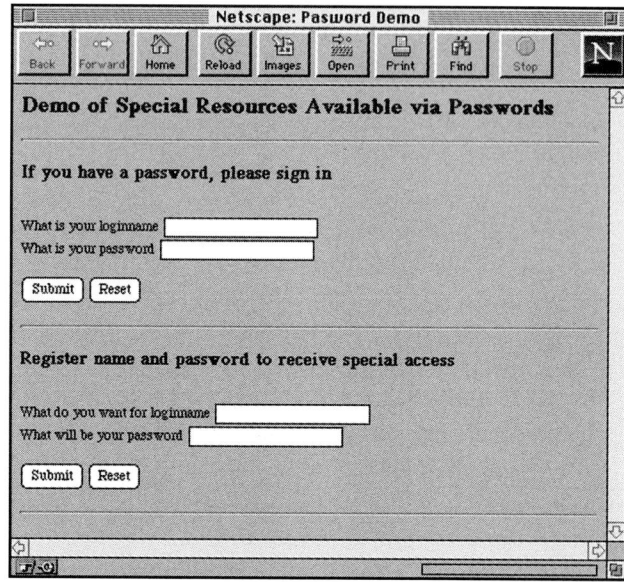

Figure 7.22:
A Web form that requests a password or allows registration of a new password.

This addition after a $ in a URL pointing to a script is called a path argument and is sent by the server as one of the CGI environmental variables discussed earlier in the CGI section of this chapter. It allows one script or program to handle many different events. Also note that the name that the person types is assigned the label *who* and the password they type is assigned the label *passwd*.

Step 3:

Wait for an Apple event sent from the server and
extract CGI environmental variables. MacHTTP and
WebSTAR Macintosh Web servers send an Apple
event called WWWΩsdoc when they receive a CGI
request. The CGI environmental variables are sent
along with this Apple event. Our script must wait for
this Apple event to jump into action. Then it must
extract the data sent from the user. In this example
the script might be called upon to perform two
different actions: check a password against its
database or register a new one. The script must
therefore branch to the proper routine based on the
path argument indicated in the original URL.

When HyperCard gets an Apple event it sends it to
the currently active stack, so our script handling
stack must be running. We place a listening script
at the stack level to wait for the Apple event
WWWΩsdoc. In addition, we build this routine to
extract the data the program will need an place
them in global variables. Here is the script for the
listening script placed on the stack level.

```
on appleEvent class, eventID, sender
 global sendstuff, pathdata, recdata
 if class & eventID is "WWWΩsdoc" then
  -- look for sdoc event, otherwise exit
  request appleEvent data
  -- get the direct
  parameter (path args) which indicates which event
  put it into pathdata
  -- puts eventname into HyperCard variable
  -- pathdata
  request appleEvent data with keyword "post"
  -- gets the data user has typed sent via the POST
  -- method
  put it into recdata
  -- puts it into HyperCard
  variable called recdata
  go card passeventcard
 end if
end appleEvent
```

When this on *appleEvent* message handler is
finished, the path argument sent by the URL (either
checkpass or *newpass*) will be assigned to the
HyperCard global variable called *pathdata*. The
information from the fill-in form will be assigned
to the HyperCard variable *recdata*. The string
sent from the client will look something like this:
who=Micky&passwd=mouse. In this example, the
script then transfers control to a HyperCard card
called *passeventcard*. It could just as well have
called subroutines instead.

Step 4:

Branch to the appropriate subroutine. The *openCard*
handler gets activated when the card is called. It
determines if the event requested (*pathdata*) is to
check a password (checkpass) or create a new one
(*newpass*) and transfers control to the appropriate
subroutines. When they are done it transfers control
back to the master card.

```
on opencard
 global pathdata
 if pathdata = checkpass then
  extractit
  checkindata
  respond
 end if
```

```
if pathdata = newpass then
 extractit
 putindata
 respond
end if
go card "master"
end opencard
```

Step 5:

Extract the needed data from the string sent by the server. The *extractit* routine retrieves the elements of the information that the user has sent. This information is put into the *recdata* variable by the *on Apple event* listening routine that is on the master card. The *extractit* routine uses the "&" symbols and the category tags ("who=" and "passwd=") to determine the elements and break apart the string. It puts the extracted name into a HyperCard global variable called *curname* and the password into a variable called *curpass*.

```
on extractit
global recdata, curname, curpass, endchar
-- this routine extracts the name and password from
-- received data (recdata)

-- get elements of incoming password data from form
-- put the number of characters in recdata into
-- numchar

-- get name into variable curname
put 5 into namebegin
-- offset for identifier "who="
put (offset ("&passwd=",recdata))-1 into nameend
-- find end of name
put char namebegin to nameend of recdata into
  ➡curname
```

```
-- get password
put nameend+9 into passbegin
-- offset for identifier "&passwd="
put char passbegin to numchar of recdata into
  ➡curpass
end extractit
```

Step 6:

Check the password against the database of known passwords. This routine makes use of a simple database of login names and passwords. It is structured so each line contains a name followed by the password. For HyperCard this database is placed in a card field called *passdata*; it could just as well have been in a separate text file. The *checkindata* handler (used only for the checking password routine) looks in the data field that contains the name password pairs for registered names for the login name the user has typed. If the handler can't find it, it puts a message "Can't find name" into a variable called *statuspass*.

If the handler does find the name, it checks the password the user has typed against the matching password in its data field. If the two don't match, the handler puts a message "Password does not match" into the variable *statuspass*. If the two do match, the handler puts the message "OK" into the variable *statuspass*. The global variable *statuspass* will be used by other routines to build an appropriate response to send back to the user.

```
on checkindata
--This routine tries to find the incoming name in
--password data
--and then extracts the password associated with it
--and then compares with password in received data
--(recdata)
--It returns ok, passwrong, or noname
global curname, curpass, statuspass
```

```
put "" into curlinenum
find curname in card field passdata
-- see if name there
put the foundline into curlinenum
if curlinenum="" then -- exit if name not listed
put "Sorry, can't find your name" into statuspass
 exit checkindata
end if

put the value of curlinenum into curline
--check the matching line
put offset ("passwd=", curline) into q
-- get password from that line
put q+7 into passbegin
put the number of characters in curline into
  ➡endchar
put char passbegin to endchar of curline into
  ➡targetpass
--Compare incoming password with the one in
passdata
--If they match put "OK" into passtatus variable
if targetpass=curpass then
  put "ok" into statuspass
else
put "Password does not match" into statuspass
end if
end checkindata
```

Step 7:

Generate an HTML document that responds accordingly and send back to the user. The *respond* routine builds a correctly formatted response based on what *statuspass* contains. It uses the standard CGI header and HTML text stored in a card field called *errorhtml* for situations that were not OK. It adjusts the details of what it says based on what the *checkindata* routine put into *statuspass*. If *statuspass* is set to "OK," it sends back HTML text that is stored in card field *okhtml* that contains the options for users with valid passwords. This field also contains the standard header composed of the required text including the carriage return/linefeed combinations. Another approach could have programmed the script to build the header and text directly rather than relying on the stored text. Here is the script for the respond handler:

```
on respond
global statuspass, sendstuff
-- if the password is ok send the html page with
-- special choices
if statuspass = "ok" then
  put card field okhtml into sendstuff
else
-- if it is wrong send back error message and
-- adjust the contents of line 7 to indicate the
-- problem
put "<H3>"&&statuspass&&"</H3><HR>" into line 7 of
  ➡card field errorhtml
put "<H3> Go back to register</H3>" into line 8 of
  ➡card field errorhtml
if statuspass = "You are now registered" then put
  ➡"<H3>Congratulations</H3>" into line 8 of card
  ➡field errorhtml
put card field errorhtml into sendstuff
end if
 reply sendstuff
end respond
```

Here are the contents of the two card fields. "crlf" stands for the actual characters representing carriage return and linefeed, not the literal characters themselves (You can generate a linefeed by pressing Control-J).

Card Field okhtml	Card Field errorhtml
HTTP/1.0 200 OK (crlf)	HTTP/1.0 200 OK (crlf)
Server: MacHTTP(crlf)	Server: MacHTTP(crlf)
MIME-Version: 1.0(crlf)	MIME-Version: 1.0(crlf)
Content-type: text/html(crlf)	Content-type: text/ html(crlf)
(crlf)	(crlf)
(crlf) <HTML><HEAD><TITLE> Special choices</TITLE> </HEAD> <BODY>	(crlf)<HTML><HEAD> <TITLE>Results</TITLE> </HEAD><BODY>
<H3>These choices are only available to those who have registered</H3> <HR>	<H3>Sorry, can't find your name/H3><HR>
<H3> Here is what is available</H3>	<H3> Go back to register </H3>
<UL>	<A HREF="passchoice. html"> Go back to main page</A>
<LI><A HREF="late.html"> Latest news</A>	</BODY></HTML>
<LI><A HREF="good.html"> Good Deals</A>	
</UL>	
</BODY></HTML>	

The contents of the appropriate card field is put into the variable *sendstuff*. The command *reply* sendstuff causes HyperCard to send it back to the server, which is waiting for a CGI response. The

server ultimately sends it back to the user's browser. Figure 7.23a shows the Web pages sent back if there is no match of the submitted password, and 7.23b shows the results when the password is valid.

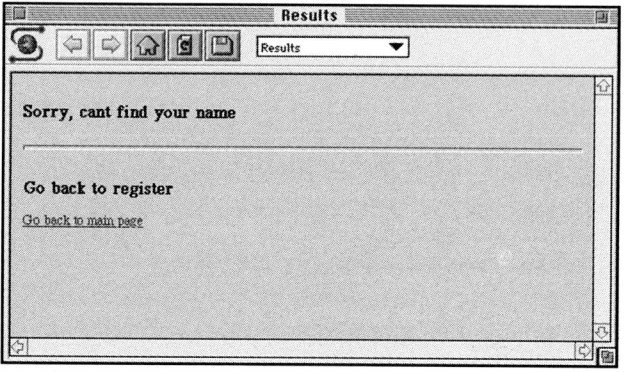

Figure 7.23a:
Web page generated when password is incorrect.

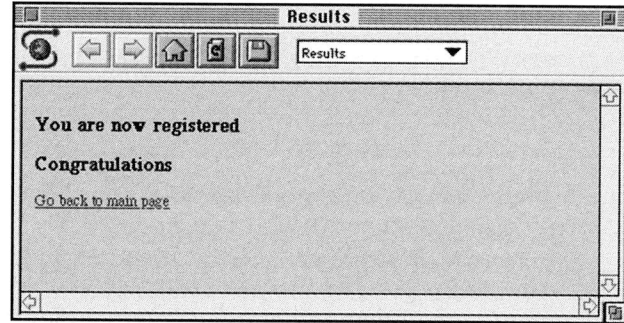

Figure 7.23b:
Acknowledgment sent for successful registration of password.

Step 8:

Create a procedure for registering new users. Now you must write the response for the second choice offered to users on your original Web page—registering a new login name and a password. The <ACTION> attribute in the tag for this form points to the same HyperCard.cgi but appends a different argument after the $ *newpass*.

```
<FORM METHOD="POST" ACTION="http://net-ad/
HyperCard.cgi$newpass">
```

Step 4 showed how the same script could handle this action as well as checking passwords. This routine to register a new password uses the same extractit and respond handlers described in Step 5 and Step 7. It replaces the *checkindata* with a different handler called *putindata*.

The *putindata* routine is only called when someone asks to register a new password. The routine checks to make sure the login name requested is not already in use. If the password is used, the routine returns the message, "Name chosen; please choose again." If the proposed name is OK, the routine adds the new login name and password pair into the card field pass that keeps the master database of passwords, and puts "You are now registered" into the global variable *statuspass* so that the respond routine will send an appropriate message. Here is the script for that routine.

```
on putindata
-- this routine adds a name to the password data
-- list if it is not already taken and informs the
-- user of what has happened.
global statuspass, sendstuff, curname, curpass
put the number of lines in card field passdata into z
find curname in card field passdata
if the foundline = "" then
put "who="&curname&&"passwd="&curpass into line z+1
➥of card field passdata
put "You are now registered" into statuspass
else
put "Name taken; Choose another" into statuspass
end if
end putindata
```

Figure 7.24 shows the HTML document that the script generates if the Web viewer's attempt to register a password is successful.

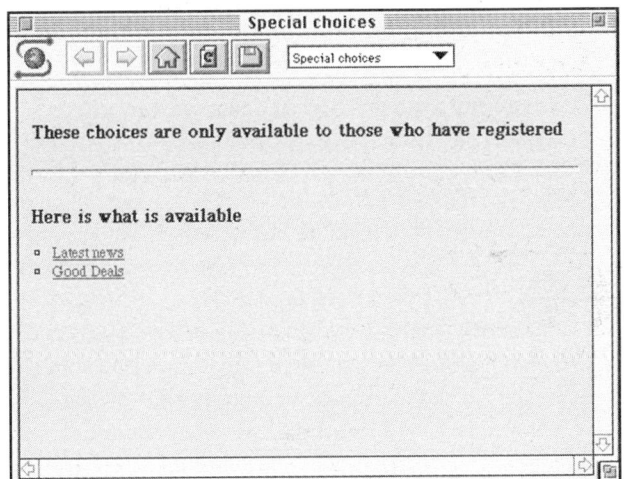

Figure 7.24:
Web page of special resources generated when password is valid.

You now have a fundamental password access system that can run via fill-in forms on the Web. To try it out you would need an Apple events capable Macintosh, a MacHTTP or WebSTAR Web server, HyperCard 2.1 or better placed in the same folder as the Web server and renamed to end with .cgi (an alias could substitute), and all <ACTION> addresses changed to point to the Internet address of your server.

Exercise 7.2b accomplishes the same password checking and recording function as Exercise 7.2a. It is designed to run on a UNIX server and is written in perl.

Exercise 7.2b:

Creating a password access system via a form sent to a UNIX-based server

Step 1:

Analyze the information system. Refer to Step 1 in Exercise 7.2a.

Step 2:

Design the HTML form. The form must accomplish two functions: check passwords that the user enters against its database and allow registration of new passwords. The HTML coding to create these two forms is the same as that shown in Step 2 of Exercise 7.2a. The <ACTION> options within the <FORM> tags might be different, however. In this example the script is called book2.cgi and it can handle both actions. The <ACTION> for the first form to check passwords would be:

```
<FORM METHOD="POST" ACTION="http://machinename/
cgi-bin/scriptname.cgi?checkpass">
```

The <ACTION> for the second form to register passwords would be:

```
<FORM METHOD="POST" ACTION="http://machinename/
cgi-bin/scriptname.cgi?newpass">
```

Step 3:

Prepare to call a library of routines, set up the header, place it in a variable, and start to create the structural parts of the HTML document: The first part of the script sets up to call on a library called cgi-lib.pl. The script creates a standard Web header in the variable called *$Header* and builds the first structural part of the HTML document to be sent back to the browser.

```
#!/opt/gnu/bin/perl
# cgi-lib.pl is a library by Steven E. Brenner
# It is freely available
require "cgi-lig.pl";

# Prints the header and beginning of the HTML
$Header = "Content-type: text/html";
print "$Header\n\n";
print "<HTML><HEAD><TITLE>CGI RESPONSE</TITLE>
</HEAD><BODY><H3>\n";
```

The URL for the cgi-lib.pl library used in this example is http://www.bio.cam.ac.uk/web/form.html.

Step 4:.

Check the user's input. Make sure the user has sent data, extract all the data, assign the name, and password sent to variables. The next routine checks that the user has passed any arguments and exits if they have not. It then calls on the *ReadParse* routine out of the cgi-lib.pl library to extract all name-value pairs that the form has sent. It places them in an array called *$in*. It assigns the name they have typed (who) to a variable called *$login* and the password they have typed (passwd) to a variable called *$passwd*.

```
# Checks to make sure there is an argument
if ($#ARGV >=0)
{
  $option = shift(@ARGV);;
}
else
{  exit 0;
}
# One function call to Steven E. Brenner's
 cgi-lib.pl
# ReadParse captures all POST name/value pairs and
# places them in
# an array called $in
&ReadParse;
# Assigns the variable $login to the login a user
# entered on the form.
$login = $in{'who'};
# Assigns the variable $passwd to the password a
# user entered on the form.
$passwd = $in{'passwd'};
```

Step 5:

Initiate appropriate subroutine. The next routine checks which form was originally activated. This is indicated in the $test variable, which will contain the name of the routine checkpass or newpass.

```
$testvariable = "checkpass"'
```

```
# This condition checks to see which form we are
# using, the checkpass or newpass
if ($option eq $testvariable)
{
 # Make a subroutine call to checkpass
 &checkpass;
$newaccount = "1";
# If it is a new account it calls the subroutine
# newpass to create a new login
 if ($output eq $newaccount)
    {
    print "New Account\n";
    &newpass;
    }
else
    {
    print "<br>$login account already exists\n";
    }
}
```

Step 6:

Check validity of name and password. The next routine makes use of a database called /tmp/ database. It finds the login name and then sees if the password just entered matches the password originally stored with that login name. If it matches it returns "Account Verified; if it doesn't match it returns "Password Incorrect"; and if it can't find the login name in its record it returns "No Such Account".

```
# Subroutine checkpass
sub checkpass {
    # Opens database called /tmp/database
    # sets up an array to hold the login you will
    # compare with
    open (DATABASE, "</tmp/database") || print
     "Cannot open Database\n";
```

```
@user = grep (/${login)/, <DATABASE>);
@tmp = split(/#/, $user[0];
$account = $tmp[0]/
$coded = $tmp[1];
```

```
# Compares the login an then checks the password
    if ($login eq $account)
        {
         if ($passwd eq $coded)
          {
           print "$login - Account Verified\n";
           $output = 0;
          }
         else
          {
           print "$login - Password Incorrect\n";
           $output = 2;
          }
        }
    else
        {
         print "No such Account\n";
         $output = 1;
        }
  close(DATABASE);
  return $output;
}
```

Step 7:

Create *newpass* subroutine to register a new password in the database. The next routine allows new users to register new login name and password pairs in the database so they can gain future access. It acknowledges their names being added to the database.

```
# Takes the login and password and creates an entry
  for it in the database
sub newpass {
        $newuser = "$login#$passwd#";
        'echo $newuser >> /tmp/database~'
        print "<br>$login added to database\n";
)
exit 0;
```

Step 8:

Set up the database. The database creates a separate line for each entry and uses # to separate the login name from the password.

```
[[DATABASE.DBS

sean#sean#
fred#fred#
sean3#sean3#


]]
```

This script will allow you to implement a simple password-checking and registration system.

Other Information Systems That Use Fill-In Forms

The password system is only one of a great variety of possible applications of the Web's form capabilities. It is impossible to discuss generic scripting techniques because any scripts would need to be adapted to your particular purposes.

Appendix C illustrates some of the possibilities by presenting examples of scripts for two other kinds of information systems:

- A system that asks for information about the user's sex and age and then generates a unique display for each category group.
- A system that cumulates user's comments about certain topics. It allows new users to browse the comments that already exist or to add their own.

Mini-Gallery of Sites That Use Forms

Forms add new dimensions to the Web's interactivity. Web designers are showing great ingenuity on the way they build on these capabilities. This mini-gallery takes a brief tour of some examples that can be appreciated for both their technical and informational design.

The UNIX server-based Cardiff Movie Database (Figure 7.25) allows the user to search its database of movie information by name, character, genre, country, and quotes. It also uses forms to invite Web navigators to vote in weekly movie ratings and to leave suggestions. The Lawrence Livermore Berkeley Lab Virtual Frog Dissection Kit (Figure 7.26) is famous for its interactive process. The Web navigator can virtually dissect a frog using fill-in forms to specify the point of view, the anatomical structures to be included, the language of labels and commentaries, and what kind of movies of the process should be made. The MIT Postcard site (Figure 7.27) allows the online visitor to create an electronic postcard. The visitors select an image and then use a form to indicate name and address of receiver and a message to be sent.

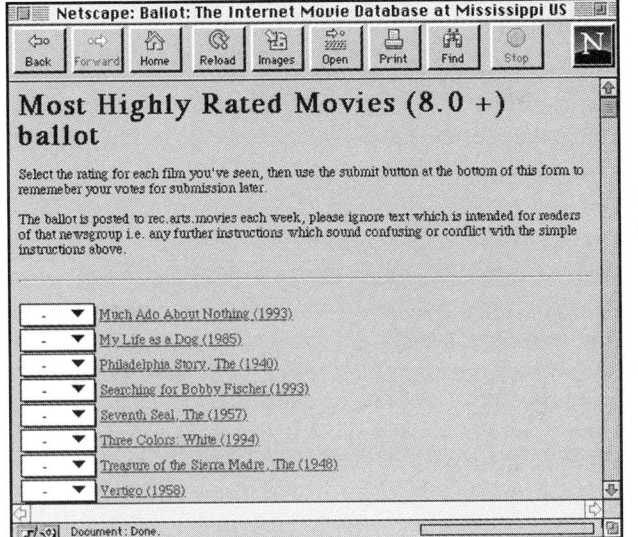

Robert Hartill, on behalf of the Internet Movie Database Team.

Figure 7.25:
Cardiff Movie Database ballot, used to rate visitors' favorite movies.
`http://www.msstate.edu/Movies/`
`Movie.Database@cm.cf.ac.uk`

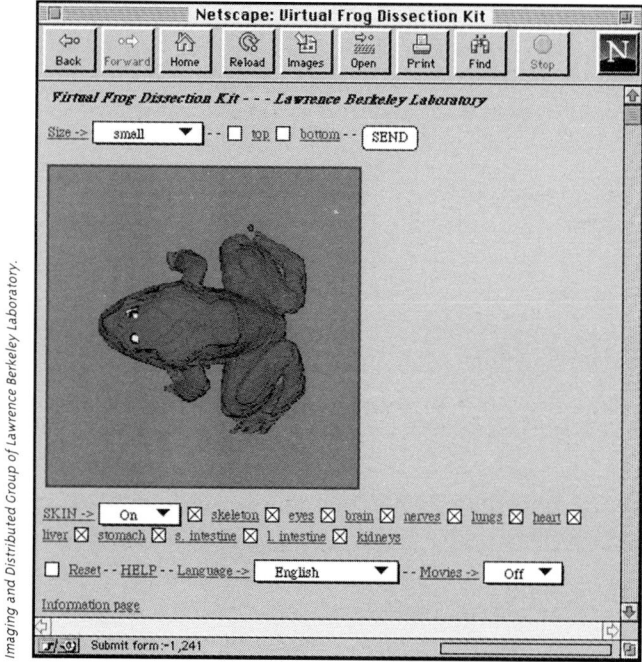

Figure 7.26:
Frog Dissection Kit.
`http://george.lbl.gov/ITG.hm.pg.docs/dissect/`
`dissect.html`

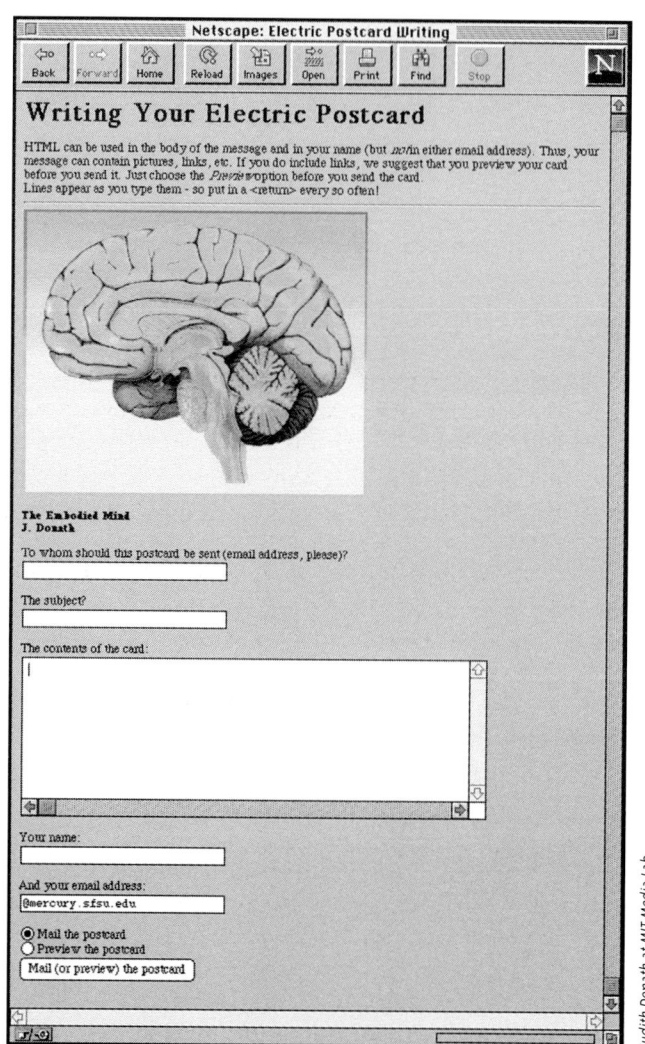

Figure 7.27:
MIT Postcard site.
`http://postcards.www.media.mit.edu/Postcards/`

HTML 3.0 Proposals for Imagemaps and Forms

HTML 3.0 proposals promise to add many exciting extensions to imagemaps and forms. They will enhance the opportunities to make Web pages that are highly interactive.

Figures with Built-In Imagemaps

Chapter 4 described the new figure structure proposed for HTML 3.0, which allows innovative features such as overlays, captions, and credits. The most radical feature, however, is a built-in imagemap capability. You no longer have to create or obtain server scripts to make imagemaps. You can include the designations of graphic hot links in an image as an intrinsic part of its HTML markup. Furthermore, the user will no longer need to wait while the server script processes the coordinates of the mouse click; the client will locally determine if the user has clicked in a hotzone and directly fetch the document that the designer linked with that area of the image.

Hotzones are indicated by a <SHAPE>= attribute included as part of link tags that are enclosed by the <FIG> tags. Each shape attribute is followed by a string that includes the name of the shape (rect,poly,circ) followed by a space followed by the coordinates that define that shape. The inclusion of the links within the figure has another benefit; browsers render the links as hot text for those users without graphics capabilities. The example that follows illustrates its potential syntax although the exact specifications are still subject to change.

```
<FIG HREF="activeimage.gif">
 <A HREF="bird.html" SHAPE="rect 10,100,60,180">
  Bird information/A>
 <A HREF="insect.html" SHAPE="rect
  220,300,50,150">Insect information/A>
 <A HREF="snake.html" SHAPE="rect
  330,200,430,300">Snake information</A>
</FIG>
```

HTML 3.0 Proposed Enhancements for Forms

HTML 3.0 proposes some fascinating additions to the input structures to be supported by forms. Users can make choices via sliders and knobs, enter drawings via a "scribble on image" feature, send audio samples, and attach files.

Authors also can provide ways to process forms other than relying on server-based scripts. Using a new <SCRIPT> attribute placed within a <FORM> tag, they can specify the URL of a script that can be downloaded by the browser. This script will then run locally in conjunction with the browser dynamically to generate responses to user provided data. The downloadable script will reduce the access and processing time associated with server-based scripts and significantly simplify logistics.

Note that these imagemap and forms features are still very tentative and subject to change.

Summary

This chapter has shown how you can create imagemaps and forms that will work seamlessly for your users; some distant server will generate custom responses based on their actions. Specifically, this chapter has shown you:

- How to create HTML documents that set up imagemaps and forms.
- How to define the hot areas of imagemaps and create files that map those areas to URLs.
- How to design information systems and server scripts to respond to information users enter in forms.

You can expect much experimentation with advanced interactive capabilities. Artists and researchers are stretching these features in fascinating ways that you will find provocative. The next chapter looks at some of this experimentation.

Chapter 8

Experimenting on the Web

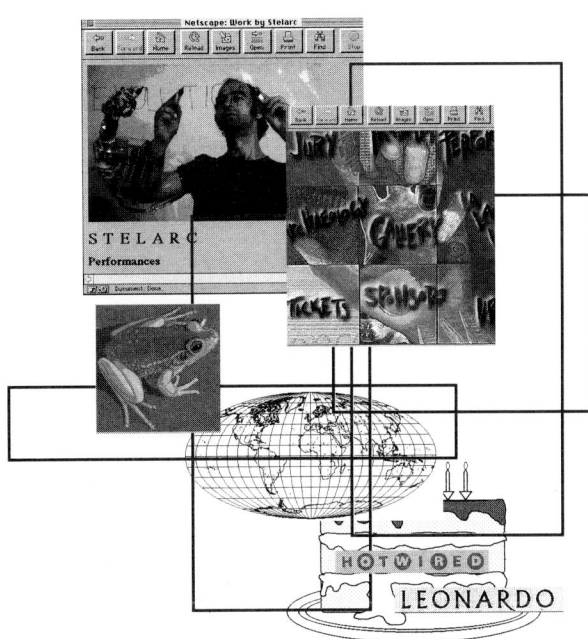

The Web is fast-changing. Views about what it is, models for organizing sites, and technologies are in constant development. Staying tuned into this development is one of your most important challenges as a Web designer.

This chapter showcases some imaginative uses of the Web and its recent trends. The best way to learn from these explorations is to think about the ideas and techniques they illustrate; maybe they can inspire you to develop some creative site design of your own! As part of your preparation to be a Web innovator, ask yourself these questions:

- What kind of experimentation is there on the Web?
- What are the experimenters trying to accomplish?
- Why is this experimentation important?

These kind of sites are often featured in "cool site" lists. While some of the experiments will certainly be dead ends, others may be the seeds of new art forms or industries that will become part of the Web mainstream. We'll look at sites that are exploring a variety of innovations, including the following:

- Off the beaten path
- Collecting and interpreting information
- Real-time reporting
- Telepresence
- Interactive distant intelligence
- Interactive media: real-time audio, Java, VRML
- Collaborative research
- Personal home pages
- Alternative art and writing

What Is Significant Information?

Early visionaries of network-based hypertext such as Ted Nelson believed that it would revolutionize the processes of publishing and dissemination of information. Anyone could make their entrepreneurial, literary, or artistic creations available to a vast online audience without needing approval from a host of gatekeepers—publishers, broadcasters, scientific review boards, censors, curators, or editors. New, unorthodox, revolutionary, and unpopular ideas would become more readily available to a wider audience. Publishing could be technically and economically feasible even if the material was not marketable.

Defining what constitutes "significant" information is one of the main challenges facing everyone in an information age. What is important information? What is useless? What might become important someday? These sites are using the Web as

a laboratory to explore these questions. You'll need to face these questions if you want to be an innovator in Web design.

The Web illustrates the slipperiness of significance. The Web destination that one site lists as useless might be listed as cool by another site. Figure 8.1 shows a screen shot from the "Useless WWW Pages" site that compiles links to sites that it considers questionable. Yahoo's list of other compilations of "useless sites" is at http://www.yahoo.com/Entertainment/Useless_Pages/. Figure 8.2 shows a well-known "Cool Site of the Day" list detailing sites the maintainer considers interesting.

Paul Phillips, lead WWW Developer, Primus Consulting.

Figure 8.1:

Useless WWW pages.

`http://www.primus.com/staff/paulp/useless.html`

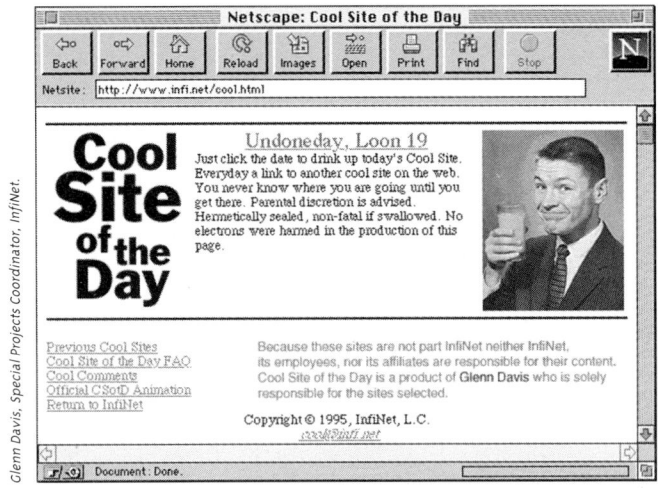

Glenn Davis, Special Projects Coordinator, InfiNet.

Figure 8.2:
Cool Site of the Day.
`http://www.infi.net/cool.html`

Off the Beaten Path

Do you want to look at pictures of all of someone's shoes, search their CD or videotape collection, find out when their phone last rang, check the balance on their discount store membership card, talk to their cat, find out what they have eaten every day, or watch movies of their everyday life? You can on the Web. Some Web designers share intimate details of their thoughts, feelings, and experiences. You can find personal details, including topics such as dream journals, lists of pet peeves, pictures from early life, and tributes to significant others.

Figure 8.3 shows one of these windows into everyday life, the Lunch Server site.

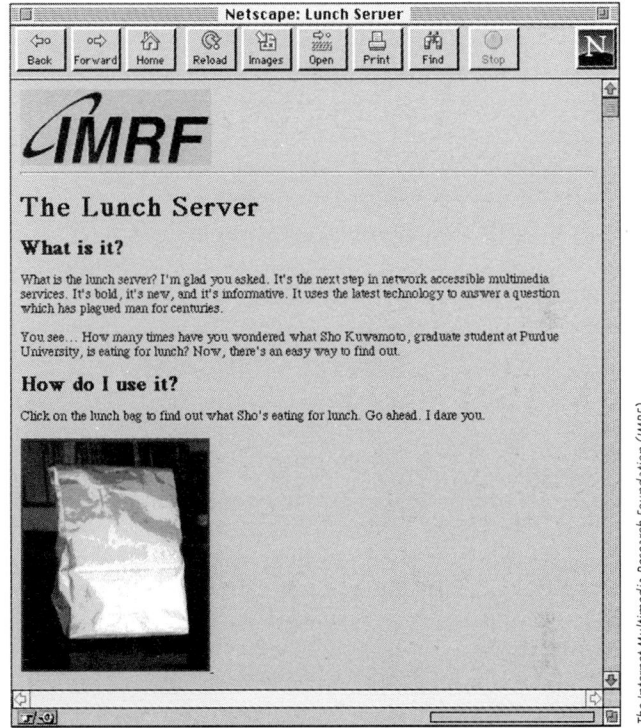

The Internet Multimedia Research Foundation (IMRF).

Figure 8.3:
Lunch Server site.
`http://physics.purdue.edu/~sho/lunch_main.html`

Collecting and Interpreting Information

The Web challenges us to think about the ways we categorize information. Many Web sites are famous for their experimentation in information organization, including such innovations as the unusual nature of the information they collect, the commentary provided, or the unique perspectives manifested in the links. With the birth of the Web, information work can become a new art form, business enterprise, political work, religious act, hobby, or some as-of-yet undefined cultural form.

Some sites provide extensive details on unlikely and occasionally distasteful topics. Other sites accumulate information on elements of pop culture, ranging from Barney the dinosaur to Lego blocks. This kind of experimentation requires a creative imagination to identify compelling topics and resourcefulness in finding relevant Web resources.

The meaning of information

Some believe the Web community is overly fascinated with the flow of data for its own sake. This issue engaged theorists even before the advent of the Web. Theodore Roszak in The Cult of Information *(New York: Random House, 1986) suggested that society is becoming overly fascinated with the flow of data, facts, and bits of information and losing touch with the importance of interpretative frameworks for making sense of this material. Coming from a different position, post-modern theorists such as Jean Baudrillard (for example, in*

Simulations—Semiotexte, New York, 1983) claimed that the historical search for meaning and hierarchies of importance was self-delusion and a doomed enterprise. The image background of an advertisement or the chance utterance of a celebrity can have more ultimate impact than the most profound political or philosophical tracts.

Figure 8.4 illustrates a page from the Lego site, which encompasses an amazing variety of information related to the children's building block toys called Legos. The figure shows unusual constructions, including a functioning automobile, built by Lego users worldwide.

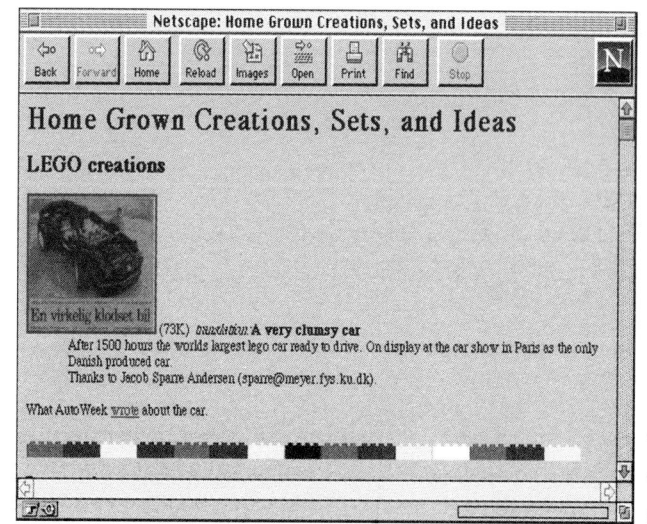

Figure 8.4:

Official Lego site page of unusual constructions made from Lego blocks.

`http://legowww.homepages.com/creations/index.html`

Figure 8.5 shows the Kite Flier's Site, another of the experiments in accumulating information. It is a massive, wide-ranging archive, all focused on kite-related materials, including images of kites from around the world, technical information on constructing and flying kites, links to weather reports, kite festivals and contests, and home pages of kite enthusiasts from around the world.

information, one leaves with new awareness that primate research may not be as "neutral" a scientific enterprise as it seems.

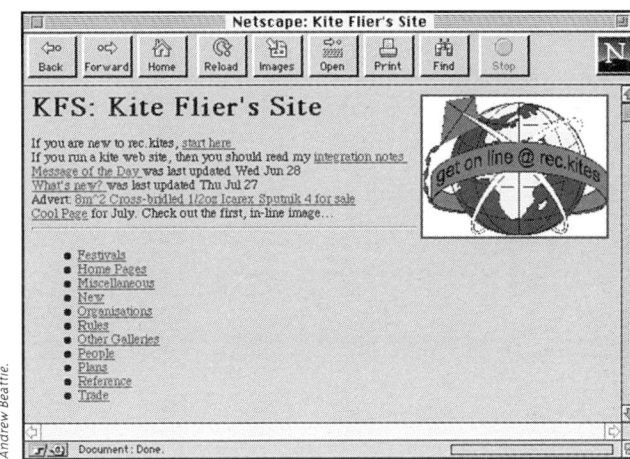

Figure 8.5:
Kite Flier's site.
`http://www.kfs.org/kites/index.html`

Figure 8.6 shows the "Primate Anatomy Matrix." It invites Web readers to understand the materials it offers in new ways by interweaving information about primate research, Tarzan stories, attitudes toward the relationships of humans and apes, and racism. Because of the way this site combines

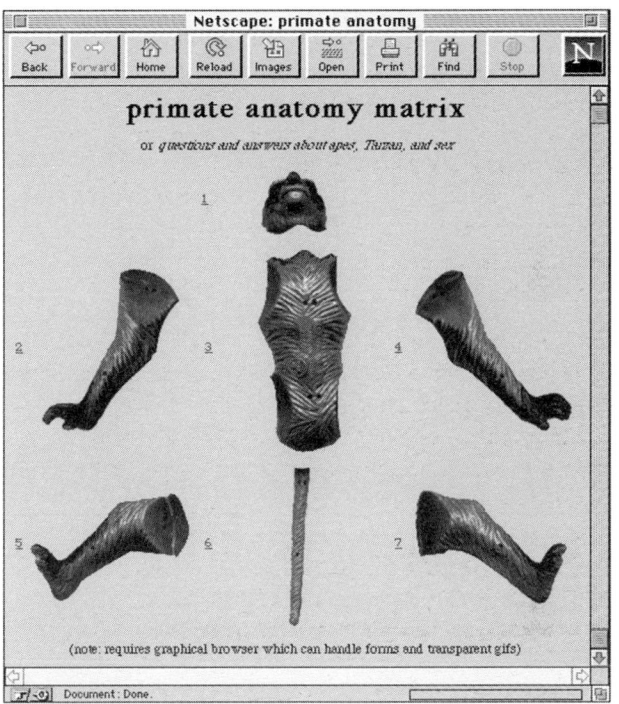

Figure 8.6:
Primate anatomy matrix.
`http://www.infoarts.sfsu.edu/infoarts/primate/`
`primatematrix.html`

Real-Time Reporting

Do you want to look into people's offices or homes, take inventory of soda and candy machines around the world, watch animals in their cages, or check the weather?

Many Web sites have used contemporary computer video scanning and data acquisition technology to make real-time observations available to the Web community. Such sites appeal to our interest in live reporting, whether it's a peek into someone's private life or an update on a trivial matter. One of the earliest pioneers was the Trojan Coffee machine site at Cambridge University (http:www.cl.cam.ac.uk/coffee/coffee.html), which continually showed the world how much coffee remained in the lab coffee pot.

Figure 8.7 shows the NetCam site, which Web-casts images from a wearable, wireless camera carried around Boston.

Indexes to Sites Offering Real-Time Reporting

- *Yahoo's list of interesting devices tied to the Internet*
http://www.yahoo.com/Computers/Internet/Interesting_Devices_Connected_to_the_Net/

- *CMU list of Internet-connected machines*
http://www.cs.cmu.edu/afs/cs.cmu.edu/user/bsy/www/iam.html

- *Anthony's list of Internet-accessible machines*
http://www.dsu.edu/~anderbea/machines.html

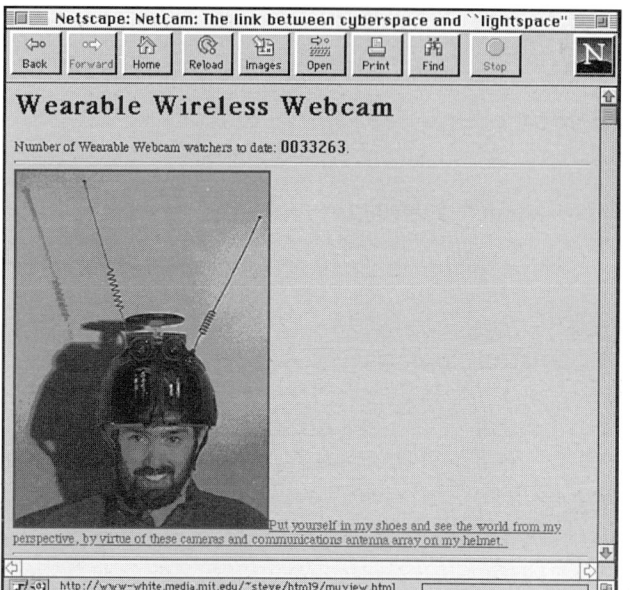

Figure 8.7:
Net.Cam—a wearable camera.
`http://www-white.media.mit.edu/~steve/netcam.html`

Telepresence

Telepresence means that a remote human cannot only observe distant happenings but actually operate a device at a distance via sensor, actuator, and network technology. The operator uses the sensor data and often video and sound information to then control the device. Probably the best-known example of telepresence is the Mars Viking Lander, which explored the surface of Mars via commands sent from earth. Contemporary research is investigating the use of virtual reality technology to make telepresence even more natural and more integrated with normal body actions.

Several Web sites offer the visitor the ability to experience limited forms of telepresence. Some sites allow visitors to control robots, telescopes, speech synthesizers, video cameras, Christmas tree lights, and even scrolling message signs located in far corners of the world. Figure 8.8 shows the home page of the "Automatic Talking Machine" a site that allows the visitor to type words that are then spoken aloud in an office in Southern California.

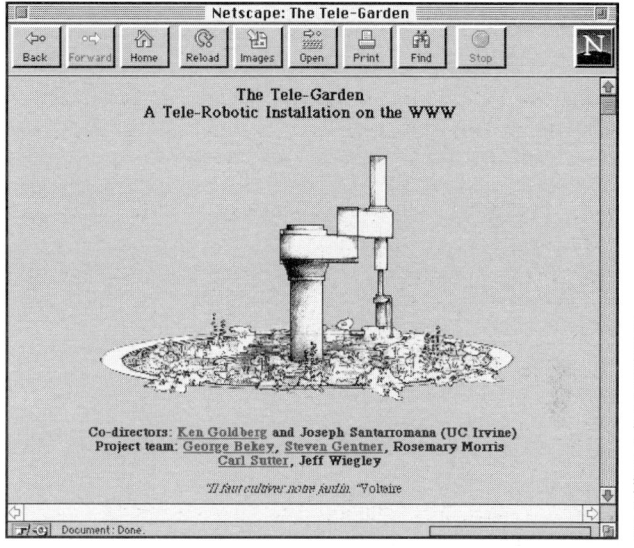

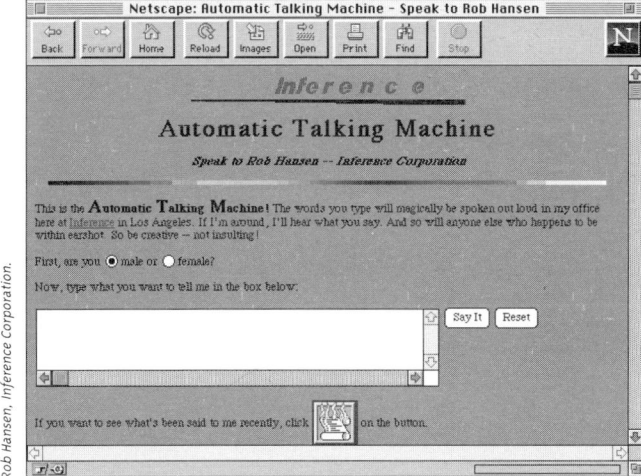

Rob Hansen, Inference Corporation.

Figure 8.8:
Automatic Talking Machine, a Web-accessible speech synthesizer.
`http://www.inference.com/~hansen/talk.html`

Figure 8.9 shows the page from the Tele-Garden site at the University of Southern California. This site lets visitors control an industrial robot arm to water and care for seedlings in a video viewable garden. Some distant participants have reportedly taken on the ongoing responsibility to plant, water, and tend their seedlings into planthood.

Ken Goldberg and Joe Santarramana.

Figure 8.9:
The Tele-Garden site lets long-distance visitors tend a garden.
`http://www.usc.edu/dept/garden`

Interactive Distant Intelligence

What is it like to interact with machine intelligence? What kinds of advanced interactive capabilities can Web sites offer? By linking their Web pages with sophisticated programs for processing information from viewers, some experimenters are extending the "intelligence" that sites can offer. Using forms to acquire user information and preferences, these offer customized responses outside of such commonplace tasks as conducting searches based on keywords.

The intelligence of most of these programs is not beyond what we would expect from sophisticated programs running on a local computer. By adapting them for Web access, however, the creators break new ground and point toward future opportunities. The Interactive Frog Dissection site described in Chapter 7 is one example. Carlos' Coloring book, shown in Figure 8.10, similarly offers complex interactive possibilities. The user is invited to pick a kind of image and interactively fill in areas of the image with various colors. The site then generates the final picture available for downloading.

Illustrating another example, Xerox PARC's Map Viewer (Figure 8.11) allows visitors to zoom in on geographic areas of the world to see increasingly detailed maps generated on the fly by the server and to pick various parameters of the map representation.

Eventually some sites may link their pages with artificial intelligence programs to respond to Web visitors with human-like sophistication. Although full AI (artificial intelligence) still eludes researchers, some sites offer experiences with limited forms of AI. For example, the Genetic Art Project (Figure 8.12) allows visitors to indicate which image out of an array they consider best and then extracts the graphic features in the preferred images to synthesize new images that manifest those characteristics.

Interactive Web games, art, and fiction offer many other examples of this experimental pushing of the intelligence of Web sites. Just as early computer pioneers used games such as tic-tac-toe, checkers, and chess to test the intelligence of their computer programs, so are Web experimenters using games to test the limits of Web interactivity. Interactive novelists and artists similarly are extending the complexity of interaction they can offer Web visitors. The reference lists

that follow present URLs to examples of interactive games, fiction, and art. Even if you are not interested in creating these kind of Web events, they serve as ideas for designing the interactivity of other kinds of Web sites.

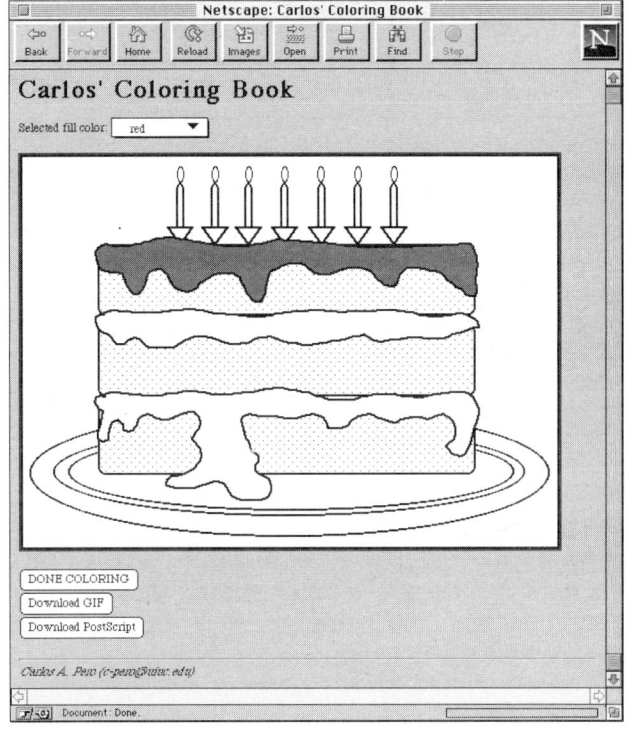

Figure 8.10:
Carlos' Coloring Book.
`http://robot0.ge.uiuc.edu/~carlosp/color/`

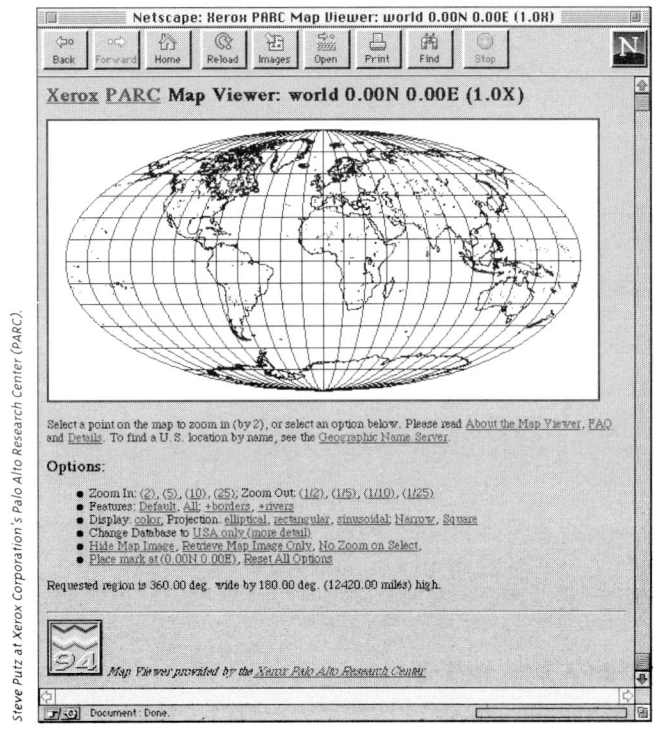

Figure 8.11:
Xerox PARC Map Viewer.
`http://pubweb.parc.xerox.com/map)`

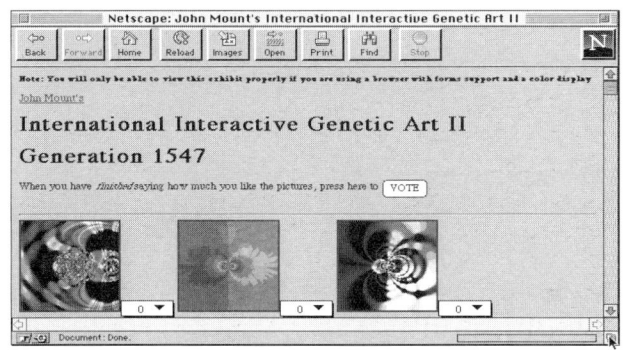

Figure 8.12:
Genetic Art.
`http://robocop.modmath.cs.cmu.edu:8001/`

Interactive Games

• *Zarf's list of interactive games on the Net*
`http://www.cs.cmu.edu/afs/andrew/org/kgb/www/zarf/`
`games.html`

• *Interactive WWW games list*
`http://www.cs.cmu.edu/afs/andrew/org/kgb/www/zarf/`
`games.html`

• *Yahoo list of interactive games*
`http://www.yahoo.com/Recreation/Games/`
`Internet_Games/Interactive_Web_Games`

Interactive Fiction Resources

• *Interactive fiction index*
`http://www.cl.cam.ac.uk/users/gdr11/tree-`
`fiction.html`

• *Yahoo list of interactive fiction*
`http://www.yahoo.com/Entertainment/Games/`
`Interactive_Web_Games/Interactive fiction`
`resources`

• *FAQ for interactive fiction*
`http://www.cis.ohio-state.edu/hypertext/faq/`
`usenet/games/interactive-fiction/top.html`

Interactive Art and Events (Single Person)

• *Links from the Underground list of interactive events*
`http://www.links.net`

• *Judy Malloy Interactive Fiction*
`http://www/tmn.com/Oh/Artswire/interactive/www/`
`scibe/home.html`

• *Arts Wire interactive fiction resource*
`http://www.tmn.com/Oh/Artswire/interactive/www/`
`interact.html`

Some sites' exploration of interactivity goes beyond what is offered on local computers. They capitalize on the Web's capability to access real-time information from anywhere in the world. They create programs with advanced interactive intelligence that modify real-time information based on user choices. For example, the Weather Map site described in Chapter 7 provided custom views of current satellite images adjusted in accordance with the viewer's desires. Figure 8.13 shows a similar processing capability in which MIT's Vvdemo project lets the Web visitor choose the kind of image processing to be applied to current live video.

Bill (William) Stasior, author of the "VV" software, and David Tennenhouse, group leader, Telemedia, Networks and Systems Group Laboratory for Computer Science, MIT.

Figure 8.13:
MIT's Vvdemo Site allowing manipulations of real-time video.
`http://www.tns.lcs.mit.edu/vs/vvdemo/vvdemo.html`

Emerging Web Technologies

Researchers are feverishly working to develop new technological capabilities for the Web that enhance its media and interactive capabilities, including real-time audio, VRML, and the Java language. These emerging technologies are discussed at greater length in Chapter 10.

Real-Time Audio

One early entrant in the emerging field of real-time audio is a company called Progressive Networks, whose product RealAudio allows inline sound that plays as it's accessed. The site presenting RealAudio needs a special server and the user needs a special player in order to experience this live audio.

Many sites have already incorporated RealAudio technology in their Web sites. For example, ABC broadcasts live news, the London Daily Mail offers zodiac forecasts, and Virtual Nashville presents an online game in which the live audio is a significant part. RealAudio allows Web designers to integrate sound into Web experience much like inline images are viewed as intrinsic parts of Web pages.

Resources for RealAudio

• *RealAudio home site*
http://www.realaudio.com/

• *Listing of sites using RealAudio*
http://www.realaudio.com/othersites.html

VRML (Virtual Reality Modeling Language)

Virtual Reality Modeling Language allows users to interact with the Web by moving about a virtual 3-D world. Users need a special player in order to make use of VRML-enhanced sites.

Experimenters have created many fascinating sites based on this technology with architectural spaces for users to move around in and inspect objects. 3-DSite's Model Market site provides a service that allows Web users to upload and download VRML models. The biomolecule site lets you move around complex molecules, the Virtual Human Body Performance lets you move through a body, the Topological Slide lets you move around strange topological objects, the Wadtoiv sites allows you to play a 3-D version of Doom, and the Johnny Mnemonic site lets you move through 3-D worlds related to the movie.

Figure 8.14 shows the home page from the University of Kansas Adding Machine Theatre event that took place in both real-time and on the Web. Web users moved around a virtual space directly related to a live performance space; Web users can still move through the virtual space.

Figure 8.15 shows a home page from the Interactive Origami site. This site instructs users how to fold origami objects and uses VRML technology to allow users to move around the object in order to understand the process better.

Mark Reaney, Associate Professor, Department of Theatre & Film, University of Kansas (mreaney@kuhub.cc.ukans.edu).

Figure 8.14:
The Adding Machine Interactive Virtual Reality Theatre.
http://ukanaix.cc.ukans.edu:80/~mreaney/

Resources for VRML

- *Yahoo VRML information list*
http://www.yahoo.com/Entertainment/
Virtual_Reality/Virtual_Reality
_Modeling_Language__VRML_/

- *On the Net listing of VRML sites*
http://www.hitl.washington.edu/projects/
knowledge_base/onthenet.html

- *New College listing of VRML sites*
http://www.newcollege.edu/vrmLab/vrmlSites.html

- *3DSite's list of VRML sites*
http://www.lightside.com/3dsite/cgi/VRML-
index.html

- *VRML information center*
http://vrml.wired.com/

- *SGI information about VRML*
http://www.sgi.com/

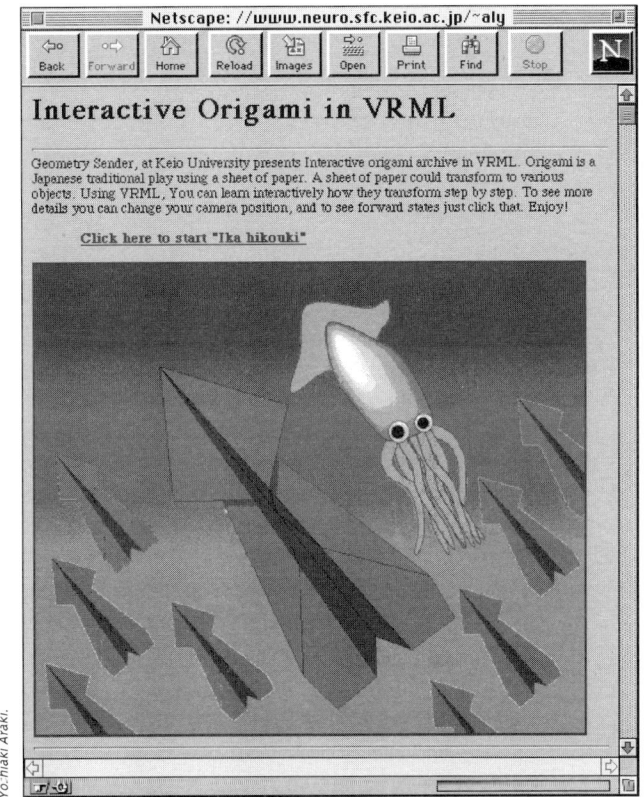

Figure 8.15:

Interactive Origami.

```
http://www.neuro.sfc.keio.ac.jp/~aly/polygon/
vrml/ika/
```

Java

Researchers at Sun developed the Java programming language, which can work with browsers as a way to allow specialized applications to run over the Web. Java requires a special browser configured to respond to Java programs. Sun has developed its own browser called HotJava, but other browsers such as Netscape will soon include the capability to enact Java programs. The Java process starts when the Web page sends an applet program along with the other customary Web information. The Java-enabled browser then does whatever the program requests.

These programs can enact multimedia displays or even more complex interactive scenarios. Experimenters have developed all kinds of innovative demonstrations, including animated "nervous text," moving bullets, and rotating helicopters. There are sites that use Java for interactive games such as Tetris, Reversi, Poker, and crossword puzzles. The HotWired site created an active animated display of links in which additional information about each link is displayed in an animated form.

Further Resources for Java

- *Sun Java Server*
http://java.sun.com/

- *Java applets*
http://java.sun.com/applets/

- *Sites experimenting with Java*
http://java.sun.com/applets/appletSites.html

Collaborative Research

Can the Web change the way people work or play together? Research in work environments, which predates the Web, focuses on topics such as groupware, workflow management, and distributed work. Scientists are developing new collaborative systems finely tuned to support scientific research. New forms of collaborative art, entertainment, and education have also been invented. Experimenters have even created some new collaborative environments such as Web-based MOOs and MUDs (multiuser online environments) in which collaboration is the focus.

Scientific Project Sites

There are collaborative electronic environments in which scientists can post work in progress and comment upon others' work. Figure 8.16 shows the "Collaborative Clickable Biology" site that allows researchers around the world to collaboratively contribute research results and commentary and to propose new ways of organizing references. The figure shows an experimental schematic map of an HIV virus that presents an innovative way of accessing research references; researchers can interactively link their research or commentary with parts of the diagram. Offering support to astronomers, the AstroVR site (http://brando.ipac.caltech.edu:8888/) provides "a 'virtual reality' where users can interact and do collaborative research almost as if they were in the same room," undertaking activities such as sharing whiteboards, inspecting telescope images, and making plots together. The international 18 nation Ocean Drilling project (http://www-odp.tamu.edu/) links several research ships out on the ocean with researchers throughout the world in an ongoing, collaborative analysis and monitoring of research results related to understanding the ocean floor.

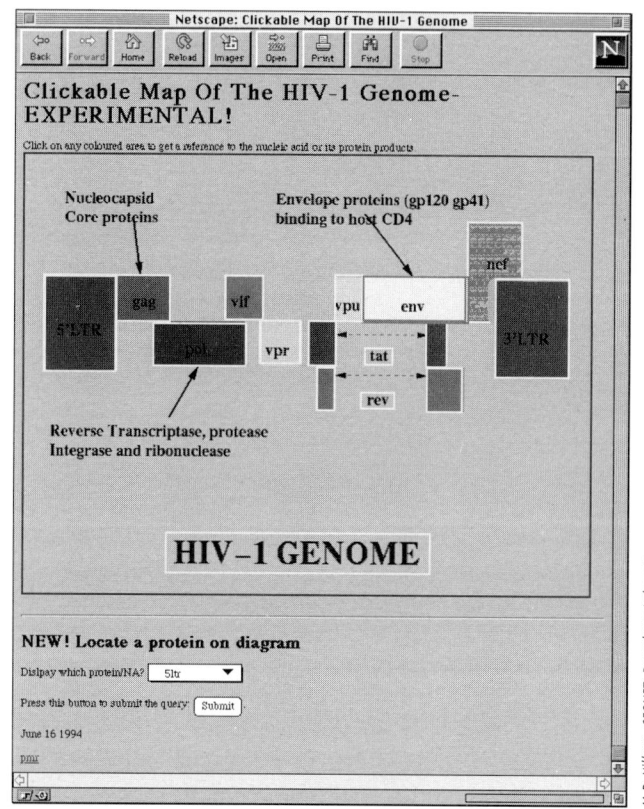

Figure 8.16:

Collaborative Clickable Biology site.
`http://seqnet.dl.ac.uk:8000/HOME.html`

Art Project Sites

Several sites have begun to test the idea that cyberculture
will unravel traditional notions of creator and audience. They
set up frameworks that encourage and organize the submissions. For example, the award-winning File Room site
assembled by Chicago artists created an interactive event
focused on the collection of information about censorship
incidents. People around the world were invited to contribute
examples of censorship via visual interfaces organized by
geography and type of censored material. (Unfortunately,
the event lost its Web location at press time, but it may
return.) The contributory possibilities take on new power
because the community of participants is anonymous,
international, and able to access automatically from anywhere in the world at any time of day.

OTIS Infinite Grid

Figure 8.17 shows the infinite grid from the OTIS art site,
which is well known for its experiments in collaborative art. A
grid is laid out and Web visitors are invited to pick a place to
which to add an image. Contributors are encouraged to
interconnect and play off others' images.

ARC Interactive Media Competition

The ARC Interactive Media Festival holds an international
interactive media competition each year. It has now started
using the Web in an innovative way by making much of the
submission, judging, and presentation process available at
its site (Figure 8.18). Anyone in the world can surf in to see
summaries of artists' work, keep up with the judging process,
and see the winners. Processes that used to be kept shrouded
in darkness are now available to open view.

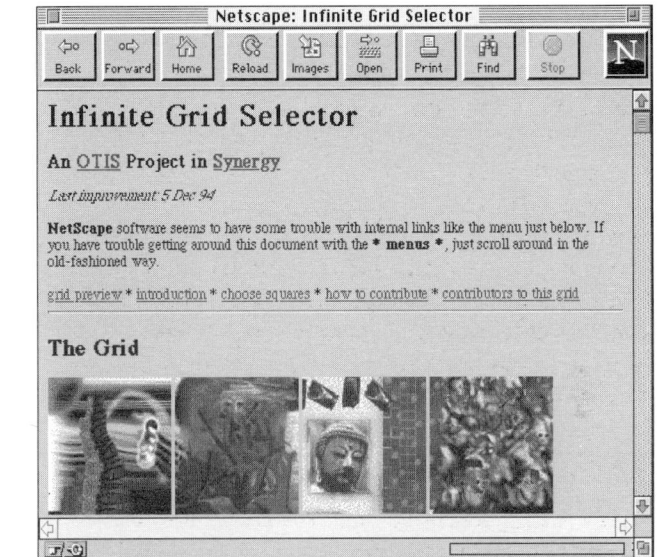

Figure 8.17:
OTIS—Infinite Grid Project.
http://sunsite.unc.edu/otis/synergy/
grid_infinite.html

Mark Meadows.

Figure 8.18:
Arc International Media competition.
`http://spark.com/`

Indexes of Experimental Collaborative Online Art

* *Yahoo interactive Web art list*
`http://www.yahoo.com/Entertainment/Miscellaneous/`
`Interactive_Web_Art/`

* *Anima guide to online Web and experimental art*
`http://www.wimsey.com/anima/ARTWORLDonline.html`

* *Hyp-art list of other collaborative art projects*
`http://rzsun01.rrz.uni-hamburg.de/World/`
`Playground/HypArt/misc/OuterArt.html`

* *Digital journey's list of art experiments*
`http://ziris.syr.edu/otherstuff/other.html`

* *Judy Malloy's paper "Making Art Online" (Analysis,*
  tools, descriptions of works)
`http://www.wimsey.com/anima/NEXUS/makingArt.html`

Entertainment

Some sites are experimenting with collaboration just for fun. They create experimental situations in which people can interact. They innovate in how they stimulate participation, organize contributions, and provide access. Web-based MOOs, MUDs, and MUSHs are part of this experimentation.

Some sites stimulate collaboration by posing a common task such as soliciting the knowledge and opinions of the Web community. For example, the Biblical Contradictions Site (http://www.ugcs.caltech.edu/werdna/contradictions/ contradictions.html) collects examples of contradictions from visitors and the One-Book Event (http://www.primus.com/ staff/paulp/one-book.txt) collects opinions about what people consider the most important book. There are voting oriented sites that accumulate the judgments of the Web community on movies, records, television shows, and just about anything else. In all these sites, the accumulation of the Web community's contributions is often as interesting as the nominal topics of the sites.

At the Find-the-Spam site (Figure 8.19), visitors are confronted with the absurd challenge to "find the Spam" when the screen is filled with an image of a Spam can. They are then invited to leave their musings on this strange topic and view what others have left. Here is a brief sample of some of the contributions:

- There are many things in this world, Horatio, that are not taught in your Spam.
- Spam Produces Artificial Minds.
- "Mean old SPAM, taught me to weep and moan..." —"When the SPAM moans"—Led Zeppelin.

Even before the Web, online phenomena such as MUDs (Multiuser Dungeons), MOOs (Multiuser Object-Oriented spaces), and MUSHs (Multiuser Shared Hallucinations) allowed multiple users to inhabit shared virtual physical spaces. People could interact online with each other and with the objects of the virtual spaces. Each person who logs on to one of these environments typically connects to a character in the space whom they can then control with simple commands. Many enthusiasts believe that this building on human proclivities for spatial orientation is the most powerful way to organize online interactions. For example, when you wander into a room, the communications from all the others become available to you. LambdaMOO, one of the most well known of these MOOs, developed at Xerox PARC research center, makes an extensive description and manual

available on the Web (ftp://parcftp.xerox.com/pub/MOO/ ProgrammersManual.texinfo_1.html).

Figure 8.20 shows the welcome page from the RealTime MUSH, which is experimenting with linking MUSHs to other media. This Canadian virtual coffee house is linked to a radio show that is on the air from 7 to midnight in parts of Canada. The live radio show and the live MUSH are allowed to bleed into each other in interesting ways—for example, listeners converse with the hosts and each other via the Web site.

What kind of shared tasks can induce people to participate in a collaborative online environment? What kinds of models can provide useful and interesting frameworks? John Mallery, who directs MIT's Intelligent Information Infrastructure Project, has assembled a valuable Web site to help you think about these questions and a rich abundance of links to related online resources (http://union.ncsa.uiuc.edu/ HyperNews/get/hypernews/related.html).

Information on MUDs, MOOs, and Other Virtual Shared Environments

- *MUD information page*
`http://www.cis.upenn.edu/~lwl/mudinfo.html`

- *Yahoo MUD and MOO list*
`http://www.yahoo.com/Computers/World_Wide_Web/`
`Programming/MUDs__MOOs__etc_/`

- *WWW MOO implementations*
`http://www.ccs.neu.edu/home/nop/mudwww.html`

Figure 8.19:

Find the Spam.

http://sp1.berkeley.edu/findthespam.html

Figure 8.20:

RealTime MUSH, a shared virtual environment linked to a radio program.

http://www.pci.on.ca/~dgilbert/RealTime.html

Personal Home Pages

Home pages are one of the quintessential Web phenomenon. Where else can individuals dream up something they want to publish or create and make it immediately available to international audiences? Many home pages are not very experimental. Other home page designers, however, have experimented with several of the approaches described in this chapter—for example, going to extremes in personal revelation, offering elaborate details of personally important information, assembling unique groupings of links, offering personal art works, constructing interactive and collaborative events, and generally pushing the envelope of the Web.

Home page authors differ on their definitions of what makes a strong page. Some focus on the assembling of information and links while others proclaim the generation of unique resources as most important. Let's look at a small sample of home pages that have achieved notoriety.

Who is on the other side of a link?

Many of the sites discussed in other sections of this book may actually be extended home pages. Because Web users have access only to the limited information that the site's maintainer chooses to send, they often cannot know if the other side of the link represents the efforts of one person or a whole organization. You can sometimes tell details about a site from the path information in the URL, although for a modest cost anyone can obtain a designer Internet domain name. The ability to construct an online persona without online correspondents knowing the "truth" is one feature of Net life that has fascinated theorists for a long time. The situation suggests analogies with the "Turing test" (proposed by computer pioneer Alan Turing), in which people attempt to guess whether their computer-linked correspondent is a computer program or a real person.

Jardin Mechanisme

The Jardin Mechanisme (http://pharmdec.wustl.edu/juju/jardin.html) shows the range of experimentation typical of some home pages. Unusual images, information, art, and links are offered under a variety of intriguing categories such as:

- The Sublimating Teleporator. The road to anywhere, with no hint of intention.
- The Surrealist Compliment Generator.
- The Gallery of Fluorescent Stomach.

Ranjit's Playground

Ranjit's Playground (see Figure 8.21) offers a diversity of options, including art, contributory events, and information on idiosyncratic topics. For example, his random portrait gallery will continually grab random personal pictures drawn from home pages on the Web and update them at a specified interval. Here is a list of some of his other projects:

- PANIC real-time, high-energy, high-speed art collaboration
- The Random Portrait Gallery
- Photomorph Project

Home Pages and Personal Web Sites Indexes

- *The Complete Home Page Directory*
  `http://web.city.ac.uk/citylive/pages.html`

- *People page*
  `http://www.nhmccd.cc.tx.us/people/rhese/people`

- *GNN Home Page "Netizens" home page site*
  `http://nearnet.gnn.com/gnn/netizens/index.html`

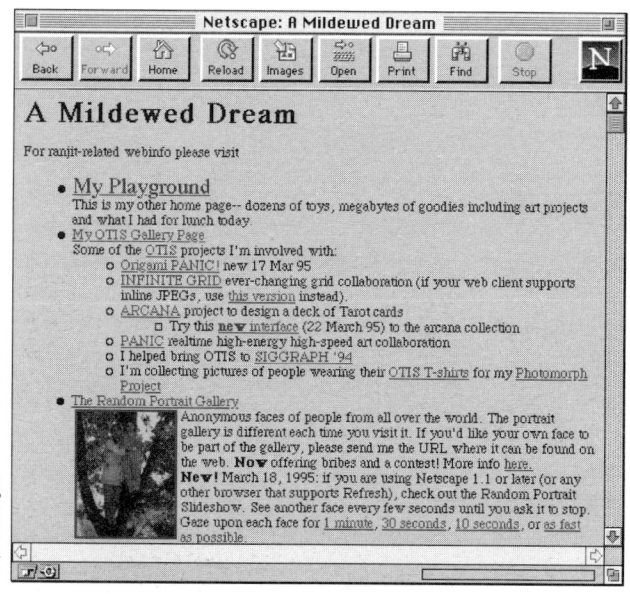

Ranjit Bhatnagar.

Figure 8.21:
Ranjit's Playground.
`http://sunsite.unc.edu/ranjit/ranjit.html`

Alternative Art and Writing

One experimental agenda for the Web focuses on increasing the ease with which artists, intellectuals, and other innovators can present their ideas to the world. The folklore of all the arts (writing, visual arts, and music) is filled with stories of difficulty finding and keeping an audience. Artists, even those who became famous, have experienced rejection. For example, James Joyce is reported to have had *Ulysses* rejected by 22 publishers before it ultimately was accepted. Publishers can be especially harsh and intolerant of works that pioneer

new approaches. Rejection of the new is not unique to the arts; it also plagues business and science innovators.

The Web can change this. Anyone anywhere with access to a Web server can make their own work public, without waiting for a gatekeeper's approval. What's more, with access to the event log of the server, they can know exactly how many people have accessed the work and from where.

Art "Galleries"

All this experimentation is giving birth to new kinds of organizations. These sites often have defined their goal as exploring the frontiers opened by the Web. They originate from many different worlds, such as visual arts, publishing, music, and political activism. Some are connected with commercial or scholarly entities such as established print magazines and some are fiercely independent, new entities. Some aim ultimately to sell work while others are more interested in public exposure without concern for remuneration. Some intend merely to present contemporary work in established media while others are interested in the experimental space where multimedia, interactivity, the Internet, information arts, and cyberculture come together.

There are too many to fully consider here. This area of activity is one of the fastest growing on the Web; new sites come online frequently, old sites change their emphases, and some disappear. They demonstrate some of the most active experimentation. This section provides a few examples to demonstrate the phenomenon.

Fine Arts Forum

Fine Arts Forum is a famous international resource focusing on art and technology. Even before the Web became popular, it provided a Gopher site. It offers online newsletters; announcements of upcoming events, shows, and competitions; pointers to other Web resources; and an online gallery.

Figure 8.22 illustrates the kind of resource found in the Fine Arts Forum. It is an online exhibit of the work of Australian performance artist Stelarc, including images from his "Drawing with Three Hands Simultaneously," "Stretched Skin/Third Hand," and "Third Hand" projects. Stelarc creates art that explores the relationships of the body and technology in the contemporary era.

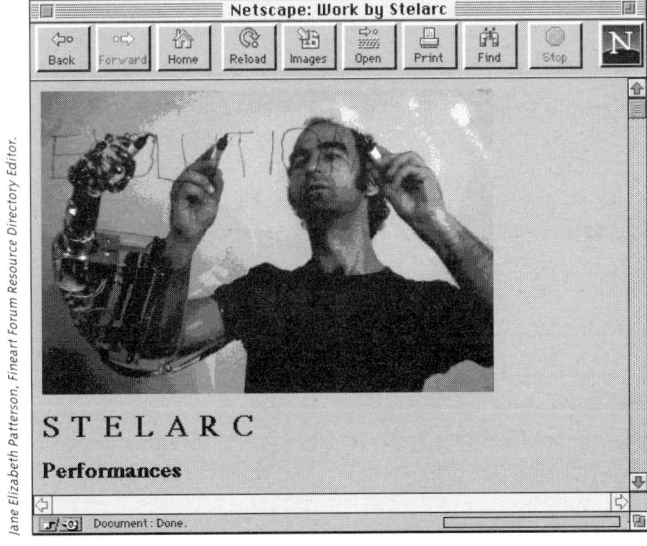

Figure 8.22:
Fine Arts Forum gallery exhibit of Stelarc.
`http://www.msstate.edu/Fineart_Online/Stelarc/`
`stelarc.html`

Anima: Arts Network for Integrated Media Applications

Anima, Arts Network for Integrated Media Applications (Figure 8.23), is a site based in Canada that both displays new technological art works and offers theory and analysis helpful in understanding Web phenomena.

Figure 8.23:
Anima, Arts Network for Integrated Media Applications.
`http://www.wimsey.com/anima/ANIMAhome.html`

Cybercafe

Cybercafe presents documentation of art events, actual in-process events, and other resources concerning the relationship of the arts and new technology (see Figure 8.24). It focuses on the domains of media and new technologies including telephones, fax, and performance in addition to computers.

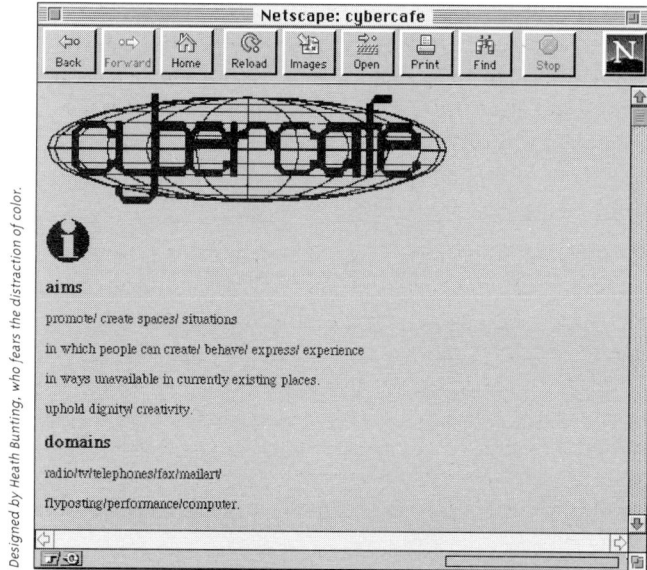

Designed by Heath Bunting, who fears the distraction of color.

Figure 8.24:
Cybercafe.
`http://www.cybercafe.org/cybercafe/`

The Asylum

The Asylum (see Figure 8.25) is an interactive art site based at California Institute of Technology. The following are examples of events offered:

- WWW Lite-Brite ("The inmates' vast art collection")
- Poll Booth (place in which visitors can express opinions on a variety of topics)
- The Revolving Door ("schizophrenics" hotlist)

- Fiction Therapy Group (place to express troubled thoughts)
- Cuckoo's Clock (interactive sound event)

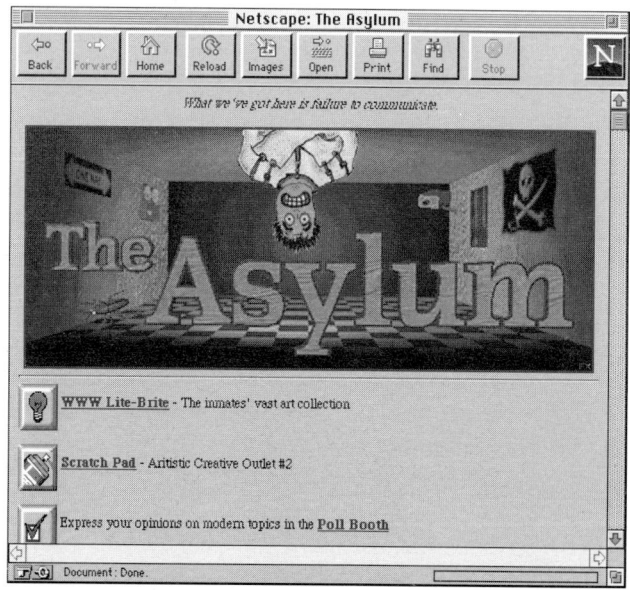

Aurelius Prochazka.

Figure 8.25:
The Asylum.
`http://www.galcit.caltech.edu/~ta/cgi-bin/asylhome-ta`

Cybersight Interactive Art Site

The Cybersight site (Figure 8.26) offers a variety of interactive art events and links such as the Graffiti Wall (collaborative art project). Illustrating the fluid boundaries of these new organizations, it also creates interactive online advertising promotions for a variety of companies.

Cybersight.

Figure 8.26:
Cybersight.
`http://cybersight.com/cgi-bin/cs/s?main.gmml`

E-Zines

A wide variety of e-zines (electronic magazines) have flourished, ranging from those linked to traditional print magazines to those started by individuals and small groups with a particular political or artistic idea. Like the online galleries, the e-zines are experimenting actively in finding new forms appropriate to the new media. In fact the

boundaries between e-zines, galleries, and the experimental collaborative events described earlier are often difficult to define. Their experimentation can be a fertile source for your own design ideas. This section offers a few examples and a reference list of indexes for more information.

HotWired

The HotWired site (Figure 8.27), which is associated with the "cyberculture"-oriented print magazine *Wired,* has earned a reputation for being cutting-edge and experimental. It covers topics such as the arts, news, technology, and commerce with full use of multiple media (text, image, sound, and video). It provides rich links to other Web resources, searches out strange information, and experiments with contributory and collaboration structures. It requires registration of a password in order to access some of its resources.

Leonardo: The International Journal of Art & Science

Leonardo is an international journal of art and science published by MIT Press. It has been in print for 25 years and was a pioneer in presenting the work of artists who explored the frontiers of technology. For several years it has had an online presence in its Leonardo Electronic Journal and in the support it gave to help initiate Fine Arts Forum.

Like many academic and trade journals, Leonardo is trying to define its role in a networked age. It asks questions about which information is best suited to print and which to present on electronic networks. How can a Web presence enhance the classic journal?

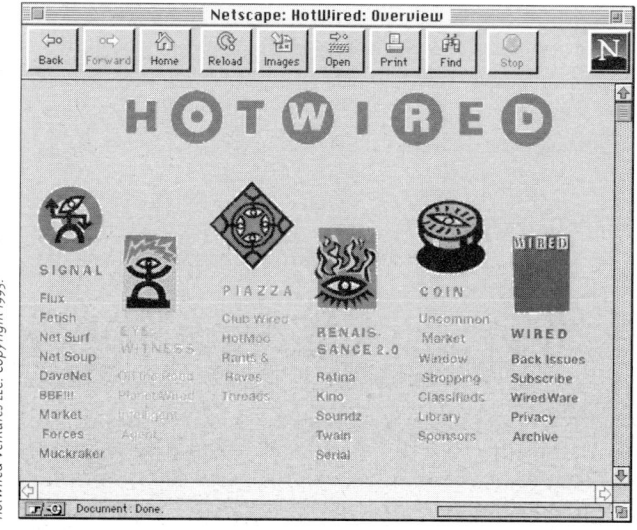

HotWired Ventures LLC. Copyright 1995.

Figure 8.27:
HotWired *site.*
`http://www.hotwired.com`

Leonardo's site (Figure 8.28) offers archives of articles, supplementary materials to printed articles, materials whose relevance or accuracy is too ephemeral for print, and online references that interest readers. Most print journals and magazines will need to contend with similar issues as they determine the role of print in an electronic age. A free access "Plaza" and a private area restricted only to subscribers is offered.

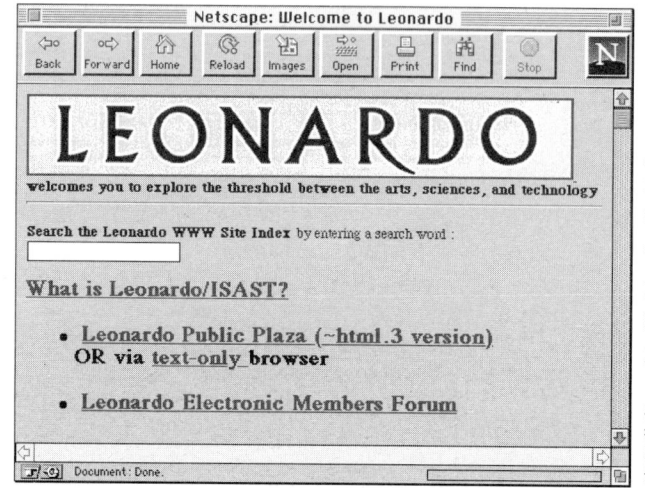

The Staff of Leonardo and the International Society for Arts, Science and Technology.

Figure 8.28:
Leonardo home page.
`http://www-mitpress.mit.edu/Leonardo/home.html`

E-Zine and Alternative Gallery Indexes

* *E-zine indexes and lists*
`http://www.acns.nwu.edu/ezines/`

* *John Labovitz E-zine index*
`http://www.meer.net/~johnl/e-zine-list/index.html`

* *Cybersight's list of online events*
`http://cybersight.com/cgi-bin/cs/s?main.gmml`

- *Derek's guide to online galleries at Anima site (includes short reviews)*
`http://www.wimsey.com/anima/`
`OnlineGalleriesGuide.html`

- *Fine Arts forum list of galleries*
`http://www.msstate.edu/Fineart_Online/art-`
`resources-galleries.html`

Summary

The Web is vibrating with innovation. Experimenters are testing the limits of what kinds of information should be on the Web and exploring new ways to organize information. They are creating new kinds of events based on real-time reporting, telepresence, and distant interactions with sophisticated computer programs. They have invented new kinds of computer-mediated collaborative structures. The Web is a virtual laboratory full of new concepts, techniques, and demonstrations that you can draw upon in your own designs.

Given what we know of Web design and Web experimentation, what kind of design principles can be extracted? Although the final word is not in yet, there are some emerging principles worth considering. We'll take a look at them in the next chapter.

Chapter 9

The Challenge of Web Design

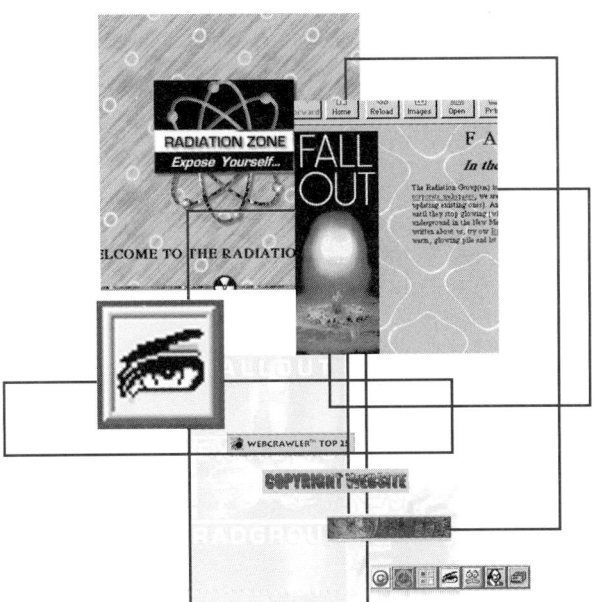

Creating an effective Web site challenges you in ways that are simultaneously very old and very new. Designing clear text, effective layout, high impact images, and compelling sounds draws upon age-old traditions of design, art, and music. Designing engaging and effective interactive Web-based hypermedia is unprecedented and draws on traditions that are just now being established. An overall goal of this book is to help you answer the following questions:

- What makes a Web site a place users find pleasing, thought-provoking, or useful?
- What should you think about in planning your own design efforts?

The expanded design framework presented early in this book can help you answer these questions. Remember, it suggested that four areas of concern underlie the design of the strongest Web sites:

- Organization of information and navigation
- Visual impact and effectiveness

- Responding to the current technological realities and future opportunities
- Knowing the site's audience and the surrounding context, as well as knowing the value of your site in the world beyond the Web

This chapter summarizes some emerging principles of Web design. It draws upon my experience and the wisdom encapsulated in the many Web style guides now available online.

A Model for Analyzing Good Web Design

Although I present guidelines and strategies for Web design that will serve you in most situations, they cannot be universal. You will need to adjust them for your particular design situation and your own opinions about the meaning of the Web. You must also be aware of significant differences of opinion that exist within the Web design community:

- Some believe the most effective sites are those that organize extensive links to external information sources. Others believe the most important function of sites is to offer original content. Your own opinions on the subject will affect what you consider a strong site.
- Good Web design cannot be totally separated from the agenda of your site. For example, the same ambiguous links that make an experimental interactive movie site inviting and provocative might be considered confusing and poor design in a information resource site.
- Design principles are useful starting points, but don't let them be a straitjacket. They cannot tell you how to

invent new design breakthroughs. The history of design and art is dynamic. Some principles now considered bedrock standard practice were considered ugly, confusing, or in bad taste when they were first introduced. The Web is so new and rapidly changing that most design principles are in flux. Avoid careless design flaws, but be willing to risk innovation.

- Ultimately, strong sites present high-quality, original, carefully crafted resources with compelling content.

With these caveats in mind, let's take a look at Web design principles in each of the four areas of expanded design.

Organizing Information and Navigation

Hypertext vertigo is a common affliction affecting Web users; many complain of being lost and frustrated. Your Web design must make it easy for users to find what they are looking for, understand where they have been, and ascertain where they might go. It must help users understand the underlying structure of your information. Navigation must be effortless. Navigational graphics and text should reinforce the user's appreciation of the site's purpose and structure and offer a predictable, comfortable basis for getting around and making sense.

Clarifying the Information Structure

- **Become an expert in your topic**. Web design means information design. The more you know about the topics your site covers, the better you can organize the site. Research is part of your role. Become a fanatical

Web surfer to related sites, read whatever you can find in traditional print sources, and join relevant newsgroups. Understanding your topic also allows you to design your Web site logically and more intuitively.

- **Clarify the logical structure of your site**. Determine what are the major divisions of information you will offer and how they relate to each other. Determine what subsections you want to offer in each category. Make clear any other relationships among categories. Decide what patterns of linkage you want to encourage, support, or discourage. Use this analysis in the layout of your site.

- **Provide a clear table of contents or orientation page**. Offer visitors a description of the sections and subsections available at your site. Write succinct but lucid descriptions so that a reader has a clear sense of what awaits them in your site. Make each entry a hot link to that section.

- **Consider using a set of orientation graphics in your introduction page.** You can reinforce the major structural divisions of your site by linking each section of the contents with a unique graphic. Be sensitive to image loading time by using small images.

- **Consider using an imagemap as your main orientation device.** Develop an image that intrigues, visually conveys information about the structure of your site, and also directly serves as the hot links. Be careful about making the visual information too dense.

- **Consider offering a search utility**. If your site is complex or multilayered, users may have trouble finding the material they are looking for, even with good indexes. A search option in which users can type keywords helps them find areas that relate to their interests.

- **Consider offering customization options**. If you are able to identify different classes of visitors who will come to your site, consider offering alternative organizational structures as an option. For example, the Web's hypertext capability allows you to construct various indexes as gateways to the same basic material or to adjust the relative prominence given different sections of your site.

Navigational Aids

- **Provide a title or a signature graphic**. Put a descriptive title near the top of the Web page. Also place the same signature graphic from the orientation page if you used one. (Remember, these graphics will take minimal time to load from the user's local hard disk cache if they are the same graphics you used on your orientation page.) The reappearance of the signature graphic in the section reinforces user's understanding of your site structure.

- **Offer navigation links in every section**. Every section should provide a link to the table of contents or orientation page. In addition, every page should offer links to the previous page and next page if your site offers linear materials, or to the major sections of your site if it is not linear. To add visual interest, some style guides recommend the use of graphic button sets or icons for these navigational aids (provided they are small, fast-to-load graphics). Avoid leading users to a page where the only way out is the *go back* option in the browser.

- **Consider using icons**. Icons used for navigational aids or for identifying certain categories of information can add visual interest to your pages and help establish a unique identity throughout your site. Be wary, however, of using icons without text; usability studies show that users are often more confused than helped by possibly ambiguous icons. Be sure to offer text alternatives for readers without graphical browsers.

- **Provide identification information on each page**. You can help users understand context by providing title, author, update date, development status (for example, "under construction"), institution, and copyright information on each page. Some designers suggest including the full URL of the page also. It's a good idea to provide mailing address and telephone number somewhere in the site.

- **Orient users who arrive directly from external links**. Some users may arrive at pages on your site via external links without going through the contents or orientation page. The titles, orientation links, and identification information on each page are essential information for them to establish a sense of context.

- **Identify your page for situations where it has been saved**. Most Web browsers allow users to save pages that interest them. After time it is easy to forget where the page came from. Identification material included on the page is useful for those situations where the page may have been disconnected from its context. Some sites provide a complete URL link to the full document for users who might later want to know.

- **Identify your links with care**. Construct your anchors so that meaningful words rather than generic phrases such as "Click here" are the highlighted active link text.

- **Modularize your sections**. Interface research indicates that users typically experience confusion if they need to scroll past three screens. Keep readability in mind and try to break up your offerings so they never exceed two or three screens. The organization of your content should help dictate which sections should be kept in one document. If you use long pages, be sure to employ techniques such as inline image section dividers, images to indicate sections, and internal document links to make navigation through the long page easier.

Managing External Links

- **Research your links**. If providing external links is an important feature of your site, maintaining and updating your links is a high priority. Strive for both depth and scope in the links you offer.

- **Provide information about potential external links**. Many sites offer undifferentiated long lists of external links. Try to add value to the links you offer by providing brief annotations of the links. Indicate the creator and context of each resource.

- **Organize your links**. Divide long lists into categories to help readers understand the informational structure of the links. Develop indexes and summaries of categories. Consider using inline graphics as dividers and section signatures.

- **Be expansive in your definition of relevance**. One way you can add value is by expanding the reader's concept of relevance. Offer non-obvious, connected links but make clear why they have been included.

- **Avoid dead and redundant links**. The Web is full of links that go stale—that is, disappear, change their addresses, change what they offer, or go out of date. You should periodically verify the links you offer.

- **Consider controlling external links**. Some sites create a two-step process for accessing external links. Remember, the readers are potentially lost once they leave your site. Offer a "vestibule" on the way out that provides information about where they are about to link to and offers them a chance to decide whether to continue to explore your site.

Usability Testing

- **Test-surf your site via third parties.** Interface designers typically ask naive users to walk through their systems and articulate their thought processes as they go. Test your system. Ask inexperienced users to tell you what sense they make of your site organization. Observe their navigation processes and where they seem confused or need more information. Adjust your pages and retest.

Moving Beyond the Guidelines

To keep up with the Web, you can do more than just adhere to guidelines. You can monitor experimentation and research that can give you new ideas for making your site special and more effective. For example, information visualization researchers at Xerox PARC are creating interactive 3-D representations of complex information spaces that they hope will better portray underlying structure and allow easier navigation.

Some sites do not want to make their structure obvious from the start; they invite visitors to engage in an exploration and discovery process that reveals hidden resources. In these cases, disorientation is not necessarily a negative factor.

Visually innovative sites are sometimes willing to experiment with section signature images and navigational icons that might be considered ambiguous.

Why is hypermedia important?

In Vannemar Bush's classic article about interactivity, "How We Think" (http://www.csi.uottawa.ca/dduchier/misc/vbush/as-we-may-think.html), he suggests that human thought is naturally associationistic—that is, thoughts give rise to avalanches of new thoughts that lead to others in a non-linear way. He suggests that devices ought to support the generation and pursuit of ideas by allowing easy non-linear movement among sources of information.

Other psychologists suggest that those interacting with computers are likely to feel more personally involved and empowered by the ability to choose paths of activity. Marketeers pose related thoughts more crassly: Interactive programs will be more fun, stimulate more engagement, and sell better.

Visual Appeal and Effectiveness

Historically, design has focused on visual design—making decisions in form, line, color, and layout that enhance the appeal and communication of one's creations. The Web poses special challenges because Web protocols such as HTML somewhat limit your control. Also, because Web pages sit somewhere between print pages and interactive computer programs, they require specially tuned approaches. Web designers, however, are beginning to develop some guidelines about ways to create visually effective Web sites.

General Design Guidelines

- **Create a coherent, consistent layout style**. Notice that magazine issues differ from each other but usually are consistent within. These styles become signatures for the publication and help readers efficiently scan the information. These style choices cover such aspects as header, paragraph, and indentation styles, placement of images, banners, and other repeating elements. Designers often use a template or layout grid to help specify placement options. The goal is not to make every page absolutely the same but to create a range of possibilities with a strong family relationship.

- **Create an overall "look."** Strive to create a consistent style for repeating inline images in your site, such as icons used for navigation. You can build that similarity by choice of image type, color, or drawing style. These visually unify your pages and can function as reassuring landmarks.

- **Judiciously use blank space**. Many Web pages appear overly dense and crowded. Open space helps set up text and images and makes it easier to focus. Dense text is especially a problem with computer media because the eye easily fatigues from reading low-resolution screen text. In print media, blank space has an economic cost because it increases page count; on Web pages blank space costs almost nothing and hypertext structures make it easy to link pages. Use blank space to create an open, balanced feeling and to set off your text and images.

- **Use emphasis techniques sparingly**. Avoid the overuse of large text, major header tags, bold style, all caps, and colored text. Some Web page creators mistakenly assume that making everything emphasized will stress the importance of all the material. Ironically, this strategy frequently backfires; the eye quickly learns to disregard all these cues. Use emphasis techniques for very special items only.

Addressing HTML and Web Features

- **Use appropriate headers and list HTML structures**. Use HTML header styles to indicate logical levels of head-ings and subheadings. Use list structures for items that genuinely constitute related items. These set up visual and logical consistency in your pages and allow automated agents to interpret your materials. Visually oriented design guides often take issue with these guidelines. Some suggest using the physical style structures such as bold to create your own standard subheading styles, rather than relying on HTML structures, which may be rendered differently in various browsers. They also do not discourage use of list structures for their purely visual impact such as the indentation they introduce.

- **Use the whole width of the page**. Early versions of HTML offered only the default placement of inline images on the left margin unless page creators used work-arounds to position them elsewhere. As a consequence, left placement predominated. Use the new align options and tables to create layouts that more flexibly place text and images. Use multiple images on the line. Weigh the fact that some readers will not have browsers that can render these new alignments.

- **Create appropriately sized pages**. As explained in the previous section on navigation, be wary of making your pages too long. Endless scrolling can frustrate and disorient viewers. Also watch horizontal width. Compose your pages to work within a width smaller than the default 470 pixel window opened by most browsers.

- **Create variation in inline image proportions**. Television and photography create expectations about "normal" aspect ratios for images. Explore the use of less common image proportions—for example, long and thin—to add visual interest to your site. Also, use the <SIZE> attribute to dynamically resize images if the manipulation does not distort the image.

- **Use transparent inline images**. Unless there is a reason for the bounding box, consider using transparent inline images, which integrate seamlessly with the page.

- **Explore use of HTML 3.0 and Netscape enhancements**. Consider using enhancements such as background images, text size, and color control. Be careful, however, that their use does not obscure essential information—for example, some complex background images make the reading of foreground text very difficult. Consider availability of browsers before you rely on these features.

- **Test your pages on various browsers**. Browsers differ in the way they render HTML. Test your pages on at least two browsers.

- **Watch out for conflicts with browser conventions.** Typically browsers indicate potential links with underlines and/or text color changes. Previously visited sites are indicated with other conventions. Be careful that your pages do not use these text styles in a way that will confuse visitors.

Variations in Visual Style

Many Web pages are visual joys; some are disasters. Borrowing from the print and computer interface design community, this section offers some guidance about what makes for strong visual design of Web pages. Realize, however, that purposeful variation from these guidelines can sometimes create Web sites that are fascinating and fresh.

For example, some sites purposely violate the principle of consistency. Some parts of the site are so different that they shock you when you arrive—you wonder if you somehow wandered into another site. Other sites violate layout guidelines by creating quirky off-balance pages with strange placement of images. Some test the boundaries of what you can do with complex backgrounds or unusual color combinations. Some of these experiments work; some don't. You should not be afraid to experiment but also to test with users to decide if the experiments work.

An Example of Design Principles in Action

Figure 9.1 and 9.2 show Web pages from the "Radiation Zone" site by the Radiation Group design co-op. The site devotes itself to experimental Web-based design, art, and music. It illustrates several of the principles described in these sections.

The site uses a radiation theme to offer a unified visual and informational presence to visitors. The concept of radiation suggests something that is hot, glowing, and dangerous—all of which are interesting metaphors for experimental artists. The theme is reinforced by the text of the site. One of the major sections devoted to news is called "Fallout"; the items are listed while "they are still glowing" and buried afterward. The group refers to itself as "mutants," suggesting people who are outside the mainstream.

The layout and visual approaches used throughout the site contribute to a design unity. The partially transparent international radiation symbol of the atom is used throughout the site. The relatively tall images of nuclear explosions serve as links and as signature graphics. All sections use similar backgrounds, layouts, and section dividers. The layout makes good use of open space and adopts a visually fresh approach in the Fallout section of placing the text margin in the center of the page. The different sections are clearly part of the same site.

Preventing scroll vertigo, each section is approximately three screens in length or less. Navigation back to the index is offered in all sections, along with identification information about the creators of the site and modification date information. The site attends to users with text-only browsers by offering a "Media-Lite" version on the first page and a text paragraph with key information and links that duplicate the links contained in the three atomic explosion images. Most external links include a short annotation about the resource to be linked to. The site offers the innovation of the "RadBot," an automated e-mail response system that can send users information they request.

The site also raises some design questions. The small, circular radiation symbol that appears at the upper part of each page is actually a link to one of a set of related sounds. While this feature is interesting, the symbol itself is ambiguous and might not be discovered by many viewers. While links are offered in each section back to the index, there are no cross links to the other major sections of the site. Generally, however, the site is rich in information and good visuals—two prime goals for site design.

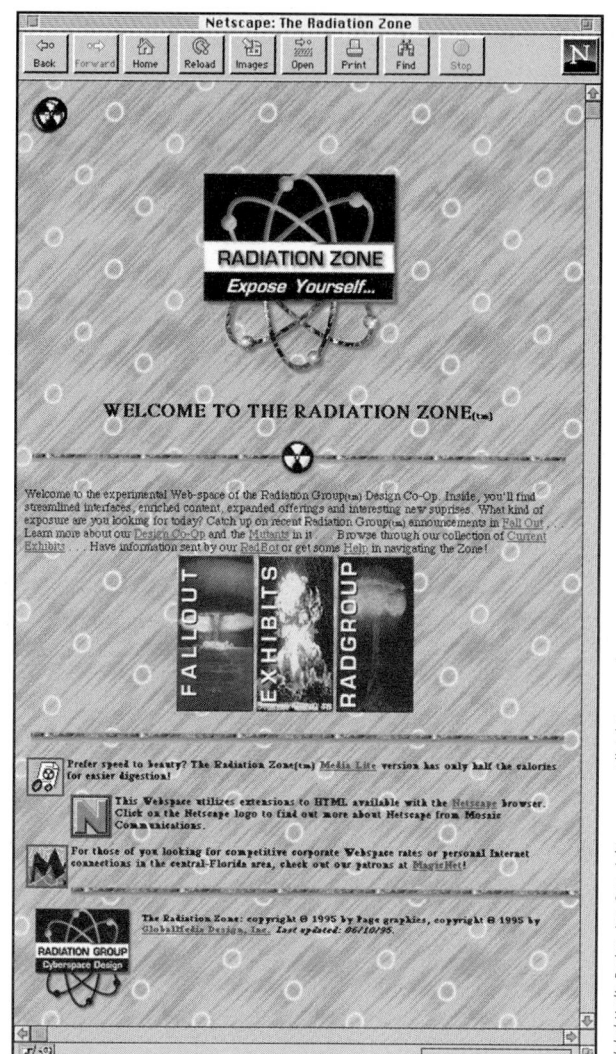

Figure 9.1:
Radiation Zone introduction page.
`http://www.magicnet.net/rz/`

Figure 9.2:
Radiation Zone Fallout page.
`http://www.magicnet.net/rz/fallout.html`

Today's Technological Realities and Future Opportunities

Good Web design takes the strengths and weaknesses of the Web into account, creating Web pages that work for users with all kinds of viewing situations, working around limitations, exploiting unique possibilities, and monitoring new developments. Understanding new technological capabilities and thinking about how they can be used to enhance your site is a critical part of Web design.

Responding to Viewers without Graphics and/or Sound

- **Provide alternative indexes**. Some of your users may be using text-based browsers such as Lynx or may have deactivated graphics viewing. Ensure that all key indexes and navigational aids (including imagemaps) provide text alternatives.

- **Provide explanatory text for images, sounds, and video**. Create short text descriptions so that media-limited visitors can derive some value from your offerings.

- **Consider offering alternative pages optimized for text-based browsers.** Many sites will offer a prominent link very near the top, leading to text-oriented pages.

Responding to Viewers with Low Bandwidth Connections

- **Minimize the size of inline images**. You cannot assume everyone has a T1 connection. A high proportion of users will be connecting via 14,400 kbps modem SLIP connections. Users get impatient waiting for large files to load. Minimize the size of images by cutting out excess space, resizing to the smallest size that still makes sense, or reducing the number of colors if full color is not necessary. Offer an optional link to full-size images for visitors who want them.

- **Take advantage of Netscape enhancements**. Use the interleaving and low-res options to offer viewers partial and low-res images as they wait for the full image to load. Use the <SIZE=> property inside <IMG> calls to specify the size of an image. Even if you are sizing an image at its original size, your explicit specification of size allows the browser to render images more quickly without waiting to determine what size they will be. (Viewers without a Netscape browser do not appreciate the advantages of these options, but also do not suffer any negative consequences.)

- **Use signature and navigation graphics carefully**. Do not make your initial home page graphic a huge inline image that requires long downloading. This is especially annoying to surfers who are just shopping around to see what is interesting. Some design guides totally discourage using "non-essential" graphics. I suggest, however, that the graphic appetite of the Web audience is such that these images can enhance your site significantly if you judiciously use small ones.

- **Reuse images**. Browsers typically load images in a local hard disk cache after downloading. You can therefore use these images throughout your site without extracting any extra downloading cost for your users. Also consider using multiple iterations of small images to create larger graphic arrays.

- **Minimize the size of sound files**. Take steps to minimize file sizes by cutting out silences and other extraneous sounds, sampling at the lowest rate, and using bit resolution that preserves the quality of your sound.

- **Minimize the size of video files**. Minimize file sizes by cutting extraneous material and minimizing frame size and frame rate as much as feasible.

- **Warn users about file sizes and describe resources as part of the link**. When you offer links to external graphics, sound, or video files, include information about file size and format with the link. Describe what the resource is. Allow users to decide whether they want to wait for the download.

- **Offer thumbnails, previews, excerpts, and snippets**. Create thumbnails of images and short samplers of long sound or video works so viewers with low bandwidth connections can get a taste of what you are offering prior to downloading.

Being Aware of Media Limitations

- **Accommodate small screen sizes**. Realize that most viewers will not be using large workstations. Currently, the 13" color monitor with 640 pixels across is the most common size and the default window opened by most popular browsers is approximately 470 pixels across. Design your pages and graphics to work at a size slightly smaller than this width. Inline images that require horizontal scrolling to view are considered annoying by most viewers.

- **Adjust images.** If you use GIF graphics, adjust your images for the 8-bit, indexed color format in which they appear—for example, by tweaking the color palette and/or contrast settings.

- **Adjust sounds.** Be realistic in your expectations about users' sound capabilities. Unless your site specializes in servicing audiophiles, most of your audience may not have the capability to hear 44kz, 16-bit, stereo playback. Make sure your sounds work well in the lower quality context most will hear them.

- **Adjust video.** Most viewers will not have capabilities to play digital video at full screen, 30 frames per second quality. Make sure your video looks good at slower frame rates and smaller window sizes.

Ensuring Adequate Access

- **Allow full-time access.** Place your site on a reliable server that is available 24 hours a day, every day of the year. One of the Web's main claims to fame is that it is always open; don't frustrate your potential viewers with the "Host cannot be contacted" message.

- **Handle multiple users.** If your site generates a lot of activity, place it on a server that can handle many users. Some of the microcomputer based servers bog down if too many browsers access them at the same time. Consider setting up "mirror" sites on other servers in other parts of the world if your site becomes extremely popular

- **Learn to use server logs.** Most server software maintains server logs that keep track of accesses. You can use this information to understand how many readers try to access your site at various times, what resources they request, how long interactions take, and what errors they encounter. This is useful for judging adequacy of access and also for other purposes such as determining popularity of pages and tracking processes of interaction.

Capitalizing on Emerging Technologies

- **Monitor developments in HTML 3.0 and beyond.** HTML is quickly changing and offering increased capabilities. Regularly monitor these developments and incorporate them in your design work where appropriate. Be wary of using them until many browsers support them or if you do, offer alternative pages for users without those capabilities.

- **Take advantage of Netscape enhancements.** Because there are enough people using Netscape browsers, it may make sense to create pages using these Netscape enhancements. If you do, however, do not rely on the enhancements to communicate absolutely essential information; test your pages with other browsers to see if they make sense, and consider offering alternative non-Netscape pages for those that do not have them. Consider using one of the server scripts available that can send different pages based on its assessment of the browser used. Also consider using Netscape's server-push/client pull mechanism that allows for automatic updates of pages as long as the client stays connected.

- **Offer access to human help and feedback.** Unlike other media, the Web can easily incorporate two-way communication for the reader. Standard Web etiquette suggests that every site make clear an e-mail address for questions and feedback. Use the "mailto" protocol to form a URL link or a form. Encourage users to send you information about their experiences with your site.

- **Take advantage of the advanced interactive capabilities offered by forms.** Forms and the scripts associated with them offer extraordinary opportunities for you to create advanced interactive capabilities for your site beyond serving documents. For example, you can provide search capabilities or customize the responses your site makes based on user preferences or characteristics. You will increasingly see sites valued for the sophistication of their interactive scripts. Learn about these capabilities and consider what features your site might offer.

- **Make your site friendly to automated agents.** Analysts suggest that automated programs such as Web robots and agents will become widespread for purposes such as automatic index building. (See Appendix A for a description of these programs.) These programs make use of HTML structures such as titles and headings to determine the content of your site. If at all possible, use HTML tags to indicate their normal structural meanings so your site will be understandable to the automated programs.

- **Monitor Web developments in new media, browser, and computing capabilities**. Developers are inventing all kinds of new capabilities for the Web—for example, inline audio and video, VRML (virtual reality markup language) that will allow interactive navigation of 3-D worlds, HotJava-like active scripts sent by servers that can increase the intelligence and multimedia capabilities of browsers, Adobe Acrobat embedding of fully formatted documents, and so on. Learn where to keep up with these developments and analyze how you can use them to enhance your site.

Emerging technologies pose significant opportunities and challenges. Keeping up with this rapid pace of Web change is not optional; it is an intrinsic component of Web design if your site is going to continue to appeal to sophisticated audiences whose appetites rapidly change. Chapter 10 offers more on these research developments and includes strategies to stay current.

Who Is Your Site's Audience and What Is Its Surrounding Context?

The Web does not exist in a vacuum. As a Web designer, you must understand the context of your site—for example, who your audience is, what it comes looking for, and where else it gets related information. You must understand the Web as a social phenomenon and monitor trends shaping its future.

Your Audience

- **Monitor who is using your site and what they want.** The more you understand your users or potential users, the better you can shape your site. Use server logs to ascertain how many users are accessing your site and what Internet domains they are coming from. Use devices such as interactive user surveys and feedback forms to gather information about what they were seeking in your site. If you want to change the access profiles for your site, adjust your site offerings.

- **Keep up with developments in Web usage**. Read trade magazines and join network newsgroups that provide information about future trends. For example, Windows 95 offers Web access as a built-in service and the major online services such as CompuServe now include Web access. These new audiences are likely to have different backgrounds and interests from early Web users. Analyze how these new audiences might change what you do at your site.

- **Disseminate information about your site**. Learn how Web users find out about sites—for example, "what's new" lists, search robots, Web indexes, cool site lists, and Usenet groups.Use non-Web information sources relevant to your site (for example, trade or academic newsletters) to spread news of your site. Make your site easy to find.

Intellectual Property and Offensive Materials

- **Be sensitive to intellectual property issues**. The Web is a tremendous system for publishing, but it also poses some intellectual property dilemmas. Don't use the creative work of others without permission or verification that your use constitutes "fair use" as defined by the copyright laws. Be careful about placing your own work on the Web if you are not prepared for readers to copy and use it. (More details are provided in the following section in this chapter on intellectual property.)

- **Develop a policy and strategy for dealing with materials that might be judged offensive**. In the United States there are strong movements by the Congress to ban online pornographic materials. Remember that young children can often access your site as easily as jaded Internet veterans. Act responsibly in what you offer. Be careful, however, in pre-censoring your materials. Many Web advocates suggest that the Web's open access is one of its major innovations. You'll likely discover that judging offensiveness is difficult because values and norms vary greatly among different parts of the international Web audience.

Responding to Future Trends

- **Include links to sites devoted to emerging developments in your fields of interest.** Monitor the trends in your area of focus; anticipate new developments. Create Web offerings that uniquely respond to these developments.

- **Decide on an economic policy for your site**. Strong forces are moving the Web toward commercialization and technologies are being developed that will make it easier to charge visitors for Web services. Popular sites are introducing advertising sponsorship of pages. Historically, the Internet has provided free services built from volunteer effort. Develop a strategy for maintaining the long-term viability of your site—either through profit or not-for-profit approaches. If you intend to charge, clarify what services will be free and which will cost. Make clear to users what the fees are and what the fee services offer.

- **Be sensitive to the international nature of the Web**. Audiences anywhere in the world will be able to access your site as easily as local audiences. Design your offerings so they make sense to international audiences. Be aware of cultural differences in the meanings of color, icons, and social propriety. Consider offering key materials in alternative languages.

- **Learn to monitor social trends affecting the Web**. Some analysts see the Web profoundly affecting the culture in many areas—for example, the role of print and entertainment media, the function of libraries, and the locus of education, government, commerce, and research. Analyze carefully what challenges and opportunities these trends pose for what you might do at your site.

Participate in the Revolution

The Web potentially revolutionizes the information power of individuals and small organizations. Recognize this potential and, if you are so inclined, help create the innovations that will make this revolution fruitful and interesting.

You can see that Web design is much more than just visual design. The Web community is by no means unanimous about good practices or what makes a strong site, although there are some areas of emerging consensus. Figure 9.3 shows the welcome page from the excellent style manual created by Yale's Center for Advanced Interactive Media.

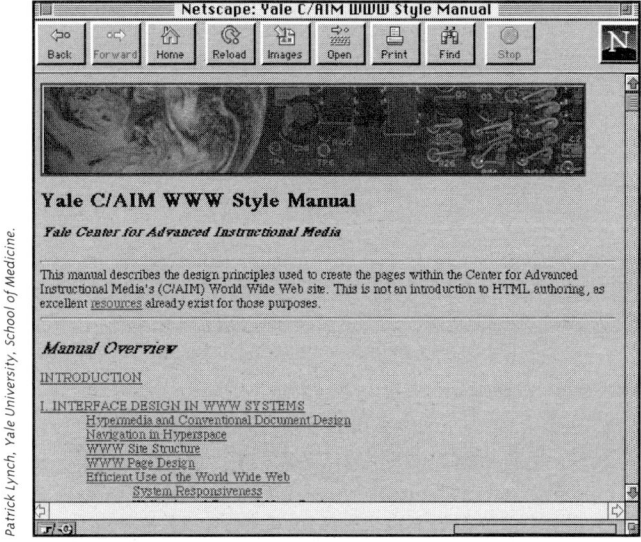

Patrick Lynch, Yale University, School of Medicine.

Figure 9.3:

Yale C/AIM style manual.

http://info.med.yale.edu/caim/StyleManual_Top.HTML

Pointers to Style Guides Available on the Web

- *W3 style guide for online hypertext*

http://www.w3.org/hypertext/WWW/Provider/Style/Overview.html

- *Yale style guide*

http://info.med.yale.edu/caim/StyleManual_Top.HTML

- *Net tips for writers and designers*

http://www.best.com/~dsiegel/tips/tips_home.html

- *Top 10 things not to do on a Web page*

http://ee.stanford.edu/eecns/www/donts.html

- *Site Design: Interface Design for WWW Documents (Anima site)*

http://www.wimsey.com/anima/NEXUS/Design/WWWdesign.html

- *Composing good HTML (focus on consistent use of tags to indicate structure)*

http://www.cs.cmu.edu/~tilt/cgh/

- *Australian National University Quality, Guidelines & Standards for Internet Information*

http://coombs.anu.edu.au/SpecialProj/QLTY/QltyHome.html

- *ANU List of truisms for Web design*

http://coombs.anu.edu.au//SpecialProj/QLTY/QltyTruisms.html

- *NASA Network Applications and Information Center (NAIC) hints for Web providers*

http://naic.nasa.gov/naic/web-info.html

- *Guide to style guides*
`http://guinan.gsfc.nasa.gov/WebStars/Style.html`

- *James Gass on "Making the Most of the World Wide Web for Your Organization"*
`http://www.gsfc.nasa.gov/documents/`
`making_most_www.html`

- *Interface Design for Sun's WWW Site*
`http://www.sun.com:80/sun-on-net/www.sun.com/`
`uidesign/`

Intellectual Property Issues

Web publishing offers unprecedented exposure for creative work. But this exposure confronts designers with two related intellectual property questions:

- Under what circumstances can you use the creative work of others in your site?

- How can you protect your own work?

Some see the World Wide Web as a potential intellectual property nightmare. The ease with which viewers can access media resources is one of its main appeals. Images, sounds and digital movies are just a click away. Moreover, the media arrive into helper applications as independent files ready to be copied to the viewer's system. Piracy is very easy if the user is so inclined.

Diverse Attitudes about Intellectual Property

Clear guidelines are difficult to derive because attitudes about intellectual property rights differ greatly. Within the Internet and microcomputer community there is a strong subculture derived from the hacker tradition that promulgates the idea that "information wants to be free." Proponents of this view freely share their own creative work and expect others to do so also.

The Web's international context also complicates intellectual property rights. In some cultures, such as the People's Republic of China, intellectual production is considered a common national resource to be freely shared. It is not private property under the creator's economic control, as is the view in the United States and other parts of the Western world. Even if copyrights are honored in one region, they might not be in other countries.

The impact of digital technology on copyright protection

Digital media has in general complicated traditional approaches to copyright and protection of intellectual property. Historically, illustrators, musicians, photographers, videographers, and other creators of media resources relied on the qualitative value of originals to help enforce copyright laws. Copies could be made, but they were usually inferior in quality to original productions. Digital technology made the copying process easy and made each copy an exact copy of the original material.

The Web and the Internet in general have further eroded traditional approaches to protection. Even with the ease of copying digital materials on local machines, a pirate had to get hold of an original. That was not always so easy. Once you place a media resource on the Web, however, it is easy for anyone anywhere in the world to call it into a local computer.

Digital technology complicates intellectual property in yet another way. Software for the editing and manipulation of sound, image, and digital video makes it extremely easy to manipulate "borrowed" files. Media can be "melded" together and transformed in millions of ways. After this manipulation, it is sometimes difficult to decide who should be considered the author.

Web developers are attempting to address copyright issues. Some are working on schemes in which users would be offered low resolution thumbnails of resources that are potentially available. To get the high resolution version they would need to register for access via passwords. The passwords and data will be sent in encrypted form so that only those who are validated will be able to access the resource.

Fair Use

In the United States the creator of a text or media resource is entitled to exclusive copyright control over the economic exploitation of the production for varying numbers of years depending on the type of production and year of origin. Others may not copy or distribute the resource except for "fair use" purposes or if the resource has entered the "public domain." Other European countries honor variations on these themes.

Can you ever use copyrighted materials without permission? Except for the fair use or public domain exceptions, copying would never be acceptable if a copyright was in force. Public domain resources have had their copyrights expire or have been explicitly placed out for free use. Fair use is a concept that allows copying without permission in some specific instances.

U.S. law has recognized the right of others to limited copying and use rights of copyrighted material for purposes such as education, parody, commentary, criticism, reporting, research, and the like.

The determination of the boundaries between fair use and infringement is not easy to specify with exactitude. Lawyers are getting rich fighting on the frontiers.

Courts use four principles to distinguish fair use:

- Is the intention of the work containing the copied material commercial or non-commercial?
- What was the nature of the original copyrighted material?

- How much of the original work was copied? How many copies were made?
- Will the publishing of the derivative work hurt the potential market or value of the original?

You would thus be less successful claiming fair use in situations where your work is commercial, a large proportion of the original was copied, or the new work will compete with the original. Also, copying from works such as factual reports is more likely to be considered fair use than copying from creative works where the individual's expressive creativity was the prime subject.

Intellectual Property Guidelines

So, what may you copy to include in your Web publications? There is no clear answer yet because the law of cyberspace is still in the making.

The conservative answer is that no copyrighted material may be included except small portions for commentary. Copying of creative media works such as images, sounds, and video are especially unlikely to be allowed as fair use. The safest course is for the Web publisher to obtain written permission for material to be included. Check with a lawyer if you believe your plans qualify as fair use.

And what should you do to protect your own work? Realize that currently to put your resource out on the Web is to make it available. Many of the individuals who access it around the world will not necessarily understand or accept your personal or your culture's interpretations of intellectual property. They may feel it is a free resource for copying and use.

Figure 9.4 shows the home page for the Copyright Website, a clearinghouse for copyright information.

Figure 9.4:
Copyright Website.
`http://www.benedict.com/`

Resources on Copyright and Intellectual Property Issues

- *Terry Caroll's FAQ (frequently asked questions) excellent summary on copyright laws from the Usenet newsgroup on copyright and patents*
`http://www.cis.ohio-state.edu/hypertext/faq/`
`usenet/Copyright-FAQ/top.html`

- *Copyright Website*
`http://www.benedict.com/`

- *Columbia U Institute for Learning Technologies Copyright Information*
`http://www.ilt.columbia.edu/projects/copyright/index.html`

- *1976 Copyright law from Cornell University's Legal Information Institute*
`http://www.law.cornell.edu/usc/17/overview.html`

- *The article "Copyright in the Electronic Age" from law book publisher Nolo Press*
`http://www.ora.com/gnn/bus/nolo/copy.html`

Web Approaches to Identifying Quality Sites

Book and magazine editors, movie and art critics, and professional accrediting agencies all attempt to determine and certify quality. Similarly, the Web community is developing its own approaches to determining notable sites. Several sites present curated lists, connoisseur choices, or voting results of the best Web sites. These are sometimes called hotlists or "what's cool" lists.

These ratings, however, should be taken with a grain of salt. You don't know who was the voting audience and what criteria they were using to make judgments. Even in the curated lists, you often don't know much about the judges or about the basis of their choices. In the statistical analyses, you can't make sense of the results unless you know about the population of users.

Nonetheless, these lists are valuable resource for Web designers for several reasons:

- They point you to sites that someone has considered superior or which a lot of people access. One of the best ways to increase your Web design skills is to fanatically study other sites.

- The variations among the lists illustrate the varying criteria of excellence that can be used to judge Web design. Study the patterns that seem to underlie the choice of sites.

- Because many Web surfers use these lists as starting points, they are important places for you to get your site listed. (Appendix A describes other ways to announce your site.)

Design Contests

There are several sites that offer contests for "Best of the Web." Typically nominations and voting are thrown open to the Web community. Users can vote via the Web and, after a specified length of time, the results are presented with live links to the winners. This kind of voting avoids the idiosyncrasies of individual cool lists by pooling the opinions of large groups.

The Best of the Web Contest offered in conjunction with the meetings of the International W3 community is perhaps the best known of the contests. For the 1994 contest, the organizers maintained a two-month online voting process; then announced their results at the meetings and online. 5,100 votes were cast and winners received around 100 votes. Figure 9.5 shows the home page of the results.

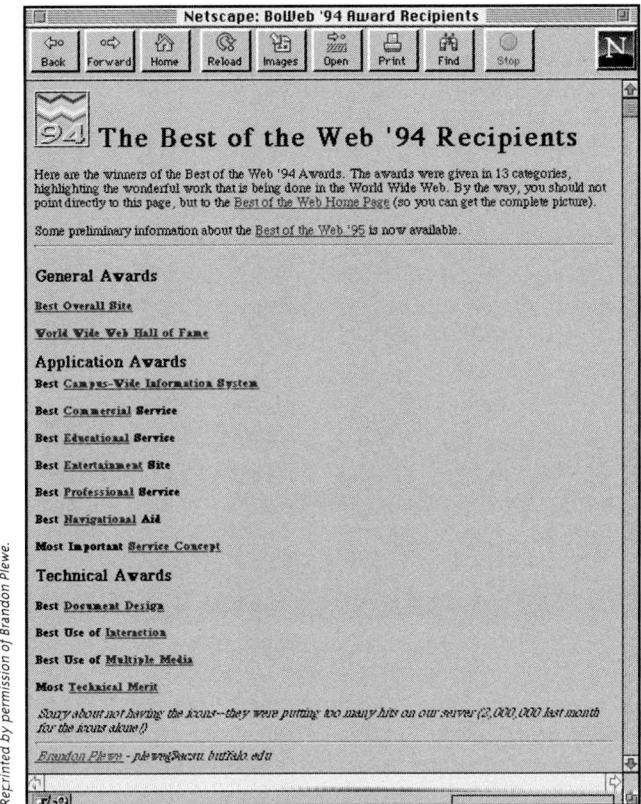

Figure 9.5:
Best of the Web home page.
`http://wings.buffalo.edu/contest/`

The categories for awards illustrate the divergent criteria that can be used to judge Web sites. Some focus on category of

service—for example, best educational—and some focus on technical accomplishment—for example, best use of interaction. Here are some of the categories proposed for the 1995 contest:

General Awards

- Best Overall Site
- Best Site by an Educational Institution
- Best Site by a Public Institution (government/non-profit)

Application Awards

- Best Educational Service
- Best Commercial Service
- Best Navigational Aid

Technical Awards

- Best Document Design
- Best Use of Interaction
- Most Technical Merit

The Australian National University ran a similar voting event (http://coombs.anu.edu.au/SpecialProj/QLTY/BEST/Best94.html). The organizers of this event put considerable care into offering resources for the voters to consider in making their quality judgments.

Voters were asked to rate the resources in two categories:

- Quality/usefulness/amount of information offered
- Presentation/ergonomics/aesthetics/accessibility

Cool Site Lists

Several sites on the Web offer "Cool Site" or "Best of the Web" lists. Usually there is little information offered about the process by which the list was derived or the individuals who determined the list. Thus, one must take these lists with some reservations. Nonetheless, because there are few resources on the Web that make quality judgments, these can suggest sites to look at.

Your personal experience of agreement with their choices and the credibility of the context in which the best list is embedded are the only bases you can use to judge their trustworthiness. These lists come from a variety of situations, ranging from those sponsored by major Web indexes (such as the Yahoo or Netscape sites) or computer magazine publishers to those that are part of individual home pages. Even those that are sponsored by large organizations might in reality represent the judgment of a few individuals.

As the Web matures you can expect more systematic evaluation systems to develop with more precise criteria. For example, the Point Communications site (http://www.pointcom.com/) solicits online raters and provides guidance for evaluating its three criteria: content, presentation, and "Web experience." The McKinley site (http://mickinley.com/) goes even further. It integrates an extensive Web index and search service with rankings. The results of any search you conduct return with rankings of based on three criteria: content up-to-dateness, organization of the content, and ease of access.

Figures 9.6 shows "Justin's Links from the Underground," a well-known, personally organized hotlist that points to interesting resources.

Figure 9.6:
Justin's Links from the Underground.
`http://www.links.net/`

Justin Hall: Yer Mama Net Productions.

Cool Sites and Best of the Web Lists

- *Yahoo's Cool Links*
`http://www.yahoo.com/Entertainment/COOL_links/`

- *Netscape's Cool Site List*
`http://home.netscape.com/home/whats-cool.html`

- *Cool Site of the Day (compiled by Glenn Davis)*
`http://www.infi.net/cool.html`

- *GNN Best of the Web (compiled by O'Reilly & Associates)*
`http://www.digital.com/gnn/botn/index.html`

- *PC Week Best of the Web (compiled by PC Week magazine)*
`http://www.ziff.com/~pcweek/pcwbests.html`

- *BBC Best of the Web (compiled by the "Babbage" Web service of the British Broadcasting Service)*
`http://www.bbcnc.org.uk/babbage/cyber.html`

- *Link of the Week (compiled at the University of Manchester in the United Kingdom)*
`http://n2t.cs.man.ac.uk/linkofweek/index.html`

- *Awesome List (compiled by a professor and Internet trainer)*
`http://www.clark.net/pub/journalism/awesome.html`

- *KZSU Hot & Cool List (compiled by student organization "UnderWorld Industries' Cultural Playground" associated with Stanford Uniersity's student radio station. Focused on sites that experiment with the Web.)*
`http://kzsu.stanford.edu/uwi/reviews-1.html`

- *Justin's Links from the Underground*
`http://www.links.net/`

- *Mirsky's Worst of the Web*
`http://turnpike.net/metro/mirsky/Worst.html`

- *Useless sites*
`http://www.primus.com/staff/paulp/useless.html`

- *Mediocre sites*
`http://minerva.cis.yale.edu/~jharris/mediocre.html`

- *Whole Internet Catalog top 50*
`http://gnn.digital.com/gnn/wic/top.toc.html`

- *Webholics top 50*
`http://www.ohiou.edu/~rbarrett/webaholics/ver2/index.html`

- *Web countdowns (analyses of various best lists)*
`http://nearnet.gnn.com/gnn/news/feature/countdowns.html`

- *Point site ratings of sites*
`http://www.pointcom.com/`

- *McKinley site ratings of sites*
`http://mckinley.com/`

- *High Five Design Awards*
`http://www.best.com/~dsiegel/high_five/high_five.html`

Statistical Identification of Popular Sites

Several index and spider sites described in Appendix A use statistical analysis in order to identify "interesting" Web locations. They measure how often certain sites are visited or how often they are referenced by other Web documents. This information can help you to identify locations that are attracting visitors or are worthy of being pointed to by other documents.

These statistics are instructive. The example that follows shows the top 11 categories during one week from Yahoo, a popular Web index. Entertainment topics are among the most accessed:

1. Entertainment

2. Society and Culture

3. Computers and the Internet

4. News

5. Entertainment: Movies and Films

6. Entertainment: Music: Artists

7. Entertainment: Magazines

8. Education

9. Business and Economy

10. New

11. Entertainment: Music

Figure 9.7 shows the "WebCrawler Top 25," which summarizes the number of times various sites are referred to by other sites. Its database includes the sites its automated program found on the Web.

Pointers to Statistical Summaries

- *Netherlands MPEG movie archive summary of site statistics*

http://w3.eeb.ele.tue.nl/mpeg/mpeg_stat.html

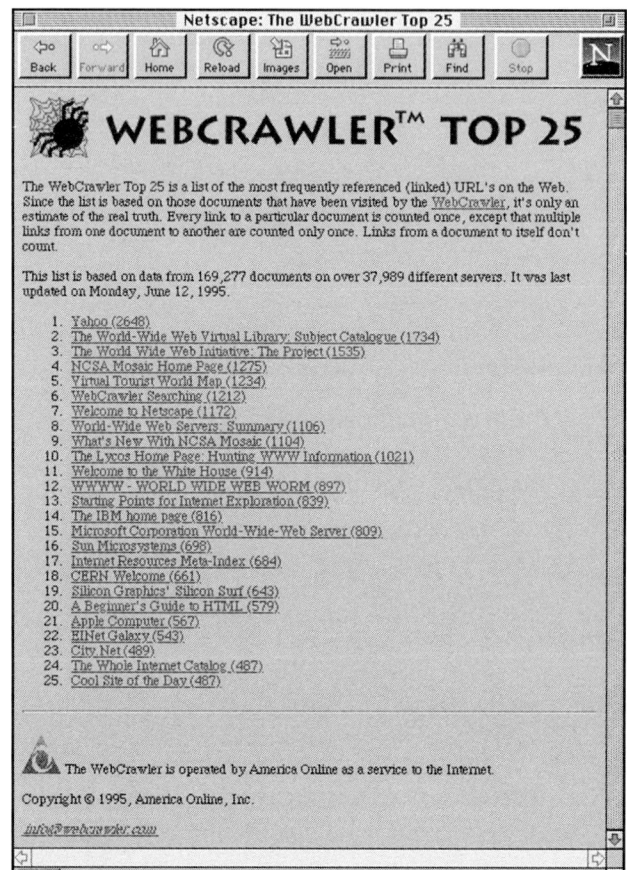

Figure 9.7:

WebCrawler Top 25.

http://webcrawler.cs.washington.edu/WebCrawler/
Top25.html

- *Yahoo weekly summary of most popular sites in its list*

`http://www.yahoo.com/popular.html`

- *WebCrawler Top 25*

`http://webcrawler.cs.washington.edu/WebCrawler/Top25.html`

- *Lycos statistics on how often URLs are referenced by other URLs*

`http://fuzine.mt.cs.cmu.edu/mlm/lycos-results.html`

- *Resources for setting up site statistics programs*

`http://www.yahoo.com/Computers/World_Wide_Web/Programming/Access_Counts/`

The Web is unusual in making these best lists and statistical summaries so easily accessible. They can help you to understand the Web better.

Summary: Building Exceptional Sites

The creation of an exceptional site requires a mix of knowledge, careful work, and inspiration. Using the expanded design framework, this book has presented the critical knowledge part.

Inspiration cannot be taught by guidebook. Still, there is much you can do. It is said that the best authors are in love with words—those of others as well as their own. Similarly, you must make the Web a passion. Learn what others are doing. Make your creations as strong as they can be and be willing to revise and experiment. Think about where the Web is going and where it might go. Chapter 10, "Web Research and Emerging Trends," offers you strategies for anticipating future developments.

Chapter 10

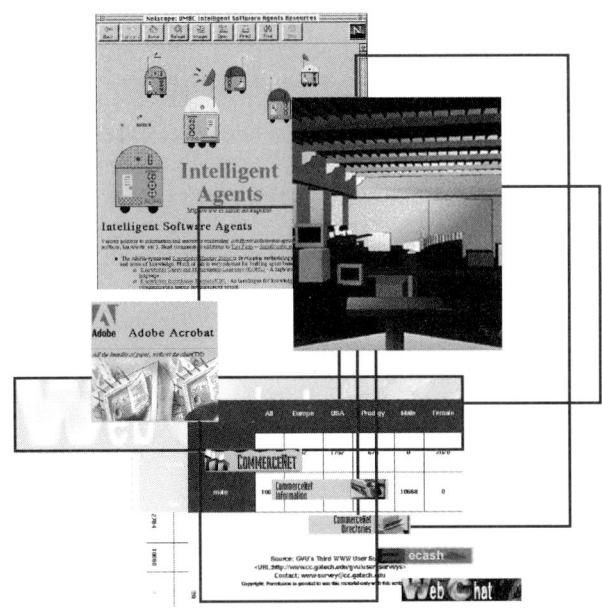

Web Research and Emerging Trends

The Web is like a wild, fast-flowing river full of rapids. It is exciting to watch and unpredictable—no one can tell you exactly where it's going. This chapter helps you keep afloat by analyzing future Web trends in the following areas:

- Faster connectivity.
- Audience access.
- Advertising and commerce.
- Enhanced media and interactive environments.
- Authoring and formatting tools.
- Research in information science and hypermedia.
- Keeping up with change.

Connectivity Speeds Up

Internet researchers are studying ways to accelerate raw speed, to respond to wireless computing, and to enable real-time, multiperson interactions.

Communication Speed

The Web depends on the speed of data communication. Improvements of delivery speed into homes, such as ISDN and Ethernet over cable TV systems, are becoming available. Communication protocols such as ATM, fast Ethernet, and FDDI (fiber optic) are out of the labs and will radically upgrade data speed to over 100 megabits per second. Bandwidth-hungry Web applications such as audio, video, two-way live interactions, and animation will become easier. Web applications will have the same speed potentials as applications that now run within local computers.

Other major projects are underway to increase transmission speeds beyond the gigabit-per-second rate. For example, the NSF-funded "gigabit testbed" project has underwritten research in a variety of strategies to increase speed. APPN (Advanced Peer-to-Peer Networking) research is developing networks that can dynamically switch routing on-the-fly in order to optimize speed and reliability. HIPPI (High-Performance Parallel Interface) research is borrowing concepts from parallel computing to make network transmission as fast as communications within current computers. Theorists such as George Gilder suggest that we must radically alter our basic models because "bandwidth will be free."

Information Sources on Networking

- Lawrence Livermore's summary of networking research
  `http://www-atp.llnl.gov/atp/`

- Virtual library index on networking
  `http://src.doc.ic.ac.uk/bySubject/Networking.html`

- Yahoo list of communication technology resources
  `http://www.yahoo.com/Computers/World_Wide_Web/Communication/`

- Don Kegel's About ISDN page
  `http://www.alumni.caltech.edu/~dank/isdn/`

- ATM forum information page
  `http://www.atmforum.com/`

- NSF gigabit testbed information
  `http://www.cnri.reston.va.us:4000/public/overview.html`

- APPN (Advanced Peer-to-Peer Networking) information
  `http://www.raleigh.ibm.com/app/aiwhome.htm`

- HIPPI (High-Performance Parallel Interface) information
  `http://www.esscom.com/hnf/html/whathnf.html`

- George Gilder's articles index
  `http://www.seas.upenn.edu/~gaj1/ggindex.html`

Mobile Computing

Some futurists suggest that the current model of the computer user tethered to power and communication lines will soon be an anachronism. Mobility researchers have created wireless personal data assistants (PDAs), which allow users to link with people and data anywhere in the world via radio and satellite communication, and they continue to work on the next generations. The Web may be a major tool for mobile computing, providing its interface and links to information resources. What future developments are likely in Web-based mobile computing?

Mobisaic is a major research project to develop some of these future scenarios, which researchers call "an Information System for a Mobile and Wireless Computing" environment. It is developing protocols such as "dynamic URLs" that change with the position of the user and "active documents" that enable a Web server to customize its response based on the user's current geographical position. Figure 10.1 shows the Virtual Library home page specializing in information about mobile computing and its implications for the Web.

Web Information Sources on Mobile Computing

- *Yahoo summary of mobile computing information*
`http://www.yahoo.com/Computers/Moblie_Computing/`

- *Mobisaic*
`http://www.cs.washington.edu/homes/voelker/`
`mobisaic/mobisaic.html`

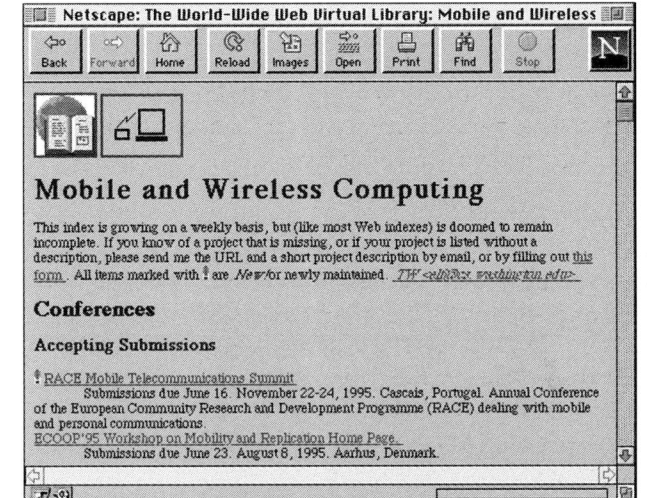

Figure 10.1:
Virtual Library resource on wireless and mobile computing.
`http://snapple.cs.washington.edu:600/mobile/`
`mobile_www.html`

Real-Time Interaction

With faster connectivity comes the opportunity for users to expand their range of online activities. Believing that the Web can serve as the major context for online collaboration, researchers are working on technical infrastructure to enable real-time interaction. These environments let users share the same virtual or text space with others.

The Internet has had a chat service called IRC (Internet Relay Chat) available for many years. Web services such as

Prospero's GlobalChat (http://www.prospero.com/globalchat/) have linked the Web to IRC. Visitors can use the chat service, which opens in a separate window, to enhance their Web experiences—for example, by having a live sales representative assist a user who is looking at a Web based catalog or by engaging in new kinds of entertainment that link live storytellers with Web navigation.

Figure 10.2 shows the welcome page from WebChat, one of the sites that allows real-time, text-based interaction. The virtual spaces where chats occur focus on particular Usenet groups, Web sites, or other topics indicated in titles. Users "enter" these spaces when they want to confer on those topics. Researchers are confident that eventually chat environments will include real-time audio and video.

Pointers to Information about Real-Time Interaction

- *Yahoo list of gateways to Internet communication services*
`http://www.yahoo.com/Computers/World_Wide_Web/Gateways/`

- *Summary of collaboration sites and technology*
`http://union.ncsa.uiuc.edu/HyperNews/get/www/collaboration.html`

- *Real-time voice communication on the Internet*
`http://www.emagic.com/`

Internet Roundtable Society.

Figure 10.2:
The WebChat welcome page.
`http://www.irsociety.com/webchat.html`

Demographic Shifts

Knowing your audience is crucial to design, but the Web is changing so rapidly that it's a very daunting challenge. One thing seems certain—tomorrow's audience will be bigger and more diverse than yesterday's audience.

Because the Web has no central switchboard, it is difficult to get reliable statistics on overall usage. The NIC (Network Information Center), which assigns domain names and addresses, is the one official organization all Internet users must contact, because they assign domain names and addresses. Analysis of NIC registrations has shown a tremendous growth rate; growing from 2.2 million in January 1994 to 4.8 million machines registered in 71,000 domains in January, 1995. The NIC statistics also provide approximate breakdowns by country for registered domains; the top rankers were North America, the UK, Germany, and Australia.

But machine and domain registrations do not tell the whole story. The registration of a domain does not tell you how many users might be connecting through that domain—for example, via shell or SLIP accounts. Universities, Internet service providers, and Information utilities such as CompuServe might have thousands of users sharing a pool of registered domains. John Quarterman, who has been tracking Internet users for years and wrote one of the first major studies of Internet growth called *The Matrix* (Digital Press, 1990), analyzes Net usage by level of access. At the end of 1994 he estimated that there were 3.5 million "core" users who had full Internet access and 27.5 "matrix" users who could send and receive e-mail. Quarterman now runs a consulting service called Matrix Information and Directory Services (http://www.tic.com/mids/index.html), which produces reports and intriguing graphs that track Internet usage.

Pointers to Internet Statistics Resources

- *U-do-it Internet estimator (access to several statistics sources)*
`http://gnn.interpath.net/gnn/news/feature/inet-demo/web.size.html`

- *Virtual library for developers (summary of statistics sites)*
`http://WWW.Stars.com/Vlib/Misc/Statistics.html`

- *NetWizards' study of the Internet viewed by domain allocation*
`http://www.nw.com/zone/WWW/top.html`

But these raw statistics miss the most important information. Who are the users? Academics and marketing research companies are trying to find out via online surveys.

Their research has found in the past that Web users are predominantly male, young, affluent, well educated, engaged in technical and research occupations, and likely to come via an academic link. New findings by these projects and others, however, indicate that Web audiences are changing to be more female, older, more likely to be married with children, more likely to be new Internet users, and more likely to come from sources other than academia. Figure 10.3 shows one of the result graphs from a 1995 GVU survey that summarizes gender differences by region. The reference list shows pointers to more information about Web surveys.

Pointers to Web Usage Statistics

- *Georgia tech usage survey*
`http://www.cc.gatech.edu/gvu/user_surveys/`

- *Hermes project (U of Michigan)*
`http://www.umich.edu/~sgupta/survey3/`

- *Turnpike online provider statistics*
`http://turnpike.net/turnpike/demog.html`

- *MIDS Matrix Maps Quarterly (MMQ) visual representations of usage patterns*
`http://www.zilker.net/mids/mmq/index.html`

- *Nielsen "Anywhere Online" service to track Web usage*
`http://www.nielsen.com/home/any.htm`

- *Internet Profiles (services to track usage of a site)*
`http://www.ipro.com/`

- *Standard Research Institute Study of Web Users*
`http://future.sri.com`

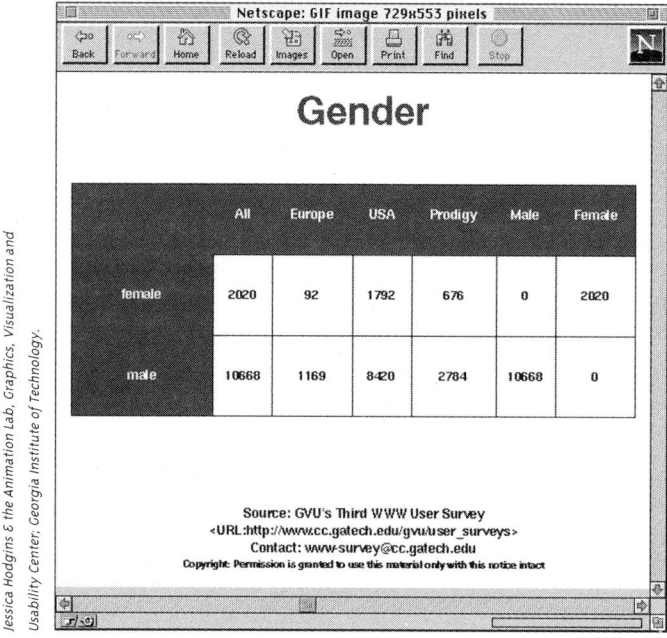

Jessica Hodgins & the Animation Lab, Graphics, Visualization and Usability Center, Georgia Institute of Technology.

Figure 10.3:
Sample Web user study graph from Graphics, Visualization, & Usability Center of Georgia Institute of Technology.
`http://www.cc.gatech.edu/gvu/user_surveys/`

So, within their limitations, what should you make of these statistics and trends? The Web is still not a universal phenomenon, but it is changing rapidly.

- Usage outside North America and Europe is projected to grow enormously.

- The move by online service providers such as AOL to add Internet access will add millions of Internet newbies.

- The inclusion of Web access as a basic feature of operating systems in Windows 95 and the Mac OS may bring millions of new users without any network experience at all. The Web will be assumed as part of what a computer can do.

- Futurists suggest that the Web may become the main conduit of governmental services, education, entertainment, and commerce to such an extent that almost everyone will be expected to be a user—as is now true of telephone service.

So what must you do? You'll need to recognize that the demographics of new users will be radically different from those of past years. Learn where the studies of Web usage are reported and monitor them carefully.

The Growth of Web Commerce

Historically, the Net was primarily aimed at researchers and others who professionally worked with computers. Commercial activity was greatly restricted. The NSF (National Science Foundation), which subsidized Net infrastructure, even included "appropriate use" rules that prohibited blatant commercial activities. The situation has changed. Audiences have expanded. Now, commercial activity is outrunning all other domain types. In the first quarter of 1995, Internet companies were infused with $47 million in venture capital, as opposed to $42 million for all of 1994.

Many businesses have discovered the Web as a resource in all aspects of their enterprises, including advertising, market analysis, corporate image projection, sales, customer support, interorganizational communication, employee recruitment, and communication with suppliers and vendors. The growing commercial potential of the Web is radically altering Web culture. Venture capitalists are buying up Web services such as Yahoo that were started as labors of love. Advertisers are willing to pay significant fees for space on the pages of popular sites such as HotWired and Netscape.

Cooperation between Sellers and Buyers

Some analysts suggest that marketing will be radically different on the Web. Because the marginal cost of providing flexibility and interactivity is so low, companies will be able to offer much more information than they do now. Also, the boundaries of business will change because information can be disseminated anywhere in the world and buyers can come from anywhere. The increasing availability of information might mean, however, that users will have to assume more of the responsibility to find relevant information.

Advertising will also change. Instead of mass media models that use large untargeted appeals, buyers and sellers will be able to cooperate. Automatic systems will allow buyers to indicate their potential interest and sellers will send relevant information targeted at the consumers' specific interests.

Some aspects of seller-buyer relations still need to be worked out. The Internet has a long tradition of free services. Some analysts suggest that businesses face a challenge of figuring out what to charge for where free services are taken for granted.

Projections about the Future of Web Commerce

- *Project 2000 study of marketing in hypermedia environments*
`http://www2000.ogsm.vanderbilt.edu/`

- *Paper on "Business of the Internet" (Rawn Shah)*
`http://www.rtd.com/people/rawn/business.html`

Security and Authorization Advances

Many businesses want to transact business on the Web. Until recently, the major technical stumbling blocks have been exchanging money, the security of sending sensitive information such as credit card numbers, and verifying the identity of the transactors. Normal Internet transmissions are easily snooped upon and manipulated.

These problems have been essentially solved. A technology called *public key encryption* has allowed the establishment of international standards for encrypting Web communications, called S-HTTP (Secure HTTP) and SSL (Secure Sockets Level). The Web community has agreed to integrate these technologies so that there will be a common standard. Web users using a browser and server conforming to these standards can count on the privacy of the information they send. Similarly, building on the same encryption technology, companies such as Verisign have created digital ID methods for authenticating transactors and verifying the untampered state of information.

For those who still have doubts, alternative transaction systems such as "digicash" and "the phantom exchange" mediate transactions through third-party agencies so sensitive financial information cannot be sent on the Web. Figure 10.4 shows Michael Pierce's Web site that provides access to information about Web payment systems.

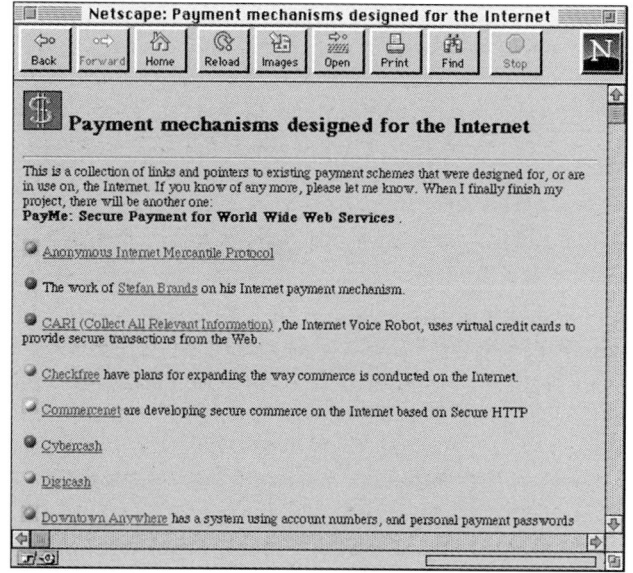

Michael Pierce.

Figure 10.4:
Payment methods on the Web home page.
`http://ganges.cs.tcd.ie/mepierce/Project/`
`oninternet.html`

Electronic Cash (E-Cash)

Even these secure transactions pose dangers to privacy. If every transaction is mediated by network computer technology, the possibility exists to accumulate this information. Real cash has a quality of anonymity that is missing in online transactions.

Theorists such as David Chaum are concerned about these dangers and have developed concepts of "e-cash" that make an untraceable online exchange medium that preserves some of the desirable qualities of cash.

He and others have developed systems called e-cash, which allow for the anonymous exchange of untraceable electronic cash and the exchange of digital credentials without revealing identity. Lower bookkeeping costs are an added bonus for the companies using this system because they don't have to keep track of credit card exchanges. Figure 10.5 shows an information page from the DigiCash ecash experimental feasibility project in which Web users could sign up to receive imaginary electronic cash that they could spend at cooperating Web providers.

Some futurists see digital cash radically altering long-standing notions of price-rationed scarcity. If a mass market really develops and bandwidth becomes cheap enough, creators of information resources can be compensated by many small payments (perhaps five cents) rather than relying on complex distribution structures and big purchases.

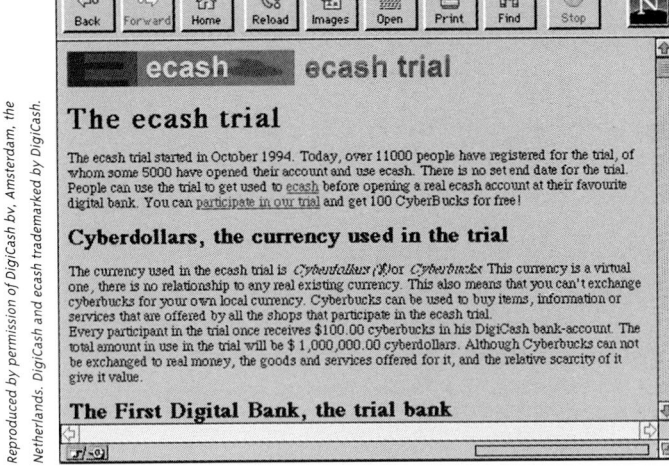

The ecash trial

The ecash trial started in October 1994. Today, over 11000 people have registered for the trial, of whom some 5000 have opened their account and use ecash. There is no set end date for the trial. People can use the trial to get used to ecash before opening a real ecash account at their favourite digital bank. You can participate in our trial and get 100 CyberBucks for free!

Cyberdollars, the currency used in the trial

The currency used in the ecash trial is *Cyberdollars* (X) or *Cyberbucks*. This currency is a virtual one, there is no relationship to any real existing currency. This also means that you can't exchange cyberbucks for your own local currency. Cyberbucks can be used to buy items, information or services that are offered by all the shops that participate in the ecash trial.
Every participant in the trial once receives $100.00 cyberbucks in his DigiCash bank-account. The total amount in use in the trial will be $ 1,000,000.00 cyberdollars. Although Cyberbucks can not be exchanged to real money, the goods and services offered for it, and the relative scarcity of it give it value.

The First Digital Bank, the trial bank

Figure 10.5:
Digicash experiment, as part of ecash information page.
http://www.digicash.com/ecash/trial.html

Pointers to Information about Secure Web Transactions

- *Netscape on summaries of security approaches*
http://home.mcom.com/info/security-overview.html

- *W3 organization on Web security approaches*
http://www.w3.org/hypertext/WWW/AccessAuthorization/Overview.html

- *Yahoo summary on digital cash*
http://www.yahoo.com/Business/Electronic_Commerce/Digital_Money/

- *Payment mechanisms for the Internet home page*
http://ganges.cs.tcd.ie/mepeirce/Project/oninternet.html

- *Verisign description of digital ID technology*
http://www.verisign.com/

- *David Chaum's article "Achieving Electronic Privacy" (Scientific American, 1992)*
http://ganges.cs.tcd.ie/mepeirce/Project/Chaum/sciam.html

Changes in Business Communication

Communications among sellers and buyers are not the only capability enhanced by the Web. Some researchers believe that other kinds of business communications may yield even more profound benefits—for example, collaboration among coworkers; connections between businesses and consultants or other expert advisers; and Electronic Data Interchange (EDI) among manufacturers, suppliers, distributors, sellers, and customers.

For example, EDI attempts to coordinate the computer information systems of everyone involved with a product, creating great efficiencies and reductions in costs. Illustrating the reach of these approaches, the Fairfax Electronic Commerce Resource Center works on approaches such as Continuous Acquisition Lifecycle Support (CALS) and Business Process Re-Engineering (BPR). In these approaches, the same electronic form might be used to track an item through all these stages: design, creation in factory, factory inventory, shipping to store, store inventory, sale, and shipping to the customer. In this view, the Web may become the basic infrastructure for most business.

Information on EDI (Electronic Data Interchange)

- *EDI standards*
http://www.premenos.com/standards/
EDIStandards.html

- *Fairfax Electronic Commerce Resource Center*
http://www.ecrc.gmu.edu/

The future of business will belong to those who understand the Web and its trends. You can keep up with this future by monitoring the work of the innovative organizations that specialize in supporting these new developments. For example, CommerceNet, located in Silicon Valley, combines research, consulting services, technical infrastructure development, compilations of resources, and reference points for consumers. Its mission is to help businesses explore the new possibilities and to provide services to facilitate the new activity. Figure 10.6 shows the welcome page from CommerceNet.

Pointers to Information Resources Related to Commerce on the Web

- *Yahoo electronic commerce*
http://www.yahoo.com/Business/Electronic_Commerce/

- *Thomas Ho's favorite Electronic Commerce WWW resources*
http://www.engr.iupui.edu/~ho/interests/
commmenu.html

- *CommerceNet information*
http://www.commerce.net/

- *Bizweb*
http://www.bizweb.com/

- *Internet Business Center*
http://www.tig.com/IBC/index.html

- *Premenos guide to commerce resources*
http://www.premenos.com/Resources/guide.html

Figure 10.6:
CommerceNet information page.
http://www.commerce.net/

Enhanced Media and Interactive Environments

Web developers are creating new Web capabilities in sound and video, animation, and virtual reality. Also emerging are new interactive environments that integrate applications such as databases, financial analysis programs, and games with the real-time communication and information service potentials of the Web.

Sound and Video

You have seen how you can transport prerecorded video and sound over the Web. But that is just the beginning. This capability is being extended to include real-time inline active video and sound for applications such as video on demand or teleconferencing. RealAudio from Progressive Systems, for example, allows Web sound that can be continually updated so users can get two-way conversations or broadcasts. Also, researchers have developed Internet telephone applications that allow two-way sound communication over the Internet much like telephone service. Some are working to incorporate this service into the Web and hope one day to challenge the telephone as the main communication medium.

Real-time Internet video poses significant challenges, but visionaries predict that the Web's descendants may one day replace cable and video rental stores, becoming the medium for distribution of video on demand, and even making videophones an everyday reality.

New video compression hardware and software such as MPEG2 and MPEG4 will help solve problems by greatly reducing the volume of data that must be transmitted.

Researchers have already developed a prototype system called Mbone (or Multicast backbone) that handles high-quality video. It sets up a special network of forwarding sites that give priority to time-based media information, allowing communication of video. You can expect these ideas to be incorporated into the Web in the near future.

Pointers to Real-Time Audio and Video Research

- *RealAudio information*
`http://www.realaudio.com/`

- *Yahoo list of voice communication on the Net*
`http://www.yahoo.com/Computers_and_Internet/`
`Internet/Internet_Voice/`

- *Yahoo list of videoconferencing resources*
`http://www.yahoo.com/Computers/Multimedia/`
`Videoconferencing/`

- *Mbone FAQ*
`http://www.research.att.com/mbone-faq.html`

- *Yahoo information on Mbone information*
`http://www.yahoo.com/Computers/Multimedia/MBONE/`

- *Live video on the Web (MIT research)*
`http://www.tns.lcs.mit.edu/publications/`
`WWW94a.html`

Animation and Virtual Reality

CD-ROM games allow users to interact with fantastic visual worlds filled with strange creatures. Researchers are bringing these capabilities to the Web.

Macromedia's Director is a well-known computer animation authoring environment. Netscape Communications promises to include an inline Director capability in its browsers. Thus, just as you can now send inline images, you will be able to send Director multimedia files that will create inline animations as part of the basic Web page. Sun's Java browser enhancement language also allows interactive multimedia to be sent over the Web.

Virtual reality offers even more amazing possibilities. Researchers are creating immersive computer-generated 3-D environments that track users' movements in order to create the simulation of being in an artificial space. Users can move through the space by moving the mouse. Researchers have developed a worldwide standard called VRML (Virtual Reality Modeling Language—pronounced "ver mal") that will allow Web-based transmission of these 3-D worlds and user movements. Spots in the 3-D world can be made into hotlinks.

VRML enthusiasts suggest that navigation of 3-D spaces is a much more natural interface and that eventually the virtual worlds might replace the current 2-D standard Web interface. Also, multiple online users will be able to jointly "inhabit" the same virtual worlds. Figure 10.7 shows a VRML experiment carried out with the 1995 Digital Media Festival. The Arc Media gallery built a 3-D model of the Variety Arts Center where the media festival took place. Web visitors with appropriate VRML helper applications could access the site and download the model, and then interactively move around the 3-D representations of the exhibit space.

Mark Meadows.

Figure 10.7:
ARC Media festival VRML gallery.
`http://vrml.arc.org/gallery95/index.html`

Pointers to Animation and Virtual Reality Information

- *VRML information center*
`http://vrml.wired.com/`

- *Yahoo list of VRML resources*
`http://www.yahoo.com/Entertainment/`
`Virtual_Reality/`
`Virtual_Reality_Modeling_Language__VRML_/`

- *SGI WebSpace 3-D interface information*
`http://www.sgi.com/Products/WebFORCE/WebSpace/`
`index.html`

Links between the Web and Other Applications

Already browsers call on helper applications to display some media. In the future the links will go also in the other direction. Applications will make use of the Web to enhance their function. Developers will be creating links between applications such as word processors, spreadsheets, databases, and desktop publishing and Web capabilities. For example, a financial analysis program might include Web access as part of what it does to update its stock values and other time-sensitive data. InternetWorks, from America Online-owned NaviSoft, uses persistent caching and progressive rendering capabilities to streamline downloading, displaying, and saving multimedia documents.

To assist this process, researchers have developed the Common Client Interface (CCI), which provides a standard way for other programs to call Web browsers. This means the capabilities of the browser become part of the functionality of other programs. In the microcomputer world, operating system functions such as AppleEvents (Mac) and OLE calls (Windows) provide a way to link applications and browsers.

In one of my research projects at Xerox PARC, I built "Inspectable Movies." Although they looked like normal QuickTime movies, they were actually hotlinked; clicking the movie, at various points activated a Web browser running in the background to make Web connections to sites linked to the content of the video. The Web was one of the "actors" in my video.

Pointers to Information on Programming Research

- *Yahoo information on Common Client Interface (CCI)*

```
http://www.yahoo.com/Computers_and_Internet/
Internet/World_Wide_Web/Browsers/
XMosaic_NCSA_for_X/Common_Client_Interface_CCI_/
```

- *HyperNews discussion of CCI*

```
http://union.ncsa.uiuc.edu/HyperNews/get/www/
cciPerl.html
```

Authoring/Formatting Tools

The desire of Web authors to facilitate the authoring process and to exercise more control over the presentation format is generating changes that will have significant future impact.

Editors

New commercial Web authoring environments such as Acrobyte, Pavillion, NaviPress, HotMetal, Internet Assistant, and Arachnid promise to simplify the HTML authoring process. Word processors such as WordPerfect and Word and page layout software such as PageMaker and QuarkXPress promise similarly to build in Web capabilities as part of their basic function. Most of these include integrated Web browsers or browser simulators so that authors can immediately see the results of their work. Many are moving toward true WYSIWYG editing so that you will be able to directly edit and position text in a browser-like environment in a format very close to what users will see.

Cross-Platform Document Formats

Other developments are challenging HTML as the universal standard. Many authors, used to the exquisite WYSIWYG control offered by PostScript illustration and page layout programs, are dissatisfied with HTML—even with HTML 3.0 enhancements. Several products such as Acrobat (Adobe), Replica (Farallon), Envoy (Novell-Word Perfect), and Portfolio (Common Ground) are offering alternative "universal" page description systems. Typically these systems convert fully formatted PostScript documents into an "exchange" format that maintains most of the layout and font details and is viewable and printable without the original application, across platforms. Adobe Acrobat, the most popular of these systems, creates files in a format called PDF (Portable Document Format). Users who have the appropriate "reader" application, usually distributed free of charge, can see the document in its full original glory. Figure 10.8 shows the orientation page for Acrobat information at Adobe's Web site. For information on other cross-platform formats, see http://www.ozemal.com.au/~paulr/docex.html.

These systems maintain some of the appealing features of HTML—application and device independence—while adding much more control over format. Users can create pages in their favorite applications without worrying about markup restrictions. These systems lack some important features of HTML, however. The original documents cannot be created in simple text editors; each requires special conversion software, usually not free, to convert the original PostScript document into the exchange format; and they create files that are typically much larger than HTML files. They require the viewer to have the free reader software as a helper application that opens the document in a separate window like an external image, and they do not effortlessly incorporate hypertext links as part of the intrinsic structure. Also, the

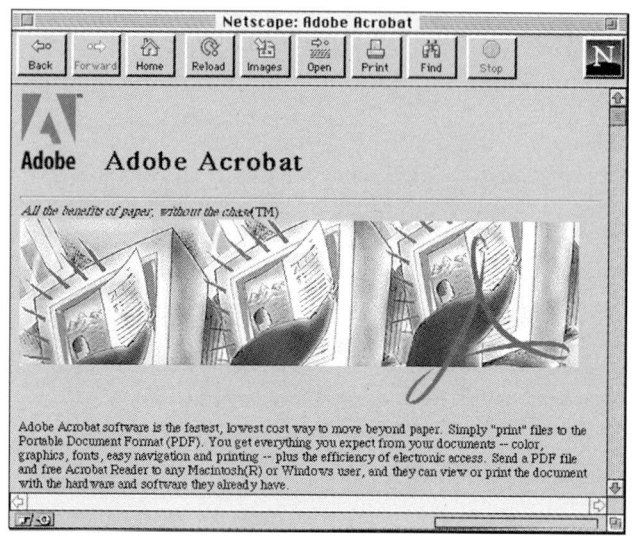

Figure 10.8:
Adobe Acrobat information page.
`http://www.adobe.com/Acrobat/Acrobat0.html`

universality is in doubt because there are so many competitors, and you cannot count on all Web users having the appropriate reader to display your files. In the future some of these limitations will disappear. For example, special add-ons such as Web Link allow authors to create links within Acrobat files, and Netscape and Adobe have an agreement to integrate a PDF reader as a built-in feature of its browsers.

The future of HTML is not clear. Will it be able to be enhanced quickly enough to satisfy the longings of page designers or will some alternative such as Acrobat supersede it?

Research in Information Science and Hypermedia

Some researchers claim that there are bigger challenges to the Web's future than hardware issues, such as increasing bandwidth. Researchers are working in areas such as information visualization, hypermedia design, and intelligent software agents that will eventually create techniques to be incorporated into the Web.

Information Visualization

Researchers are creating computer-based systems that take advantage of human perceptual, cognitive, and sociocultural characteristics to enable creative and productive work. For example, the user interface research group at the Xerox PARC research center is exploring the use of contemporary computer graphics and animation to address the "problem of visualizing and making sense of larger information sets."

One of their many projects explores ways to facilitate researchers' work with scholarly papers. This information visualization technique creates artificial 3-D representations of the citation structure that underlies bibliographies. At a glance you can see all the papers that a target paper cites and all the other papers that, in turn, cite the target paper. Furthermore, you can the see the relationships among the cited papers—for example, temporal relationships and clustering of authors.

Xerox PARC Research Summaries

- *Digital Libraries and Xerox PARC (summaries of several areas of interface research)*
`http://www.xerox.com/PARC/dlbx/library.html`

- *User interface research at PARC (information visualization and other strategies)*
`http://www.xerox.com/PARC/dlbx/uir.html`

- *Magic lens at PARC (interface that modifies view based on interest level)*
`http://www.xerox.com/PARC/istl/gir/gir.html`

Hypermedia Design

Another group at PARC has been studying hypermedia structures for many years. Hypermedia structures can be fine-tuned; instead of each link invariably leading to a particular resource, authors could create pointers that could be dynamically modified based on previously visited sites or on other user characteristics. Links could be designed to differentially show the nature of the relationship between nodes, a variety of "maps" could show users where they had been and might go, and annotation systems could be provided so that users might add their own navigational aids beyond the current bookmarks

Many other researchers around the world are focusing on similar inquiries for improving the Web. The W3 organization considers hypertext research so essential to the Web's future that they maintain a research summary page at their main site. Figure 10.9 shows a Web page from SIGLINK, one of the major international organizations devoted to promoting research on hypermedia. You can count on the Web's approach to hypermedia growing more sophisticated in the future.

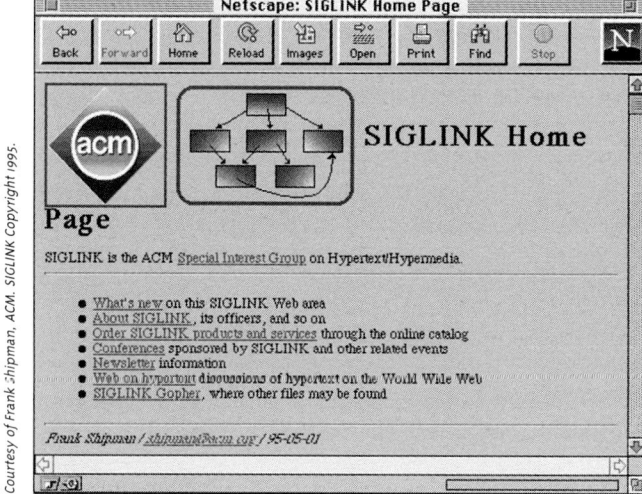

Courtesy of Frank Shipman, ACM. SIGLINK Copyright 1995.

Figure 10.9:
SIGLINK Web page.
http://www.acm.org/siglink/

Information about Hypermedia Research

• *W3 list of Web design issues related to hypertext*
http://www.w3.org/hypertext/WWW/DesignIssues/
Overview.html

• *Yahoo summary of hypermedia resources*
http://www.yahoo.com/Computers/Multimedia/
Hypermedia/

• *ACM special interest group on hypermedia*
http://www.acm.org/siglink/

• *Hypermedia Research information page*
http://www.inf-wiss.uni-konstanz.de/Res/
hypertext_e.html

• *Hypertext information page*
http://www.lawrence.edu/www/hypertext.html

Intelligent Software Agents

Many researchers believe the information management challenges of the Web will necessitate techniques such as intelligent software "agents." This software takes on some significant parts of users' information management and navigation work. Past research at MIT illustrates some of what agents could do. They developed a news watching agent that systematically monitored many online news sources every day to extract news that the user might be interested in. Similarly, the Web walking "robots" described in Appendix A are automatic programs that search the Web looking for new resources and try to digest them into an indexable form that users can use to find what they are looking for. Verity Corporation (http://www.verity.com/) offers a line of agent-based products that help individuals and organizations "to filter, search, retrieve, analyze, and navigate all available information sources that get the personalized, relevant information they need."

In the future browsers might include agents that you could set out to do your bidding, or sites might offer agents that visitors could temporarily use to navigate the site's resources. General Magic's Magic Cap (http://www.genmagic.com/) has extended the agent concept beyond information work into other kinds of transactions. Figure 10.10 shows the welcome page from the Intelligent Agents site that points to resources related to agents.

Tim Finin, University of Maryland Baltimore County (UMBC).

Figure 10.10:
UMBC Intelligent Agents information site.
`http://www.cs.umbc.edu/agents/`

Information about Intelligent Software Agents

- *Agents information site*
`http://www.cs.bham.ac.uk/~amw/agents/`

- *Intelligent agents information page at University of Maryland*
`http://www.cs.umbc.edu/agents/`

This section has presented just a few samples of the kind of interface and hypermedia research that will be shaping the Web's future. Researchers are also studying topics such as the nature of work and collaboration, interfaces optimized for sound and video, multimedia indexing and retrieval, cognitive models of searching and browsing, and gesture-based interfaces.

Keeping Up with Change

To succeed as a Web designer you must continually monitor the trends affecting the future of the Web. Two of the major forces shaping these changes are (1) The quasi-political international process that sets Web standards and conventions and, (2) the activities of researchers and artists inventing new Web approaches. Luckily, the Web makes it relatively easy to monitor these developments.

W3 Organization and International Standards

Because the Web is an Internet-based service, the standards consideration bodies have been open, dispersed, voluntary groups composed of researchers and practitioners interested in the future of the Web and its conventions. Proposals are solicited from the Web community for new enhancements; they are debated online and face-to-face and revised; demonstration software is written that uses the tentative specifications; and ultimately the standards are formally adopted.

Decentralization and Internet culture

The conceptual underpinnings of the Internet are significant determiners of its present reality. The military's ARPA (Advanced Research Projects Agency) funded much basic research in computer science including computer networking. APRAnet, the precursor of the Internet, connected government, military, and university computers in order to facilitate research.

The military origins of this network influenced the decentralization of its design. Developers wanted a system that could stand the disruption of military attack. That is, if some computers and links became disabled, this flexible system could adjust and dynamically select new links to send the packets happily on their way. Technical decentralization significantly shaped features of Internet culture such as volunteerism and cooperative individualism. Because there needed to be no centralized authority, each domain could act independently as long as they met network-wide standards. Joint decisions required the convening of volunteer committees that addressed problems and coordinated activities. Individuals took on the responsibility to write new software that was offered freely to the Internet community. These cultural processes continue today and have shaped the way that the Web developed.

The organization charged with overseeing these considerations is the W3 Organization. Many of the developers responsible for the birth of the Web are active members. The exploding popularity of the Web means that its deliberations have accelerated and grown more complex. Commercially initiated innovations such as those introduced by Netscape Corporation begin to shape future standards. The W3 consortium describes its mission as to "ensure the evolution of the World Wide Web (W3) protocols into a true information infrastructure in such a fashion that smooth transitions will be assured both now and in the future." Its activities are described in great detail in the organization's Web site.

Information about the W3 Organization and Standards Deliberations

* *W3 organization*
`http://www.w3.org/hypertext/WWW/`

* *W3 organization statement of its agenda and areas of interest*
`http://www.w3.org/hypertext/WWW/Consortium/`
`Agreement/Technical.html`

* *Netscape's approach to standards*
`http://home.mcom.com/info/open-standards.html`

* *How to participate in refinements to HTML*
`http://www.w3.org/hypertext/WWW/MarkUp/html3/`
`intro.html#participate`

You do not need to be a passive observer of these processes. These organizations welcome participation by interested members of the Web community. Usually there are online discussion and work groups devoted to the various topics.

Web Conferences and Trade Publications

Because the Web is an international phenomenon, conferences have been very important in coordinating Web development and promoting and disseminating research. Researchers and practitioners who are developing new ideas for the Web usually share them eagerly in conference sessions and forums. These events are a major resource for anticipating future Web directions.

The conferences usually cover a wide array of topics. For example, a recent Web conference included tracks on topics such as agents, commercialization, computer-supported collaboration, free nets, interface design, searching, security, virtual reality, and sessions on many application areas such as science, education, medicine, art, and humanities. Luckily for those who can't attend, the proceedings of these conferences are actively described in Web sites such as those listed in the reference list. Also, researchers make their papers available online even if they are not presented at conferences.

Special Web-focused trade journals also offer extensive information on trends and late-breaking developments. For example, *Web Week*, *Interactive Age*, and *Interactive Week* all present vital news for those trying to keep up with the Web.

Information about Web Conferences and Bibliographies

- *Yahoo list of conferences*
`http://www.yahoo.com/Computers/World_Wide_Web/Conferences/`

- *Overview of conferences*
`http://www.w3.org/hypertext/Conferences/Overview-WWW.html`

- *W3 Web Bibliography*
`http://www.w3.org/hypertext/WWW/Bibliography.html`

- *Academic papers on the Web*
`http://www.w3.org/hypertext/WWW/Bibliography/Papers.html`

- *Papers on WWW-related research*
`http://itdsrv1.ul.ie/Research/WWW/www-research.html`

- *Mecklermedia's iWorld site (links to* Internet World *and* Web Week*)*
`http://www.mecklerweb.com/`

- *CMP's TechWeb site*
`http://techweb.cmp.com/`

- *Interactive Week* Web site
`http://www.interactive-week.com/`

Summary

Some analysts consider the Web the most profound development in the computer revolution. Individuals have incrementally been empowered to work with numbers, text, sound, image, and video. And now, the World Wide Web enables anyone to instantly publish to an international audience. The ultimate ramifications of this development are still unclear, but most agree they will be profound.

With opportunity comes responsibilities. Web publishers must develop the technical and analytical skills necessary to create high-quality offerings. They must learn skills of experimentation and artistic risk-taking in order to respond creatively to the Web's challenges and to help shape its future.

Some analysts predict that the Web may become the center of our private and public lives. It will mediate communication like the telephone, transmit documents like the mail, entertain like the television, and inform like books. We will work, learn, and play via the Web. It will put access to the world's libraries, museums, and research centers at our fingertips. And it will do things we can't even yet imagine.

There is much work to be done, however, in reaching toward this future. The information space of the Web could be filled with richness and beauty or it could be filled with garbage. Just as the Web allows new millions to become publishers, these new publishers must also become designers in the broadest sense of the word.

Appendix A

Research and Publicizing Yourself on the Web

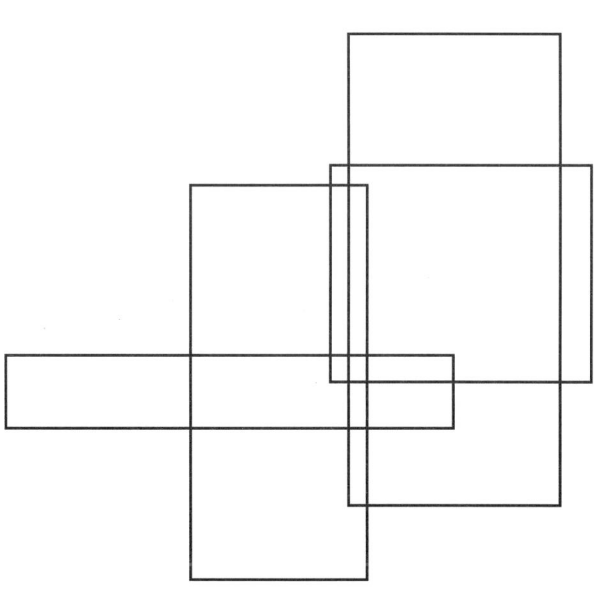

Creating your Web site is just the beginning—there's still much maintenance and marketing to be done! The more you know about how Web users search and find resources on the Web, the more effective you can be in creating site awareness. Some beginning questions you'll need to consider include:

- How can you let your potential audience know about your site?

- In preparing your own site, how can you study similiar sites?
- How can you find other Web-based information that you might want to include in your site?

This appendix helps you become proficient at using these services to find what you need on the Web and to spread the word about your own site. Research is essential in developing the content and links of your site.

In spite of its youth, the Web community has developed a variety of services to help users find what they are looking for. These include various managed comprehensive indexes, user-generated indexes, and automated search programs.

Unfortunately, searching the Web can be much more difficult than it should be. Many users experience information anxiety, uneasily sensing that there are many useful resources hidden in unknown places. Some analysts believe that the Web's future depends on the development of new search structures that are up to the task.

Comprehensive Indexes and Managed Lists

Comprehensive indexes and managed lists are resource locators maintained by persons, as opposed to automated systems. Web users can suggest noteworthy URLs for inclusion and designated managers organize the resources into searchable lists. You can find out about even more by consulting Yahoo's index of indexes at http://www.yahoo.com/Reference/Indices_to_Web_Documents/.

W3 Organization Virtual Library Organized by Geographical Area

CERN, the Web's founder, initiated a listing of Web resources organized by geographical area. The list is now maintained by the W3 Organization. Web searchers can browse this list by selecting continent, country, and (in some countries) by state or region. Web users are encouraged to submit announcements of new sites to coordinators for their countries.

Registration is completed via a fill-in form. The list of coordinators is available in the same HTML document. Anyone can propose to be the coordinator if none exists for a particular country. Figure A.1 shows the welcome and registration pages for the W3 Organization list.

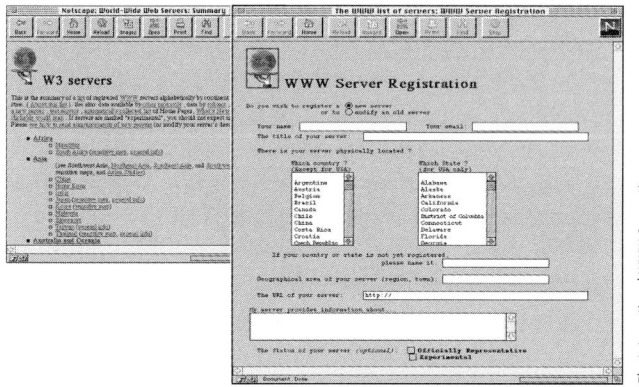

The International WWW Consortium.

Figure A.1:
W3 Organization list of servers organized by country and registration page.

W3 Organization Virtual Library Organized by Topic

The W3 Organization also maintains a list of servers organized by topic. The procedures and kind of information solicited are similar to the list organized by geographical area. A set of topics serves as the main organizing feature of this list. Correspondents who want to submit resources look through the list and identify the appropriate topic heading for their URL, and then submit the information to the maintainer who oversees that topic. If no topic is appropriate, the correspondent can propose to become a maintainer for a new topic.

Access to W3 Organizations's List of Resources Organized by Topics

- *Main access to list of resources organized by topics*
`http://www.w3.org/hypertext/DataSources/bySubject/Overview.html`

- *Location for registering a new URL under a topic*
`http://www.w3.org/hypertext/DataSources/bySubject/Maintainers.html`

- *E mail address to propose a new topic*
`vlib@info.cern.ch`

`http://www.w3.org/hypertext/DataSources/bySubject/coordination.html`

Mosaic What's New List

The National Center for Super Computing Applications at the University of Illinois maintains a list called *Mosaic What's New List*, which is updated several times a week. This list is a major starting point for many Web users because it is a preconfigured location on Mosaic browsers. This list is also a major source for other indexers who regularly check this list for indications of URLs that should be included in their lists because it has a history of being where most page creators tried to register their sites. The list makes no attempt to categorize the material other than by the descriptions that the correspondents have sent in as part of the submission. Figure A.2 shows a sample listing from Mosaic's What's New site.

You can send in submissions to this list through an online fill-in form or e-mail. You need only send in identification information including a title, URL, geographical and organizational information, and a descriptive paragraph of 25 words or less. The site's maintainers say they will not publish "personal home pages, material of an offensive nature, or adult entertainment listings."

Access to NCGA What's New in Mosaic

- *Mosaic What's New List*
`http://www.ncsa.uiuc.edu/SDG/Software/Mosaic/Docs/whats-new.html`

- *Submission address for the Mosaic What's New List*
`http://www.ncsa.uiuc.edu/SDG/Software/Mosaic/Docs/whats-new-form.html`

- *E-mail*
`whats-new@ncsa.uiuc.edu`

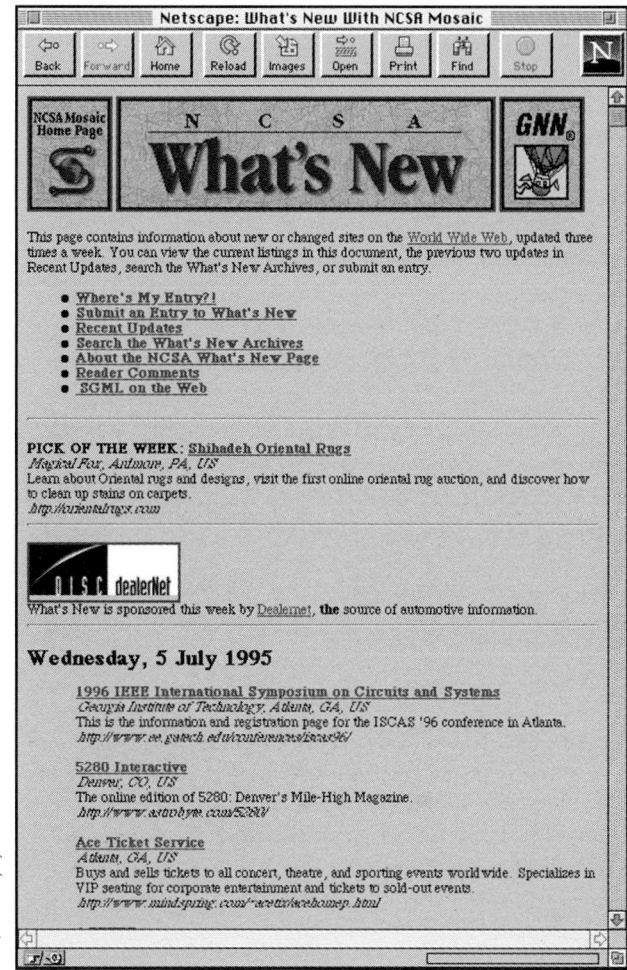

Figure A.2:
NCSA's Mosaic What's New list.

Netscape's What's New

Netscape's What's New page is another important place to register. Because Netscape includes a button that leads directly to this list, many readers use it as a launch pad for browsing. You submit your site through an online form with the same kind of information requested by other sites. Netscape's maintainers make an effort to curate their What's New section. They are looking for sites that are "not only new to the Net but that use or advance the technology of the Net in new ways." You will have to make clear what is special about your site in your submission.

Netscape's What's New

• *Access to Netscape's What's New list*
`http://home.netscape.com/home/whats-new.html`

• *Page to register a site*
`http://home.netscape.com/escapes/submit_new.html`

Yahoo Site

Yahoo, originally started by Stanford students, has become one of the most appreciated Web index sites. It is now part of a commercial enterprise to develop new resources for the Web. It offers a hierarchical, topically organized list that is easy to navigate. Its database is searchable by a menu of subjects areas or by keyword search. Yahoo focuses on Web resources but also includes some Gopher, FTP, and Usenet material. It is especially well-stocked in computing, Web, and Internet resources. Topics include categories such as Computers, Economy, Education, Entertainment, Environment and Nature, and Events. Users are encouraged to submit sites for consideration via an online form that asks for title, URL, description, category, additional categories, and contact information.

Access to Yahoo Service

• *Basic access location for Yahoo*
`http://www.yahoo.com/`

• *Form to add to the Yahoo database*
`http://www.yahoo.com/bin/add`

McKinley

The McKinley site is an ambitious information resource created just for the Web. Its database includes full text of a wide range of sites and powerful search engines for users. It tries to improve on the unsystematic approaches used by many other indexes. It provides information seekers with summaries of site content so they can decide if the site might be useful. It also provides evaluations of the content organization, currency, and ease of access of each site. It offers a search engine that provides the user with sophisticated techniques such as fuzzy logic. Its categorical index was developed by professional indexers specifically for the Web.

Access to McKinley

• *Main access*
`http://mckinley.com/`

• *Registration of site*
`http://mckinley.com/Template_new.html`

Virtual Tourist

Virtual Tourist is a geographically based database that users search by clicking imagemaps. The resources listed are based on the W3 Organization's list of servers and geographic lists, resources that the maintainers become aware of, and by direct submissions from users. Web authors are encouraged to send notices of new Web sites by e-mail.

Access to Virtual Tourist

• *Virtual Tourist Map*
`http://wings.buffalo.edu/world/`

• *Virtual Tourist e-mail address to receive notices of new services*

• *Send to the country maintainers of W3 Organization's server list*

`(http://www.w3.org/hypertext/DataSources/WWW/`
`Geographical_generation/new-servers.html)`

CityNet

CityNet provides another geographic metaphor for organizing Web resources. This index seeks resources that relate to particular cities or regions. It is billed as the "sequel" to Virtual Tourist. Web users are encouraged to send in new resources. The registration page asks for the URL, city and country, languages supported, maintainer information, and a description.

Access Locations for CityNet

- *Main access to CityNet*
`http://www.city.net/`

- *Location to add a resource to CityNet*
`http://www.city.net/forms/city_registration.html`

EINet Galaxy

EINet (Enterprise Integration Network) Galaxy is especially interested in the problems of organizing access to resources. Its mission statement notes that Web information is different from that in libraries and that "much of it is transitory, difficult to classify, and of uncertain origin... and spans an incredible range of topics." Its "Galaxy" indexes to Web resources tries to address these problems. Site designers are encouraged to register their pages. Topic lists are maintained by volunteer guest editors.

Access to EINet Galaxy Information Service

- *Galaxy home page*
`http://galaxy.einet.net/galaxy.html`

- *Submission form*
`http://galaxy.einet.net/cgi-bin/annotate?Other`

User-Generated Lists

User-generated lists normally use a highly automated process for managing topics and listings. Because the categories in these lists are usually proscribed by the contributors, these list of topics can look very different from the more highly organized ones used by comprehensive indexes and managed lists.

GENBBB

GENBBB (Generic Bulletin Board Builder), the "mother of all bulletin boards," is an automated bulletin board system that allows those who visit the Web site to add topics or resources. This very popular index is highly idiosyncratic in topic coverage but is a good place to register your site (via an online form) if some of the topics match your site's focus. Topics range from Northern Minnesota fishing to philosophy. Figure A.3 shows the site's welcome page.

Access to GENBBB (Mother of all Bulletin Boards)

- *Main Access to GENBBB*
`http://www.cs.colorado.edu/homes/mcbryan/public_html/bb/summary.html`

- *GENBBB location to register URL to be indexed*
`http://www.cs.colorado.edu/homes/mcbryan/public_html/bb/add.html`

Aliweb

Aliweb is supported by the Nexor Company in the United Kingdom. Users are invited to register their own sites with the database. The site asks you to create an index file in the IAFA (Internet Anonymous FTP Archive) format being developed

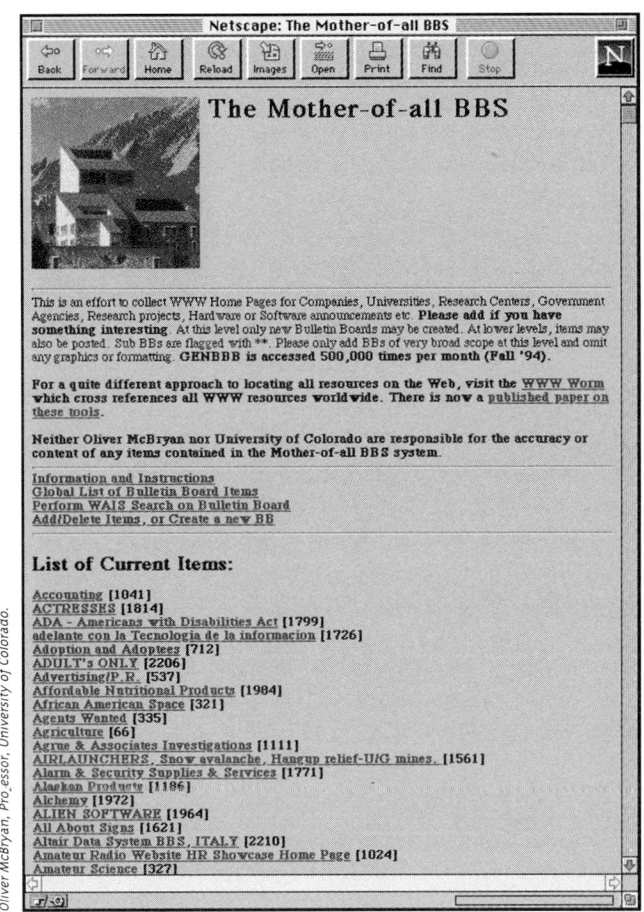

Figure A.3:
GENBBB main access page and list of topics.

by an IETF subcommittee (described in the documentation). This format makes it easy for search programs to extract key information. You then notify Aliweb of your index file's location and it will be added to the database.

Access to Aliweb User Generated List

• Access to Aliweb
`http://web.nexor.co.uk/public/aliweb/aliweb.html`

• Location to register a URL
`http://web.nexor.co.uk/public/aliweb/doc/registering.html`

Hidden Index Treasures

The indexes described previously are extremely valuable, especially when one of the subtopics matches your interests exactly. But there are many other useful indexes, often maintained by individuals, that are made available as an unofficial resource for devotees of a specific subject or interest. Often it is these kinds of curious and ingenious individuals who are most successful in discovering and organizing Web resources. The topic could be anything: body art, Buddhist ethics, karate, international banking, or jazz. These "personal" indexes can be a great boon to your research; they can also be good places to announce your site. Keep track of these sites in your area of interest and correspond with their maintainers.

Automated Search Programs

Automated search programs go by a variety of colorful names such as spiders, worms, and webwalkers. These programs attempt to locate and index new Web resources, and to make their parent indexes available for search. In addition to automated searching, most of these sites will also accept submissions for new URLs.

You need to understand how these programs function because your knowledge of their workings will enable you to ensure that elements of your documents such as titles and headings facilitate the search programs' capability to find your work.

Lycos

The automated program with perhaps the largest database is the Lycos program, which is a joint project of Carnegie Mellon University and Lycos, Inc. By July 1995, it had a database of over 4.5 million URLs. Lycos is the name of a species of spiders that catches its prey by active pursuit rather than by spinning a web.

The approach it uses to search is described in the documentation available online. It stores information about the site's title, heading and subheadings, the first 20 lines, and the 100 most "weighty" words, which are assigned value by how near the top they appear and how often they occur.

Figure A.4 presents the home page for the Lycos engine. The Lycos project welcomes registration of a URL for possible exploration. The site notes that submission, however, is no guarantee that your site will be explored or kept in the database.

Access to Lycos Spider

- *Main home page for Lycos*
`http://lycos.cs.cmu.edu/`

- *Documentation for using Lycos*
`http://lycos.cs.cmu.edu/lycos-docs.html`

- *Description of Lycos project*
`http://fuzine.mt.cs.cmu.edu/mlm/lycos-post-01.html`

- *To register a URL for possible exploration by Lycos*
`http://lycos.cs.cmu.edu/lycos-register.html`

WebCrawler

WebCrawler is an automatic search program originally developed at the University of Washington. It is part of AOL's Internet services. It uses a *breadth-first* search technique to scan possibilities and indexes the contents of the URLs, which means the search looks widely at the header level rather than pursuing much depth for each URL. It uses the W3 Organization's tables of servers and other sources. It welcomes suggestions from users about URLs to visit and provides an online fill-in form for submitting information.

Access to WebCrawler

- *Home search page for WebCrawler*
`http://webcrawler.com/WebCrawler/Home.html`

- *Registration page to submit URL*
`http://webcrawler.com/WebCrawler/SubmitURLS.html`

Lycos.

Figure A.4:
Lycos automated search program home page.
`http://lycos.cs.cmu.edu/`

Issues confronting spider, worms, and webwalkers

The issues surrounding the design and implementation of these automated programs are not trivial. All of the following must be addressed:

- *How can the program find Web resources?*

- *How can the program navigate to explore other resources referenced by the initial resources?*

- *Should the programs use breadth- or depth-first search techniques?*

- *How can the program keep track of where it has been and where it needs to go?*

- *How can the program be graceful in its activity so it doesn't overwork servers and hog Web resources?*

- *How can the program efficiently and thoroughly index what it finds so the information can be available to those who want to use the data?*

Locating starting places is not trivial. Most of the spiders are seeded with lists to start with. They then systematically follow those links to discover new links, which are then used recursively to find more links. It is to the advantage of the Web author to get their Web event listed in as many places as possible. This listing will also serve as a seed for the auto-mated searchers.

Unfortunately, automated programs can cause problems for servers and the Net in general. For example, they can get out of control and tie up servers. A full discussion of Robot issues can be found at http://web.nexor.co.uk/users/mak/doc/robots/robots.html.

InfoSeek

InfoSeek is a full text search service that uses human indexers and robots to collect references for its archive. It claims to have one of the most comprehensive information archives on the Web. InfoSeek indexes every word of the documents, not only titles and headers. It uses a very efficient and precise search engine that it claims gives better results than others on the Web.

InfoSeek is in the business of selling information. Although it offers a limited free search service to the Web, it offers a more comprehensive service for a fee. Because InfoSeek is the first search service accessible via the Netscape "Net Search" button, it is a very popular service and a good place to register your site.

Access to InfoSeek

* *Home page for InfoSeek*
http://www.infoseek.com:80/Home

* *Register your site by sending e-mail*
mailto:www-request@infoseek.com

Harvest System

Harvest is part of the Internet Research Task Force Research Group on Resource Discovery (IRTF-RD) project based at the University of Colorado, designed to develop tools for retrieval of information on the Internet and the Web. It is funded by the Advanced Research Projects Agency (ARPA), the Air Force Office of Scientific Research, the National Science Foundation,

Hughes Aircraft Co., and Sun Microsystems. Its researchers have developed several kinds of software to facilitate work with Internet information including resource discovery programs (gatherers), indexers (brokers), and replicators (programs that disperse indexed resources in order to reduce network traffic). The indexes are called "brokers" because they negotiate between the reader's needs and the resources available. Submissions of URLs are accepted.

Access to Harvest Project

* *Harvest home page*
http://harvest.cs.colorado.edu/

* *To register a URL with Harvest project*
http://harvest.cs.colorado.edu/brokers/register-with-CU-gatherers.html

W4: The WWW Wanderer

The World Wide Web Wanderer is an information robot run out of MIT. Its flexible search capability allows users to search by terms or by hosts. Lists of sites are available by IP number (basic Internet numerical address), geographic region, or type of domain (.edu, .gov, .net).

Access to WWW Wanderer

* *Home page*
http://www.netgen.com/info/wanderer.html

* *Add a site to the list*
http://www.netgen.com/cgi/addhost

Submit It

The Submit It site has automated the process of submitting your site to many of the indexes and robots described in this appendix. The author offers a generic form in which you enter the information about your site that most of the indexes require—for example, title, URL, description, and contact information. It then allows you to select which services you want to submit your site to. It automatically fills out the forms for each of the sites, using your generic information. This approach might not work for you, however, if you want to customize the description or title for particular indexes. Figure A.5 shows the Submit It home page.

Access to Global Integrated Search Pages (Meta-Indexes)

- *Meta-index NCSA*

`http://www.ncsa.uiuc.edu/SDG/Software/Mosaic/Demo/metaindex.html`

- *Meta-index CUI (Centre Universitaire d'Informatique of the University of Geneva)*

`http://cui_www.unige.ch/meta-index.html`

- *Nexor configurable unified search interface (CUSI)*

`http://web.nexor.co.uk/public/cusi/cusi.html`

- *University of Twente external info (meta-index)*

`http://www_is.cs.utwente.nl:8080/cgi-bin/local/nph-susi1.pl`

- *Allinone search page*

`http://www.albany.net/~wcross/all1srch.html`

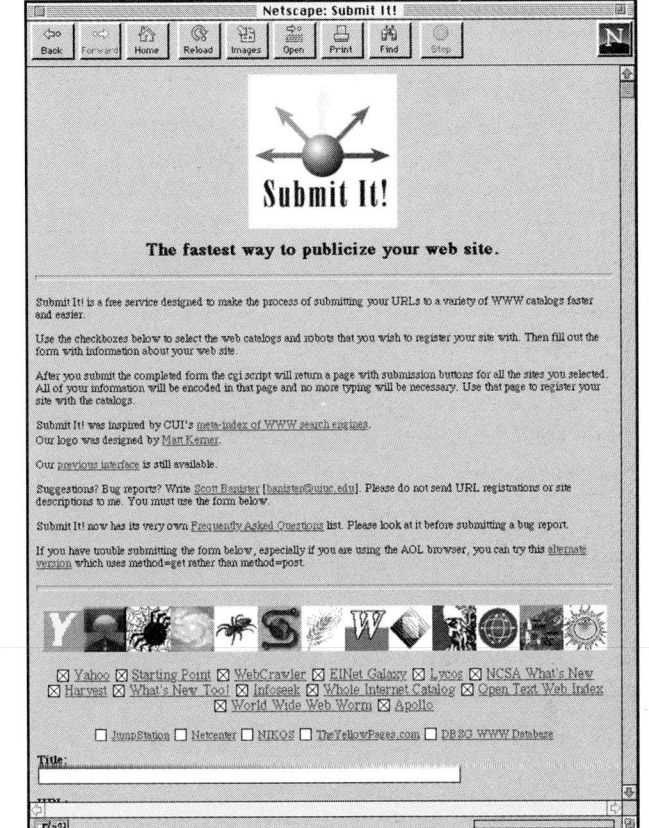

Figure A.5:
Submit It.
`http://www.cen.uiuc.edu/~banister/submit-it/`

Understanding How Search Engines Work

Many automated search programs and indexes offer users a search "engine" to find resources. Understanding how these search programs work will help you in your own research.

In order to optimize a search, you should be specific enough to exclude irrelevant materials but general enough not to overly restrict the search. For example, I conducted searches on several of the services described in this appendix for materials related to the search term *design*. *Design* returned links to resources ranging from electronics fabrication to building design, as well as some resources related to visual design—which is what I was really looking for. Searching on the term *visual design* failed to turn up some resources that would have been appropriate because the authors of those resources used other terms—such as *graphic design*—instead of *visual design*. Many users new to searching fail to realize how literal the computer is and how much like a detective they must be in finding alternative terms to search on.

There are new companies on the Web that offer sophisticated search engines. For example Architext (http://www.atext.com/index.html) has created software that allows "Concept-Based Searching" that has the intelligence to search for terms related to those stated in the query.

Search Criteria

Search engines differ in the options they give you to specify combinations of search terms. For example, some will assume that the user's typing of several words separated by spaces means that the search should look for resources that contain all terms. This is called a logical AND connection. Other services require that the user actually type the AND if that is what is required and offer many other logical combinations such as OR and NOT (called Boolean searches).

Figure A.6 shows the search page from the Yahoo site with some of the options it offers, and the partial results of a search using the term "design."

A full-featured search engine can greatly increase the power and efficiency of your searches. Because they differ, a general template cannot be specified. To best use each information service, consult the online documentation.

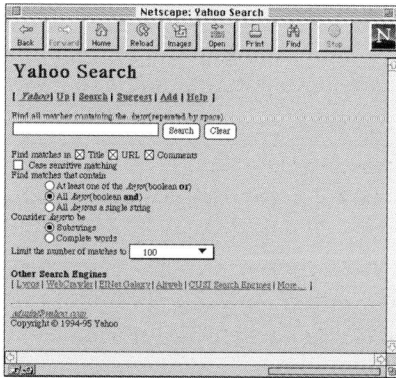

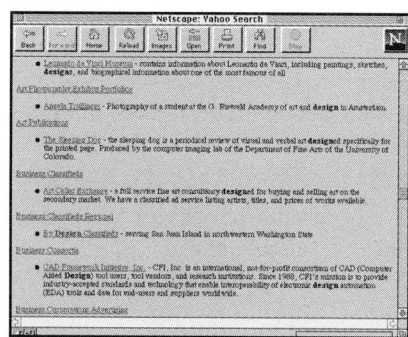

Yahoo! Corp.

Figure A.6:

Yahoo search page and sample of results from search for term design.
`http://www.yahoo.com/search.html`

Interpreting Results

Several of the services provide an automatic ranking of the relevance of the resources they retrieve. The retrieval engine makes the judgment based on the fit between the words in a resource and the words specified in the search terms. More occurrences of a term and earlier occurrences of a term earn more points. See the documentation for the services for a fuller explanation of the ranking systems.

Making Your Site Accessible

Here are some hints for making your pages more accessible:

- Include several descriptive terms in your HTML title if feasible. Be careful not to exceed the 64-character limit some browsers require.
- Make sure your higher level heads (H1 and H2) include terms that are descriptive of the sections of your site.
- Near the top of your document offer a short paragraph that includes phrases descriptive of topics in your site. For some kinds of sites it is appropriate to provide an explicit keyword list. You can use any HTML structure you want.
- Watch out for formatting tags that can confuse a search engine. For example, using the <FONT> tag to change the size of the first letter in a major header can fool it into thinking the word is two words instead of one.
- If you are applying for a new domain name, select one that's fairly obvious to your purpose, e.g. Adobe's site at http://www.adobe.com.

Best of the Web Sites

Chapter 9 described Best of the Web sites, which are another important place for you to try to publicize your site. The lists, spiders, and other resources described previously in this appendix do not make determination of quality their major agenda. The user-generated lists by definition are open to whatever the community generates. The lists maintained by humans technically could facilitate quality judgments but most maintainers do not emphasize this function. Chapter 9 provides descriptions and access pointers to several of the Best of the Web sites.

There are some things you can do:

- Make your site special
- Learn the winning criteria
- Nominate your site

Random Access and Free-for-Alls

When all else fails, Web users can use chance to access Web sites. In fact, relying on chance can be seen as a comment on the frustration that Web navigation can provoke. Several sites offer chance based links to Web resources. Free-for-alls are a similar Web structure. Anyone can add text and links to a cumulative list that is open to inspection by other Web users. Some users consider these kinds of whimsical, random starting points a valuable place to start browsing. It is easy to add your site to their databases so you can make your site available to these audiences.

Random Access

The University of Kansas roulette wheel, one of the best known random access sites, presents visitors with a roulette wheel. The event is called "URouLette." The user can click the image of the roulette wheel and be connected to random Web locations. The site notes, "Sometimes you'll be taken to an interesting place, sometimes you won't." Figure A.7 shows the main roulette wheel. The reference list points to the URouLette site and other random jump sites. Instructions for registering your site are available on the home page.

Random Access Sites

- *Main access to U of Kansas roulette wheel*
`http://kuhttp.cc.ukans.edu/cwis/organizations/`
`kucia/uroulette/uroulette.html`

- *To add a resource to U. Kansas roulette wheel*
`http://lark.cc.ukans.edu:8000/~angell/`
`add_form.html`

- *1,000 points of site random jump site at UCSD*
`http://inls.ucsd.edu/y/OhBoy/randomjump1.html`

- *Cool Roulette Magicurl mystery trip*
`http://www.netcreations.com/magicurl/index.html`

- *Random jump site at Yahoo site*
`http://www.cen.uiuc.edu/cgi-bin/ryl`

- *Information supercollider (random mixes of Web info)*
`http://www.eecs.harvard.edu/collider.html`

- *Web autopilot (automatic continual retrieval of sites)*
`http://www.netgen.com/~mkgray//autopilot.html`

Free-for-Alls

Some sites have created a less structured version of the user generated list called the free-for-all. These lists allow anyone to add their own pointers to Web sites they have created or others they find interesting. Some allow addition of inline images. The method of adding references is made clear at the sites.

Matthew T. Abrams.

Figure A.7:
URouLette event that uses roulette wheel to identify Web sites to visit.
`http://kuhttp.cc.ukans.edu/cwis/organizations/kucia/`
`uroulette/uroulette.html`

Access to Free-for-All Sites

- *Free-for-all (at Artemide in Italy)*
`http://artemide.cselt.stet.it/ex1_html.html`

- *Dave's site*
`http://www.eg.bucknell.edu/cgi-bin/webula/index.html`

- *Matt's site*
`http://alpha.pr1.k12.co.us/~mattw/links/links.html`

Internet Resources Outside the Web

The Internet is much more than the Web. Services such as Gopher, FTP, list severs, WAIS, e-mail, USENET, Jughead, Veronica, and Archie offer rich resources that might not be available via the Web. Developers of the Web made it extremely easy to access these services from within the Web.

Many Internet users rely on non-Web sources to obtain information—for example, Internet resource collections and newsgroups. It is to your advantage to know about these sites for your research and as possible places to announce your site.

John December's Guides to the Internet

John December is a professor at Rensselaer Polytechnic University who has made it his professional mission to collect and organize Internet resources. He categorizes his resources as being related to NIR (Network Information Retrieval) and

CMC (Computer Mediated Communication). He is eager to hear about additional resources and welcomes suggestions from the field.

Access to December's Internet Guides

- *Main access to John December's Internet Guides*
`http://www.rpi.edu/Internet/Guides/decemj/internet-tools.html`

- *Suggest additions*
`http://www.rpi.edu/Internet/Guides/decemj/itools/add-itools.html`

Big Dummy's Guide to the Internet

Adam Gaffin wrote the first version of the *Big Dummy's Guide to the Internet* for a joint project of Apple Computer, Inc. and The Electronic Frontier Foundation (EFF). Many others contributed to its creation and now its maintenance is coordinated by EFF. It was inspired by an online book called *Zen and the Art of the Internet: A Beginner's Guide to the Internet*, by B.P. Kehoe, which is now available in printed form (Prentice Hall, 1993). *The Big Dummy's Guide* is now also available in print as *Everybody's Guide to the Internet* (A. Gaffin, MIT Press, 1994). *The Big Dummy's Guide* provides information about Internet services, substantive topics, and philosophical and social issues related to the Internet.

Access to Big Dummy's Guide to the Internet

- *Sample access location*
`http://www.cs.dal.ca/dummy.html`

- *Main access to update (called the Extended Guide)*
`http://www.eff.org/papers/eegtti/eeg_toc.html`

- *Access to online version of Zen & the Art of the Internet*
`ftp://ftp.cs.widener.edu`

Gopher Jewels

Before the current popularity of the Web, Internet proponents identified Gopher sites that they felt were exemplary. One set of such lists is called Gopher Jewels. Many Internet users around the world still rely on Gopher as their main user friendly window to the Net so the Jewel collection is a valuable source of research information and a good place to announce your site.

Access to Gopher Jewels

- *Web access to Gopher Jewels*
`http://galaxy.einet.net:80/GJ/`

- *Comments and suggestions, suggestions for additions*
`http://galaxy.einet.net:80/GJ/#CONTRIBUTE`

- *Gopher access to Gopher Jewels*
`gopher://cwis.usc.edu/11/`
`Other_Gophers_and_Information_Resources/Gopher-`
`Jewels`

Usenet Newsgroups

The Usenet is a valuable resource for research and publicity. You should regularly monitor newsgroups covering topics related to your site and post listings of your site in these groups. In addition there are two newsgroups that have become standard places to announce Web sites. You can find the details for how to post to these groups in the FAQ for these groups.

- Comp.infosystems.www.announce—World Wide Web announcements. The FAQ that explains how to post is at http://www.halcyon.com/grant/charter.html

- Comp.internet.net-happenings—The FAQ that explains the site and how to announce your site is available at http://www.mid.net:80/NET/

Summary

The Web has developed many helpful search services, including indexes, automated search programs, and curated lists. But how will search services meet the unprecedented challenge of providing access to a structure that consolidates all information and media—ranging from fundamental philosophical texts to stock quotations and jokes of the day? Some Web visionaries suggest we will need radically new models of information work. Remember to monitor these developments carefully in order to continue to be successful as an information finder and provider.

Appendix B

Preparing Servers to Respond to Imagemaps

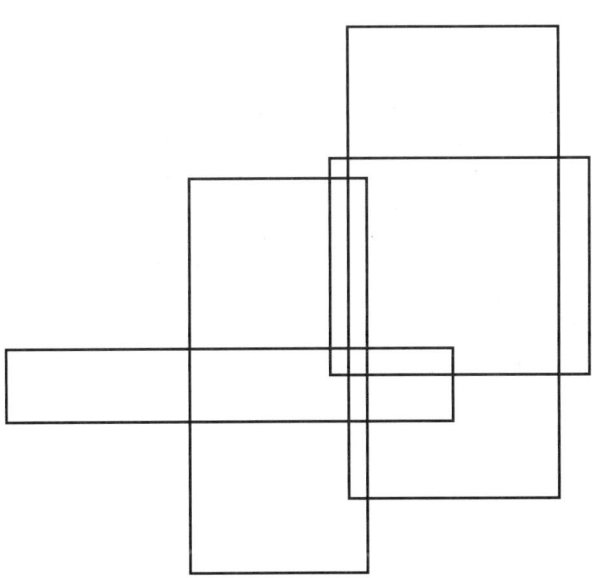

Chapter 7 explained that imagemaps are Web images that are sensitive to user mouse clicks. You accomplish this easily by including the <ISMAP> attribute inside of the <IMG> structure. For example:

```
<IMG SRC="liveimage.gif" ISMAP>
```

You must also designate particular areas as significant and decide what should happen when the Web reader clicks within a hot area. The most common response is that the server finds a URL that you linked with that area and accesses it to send back to the browser. This response requires that the server run a script or program that has the intelligence to determine whether the user clicked a significant area, and then to make the required response. This appendix explains the details of setting up imagemap systems on UNIX and Macintosh platforms.

Arranging an Imagemap System on a UNIX Server

There are several server programs that run on UNIX computers. The httpd software distributed free by the NCSA group that created Mosaic is one of the most widely used. This section describes how to set up that server to service imagemaps. The server must be version 1.05a or later. Other servers might be able to respond to imagemaps; you need to refer to the documentation for those servers for the details of getting prepared to respond to imagemaps.

Setting Up UNIX Servers to Respond to Imagemaps

- *Httpd server*
`http://hoohoo.ncsa.uiuc.edu/docs/Overview.html`

- *Tutorial on imagemaps*
`http://wintermute.ncsa.uiuc.edu:8080/map-tutorial/`

If you are not the system operator, you need to consult the persons who control the configuration of the UNIX server. Here are the steps:

1. **Compile and place the imagemap program.** A free imagemap program is distributed with the httpd server software that provides the ability to respond to clicks within imagemaps. The imagemap software must be compiled and placed in the htbin directory, or in whichever directory is designated for CGI scripts (this can be defined in the httpd.conf file). UNIX systems are arranged with a hierarchy of privileges for who may place files where. It is highly likely that only system operators have access to this directory.

2. **Prepare the imagemap file that contains coordinates of the imaginary shapes.** Figure B.1 presents a world map image with some sample shapes; clicking the image of each continent links to a different document.

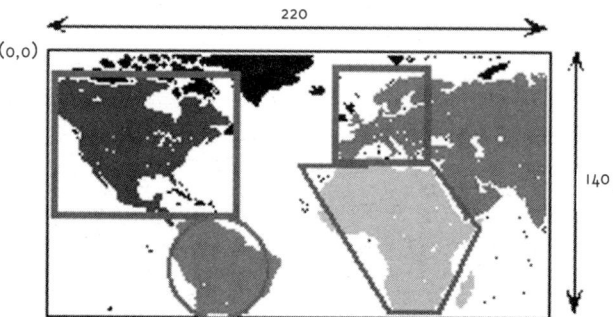

Figure B.1:
World map with designated hot areas.

For the sake of illustration, I call it *WorldMap.GIF.* The imagemap file is a record of those shapes specified in the format that your particular imagemap program expects. Here is an example of that file, called WorldMap.map, in NCSA format:

```
!-- Map file for world map (in NCSA format)
default http://net.add/no.selection.html
rect http://net.add/NorAm.html 1,7 82,65
circle http://net.add/SouAm.html 74,89 100,140
rect http://net.add/Eur.html 125,4 165,45
poly http://net.add/Af.html 107,44 148,106 172,106
➡187,72 164 44
```

That format consists of a series of lines that each have the following elements:

- The term *rect* (indicating it is a rectangle bounding shape), *circ* (indicating a circle or oval), and *poly* (indicating a polygon).

- The address of the URL that should be retrieved if that element is clicked. In this example, each is named in accordance with the continent represented on the map (e.g., clicking within the image of Europe will jump the user to a file called Eur.html) and is present on the same machine as the response script. Any name could be used.

- The coordinates that designate the invisible shape that encloses the hot area—the upper-left and lower-right corners of rectangles, upper-left and any edgepoint coordinates that define a circle, as well as the list of vertices that defines a polygon. Each item is separated by spaces. The first line is a default URL that should be retrieved

if the click fails to fall within any of the bounding shapes. In this example, this file is named *summarylocs* and is in the same directory as the HTML pages returned when the user clicks the multishape.gif image *(/net.add/ summarylocs)*.

3. **Set the configuration file of the server to know where to find the files that contain definitions of the hotlink rectangles.** The imagemap software needs to know where to find the file of shape definitions for each image file to which it is going to respond. UNIX software often needs redirection instructions so it knows which directories contain necessary resources. Again, it is likely that general users will not have access to this configuration file. New enhancements to imagemaps allow for virtual file paths to imagemaps in order to accommodate multiple imagemap directories.

There is a special configuration file that tells the imagemap software where to find these files. The configuration file (usually named conf/ imagemap.conf) has a line for each imagemap file. Each line has a symbolic name for the file, followed by its full location. Assuming this file had the symbolic name *worldevent,* the line would look like this:

```
worldevent /net.add/summarylocs
treeevent /net.add/summarytrees
```

The file would need other lines to define the imagemap files for other images. In the example, another imagemap location file called *summarytrees* was added just to illustrate.

4. **Construct an HTML tag for the image.** Create a standard inline image call, adding the <ISMAP> tag.

Make the image into a link by indicating the appropriate link tag. The link, however, must point to the imagemap program and it must include the symbolic name of the file that contains the location information. The standard program provided by NCSA is called imagemap and it is typically located in a directory called cgi-bin. There is also a set of aliases to map the file WorldMap.map to just WorldMap because imagemap expects a GET method. In the example here, the tag would look as follows:

```
<A HREF="http://net-ad/cgi-bin/imagemap/WorldMap">
<IMG SRC="WorldMap.GIF" ISMAP></A>
```

This example demonstrates a fairly simple process. The clickable coordinates are passed to the response script. It sequentially checks its list to see whether the click is within any of the shapes. When it finds one, it sends the URL indicated. Each click on one of the defined areas leads to a particular URL. More complex actions are possible with a custom response script.

Arranging an Imagemap System on a Macintosh Server

Each kind of server must be prepared to respond to imagemaps in its own way. Although the basic processes are often similar across platforms, the details differ. If you want only to arrange for hot areas of your image to link to particular URLs, there is a canned program called Mac-Imagemap.cgi that makes this relatively easy. If you want to create more complex responses, however, you must write your own script.

Both approaches assume that you have created the imagemap image in GIF format, identified hot areas, and determined the coordinates of the imaginary shapes that bound the hot areas.

Mac-Imagemap.cgi is a standardized program that can respond to user clicks in an imagemap image. Working with the MacHTTP or WebSTAR Web servers, it can determine which hot area a user has clicked. It then returns the URL that the author has linked with the hot area. Note this is the only action it is capable of doing; it will not allow any other kind of interactive response such as generation of HTML pages on the fly.

This program works similarly to the imagemap program for UNIX described previously. It requires a map file in standard format, linking the shape coordinates with URLs and a setting in its configuration file to identify where the map is located. It uses the CGI interface conventions discussed in Chapter 7. It assumes you are using a version of the Mac operating system that is AppleEvents capable and you are using Web server software MacHTTP 1.03 or later. Here are the steps:

1. **Prepare the image that serves as the imagemap in GIF format.**

2. **Prepare an HTML page that contains a reference to an imagemap.** The link reference should point to the imagemap program itself followed by a $ with the symbolic name of the particular image appended. (In this example the image is called *sample*. Using a name after the $ allows the imagemap.cgi program to deal with many different images each specified by a name.)

```
<A HREF=http://net-ad/imagemap.cgi$sample> Pick the
part of the image you like <IMG SRC = http://net-ad/
folder/sample.GIF ISMAP></A>
```

3. **Prepare a map file of hot areas for that particular GIF image.** Use plain ASCII text format for this file. Each hot area must be specified by the coordinates of a rectangle, circle, or polygon that encloses it.

You can determine these coordinates by using a drawing program or a special purpose program such as WebMap. (Access locations for this program and Mac-Imagemap.cgi mentioned earlier appear in Chapter 7.) Rectangles are specified by the coordinates of the upper-left and lower-right corners. Circles are specified by the coordinates of the center and of any edgepoint. Polygons are specified by a list of the coordinates of each vertex. (The WebMap program automatically generates this map file by allowing the user to place shapes over areas of the GIF image and then generating the list of coordinates in a text file.)

Create this map file in a standard format such as that used by the NCSA or CERN servers. This format requires each line to contain the following items separated by spaces:

- Abbreviated name of the shape
- The URL that the hot area links to
- The coordinate specifications

These URLs can be local files generated by the author or any other resource available on the Web. The map file needs to end with the ".map" suffix. The file should also contain a default URL that is accessed when someone clicks an area not specified as hot.

These files are in NCSA standard imagemap format and thus can be switched to a UNIX computer if the server moved. The imagemap.cgi program allows other kinds of mapping functions, such as nearness to an arbitrary point. These files are in NCSA standard imagemap format and thus could be switched to UNIX if the server moved. The imagemap.cgi program allows other kinds of mapping functions such as nearness to an arbitrary point, which are also available with the NCSA standard imagemap programs.

Example map file "sampleimage.map"

```
default http://net-ad/folder/youmissed.html
circle http://net-ad/folder/eye1.html 42,16 71,39
circle http://net-ad/folder/eye2.html 89,18 117,45
rect http://net-ad/folder/nose.html 63,40 95,63
poly http://net-ad/folder/mouth.html 52,70 72,127
➡99,67 52,70
```

4. **Add a line to the imagemap.config file that the imagemap.cgi program uses to find where the map files are located.** There is only one imagemap.config file for the program. Each image has its own line in this file. This file contains the symbolic names of images (the part of the reference following the $ in the original link) to be served followed by the location of the ".map" file that relates to that image.

Example lines from the imagemap.config configuration file

```
sample : netaddress/folder/sampleimage.map
lion : netaddress/lionfolder/lionimage.map
```

After these steps, you should be ready to go. When the user clicks a particular part of your imagemap, the client will send a request to your server consisting of the address of your imagemap.cgi program and the name of the image and the coordinates of the click. It might look as follows:

```
net-ad/imagemap.cgi$sample?100, 200
```

The server will determine that it needs to send the information to the imagemap.cgi program. That program will look at the name of the image after the $ and check its configuration file to find out where the map file is for that image. It will then determine if the coordinates of the click fall within any of the defined hot areas. If they do, it will send back the URL you have linked with that hot area; otherwise it will send back the default URL you have specified. For example, you might design that document to respond with text such as "You have not clicked in a live area—please try again."

Writing Your Own Scripts for Imagemaps

This section shows you how to write your own scripts. Although I focus on the Macintosh MacHTTP and WebSTAR servers, the basic concepts apply to all platforms.

As with the UNIX httpd server, the raw server software is not able to make use of the information about the coordinates of the user's click within an ISMAP inline image. This example is presented to show you the underlying function of imagemap scripts and also to show you how you can write a script to do something other than return a URL mapped to each hot area. Your program needs to perform some of the same functions as the canned programs and then add the special functions you build:

- Extracting the coordinates that the client browser has sent with the URL.
- Checking them against some data set that lists the active areas of the image.
- Identifying a response if the clicked coordinates are within an active area.
- Preparing an appropriately formatted document for Web protocols.
- Sending that document back to the server to be relayed to the original requester.

Using AppleEvents and HyperCard

There are many approaches possible to generating that supplemental program. The one illustrated here makes use of AppleEvents and HyperCard. AppleEvents is the interapplication communication system that Apple includes in the Macintosh operating system. Applications can send commands to other applications that understand Apple-Events and retrieve information generated in those programs. You will need a Macintosh that is AppleEvents capable and HyperCard 2.1 or later.

AppleEvents can be used easily to carry information between the MacHTTP or WebSTAR Web server and the application that processes the data about the clicks. HyperCard does the actual processing, such as checking if a click is in an active area. It is used because it is a full programming environment that is widespread and uses fairly easy syntax. As is true of computer programming in general, there are many ways to accomplish the same outcomes. For example, a simple imagemap response system can be programmed only in AppleScript. The reference list in Chapter 7 points to examples of different interactive scripts to respond to imagemaps.

Obviously I can't offer a full introduction to AppleEvents, AppleScript, and HyperCard here. Nonetheless, I attempt to provide enough details so you can see how the process works. Those of you with scripting background will quickly see how you can create your own scripts to build interactive Web events.

Those without this background may be able to adopt the templates offered and will hopefully be inspired to learn more about these development environments in preparation for creating interactive Web events. Note that the conceptual models work with almost any kind of programming or scripting language on any kind of computer.

The Logical Structure of a Script

When a browser such as Mosaic sees an <ISMAP> tag attached to an inline image, it sets up to get the coordinates of the click should one occur. When the user clicks in the image, the browser identifies the URL link connected to the image. It requests from the server connection to the file indicated and it attaches the coordinates to the end of the filename. It is said to pass the search arguments. With interactive scripts, the URL points to a program or script, not to an HTML document. In this example, the URL points to HyperCard, which is functioning as the interactive script.

The server receives this request and automatically sends out a particular AppleEvent called *sdoc* when it receives a link request that involves forwarding information such as an imagemap, form, or index. This *sdoc* event contains information about the user's actions—for example, what was typed into a form or where the user clicked. The information is designed to conform to CGI specifications about what variables must be available to a supplementary program.

HyperCard is AppleEvents-aware and can be programmed to extract this information and respond. Then HyperCard must prepare the response in an appropriately formatted document with the required CGI header information.

For this arrangement to work, HyperCard must be running as well as the MacHTTP server. This response stack must be the active stack. Also HyperCard must be renamed to have a ".cgi" after it so that the server knows it is going to function with the cgi standard. The image called branch.GIF is the active image. The <ISMAP> tag is appended to indicate an active image. The image and stack is a fragment from the author's prototype Web art event to reflect users' information styles back to them.

```
<A> Pick a shape<SRC= http://net-ad/branch.gif ISMAP>
HREF = http://net-ad/hypercard.cgi$Shapehtml</A>
```

HyperCard is best placed in the same folder as the server in order to avoid path finding confusion. The renaming and positioning of HyperCard can be easily accomplished by making an alias of HyperCard, placing the alias in the MacHTTP folder, and adding the CGI suffix after its name.

Also note that a path argument, arbitrarily called *shapehtml,* is appended after a $ symbol in the name of the program link. The server allows passing of this item as a method to let the HyperCard stack know specifically what event is calling the script and which routines should be accessed. Use of other identifiers may cause the same stack to be able to respond to many kinds of events.

This example illustrates a HyperCard stack that can respond in two ways to clicks in hot areas. It can either send back a URL that has been linked to that hot area, or it can dynamically generate an HTML page that confirms the choice the user has made and tells how many people previously made that choice. This first option duplicates what the canned programs do. The second option shows the skeleton of what could be a sophisticated response.

The stack contains two cards: a master card (containing the listening script) and a card called *shapec* to handle the two imagemap illustrated events. Here are the steps to create this script:

1. **Prepare the GIF image and the list of coordinates that designate hot areas.** The first steps in creating an imagemap event are preparing the GIF image that users will see, deciding which areas in the image will be hot, and determining the coordinates of the shapes that bound the image. These are the same steps you need to perform when using the canned imagemap programs.

2. **Create an HTML page that presents the imagemap.** You must also prepare the HTML page that presents the imagemap to the user. Note that the link will point to the script that was written to process the user's clicks the imagemap. In this example the imagemap tag might look as follows:

```
<A HREF="net-add/hypercard.cgi$shapehtml">
<IMG SRC=shapechoices.GIF ISMAP></A>
```

These next steps walk you through creation of the actual script.

3. **Wait for the AppleEvent sent from the Server, extract the variables containing essential information, and branch to the appropriate card to handle different events.** In this example, there is a master routine that is always listening for AppleEvents sent from the server. This script is placed on the stack level. When an event comes in, the routine extracts information about which event has called the script; reads the critical data from

the event, such as the coordinates on which the user has clicked; places that data in local variables; and then transfers control to the appropriate card designed to respond to that event. In this example, the same card *shapec* handles both events related to imagemaps. The listening script and the processing script are each placed on a separate HyperCard card because that makes for a clear logical separation. You can use other approaches such as making all handlers into subroutines on one card. Here is the listening script:

```
--Script from Stack that Will Respond to Imagemap
--Clicks
--(Place at the stack level)

on appleEvent class, eventID, sender
-- wait for AppleEvent
    global sendstuff,pathdata,recdata
    if class & eventID is "WWWΩsdoc" then

        request appleEvent data
        put it into pathdata
        request appleEvent data with keyword "kfor"
        put it into recdata
        -- in this example, control goes to card
        --shapec
        -- if the event requested is shapehtml or
        --shapeurl
        if pathdata = "Shapehtml" then go card shapec
        if pathdata = "Shapeurl" then go card shapec
        if pathdata = "Lionmap" then go card lionc
    end if
    reply senstuff
end appleEvent
```

The script on this card contains an *on AppleEvents* message handler that is waiting for AppleEvents. It checks to see if the AppleEvent is of the type "WWWΩsdoc," which the MacHTTP server sends whenever it receives a request from a client for a CGI event. The script extracts the direct data information that indicates which specific event is called for (the term after the $ symbol). It places it in a global variable called *pathdata*. It also extracts other information sent from the server and places it in global variables that are available to all the other routines.

The *sdoc* AppleEvent attaches information by certain keywords. The request for AppleEvent data with the keyword "kfor" yields the coordinates of the click. The stack puts this data into a global variable called *recdata* (received data). The *sdoc* event also carries other environmental variables which were discussed in Chapter 7's section on CGI variables.

The routine then uses a series of *if* statements to inspect the *pathdata* variable and to transfer control to the appropriate card designed to handle the events that match that keyword. In this example, *pathdata* variables of the value *shapehtml* and *shapeurl* will both send control to a card arbitrarily called *shapec*. If a different event with a different image called for an event called *lionmap*, control would be sent to a card called *lionc*.

To work with this listening script, these cards and their scripts must be designed to process the information and ultimately prepare a response to send back to the server. They put that response into a global variable called *sendstuff*. When they return control to this script, the *reply senstuff* command sends the information to the server.

4. **Design card to handle two kinds of events.** The card *shapec* must have scripts and data structures that enable it to respond to clicks in an imagemap. Some of the same tasks must be accomplished as with the canned program examples—check if the click is within a hot area, respond appropriately if it is, and send back a default if the click is not in a hot area. In HyperCard, data structures are often put in card fields. This script requires three fields:

Shape: Contains the list of coordinates defining the hot area rectangles and the URLs that they lead to, the keywords the script associates with each of them, and a running total of the number of people who have chosen each option. (Step 7)

Html: The script responding to event *shapehtml* dynamically builds a Web page to send to the server. (Step 9)

Redirect: The script responding to event *shapeurl* composes the Web page to send to the server. (Step 10)

Use of a full scripting environment such as HyperCard allows for more complex reactions. In this example, the card *shapec* supports two kinds of events: generating an HTML page differentially in response to clicks on particular parts of the image (called *shapehtml*), and sending a new URL to be accessed depending on where the user clicked (called *shapeurl*). Figure B.2 shows a flow chart of how these scripts work.

5. **Decide which event is requested and call the appropriate subroutines.** The script to respond is put in the *On Opencard* message handler so it is automatically activated as soon as the control is transferred to it by the master card listening script. Because this example demonstrates two kinds of actions, the script

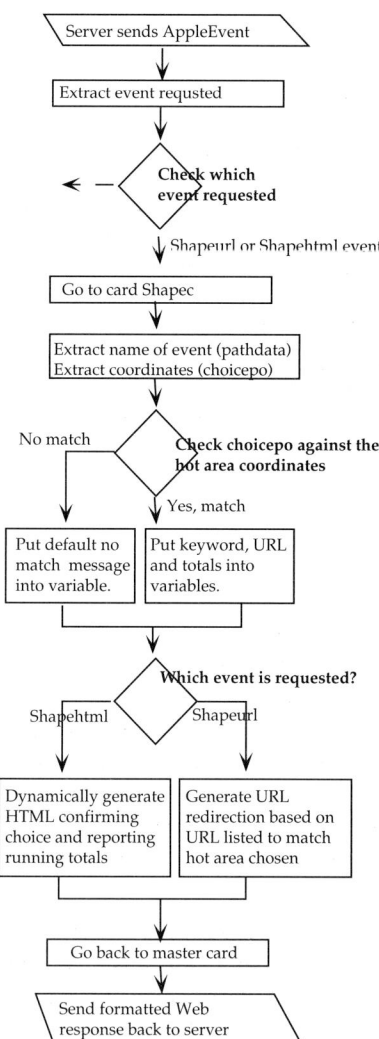

Figure B.2:
Flow chart of card script to respond to clicks on an imagemap.

must first determine which kind of action is requested. Here they are called *shapehtml* (for the one that will dynamically generate an HTML page) and *shapeurl* (for the one that will redirect the user to Web documents related to the clicks). The listening script has put this action term in the variable it called *pathdata*.

The script checks first to make sure that the value of *pathdata* matches one of the events it can deal with— *shapehtml* or *shapeurl*. Then it calls two routines that are common to both: *Extractit* gets the coordinates out of the variable *recdata* that the master has created. *Shapehandle* goes through a list of hot areas in the image defined by coordinates of the rectangles. It then differentially calls *replybuild* or *redirectbuild*, which are routines to reply to the two events. Here's the script:

```
on opencard
  global sendstuff, pathdata
  put "shapehtml, shapeurl" into list
  if list contains pathdata then
  extractit
  shapehandle
  if pathdata = shapehtml then
   replybuild
  end if
  if pathdata = shapeurl then
   redirectbuild
  end if
  else
   exit opencard
  end if
end opencard
```

6. **Extract the coordinates of the user's click and put them into a local variable.** The *extractit* routine extracts the coordinates of the click from the *recdata* variable, into which the master listing routine has placed it. The URL sent from the user contains the coordinates at the end as illustrated. The *on AppleEvent* handler illustrated in Step 2 puts the coordinates into a variable called *recdata*. The original string sent from the user looks like this:

```
http://net-ad/hypercard.cgi$Shapehtml?300, 100
```

This *extractit* routine places the coordinates in a variable for this card called *choicepo* (for choice point).

```
on extractit
 global pathdata, choicepo, recdata
 -- This extracts the coordinates of click received
 -- data (recdata)
 -- and puts it into a variable called choicepo
 -- (choice point)
 put recdata into choicepo
end extractit
```

7. **Check if the coordinates are within one of the hot rectangle areas.** The *shapehandle* routine steps through a list of hot areas bounding rectangles stored in a card field called *shape*. To simplify this example, all the hot areas are defined as rectangles. More sophisticated programming may use other shapes as well. The script is illustrated here:

```
On shapehandle
 global pathdata, choicepo, realreply, temprec
 global temp, tempreply, newtot, urlloc
 -- This routine checks if the click occurred within
 -- a hot area
```

```
 -- It then extracts the keyword, running total, and
 -- URL linked to that hot area
 put "no valid item" into realreply
 put "" into urlloc
 put the number of lines of card field shape into z
 repeat with n = 1 to z
  put line n of card field shape into temp
  put word 1 of temp into tempreply
  put word 2 of temp into temprec
  if choicepo is within temprec then
   put tempreply into realreply
   put word 3 of temp into temptot
   put temptot+1 into newtot
   put newtot into word 3 of line n of card field
    ➡shape
   put word 4 of temp into urlloc
   exit repeat
  end if
 end repeat
end shapehandle
```

When it finds that the coordinate of the click (*choicepo*) is within one of the bounding rectangles (*temprec*) it extracts the values on that line of the table of hot spots. It places them in variables that it uses later. Word 1 of the line, the keyword, is put into *realreply*; word 3 of the line, the running total of the people who have chosen that option, is put into *temptot;* and word 4, the URL for linkage if there is one, is put into *urlloc*.

The example that follows shows a sample of the contents of card field shape, which contains all the key information about the shapes including the bounding rectangle's coordinates, the keyword to be sent back to the users when they click in that area, the running totals, and the URL that should be returned in the *shapeurl* event.

Notice that the data structure of the list of shapes and the script must be tightly coupled. This example is derived from a Web art event I ran in which Web visitors were asked to click on their preferred style of information organization. The keywords are linked to the symbolic representations of information structures in the original image. Table B.1 shows the contents of card field shape.

Table B.1

Contents of Card Field Shape

linear	0,0,37,99	4	http://net-ad/lin.im.html
Indexed	61,12,181,68	2	http://net-ad/in.im.html
branching	50,97,142,187	4	http://net-ad/bra.im.html
hypermedia	169,61,266,154	5	http://net-ad/lhyp.im.html

The running total is not a standard feature; it is just one of the capabilities that this particular example is illustrating. To keep track of the running total, it adds 1 to *temtot* and puts it back in word three of the line so it will become part of the permanent record. (Note that *word* here refers to the technical HyperCard term of text units separated by spaces.) It then exits the routine satisfied that it has found a valid area of the image.

The variable *realreply* was preloaded with the default value of "no valid item." If a valid area is found, this value will be replaced with the keyword from the line of the valid area; otherwise, the user is informed that the click was not in a valid area.

Note that the information on each line is not intrinsically necessary except for the bounding rectangle. This stack is designed to accomplish the simple outcomes of reporting back what shape the person has picked and how many people picked that shape before them. The items on each line are linked to those purposes. The *urlloc* is not necessary for this purpose but will be used in the example of the other event that takes the user to a new URL based on the click. One could design the stack to respond in an infinite number of ways. This script is intended to provide a basic understanding of how a response script might be structured and to provide a framework on which you can build.

8. **Build a different response based on which original event the user requested.** The *if* statements that ascertained which of the two events were selected now branch based on that information. If the event was *shapehtml*, it branches to the routine *replybuild* that generates an HTML page on the fly. If the event was *shapeurl*, it branches to *redirectbuild* that sends instructions for the client to fetch a URL based on where the user clicked.

9. **Build an HTML document on the fly (shapehtml event).** The *replybuild* routine constructs a document to send back to the server. The field HTML, which will ultimately constitute the document to be sent, is preloaded with the header information in the required format to be sent by the server. The next part builds an HTML document on the fly by applying appropriate tags for a title and for the text that follows. In this example, it creates two lines—one that presents the keyword associated with what the person has picked (*realreply*) and the other that tells how many people picked that item before (*newtot*). It puts the card field

that contains the whole document into a variable called *sendstuff* that the master routine sends to the server. This is the *shapethml* event referred to in Step 4. Here is the script:

```
on replybuild
 global pathdata, searchdata, realreply, newtot
 global sendstuff
 put "<HTML><HEAD><TITLE>" & realreply & "</TITLE>
 ➥</HEAD><BODY>" into line 6 of card field html
 put "<H2>" &"The info style chosen:"&& realreply &
 ➥"</H2><BR>" into line 7 of card field html
 put "<H3>" &"Number who chose this style before
 ➥you:" && newtot-1 & "</H3><br>" into line 8 of
 ➥card field html
 put "</BODY></HTML>" into line 9 of card field html
 put card field html into sendstuff
end replybuild
```

The response that is sent back must be constructed in accordance with Web protocols. The following code shows the card field html that contains the whole constructed reply that is sent. The non-printing *[lf]* character in the lines represents a linefeed that can be generated by chartonum(10) in HyperCard or by Control-J. It is needed for some UNIX communication protocols that require carriage returns and linefeeds.

The first line contains a report of server protocol (HTTP/1.0), status ID number (200), and status string (OK). The following line contains the server software name (Server: MacHTTP). The next lines inform the server of the kind of information to be sent in standard Internet MIME format. This document is a valid http form that can be sent back to the client. Thus, the users' clicks result in a confirmation of what they chose and a notification of the number of people who previously chose that item.

HTTP/1.0 200 OK
[lf]Server: MacHTTP
[lf]MIME-Version: 1.0
[lf]Content-type: text/html
[lf]
<HTML><HEAD><TITLE>Branching</TITLE></HEAD><BODY>
**<H2>The info style chosen: Branching</H2>
**
<H3>Number who chose this style before you: 4
**</H3>
**
</BODY></HTML>

10. **Direct the client to fetch a linked URL (*shapeurl* event).** The other option illustrated uses the active areas of imagemaps as links to URLs. That is, the user's clicks on hot areas of the image results in a link to another URL. Technically this is accomplished by sending a document formatted with Web protocols that instructs the client to fetch another URL. This is the same result effected by the canned programs illustrated earlier in this appendix. The *redirectbuild* routine accomplishes this end. This routine illustrates a slightly different approach than the one illustrated in Step 9.

```
on redirectbuild
 global pathdata, urlloc, sendstuff
 put numtochar(13)&numtochar(10) into crlf
 put "HTTP/1.0 302 Found" & crlf into card field
 ➥redirect
 put "Location: " & urlloc & crlf & crlf into line 2
 ➥of card field redirect
 put card field redirect into sendstuff
end redirectbuild
```

Somehow, a URL must be associated with each live area of the image. There are many ways to set this up. In the example the field named *shape* was adapted to that purpose. Each line of the card field contains the URL associated with the area of the image described on that line. Remember that the *shapehandle* routine assigned word 4 of each line to the variable called *urlloc.*

Also, the header sent back to the server must reflect the fact that a redirection instruction is being sent and not an HTML document. The *redirectbuild* script shown previously constructs a redirect instruction document and uses *urlloc* to identify the appropriate link for the area of the image that was clicked. It builds this document in card field redirect.

The routine can build the document based on a field with the relevant header information preinstalled, as it did with the *replybuild* example. Just to illustrate another possibility, however, it shows how the document can be built totally from scratch. The routine uses a special variable called *crlf* that contains a carriage return and linefeed character as is sometimes required by UNIX. The first line of the header starting with "HTTP…" can be preloaded as in the first example. The "3.02 Found" status indicates redirection.

The next line builds the line of the header starting with "Location:" by appending the *urlloc* in the appropriate place and the appropriate number of carriage returns and linefeeds. Remember the *[lf]* symbol represents a linefeed character. This is the line that tells the client ultimately where to go to get the URL linked to the particular live area of the image. The contents of card field redirect containing the constructed document are illustrated in the following code. The URL is the one linked with the part of the image that our hypothetical user clicked. The example shows the contents of that field.

HTTP/1.0 302 Found
[lf]Location: http://net-ad/bra.im.html
[lf]
[lf]

These routines can be separated into two separate scripts, but they are connected to show how the same database can serve several purposes. Also, the first example kept a running total of the number of people who previously chose each particular area of the image. This capability demonstrates that the stack can generate more complex responses than invariant text.

It demonstrates how information about the user's actions can be used to create the experience. This model is similar to that used in games and in educational and other multimedia software. These complex responses are still relatively rare on the Web and will continue to be so until Web authors become more familiar with the linkage of interactive scripting to Web events.

Appendix C

Examples of Scripts Responding to Web Forms

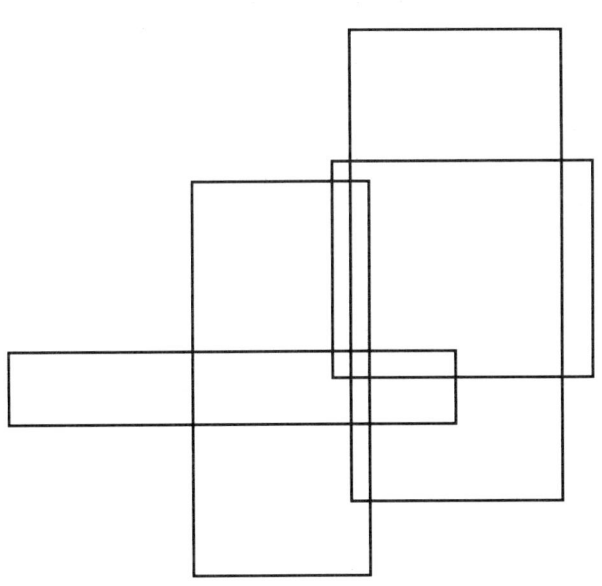

Chapter 7 explained how to create fill-in forms and the server scripts that respond to them. To help clarify the design of forms and their associated scripts, I present two more examples. This appendix shows you how to create these two systems:

- A system that maintains several bodies of information customized for users with different characteristics accessible after users enter information about them-selves. This particular example asks for information about the user's age and gender and then generates a unique display for each category group.

- A system that accumulates user's comments about certain topics. It allows new users to browse the comments that already exist or to add their own.

These systems will probably not match exactly your needs or goals. Still, they should give an idea of structures and strategies that you could use to accomplish your goals. These examples use HyperCard as the script engine. They assume you are running an AppleEvents-capable Macintosh with either MacHTTP or WebSTAR Web servers. The principles apply no matter what kind of server you are running.

Customizing Web Pages

This example maintains a set of databases of unique interest to particular age/gender groups. The form asks the user to indicate age and gender and sends this information to the response script. Gender is given the symbolic name *sex* and age is given the name *age*. The script extracts the user's information about these categories and then accesses the information it has stored relevant to that group. It prepares or constructs an HTML document with that information and with the appropriate CGI header and then sends it back to the server. The server sends it back to the client and users get customized information based on information they provided. Figure C.1 shows the flow chart of the system.

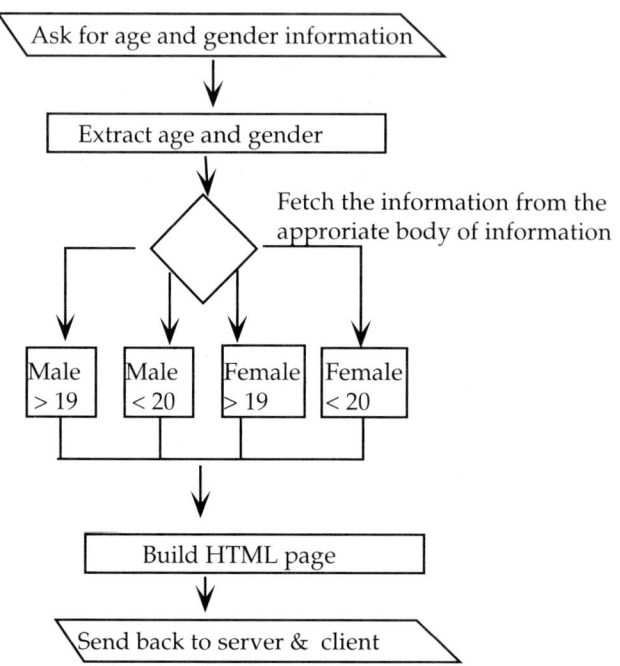

Figure C.1:
Flow chart of system to retrieve age/gender-based information.

Here is the basic approach used by this script:

1. There is a master listening script waiting for messages from the server.

2. When a message arrives, the script extracts other information that may be needed by subroutines such as the data sent from the various categories indicated on the HTML document.

3. It then transfers control to the appropriate subroutine.

4. This subroutine processes the information, checks against databases if necessary, and then constructs a properly formatted Web document to send to the user.

5. The subroutine transfers control to the master routine, which sends the response to the server, which then sends it to the user.

In HyperCard, databases are often maintained in structures called card fields. The script illustrated in this section requires the card to have six card fields. Four of the card fields contain the data to be sent to different kinds of users and are named by category of user: *Adultmale*, *Adultfemale*, *Youngmale*, and *Youngfemale*. Another field called *header* contains the text that Web protocols require at the head of a Web document. The script also uses a card field called *outgoinghtml* to assemble the final Web document with header and customized data.

Sample Form and Script: Asking Users for Age/Gender Information

Here are the steps to create this system:

1. **Create a form that asks users about their age and gender.** Figure C.2 illustrates an HTML form that asks for the users' age and gender as a prelude to offering them custom information. The example that follows shows the code that generates that Web page.

```
<HTML>
<HEAD>
<TITLE>Category Demo</TITLE>
</HEAD>
<BODY>
<H2>Demo of form to retrieve category of
   information</H2>
```

```
<HR>
<H3>Different information will be made available<P>
depending on your age and gender<P></H3>
<HR>
<FORM METHOD="POST" ACTION="http://net-ad/
  HyperCard.cgi$agesex">
Please indicate your gender: Male
 <INPUT TYPE="radio"
 NAME="Sex" VALUE="Male">
Female <INPUT TYPE="radio" NAME="Sex"
 VALUE="Female" CHECKED>
<P>
Please indicate your age: <INPUT TYPE="text"
 NAME="age" SIZE="5" MAXLENGTH="5">
<P>
<INPUT TYPE="Submit" VALUE="Submit">
<INPUT TYPE="Reset" VALUE="Reset">
</FORM>
<HR>
</BODY>
</HTML>
```

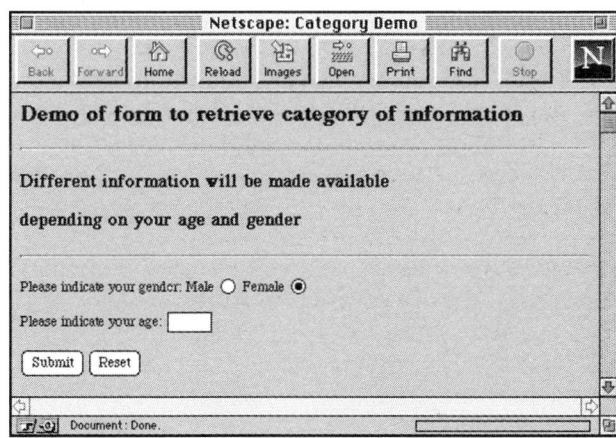

Figure C2:
Web page that asks the user to indicate age and gender.

2. Set up the script to listen for an AppleEvent sent from the server and extract variables that later scripts will need. Both of the example stacks make use of a listening script to wait for the AppleEvent *sdoc*, sent automatically by the server when a supplementary script is requested. This script is placed on the stack level.

The example that follows illustrates a listening script that waits for Web events. Compared to the imagemap example in Appendix B, it extracts more information, including the *Method* argument, which tells which kind of action the form used to send the information—GET or POST. (*Request AppleEvent data with keyword "meth"*). This distinction is important because the information will come in a slightly different style depending on the method used. Also, this example shows how one can extract information about user address, user name, and formal passwords. This data is not used in the examples that follow, but their extraction is shown for general interest.

The HTML document that describes the form must be intimately linked with the script that processes the information. The document creates two categories of information that are sent to the script—sex= and age=. When the user clicks the submit button, the browser sends the following URL with the information attached:

```
http://net-ad/HyperCard.cgi$agesex&sex=female&age=33
```

The link points to HyperCard. The direct argument (the section after the $) lists a path of "agesex". This lets HyperCard know which event is sending the form and which scripts should handle it. The data is attached indicating that the category sex has a value of "female" and the category age has a value of "33". Data

elements are separated with & symbols. The master listening program described next extracts the event requested and puts it into a variable called *pathdata*. It extracts the data and puts it into a variable called *recdata*. It then transfer control to a card called *agesexcard* that has the script to respond.

```
on appleEvent class, eventID, sender
  global sendstuff, pathdata, recdata, add, meth
  global user, pas
  if class & eventID is "WWWΩsdoc" then
  -- look for sdoc event
    request appleEvent data
    -- get the direct parameter (path args)
    put it into pathdata
    request appleEvent data with keyword "meth"
    put it into meth
    request appleEvent data with keyword "kfor"
    put it into searchdata
    if meth= "GET" then put searchdata into recdata
    request appleEvent data with keyword "post"
    put it into postdata
    if meth = "POST" then put postdata into recdata
    request appleEvent data with keyword "addr"
    put it into add
    request appleEvent data with keyword "user"
    put it into user
    request appleEvent data with keyword "pass"
    put it into pas
  end if
  go card agesexcard
  reply sendstuff
end AppleEvent
```

The information from imagemaps always came in via the GET method so the previous example did not deal with method. The information from forms can come in via either method depending on how the you have set up the original form HTML attribute ACTION=. Therefore, this script determines which method was used and puts the data that has been sent into a variable called *recdata*. All subroutines can then be structured to use this variable. This script could have just as well been used for the imagemaps illustrated in Appendix B; that script was simplified for the sake of illustration.

3. **Check that the event name is correct and then activate each of the subroutines needed to process information from the form.** This script is placed on a card called *agesexcard*. It could have been structured as subroutines on one card. When the master routine accesses this card the *opencard* routine takes over. It calls the handlers needed to process the information and then returns to the master card. Here is the script for the *opencard* script:

```
on opencard
  -- This card will take extract age and gender from
  -- a form
  -- and send back a custom HTML page for the four
  -- groups of
  -- young males, adult males, young females, adult
  -- females
  global sendstuff, pathdata, recdata
  if pathdata = "agesex" then
    extractsexage
    whichdata
    respond
  end if
  go card master
end opencard
```

4. **Extract the information that the user has entered into the form.** The *extractsexage* routine takes the incoming data in the variable *recdata* and separates out the elements. It looks for the "sex=" and the "age=" text and the "&" symbols to determine the boundaries. Sex is put into *cursex* and age is put into *curage*.

```
on extractsexage
  global sendstuff, pathdata, recdata
  global cursex, curage
  -- this extracts the sex and age from received
  -- data (recdata)
  -- get elements of incoming data from form
  -- put the number of characters in recdata into
  -- numchar
  -- get sex into variable cursex
  put 5 into sexbegin
  -- offset for identifier "sex="
  put (offset ("&age=", recdata))-1 into sexend
  -- find end of sex
  put char sexbegin to sexend of recdata into cursex

  -- get age
  put sexend+6 into agebegin
  -- offset for identifier "&age="
  put char agebegin to numchar of recdata into
    ➥curage
end extractsexage
```

5. **Decide which category the user fits and retrieve the information targeted to that category.** The *whichdata* routine determines which data to send back. It determines adult age status by seeing if the curage is greater than 19. It then picks one of the four HTML-formatted data sets to send back (*Youngfemale, Youngmale, Adultfemale, Adultmale*). These data sets are contained in fields in HyperCard that are named to correspond to these categories. In other systems they could be external text files. They already contain HTML formatting tags.

```
on whichdata
  --This routine decides if age qualifies as adult
  -- and then identifies the field of data to send
  -- based on age and gender

  global sendstuff,pathdata,recdata
  global curage, cursex, statuspass, tarfield

  -- Decide if person is adult
  if curage > 19 then
    put "Adult" into astatus
  else
    put "Young" into astatus
  end if

  put astatus&&cursex into tarfield
end whichdata
```

The following code shows a sample of what card field *Adultmale* might contain. The card fields for the other three categories would be set up similarly.

```
<H2> Here are some net resources especially for
 adult males </H2>
<UL>
<LI> <A HREF = journal.html>Men's Journals</A>
<LI> <A HREF = images.html>Web resources for men</A>
</UL>
</BODY></HTML>
```

6. **Build a correctly formatted response with header to send back to server and return to user.** The *respond* routine builds a Web formatted document to send back by putting the appropriate header, stored in a card field called *header*, in front of the special resource text described previously. It puts this into the standard variable called *sendstuff* that the master routine will be looking for. It also puts it into a card field called *outgoinghtml* so the author can inspect it if needed.

The following code example shows the respond script:

```
on respond
  global statuspass, sendstuff, tarfield
  -- send the HTML document that matches the user's
  -- category
  put card field header &return&card field tarfield
    ➥into sendstuff
  put sendstuff into card field "outgoinghtml"
end respond
```

The following code shows the contents of the card field header. The characters *[lf]* stand for the non-printing linefeed character required to end each line in addition to the carriage return:

HTTP/1.0 200 OK [lf]
Server: MacHTTP[lf]
MIME-Version: 1.0([lf]
Content-type: text/html[lf]
[lf]
<HTML><HEAD><TITLE>Age/Gender Response
</TITLE>
</HEAD><BODY>

The script sends data about gender and age, the routines determine which card field contains the information appropriate to that age/gender group, and the script then builds an appropriately formatted document to send to the server.

Fill-In Form Script to Allow Users to Sign a Guestbook

This system asks users to pick a topic that interests them and to leave comments or browse the comments of others. The comments are added to the other comments already left by previous viewers. The system uses forms to dynamically build a database of comments for each category. Figure C.3 shows the flow chart of the system.

Visitors can choose to browse the comments others have left or to add their own. The script handles the details either by adding their comments to the card field related to the topic they chose or by sending back the record of already existing comments. This script assumes that the card has four card fields: *Warcom* to store comments on war; *Lovecom* to store comments on love; *header* that stores the standard Web header lines that must start a page to be sent to the server; and *outgoinghtml* in which the script assembles the Web page to send to the server.

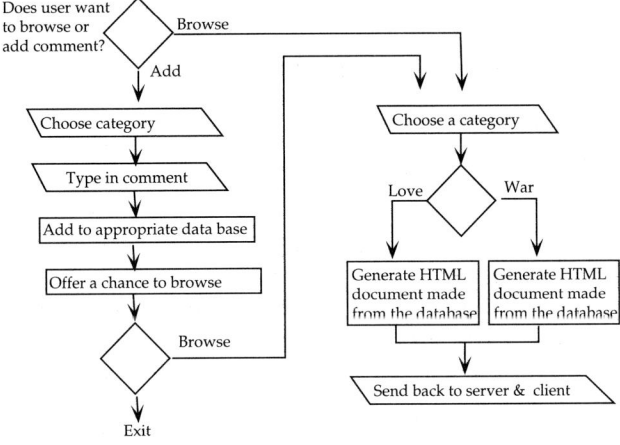

Figure C.3:
Flow chart of system to allow visitors to add comments to a cumulating database.

Here are the steps to create the form and HyperCard stack that enable this event:

1. **Create a Web form so users can choose whether to browse or submit a comment.** The example shows the HTML document that creates the form; Figure C.4 shows what browsers show. There are two actions possible: Reading the comments others have left (*readcomment*) and adding a comment to the record of comments (*addcomment*). The user can use a set of radio buttons to select the topic—Love or War—for browsing or adding a comment.

```
<HTML>
<HEAD>
 <TITLE>Comment Demo</TITLE>
</HEAD>
<BODY>
<H2>Guestbook form</H2>
<H3>You may either look at comments people made
 before you<P>
or add your own comments<P></H3>
<hr>
<FORM METHOD="POST" ACTION="http://net-ad/
 HyperCard.cgi$readcomment">

Please indicate the topic you would like to look at:
War <INPUT TYPE-"radio" NAME="cat" VALUE="War"
 CHECKED>
Love<INPUT TYPE="radio" NAME="cat" VALUE="Love"><P>
Click here to read other's comments
<INPUT TYPE="Submit" VALUE="Read Comments">
</FORM>
<hr>
<FORM METHOD="GET" ACTION="http://net-ad/
 HyperCard.cgi$addcomment">
```

```
Please indicate the topic you would like to add
  comment to:
War <INPUT TYPE="radio" NAME="cat" VALUE="War"
  CHECKED>
Love<INPUT TYPE="radio" NAME="cat" VALUE="Love"><P>
<TEXTAREA NAME="com" ROWS=2 COLS=40></TEXTAREA><P>
Click here to submit your comments
<INPUT TYPE="Submit" VALUE="Submit">
<INPUT TYPE="Reset" VALUE="Reset">
</FORM>
<HR>
</BODY>
</HTML>
```

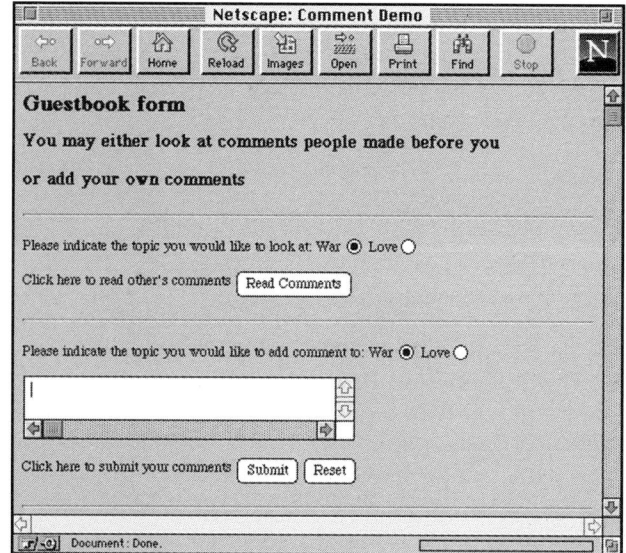

Figure C.4:
A Web form that allows readers to browse a record of comments or to add to the record.

To illustrate different approaches, this form uses both the GET and POST methods to send data. The GET method is used for the added comments in order to avoid the complexity of the way the POST method sends multiword text. Every space and special character is explicitly indicated with the hexadecimal number for the ASCII code for that character—for example, all spaces would be represented by %20 (hexadecimal 20 = decimal 32, which is the ASCII code for space). The GET method just sends the text as it was typed. Certainly a routine can be written to convert all the hex codes into their proper characters, but for the sake of simplicity, this example used the GET method for the added comments.

There are actually two forms on this page. The reading comments section invites the user to use a radio button to indicate a topic of interest—Love or War. Then clicking the read comments button sends a submit message to the browser and the information is sent to the server with the event requested equal to *readcomment.* The URL might look like this:

```
http://net-ad/HyperCard.cgi$readcomment&cat=Love
```

The adding comments section is a separate form that invites the reader to select a topic and to type comments into the *textarea* field. When done, the reader clicks the submit button and the URL is sent to the server. It might look like this:

```
http://net-ad/
HyperCard.cgi$addcomment&cat=Love&com=Love is a
Mystery
```

2. **Listen for AppleEvent sent from server and extract variables that later scripts need.** The script that supports this form again relies on a master card with

the listening routine to wait for server events. The master routine also extracts the *pathdata* information about which event is requested and extracts the information sent by the user. It then transfers control to the card that handles the events. In this example, the *commentc* card handles both the reading and adding comments. The listening routine is the same as that described in Step 2 in the previous example.

Indeed this one stack can handle multiple events with the same listening routine. Instead of invariably going to one card, it can go to different cards depending upon which event came in. For example, an if-then structure can check the value of *pathdata* and branch accordingly to the appropriate card to handle that incoming event.

```
on appleEvent class, eventID, sender
  global sendstuff, pathdata, recdata
  global add, meth, user, pas
  if class & eventID is "WWWΩsdoc" then
  -- look for sdoc event
    request appleEvent data
    -- get the direct parameter (path args)
    put it into pathdata
    request appleEvent data with keyword "meth"
    put it into meth
    request appleEvent data with keyword "kfor"
    put it into searchdata
    if meth= "GET" then put searchdata into recdata
    request appleEvent data with keyword "post"
    put it into postdata
    if meth = "POST" then put postdata into recdata
    request appleEvent data with keyword "addr"
    put it into add
    request appleEvent data with keyword "user"
    put it into user
    request appleEvent data with keyword "pass"
```

```
    put it into pas
  end if
  go card commentcard
  reply sendstuff
end AppleEvent
```

3. **Determine which event is called for, transfer control to the subroutines to handle that event, and send the document back when the processing is done.** The *opencard* routine checks the *pathdata* variable to see which event was requested—*readcomment* or *addcomment*. It then transfers control to the appropriate subroutines. When control comes back, it returns to the master card.

```
on opencard
  -- This card will allow visitors to record text
  -- comments and see the comments others have left.
  global pathdata

  if pathdata = "addcomment" then
    extractcatcom
    addcomment
    respond
  end if

  if pathdata = "readcomment" then
    extractcatcom
    respond
  end if
  go card master

end opencard
```

4. **Extract the data that the user entered into the form.** The *extractcatcom* routine extracts the elements of the incoming data in the variable *recdata*. For the *readcomment* event it needs only to get the category

requested (cat=) and put it into a variable called *curcat*. For the *addcomment* event, it also needs to get the information that the user has typed (com=) and to place it in a variable called *curcom*.

```
on extractcatcom
  global sendstuff, pathdata, recdata
  global curcat, curcom
  -- this extracts the category of comment the user
  -- has selected (recdata)

  -- get elements of incoming data from form
  put the number of characters in recdata into
    ➥numchar

  -- get category into variable curcat
  put 5 into catbegin
  -- offset for identifier "cat="
  put (offset ("&com=", recdata))-1 into catend
  -- find end of category
  if pathdata = "readcomment" then put numchar into
    ➥catend
  put char catbegin to catend of recdata into curcat
  if pathdata = "readcomment" then exit
    ➥extractcatcom

  -- get comment
  put catend+6 into combegin
  -- offset for identifier "&com="
  put char combegin to numchar of recdata into
    ➥curcom
end extractcatcom
```

5. **For the *addcomment* event, append the user's comments to the end of the relevant field and format it for HTML.** The *addcomment* routine only applies for the *addcomment* event. It determines which category the person has commented on, places the comments at the end of the card field that holds those comments, finds the number of comments in that field (stored on line 1 of the data field), adds 1 to the total, and adds a <BR> tag at the end of each line so they will be properly formatted for HTML. This routine depends on the existence of a field for each category of comment with a composite name made up of the category and the string "com"—that is, *lovecom* or *warcom*. External text files can also store comments.

```
on addcomment
  --This routine takes the Web visitor's comments
  -- and adds them at the end of
  -- the field relating to category chosen

  global sendstuff,pathdata,recdata
  global curcat, curcom, tarfield, statuscom

  -- Decide on which category field, get present
  -- number, prepare to add
  put curcat&"com" into tarfield
  put line 1 of card field tarfield into curnum
  put return & "comment #"&curnum+1&return&curcom
    ➥after card field tarfield
  put curnum+1 into line 1 of card field tarfield

  -- add <BR> to end of each line
  put "comment #"& curnum+1 into lastcom
  find string lastcom
  put word 2 of the foundline into z
  put the number of lines in card field tarfield
    ➥into z1
  repeat with n = z to z1
    put "<BR>"after line n of card field tarfield
  end repeat
```

```
put "<H2>Your comments on"&&curcat&&"recorded
    ➡</H2>" into statuscom
end addcomment
```

The following code shows an example of what the comments on love in the *lovecom* field might contain:

3
**Comment #1
**
**Where can you find it ?
**
**Comment #2
**
**It is kind of sweet and sour
**
**Comment #3
**
**I love its mystery
**

6. **Build a response for the two events by combining a standard header, and dynamically generated information appropriate to the user's action.** The *respond* routine builds an HTML page to send back to the server. It prefixes a preloaded header from the field called *header* and then builds a page for each kind of event. It builds it in a card field called *outgoinghtml*. For the *readcomments* event, it creates lines confirming the choice of topic and then adds the comments from the data field that has the record for that topic. For the *addcomment* event, it confirms that the comment was added to the topic. In both cases, it puts the text into a variable called *sendstuff* that the master routine sends to the server. The *[lf]* stands for the non-printing linefeed character that must end each line in addition to the carriage return.

```
on respond
    -- This routine sends answer back to server
    -- It sends back all comments if the person wants
    -- to read
    global statuscom, sendstuff, tarfield, pathdata
    global curcat
```

```
    -- send the HTML document that matches
    if pathdata = "addcomment" then
        put card field header &return&statuscom into
            ➡sendstuff
        put sendstuff into card field "outgoinghtml"
    end if
    if pathdata = "readcomment" then
        put "<h2>Here are the views
            ➡on"&&curcat&&"</h2><br><hr>"
            ➡& return into statuscom
        put curcat&"com" into tarfield
        put card field header & statuscom& card field
            ➡tarfield into card field outgoinghtml
        put "Number of comments: " before line 8 of card
            ➡field outgoinghtml
        put "<br>" after line 8 of card field
            ➡outgoinghtml
        put card field outgoinghtml into sendstuff
    end if
    put return&"</BODY></HTML>"after card field
        ➡outgoinghtml
    reply sendstuff
end respond
```

The following code shows the card field called *header* that contains the standard header and dynamically generated title. The last lines in the header change depending on the event to which the script is responding:

HTTP/1.0 200 OK [lf]
Server: MacHTTP[lf]
MIME-Version: 1.0[lf]
Content-type: text/html[lf]
[lf]
<HTML><HEAD><TITLE>Comments Reply</TITLE>
</HEAD><BODY>
<HR>

This stack allows your Web readers to read comments that others have made on particular topics and to add their comments to the list.

These scripts are offered only as templates on top of which you can build your own environments. As you continue your Web surfing, you'll discover there are many basic scripts and fill-in forms you can find online, although you need to invest time and effort to adapt them to your specific purposes. Hopefully, by now you can see that there's nothing mysterious about scripting. Clarifying the logic of what you hope to accomplish is a major part of the task.

Index

H

M

N

newsgroups (Usenet), 332
    URLs, 96
NIC (Network Information Center), 300
<NOFLOW> tag, 132
<NOTE> tag, 70
numbering lists, 67

O

object-oriented file formats (graphics),
    108-110
<OL> ordered lists, 42
on-line documentation
    backgrounds, 131
    CGI (Common Gateway Interface), 204-211
    color, 131
    computer mediated sound, 157
    converters, 78-79
    editors, 78-79
    forms, 223
    graphics, 113
    images
        archives, 144-145
        interleaving, 139
        transparency, 139
    intellectual property rights, 289
    markup tags, 51-52
    MIDI, 159
    Netscape extensions, 122
    network research, 298

real-time reporting, 252
sound, 157
    file formats, 161
    standards (HTML), 53-77
    templates, 78-79
    video (MPEG), 182
    W3 organization, 314
    see also URLs
ordered lists, 65
organizing sites (structure), 103
OTIS Infinite Grid (art), 261

P

<P> markup tag (paragraph), 34, 39-40
padding cells (tables), 59
page dividers (images), 146
pages
    initial images, 145
    site design, 278
paragraphs, <P> markup tag, 34, 39-40
passwords
    forms, 229-231, 234
        Macintosh, 233
        putindata routine, 239
        UNIX, 240
pathnames (URLs), 91
    absolute, 84
    relative, 84

PDAs (personal data assistants), 299
persistence of vision (video), 178
personal data assistants (PDAs), 299
physical style tags, 46-48
    <BIG>, 72
    <SMALL>, 72
    combining, 48
    embedding, 48
pixels, 108
PLAIN (lists), 66
platforms
    CGI, 206
    cross-platform documents, 310
ports (URLs), 91
<POST> tag, 223
POST_ARGS (CGI), 206
<PRE> tag (formatting text), 45, 126
preformatted text, 45
programming URLs, 309
proprietary markup tags, 32
protocols (URLs), 91
public key encryption, 303
publishing, 21
    resposibility, 24
putindata routine (forms), 239

Q

QuickTime
    converting to MPEG, 192
    video compression, 182-183